A Survey of
Religious Education

J. M. PRICE
DIRECTOR EMERITUS OF THE SCHOOL OF RELIGIOUS EDUCATION
SOUTHWESTERN BAPTIST THEOLOGICAL SEMINARY

JAMES H. CHAPMAN
PROFESSOR OF RELIGION
HOWARD COLLEGE

L. L. CARPENTER
EDITOR OF *Biblical Recorder*
FORMERLY CHAPLAIN AND PROFESSOR OF BIBLE
UNIVERSITY OF SOUTH CAROLINA

W. FORBES YARBOROUGH
DISTINGUISHED SERVICE PROFESSOR OF RELIGIOUS EDUCATION
OKLAHOMA BAPTIST UNIVERSITY

SECOND EDITION

THE RONALD PRESS COMPANY • NEW YORK

Library of Congress Catalog Card Number: 59–6624

PRINTED IN THE UNITED STATES OF AMERICA

PREFACE

A Survey of Religious Education was written to meet the need for a comprehensive introductory college textbook in the field of religious education. Because it is important that religious education take account of developments in the field of general education, the second edition of this book makes judicious use of new material based on recent developments in psychology and education. The basic philosophy of the Christian religion remains, as it must, unchanged, but the authors have given full consideration to advances in educational methods and principles.

The book is designed to meet today's needs for a practical introduction to the total educational program of the church. Although written primarily for use as a textbook, it has been the deliberate purpose of the authors to avoid the use of technical, philosophical, and theological terminology so that the book may be as valuable to the layman as to the student planning to enter some church-related vocation. Modern social and religious conditions are presented as a challenge to the churches to find a more effective way to build character into the lives of a "greater generation"—men and women who can face and solve these problems individually and collectively. The psychological and philosophical principles and educational techniques necessary to such a program are fully discussed in nontechnical language in the first half of the book.

The second half of the book is devoted to the agencies within the church and to the agencies beyond the local church. Part III considers the organization and administration of the church agencies. In dealing with this extensive field, this part concentrates mainly upon Southern Baptist church agencies. But teachers who prefer to present in more detail the organizational structure of a different denomination may supplement the text by the use of their own church manuals and guidebooks. Again, in the treatment of the agencies outside the immediate range of the church—from leisure-time activities to the modern mass media of communication—stress is placed on the great problems and challenges of the modern world, particularly as they affect the character of growing persons.

Thus, *A Survey of Religious Education* is a practical guide to the educational techniques implicit in Christian principles. It is the fervent hope of the authors that it will serve as a genuine inspiration to the many Christian college students, volunteer church workers, and religious leaders working in this vital field.

J. M. Price
James H. Chapman
L. L. Carpenter
W. Forbes Yarborough

February, 1959

CONTENTS

Part I

PHILOSOPHY OF RELIGIOUS EDUCATION
J. M. Price

Part II

PRINCIPLES OF RELIGIOUS EDUCATION
James H. Chapman

v

Part III

RELIGIOUS EDUCATION IN THE CHURCH
W. Forbes Yarborough

Part IV

RELIGIOUS EDUCATION BEYOND THE CHURCH
L. L. Carpenter

Part I

PHILOSOPHY OF
RELIGIOUS EDUCATION

CHAPTER 1

NATURE AND SCOPE OF RELIGIOUS EDUCATION

The term "religious education" has been used in various ways. To different people it has different meanings. Some regard it as so liberal an expression that they prefer the term "Christian education" instead. Others use the two practically interchangeably. Still others identify Christian education with the work of the Christian college and consider religious education as the more comprehensive term. It is well, then, to consider just what is meant by the statement as used in this book.

MEANING OF EDUCATION

Some confusion has existed with regard to the word "education" itself. In fact, often it has about as many meanings as there are individuals using the word. Frequently the idea is very vague and far removed from the real truth. There are several approaches that will help to clarify the matter.

Based on Etymology

Generally, the idea obtains that the word education comes from the Latin term *educere* which is of the third conjugation and means "to lead out." Education is thought of, therefore, in terms of drawing out the powers inherent in the person and developing them. It carries the idea of expression. The idea is good as applied to education, but unfortunately it is not involved in the word itself. For were the word derived from the third conjugation it would have to be "eduction" instead of "education."

Looking a little further, it is found that the word is from the first conjugation and the form is *educare*. This term, however, has a very different meaning. Instead of signifying "to lead or draw out" it means "to nourish or nurture." This carries the idea of supplying food or sustenance rather than drawing out or exercising. It is the "impressional" rather than the "expressional" idea. From this viewpoint education consists of supplying ideas or inspiration more than of securing responses.

A full conception of the educational process, however, requires both ideas. First there is an in-filling process which includes the inculcation of ideas and the forming of ideals. Second, there is a drawing-out aspect which includes the activity side. In other words, a complete process of education includes both impression and expression — nourishing and exercising. In this book "education" is used in this twofold sense.

Based on Aims

Some definitions grow out of aims or objectives. The end in view determines the concept of education. The approach to education from the viewpoint of the materials used in acquiring it may be considered as *familiarity with the cultural inheritance* of the race. Education therefore consists of acquiring a mass of materials. This is the older view that obtained when the material-centered and cultural emphasis held sway. It is the transmission idea in education. Recently this material-centered stress has been discounted.

Viewed from the standpoint of the individual and the maturing of innate potentialities, education may be defined as the *development of unfolding powers*. Instincts hold a prominent place in this definition, and the idea of mental discipline is involved in part. This is a subjective approach and is rather individualistic in nature. The aim is the growing of a well-rounded and symmetrical personality.

Looked at from the angle of society, education may be considered as *preparation for efficient living*. From this point of view the purpose of the school is to fit the individual to take his place in the life of the world. It is an objective approach to education and stresses the utilitarian emphasis in which social studies and practical arts play a prominent part.

Based on Procedure

Definitions of education also grow out of the concept of the process or activity employed as well as out of the aim or objective to be attained in the life of the individual.

One emphasis based on activity is that education is the *guidance of growth*. This definition proceeds from the point of view of the person rather than from the materials and also from the viewpoint of the unfolding life. Hence, education is a continuous process rather than a completed one. The emphasis is on guidance rather than on the instilling of ideas or the determining of a course of conduct. This view gives more emphasis to the creative aspect.

Another definition growing out of procedure is that education is the *introduction of control into conduct*. From this point of view the thought is not so much the intellectual or emotional aspect of life as the volitional. Conduct is the goal. This is to be determined by the ideal, and this ideal is stimulated by education. Properly facing and solving life's problems is the emphasis here. This theory looks toward a life controlled and directed by dominant ideals.

Other definitions shading off from these might be given, but these are adequate. The whole truth does not lie in any one of them but rather in the combined elements of all, together with other features involving emotions, attitudes, and desires. Education is a process involving life and a lifetime.

NATURE OF RELIGIOUS EDUCATION

Upon consideration of the nature of education in general, these questions naturally arise: What is its relation to religion? How far can religion be taught? What is religious education? How is it differentiated from other education?

Relation of Education to Religion

Education involves religion. Since religion has to do with man's thoughts, feelings, and actions in relation to the supernatural, it is very evident that it has a place in education. In fact, any system of education that ignores the spiritual aspect of man's nature is incomplete. Training the intellect without relating it to God makes a cynic or an atheist. Training in skills without stressing the spiritual makes a materialist. Since man has moral and spiritual inclinations, education, to be complete, must develop these. Religion, therefore, is involved in a complete process of education.

But religion also involves education. There are some extremists who think that religion is a matter of feeling and so does not require any education. There are others who overemphasize the divine aspect and think no education is needed. But any common-sense point of view makes it clear that, if the religious life is to be balanced and complete, education is necessary. Information is needed for an enlightened experience. Without such it tends toward bigotry and mere emotionalism and gets practically nowhere in the life of the individual.

Education and religion, then, are vitally interrelated. Each is incomplete without the other. Frank M. McKibben says:

> The goals of education have been conceived as spiritual values. . . . These spiritual values, which are the confessed objectives of education, are most commendable. Any educator, parent, or citizen would give hearty approval of them as goals of education. Anyone interested in the more adequate religious education cannot help sensing the identity of these objectives with much that church leaders are primarily concerned for.[1]

They are essentially the same in aims, spirit, means, methods, and results. No system of education is complete that does not include the religious element, and no system of religion is adequate that does not involve education. It is inaccurate to call anyone fully educated who is not religious and just as

---

[1] Frank M. McKibben, Philip H. Lotz (ed.), in *Orientation in Religious Education* (Nashville: Abingdon Press, 1950), p. 57.

inaccurate to think that religion can reach its climax without education.

Can Religion Be Taught?

The conclusion that education is involved in religious experience does not fully clarify the matter. How much of religious experience is communicable from one person to another? *Negatively* it is evident that the supernatural element in the experience cannot be humanly imparted. The educational process cannot control or supplant the operation of the Holy Spirit in the heart and mind of the individual. There is that divine element in the new birth and Christian growth which teaching can stress but cannot impart. As was said by Zechariah, it is "Not by might nor by power, but by my Spirit saith Jehovah. . . ." (Zech. 4:6) It has been the fear of leaving God out of the process that has made many fearful of education. Nor can the crisis in Christian experience be determined by education. The teacher may give information about, and lead the pupil to the entrance into the kingdom of God; but the final step in that experience must be taken by the individual. Neither God nor man can override the human will. There is a personal, private element in conversion that no one can experience for another.

Positively considered there are a number of things that teaching may do for the individual. It may help him to understand his natural condition, what God has done for him, and what he must do for himself. It is through instruction that the plan of salvation is made clear. Moreover, it is through education that attitudes, conducive to entering the Christian life, are built up. In this way a subconscious basis is laid for the conversion experience, and to this extent the will is influenced.

Nor is this all. After one has entered the Christian life, there is much more that teaching and training may do for him. The responsibilities of church membership, the obligation of stewardship, and the applications of Christianity to current life are matters that require a great deal of instruction and guidance. Dr. J. B. Gambrell spoke wisely when he said: "We have evangelized, and we have baptized; but we have not taught, and out of that have come the most of our troubles." No one is born full-fledged into the kingdom of God. Character must be grown. And education plays a large part in furnishing the information and inspiration to that end.

What Is Religious Education?

From the preceding discussion something of the nature of religious education is evident. It is in the realm of religion and morals, and it is more interested in the right kind of attitudes and conduct than it is in knowledge, even Biblical. It involves the whole personality in relation to God, self, and man. There are at least three aspects of the complete process.

For one thing, religious education involves *inculcating religious truths*. This includes not only the teaching of the Bible in general but especially that part of it of particular need and value to the pupil at the time. George H. Betts has termed it "fruitful knowledge." This is necessary as a basis for intelligent conversion, church membership, Christian living, and kingdom service. By this means Christian ideals are formed for the guidance of life.

It includes also *stimulating right attitudes*. To know is one thing. To feel the value and weight of that knowledge is quite another thing. No person lives up to his standards. Man must contend with the world, the flesh, and the devil — also with the habit-set of life. There is ever present "the lust of the flesh and the lust of the eyes and the vainglory of life" (I John 2:16). So motivating is at least as important as informing.

And to fill out the cycle, there is involved the problem of *securing proper responses*. A thing has not been learned in its completeness until it has been experienced. An act of the will is as necessary as that of the intellect or the emotions. So religious education includes response in conversion, church membership, and Christian living. Religious education has been defined as the introduction of control into conduct in terms of religious ideas and ideals.

How It Differs from Other Education

It can readily be seen that religious education differs greatly from *public education.* The latter is under the direction of the state and is therefore secular in nature, while the former is under the control of the church and other religious agencies and is religious and moral. Public education deals largely with knowledge and skills, while religious education is more concerned about motives and attitudes. Religious education is not something tacked on to general education but rather supplies a part not provided. As Miller's book title states, it is *Education for Christian Living.*[2] And, too, it seeks to provide the spirit and dynamic which will motivate all education.

Differentiated from *Christian education,* as the term is most commonly used, religious education is broader in scope and different in its point of view. The term "Christian education" for the most part has been used to designate the work of the denominational college and deals, therefore, with college subjects from a Christian point of view. The term "religious education," on the other hand, is used to cover religious and moral instruction and guidance in the home, the church, the school, and the press. It is definitely from the Christian point of view as evangelicals use it today.

FACTORS IN RELIGIOUS EDUCATION

A number of factors are involved in the process of religious education if it is to be complete. Each is important and has its part to play. Without any one of them, the activity would be incomplete. With them, religious education can go a long way toward growing Christian character and building a Christian civilization.

The Pupil

The first and most important factor in religious education is the pupil. All else exists for, and centers around, him. For

[2] Randolph Crump Miller, *Education for Christian Living* (Englewood Cliffs, N. J.: Prentice-Hall, Inc., 1956).

him, buildings are erected, teachers employed, teaching materials provided, and the whole activity of teaching carried on. He is, therefore, the most significant factor in the educational task. Religious education today, like Christ of old, puts the child or pupil in the center. The development of this immature being is the first consideration. Martin Luther believed that adults exist to nurture the young. Pupils of all ages are immature and in need of development.

The Teacher

The second most important factor in the religious-educational process is the teacher. All remaining factors are secondary to him. This idea is dominant in the statement attributed to President James A. Garfield that his idea of a college was a log with Mark Hopkins on one end and himself on the other. The teacher is supposed to be more mature than the pupil, at least so far as the immediate thing being taught is concerned. It is his business to serve as instructor, inspirer, and guide in the process of religious training. He works on the soul and fashions life. No wonder the Jews considered the teacher the true guardian of the city. A recent appraisal designates him as "the keeper of the gates of tomorrow!"

The Aim

Probably next in importance is the aim or objective. This is the goal toward which the teacher leads and the pupil strives. It is determined in part by the definition of religious education. The stage of development already attained helps also to fashion it. This goal is a moving rather than a fixed one. It includes Christian conversion, character development, and kingdom service. Since objectives will be discussed in detail in another chapter, they will not be developed here. It may be said, however, that one of the greatest weaknesses in the average teacher is his lack of clear-cut aims. Nothing helps more to give definiteness, furnish incentives, and provide a measuring rod than worthy objectives.

The Curriculum

The fourth factor in the process of religious education is the curriculum. This includes all the materials to be used in the teaching and training activities. In a large measure what comes out in the final product is dependent on what is put into the process. On the whole, not enough attention has been given to this phase of activity, especially in the Sunday school and particularly with regard to the Uniform Lessons. Much of the effectiveness of grading, equipment, and improved methods may be lost through inadequate materials. These materials are determined in a large measure by the objectives and naturally vary according to the age group. More will be said about the curriculum in Chapter 9.

The Equipment

Although equipment is not as important a factor as the others mentioned, it is very significant. As an evidence of this fact, one needs only to stand near the center of a one-room church building while eight or ten classes are being conducted, particularly without curtains. Under such conditions, it almost seems that the equipment is the most important factor in efficiency. By equipment is meant not only a building but also departmental assembly rooms and classrooms; and in addition, suitable chairs, tables, chalk-boards, maps, visual aids, record systems, and such provision for the library and recreational life as will enable a church school to carry on to the best possible advantage. In a sense the equipment is a part of the materials.

The Time Element

Probably there is some question as to whether or not the time element should be considered in discussing the factors in religious education. It is, however, a very important factor in the religious-educational process. Education, whether in the field of religion and morals or elsewhere, cannot be forced. It takes time to grow a mind and a character. Mushrooms may be developed overnight, but it takes decades to grow a tree. Maltbie D. Babcock well says: "Good habits are not made on birthdays nor Christian character at the new year. The vision may dawn . . . the heart may leap with new inspiration on some mountain-top, but the test, the triumph is at the foot of the mountain on the level plain." Education requires time.

RELIGIOUS EDUCATIONAL ACTIVITIES

Though previously mentioned and to be discussed more fully in a later chapter, a brief statement of the activities involved in religious education will be given here in order to understand more clearly the full meaning of the term.

Instruction

Teaching is foundational. By whatever method, the inculcation of ideas and the building up of ideals is the first responsibility of religious education. Helpful knowledge is essential to right living. W. S. Athearn was right in saying: "Ideals are the pulleys over which we lift original nature to higher levels." Whatever stress may be given to habit formation, instruction must not be minimized. The transmission of truth from teacher to pupil is necessary. What one believes is as important as how he feels or what he does. Satisfaction must accompany information for it to be effective.

Evangelism

Evangelism may be defined as the effort to lead the individual to a personal acceptance of Christ and his way of life. This, evangelical Christians regard as the activity next after instruction and the most important until accomplished. It may be done privately, in a class, a department, or a school assembly either during a revival meeting or apart from one. Some religious educators think this activity is out of harmony with the educational method. Betts devotes four pages to contrasting the educational and evangelistic points of view. He thinks they are antagonistic and mutually exclusive, but such is not the case.[3] If education includes response to truth taught, then it involves evangelism; for it is leading the pupil to respond to the truth taught about Christ.[4]

Worship

More and more emphasis is being placed on the importance of worship in order to keep a vital touch with God, to give a true perspective to life, and to help keep a grip on ourselves in this materialistic, nerve-strained, pleasure-loving age. Increasingly, it is being recognized that, to be most effective, worship must be adapted to the age and experience of the individual. Too often it has been on the adult level only. It should be graded and made a part of the educational program of the church. This is being done in an increasing measure with suitable songs, scriptures, and other materials provided in various departmental programs.

Giving

In recent years it has become increasingly evident that occasional, spasmodic collections based largely on emotion are not an adequate means of developing a generation of givers. It is more and more felt that the giving of money should grow out of an enlightened conscience and be a regular, systematic, and proportionate expression, based on love. In other words, training in giving should relate to teaching about it and become a regular activity of the educational program. The Sunday school is especially suitable since it reaches most people and is best adapted to this procedure. Consequently, development in giving is being made a regular activity with excellent results both in developing character and in securing adequate funds.

Recreation

Educators have come to recognize that developing the

---

[3] George Herbert Betts, *The New Program of Religious Education* (Nashville: Abingdon Press, 1921), pp. 28–31. For a more recent discussion see Harold C. Mason, *Abiding Values in Christian Education* (Westwood, N. J.: Fleming H. Revell Co., 1955), pp. 55–60.

[4] Harry C. Munro, *Protestant Nurture* (Englewood Cliffs, N. J.: Prentice-Hall, Inc., 1956), chap. vi.

social instinct and giving relaxation to jaded nerves are vital elements in personality development. Also they have come to realize that what people do during hours of leisure enters as vitally into character as what they do during the time of work. Since recreation has come to be recognized as an important activity in religious education, emphasis has been given to the various social-recreational organizations as well as to the graded social activities in church life. New results in character education are emerging as a result of the positive emphasis along this line.

Service

Since religious educational activity includes the development of habits and skills as well as the imparting of proper information and the forming of right attitudes, it is natural that service activities should be included in the religious-educational procedures. Increasingly this is being done through the enlistment work of Sunday school organizations, the personal service phase of missionary agencies, and the expressional activities of the Training Union. Through these means people are led to grow in Christian graces since they express them as well as hear about them. In other words, the principle of learning to do by doing is followed.

AGENCIES FOR RELIGIOUS EDUCATION

Since a somewhat detailed discussion of the agencies involved in carrying out the program of religious education will be found in Parts III and IV of this book, only brief attention will be given to them here — merely enough to explain something of the scope of religious education.

The Home

Naturally, education in religion as in all other matters begins in the home. It was first in the history of the race, is first in the life of each individual, and should be first in emphasis. Because the home has the child before any other institution, at the most impressionable period in life, for the longest period of time, when external control is greatest, and

under the most impressionable circumstances, it has possibilities beyond any other agency. No one ever gets away
from the good of the positive religious influences of the home
or the harm of the nonreligious or antireligious elements.
This is true whether the method is the unconscious influence
of the life and activity of the parents or their conscious and
deliberate efforts. Wesner Fallaw well says:

> The attitudes, values, and conduct of parents constitute the pattern
> for living by which the child fashions his early behavior. . . . A large
> part of the practices and customs of a given family constitute the raw
> material with which the growing child structures his life.[5]

The Church

Next to the home comes the church. With the modern
emphasis on the Cradle Roll, the Nursery, and the Nursery
class, the child comes under the influence of the church very
early in life. Several educational organizations function in
the church.

The *Sunday School,* designated as the teaching agency, is
set for the task of teaching the Bible to all ages through
graded classes and by means of adapted materials and methods. It utilizes more workers, reaches more people, has them
for a longer period of time, covers a wider range of activity,
and probably accomplishes more than any other educational
agency in the church. It is still primary.

Along with the teaching agency comes the *Training
Union,* whose primary task is to train immature Christians
into full-fledged church members. Its emphasis, therefore, is
on the expressional side of education. Through the discussion
of topics, discharging official responsibilities, and participation in various kinds of service activities, young Christians
are developed as Kingdom citizens. It has helped greatly in
creating Christian morale.

Woman's Missionary Union has developed as the particular agency for training in the field of missions. While originally for older women, girls and younger women now

---

[5] Wesner Fallaw, in Philip H. Lotz (ed.), *Orientation in Religious Education* (Nashville: Abingdon Press, 1950).

are given a prominent place in the organization. Through weekly meetings, reading courses, personal service, prayer, and giving, they have accomplished much. In fact, they have led the way in missions.

While the *Brotherhood* is not so thoroughly organized, generally promoted, or definitely educational, it is seeking more and more to enlist the men and develop them in fellowship, stewardship, and general church responsibility. Also it is fostering the Royal Ambassador organization for boys. It has helped greatly to stimulate morale.

The *Vacation Bible School* has come to fill a unique and large place in the educational work of the church. Coming during the vacation period when boys and girls are idle and subjected to temptation, it meets daily with emphasis on recreation, handwork, and moral and patriotic topics as well as definitely religious ones. It is attracting many and rendering a distinct service.

Growing in recognition is the *weekday class* for religious instruction. It meets once a week during the school year and is correlated with, if not credited by, the public school. Since it has the possibility of reaching more people and giving more thorough instruction than the other agencies, it is exceptionally valuable. The future will see more of it.

Also there is the *Christian day school.* It may be for the elementary grades or the high school or both. It operates all day for five days a week. The Bible is taught for one period daily, and all other subjects are approached from the Christian point of view. It has been Catholicism's most powerful agency, and on the mission field is Protestantism's most effective means of evangelizing today.[6]

The College

The *Christian college* carries on beyond the range of the home and the church. The period covered is a critical one in the life of the individual because of the type of subjects studied and also because the student is away from the influ-

[6] See Frank E. Gabelein, *Christian Education in a Democracy* (New York: Oxford University Press, 1951), chap. v.

ence of the home and the home church. The denominational college has an advantage over the state school in having Christian teachers, chapel exercises, the Christian point of view, and an atmosphere of religious influence. It has not only trained Christian leaders but has also been a leavening influence in the educational world.

In recent years more attention has been given to *student work* in state schools. This is due in part to the increased realization of the need within the school but more particularly because so many more students are now attending state institutions than denominational schools. Student secretaries and teachers have been employed. Bible courses for credit have been instituted in many places. Baptist Student Union and other denominational student-led religious organizations have been formed to head up religious life. In some cases dormitories under Christian influence have been erected. This work constitutes one of the ripest and most vital fields for service.

Other Agencies

Prominent among character-building organizations are the *recreational* agencies such as Boy Scouts and Camp Fire Girls. Although frequently sponsored by local churches, they are independent in their control and have national leadership. Hence, they are not definitely denominational. However, by virtue of the appeal that they make to the interests of youth and the emphasis they give to character, they are very effective agencies for religious education.

The *religious press* is another outstanding agency. The religious paper published by the local church, the state denominational paper, and the various South-wide magazines have tremendous opportunities in shaping the thoughts and lives of people. In addition, good books and tracts circulated in homes directly and through church libraries may accomplish much. And while somewhat different, the possibilities for religious education through the use of the radio and television are now being realized.

In this introductory chapter the nature of religious education, the activities involved, the factors included, and the agencies for promotion have been briefly discussed. It has been seen as a major rather than a minor task. In fact, it is central in the work of the kingdom of God.

QUESTIONS FOR DISCUSSION

1. Find several definitions of religious education. Select from your library a number of books on religious education and compare the definitions given by each author. Then formulate your own definition.

2. Plan a calendar of activities for your own age group in your church.

3. In recent years there has been an effort to restore the Bible to the public school curriculum. Do you think this is a wise thing to do? Give reasons for your position.

4. How does religious education differ from other education? Consider the material, methods, and the qualifications of the teachers.

CHAPTER 2

EDUCATIONAL ACTIVITIES IN OLD TESTAMENT TIMES

The Jewish people have always placed a great emphasis on education as a means of promoting religion. In fact, preaching has been secondary to it. Alfred Edersheim, an authority on Jewish customs, says:

> To impart to the child knowledge of the Torah conferred as great a spiritual distinction as if a man had received the Law itself on Mount Horeb. Every other engagement, even the necessary meal, should give place to this paramount duty; nor should it be forgotten that while here real labour was necessary, it would never prove fruitless. That man was of the profane vulgar (an *Am Ha-arets*), who had sons, but failed to bring them up in knowledge of the law.[1]

A prominent modern Jewish scholar, Israel S. Chipkin, has stressed the Jewish emphasis in these strong words:

> Learning and conduct, culture and custom, become integrated to form the personality of the individual and to give distinctive character to the community. Jewish education, the study of Torah, therefore, became traditionally the religious preoccupation of the individual Jew and the basic obligation of the Jewish community.[2]

It is important to begin these background studies with an

[1] Alfred Edersheim, *The Life and Times of Jesus the Messiah* (Grand Rapids, Mich.: Wm. B. Eerdmans Publishing Co., 1953), Vol. I., p. 230.

[2] Israel S. Chipkin, in Philip H. Lotz (ed.), *Orientation in Religious Education* (Nashville: Abingdon Press, 1950), p. 501.

investigation of what the Jews have done. In this one chapter it is impossible, of course, to give a thorough treatment of educational activities in the Old Testament. Only a general survey from an institutional angle will be given.

THE HOME

The home was the first institution for religious and moral training in the history of the race, as it is in the life of each individual now. Everything considered, it has always been the most powerful one, at least potentially.

Commands

The Lord selected *Abraham* as national leader and put upon him the responsibility to "command his children and his household after him, that they may keep the way of Jehovah, to do righteousness and justice; to the end that Jehovah may bring upon Abraham that which he hath spoken of him." (Gen. 18:19). God's immediate purpose in calling Abraham into a separated life was that he might engage in a process of domestic education.

Moses urged the Israelites to teach in the home, saying: "Thou shalt teach them [these words] diligently unto thy children, and shalt talk of them when thou sittest in thy house, and when thou walkest by the way, and when thou liest down, and when thou risest up. And thou shalt bind them for a sign upon thy hand, and they shall be for frontlets between thine eyes. And thou shalt write them upon the door-posts of thy house, and upon thy gates." (Deut. 6:7-9).

The oft-quoted exhortation in *Proverbs*, "Train up a child in the way he should go, and even when he is old he will not depart from it" (22:6) was primarily an emphasis to parents. All along the importance of parental instruction was stressed.

Other Old Testament scriptures emphasize home training, some implying the training of servants and retainers as well as children in the immediate family, by the patriarchal head, as in the case of Abraham and his 318 trained men. (Gen. 14:14). Edersheim says:

There could not be national history, nor even romance, to compare with that by which a Jewish mother might hold her child entranced. And it was his own history — that of his tribe, clan, perhaps family; of the past, indeed, but yet of the present, and still more of the glorious future. Long before he could go to school, or even Synagogue, the private and united prayers and the domestic rites, whether of the weekly Sabbath or of festive seasons, would indelibly impress themselves upon his mind.[3]

Teachers

The *parents* were of course the chief teachers in the home, both emphasizing morals and religion, with the father instructing the son in industrial activities and the mother instructing the daughter in domestic arts. Children were urged to "hear the instruction of thy father and forsake not the teaching of thy mother." (Prov. 1:8). It also seems that the *patriarch* was expected to teach all the children of the families under his leadership. The writer of Genesis records that Abraham "led forth his trained men, born in his house, three hundred and eighteen." This reference would presuppose a process of school instruction under Abraham's oversight.

In addition to parents and patriarchs there were various *private* teachers, often professional or semiprofessional in nature. Nursing fathers and nursing mothers, who were guardians or governesses, carried on nurturing or teaching activity (Num. 11:12, Isa. 49:33); Naomi served as such to Ruth's child (Ruth 4:16); and the great men of Samaria to Ahab's son (II Kings 10:5). It is possible that other private, professional teachers were employed from time to time (Prov. 5:13, Ps. 119:99). There are also specific instances of individual instruction, such as Melchizedek teaching Abraham with regard to the tithe (Gen. 14:18 f).

Teaching

The elements of *culture* were included in the instruction. This involved the rudiments of learning, such as reading, writing, and calculation. The history of the chosen people

[3] Edersheim, *The Life and Times*, Vol. I, p. 228.

was inculcated in various ways. Manners relative to eating and to right relationships to parents and others were instilled.

Much attention was given to *practical arts*. The child learned of suitable and forbidden foods and other matters relative to health. The boys were skilled in agricultural and mechanical activities. Girls were taught domestic arts. Some attention was probably given to music, athletics, and military tactics.

Morals received particular emphasis. This covered the whole range of ethical virtues, such as temperance, purity, honesty, obedience, and industry. Right relationships to others were stressed. In fact, the Book of Proverbs is a rather comprehensive manual of practical ethics.

Religion was of course stressed. In various ways ideas relative to the true God, providential dealings, stewardship of money, the Sabbath, worship, and other matters pertaining to religion were emphasized. The religious attitude permeated all of the other instruction given.

Characteristics

The teaching was *informal*. A formal system of instruction had not been thought of. Conversation, imitation, and example played a large part then as they do in rural life today. Often this is the most effective kind of instruction.

The instruction was *vital*, centering around the problems and needs in everyday living. This is the element that educators have been striving recently to get into modern education. Life-centered activities and problems are prominent in all educational discussions these days. Jewish education centuries ago was similar.

Participation played a large part. While stories, questions, and memorizing entered in, they were not the dominant methods. Ceremonial rites as in circumcision, festivals such as the Passover, garbs worn during prayer and at meals, and other activities gave ample opportunity for participation. While the project method as such had never been heard of, its principles were being carried out.

Achievements

The training in the home in the patriarchal as well as in later periods of Hebrew life resulted in high *ideals* in religion and morals. The concepts of God, the Sabbath, holiness, and obligation to man and God were far above those of surrounding peoples. One of Judaism's distinctive contributions has been the loftiness of its ideals.

Outstanding *characters* developed as another result. Joseph was so instructed as to withstand Egypt's temptations and become a ruler; Moses became the outstanding leader and author of his day; Samuel developed into a great judge and ruler; and David, Solomon, Daniel, and others made pre-eminent contributions.

National greatness was another outcome. Surrounded by peoples with civilizations of long standing, the Hebrew nation came to a place of pre-eminent influence. This was due to the character of its people which, in turn, was largely the result of its home life.

THE FESTIVALS

The various festivals may very well be viewed as educational activities since they did much to impress certain significant facts as well as provide occasions for social fellowship.

Number

Apart from the ceremonials accompanying birth, marriage, and other such occasions, and those connected with the weekly, monthly, and other fast days, there gradually developed a number of outstanding feasts.

Prominent among these were the Passover, commemorating the death angel's passing over the first-born in Egypt and the exodus from that country; Pentecost, celebrating the giving of the Law; and Tabernacles, recalling the period of wandering in the wilderness.

As time went on and significant events happened, others were added, such as the Day of Atonement, Dedication, and Purim, commemorating outstanding occasions. During later

Judaism, the number had so grown that approximately a month during the year was given to such celebrations. Sometimes one day emphasized several events.

Nature

These occasions were of the nature of festivals, sometimes involving feasts commemorating happy events and sometimes fasts commemorating tragic events. Social as well as commemorative features were usually connected with them. The length of time they lasted varied from a day to a week or more.

Passover is a good illustration of a feast. It was observed annually at night, and portrayed the eating of the last meal before leaving Egypt while the death angel passed over the Hebrew homes and slew the first-born of the Egyptians. One or more families dressed in the garb of travelers and with staff in hand stood around a table and ate hurriedly the roasted paschal lamb or kid served with bitter herbs and unleavened bread. At a certain time during the procedure the youngest child asked what it all meant, and the head of the household explained the occasion. Following this, all leftovers were burned, and the family remained in the house until morning.

Characteristics

A number of features distinctively educational characterize these various festival occasions.

For one thing, they were *objective*. They made distinct appeals to the eye and other senses. This made them much more effective than speeches and books, especially for little children. Modern education is putting much stress on the use of visual aids in teaching.

They involved *activity*. Since the people themselves participated in the occasion rather than merely listened to someone read or tell the story, it was more powerful educationally. This principle of activity is emphasized today as being an essential element in the most effective educational procedure.

These feasts were also *dramatic*. The participants re-en-acted the scenes in an appropriate garb and in the natural setting, as far as was practicable. Acting added greatly to the didactic effectiveness. It involved movement and costume and appealed to the eye.

Intensiveness was another very effective feature. Some lasted for a week or more. All of the attention during this time was centered on this festival. By such means attention was focused and continued, and the impression deepened, as in a Vacation Bible School or continued revival meeting.

Results

These feasts helped to fix in mind significant *historical* events in the life of the chosen nation as could not have been done by merely reading about them or hearing them described. It was a wise piece of educational strategy and accomplishment.

Interest in things Jewish was stimulated by these periodic gatherings with their social, patriotic, and religious emphases. They were to the Hebrews what the Fourth of July or Lincoln's birthday is to Americans. Zeal for things Jewish was naturally stimulated.

National and religious *solidarity* was the final result. There was gradually built up a sense of divine leadership and unity that has persisted through the centuries, for even now it is difficult for a Jew to desert his religion or to marry a Gentile.

TABERNACLE AND TEMPLE

At first thought it would not seem that the activities of the Tabernacle and Temple were in any particular sense educational. But on more careful consideration it is evident that they were in many ways very much so. Since the Temple was largely just an enlargement and amplification of the Tabernacle, the main treatment will be given to the latter.

Construction

Surrounding the Tabernacle was a wall made of colored, embroidered curtains fastened on silver-tipped posts. Within the enclosure was an altar overlaid with gold. The Taber-

nacle proper was a tent, two-thirds of which was the Holy
Place and one-third the Holy of Holies, containing the Ark
of the Covenant, which enclosed the Ten Commandments.
The Temple was much more elaborate and substantial in its
construction than the Tabernacle.

This striking construction had educational significance
because it impressed upon these Hebrew people who had
been influenced by the animism of Egypt, the grandeur of a
personal God and the beauty of religion as against the animal
worship of heathenism. It raised their sense of values and
their appreciation of religion even as a beautiful church
building today is more impressive than a crude one. A new
sense of the worth of religion naturally emerged.

Arrangement

As previously indicated, a curtained wall surrounded the
Tabernacle and the enclosure, thus keeping the masses on the
outside. They could bring their offering only to the entrance.
Within the general enclosure and the Holy Place only the
priests were allowed. Within the Holy of Holies only the
High Priest went and then only once a year on the Day of
Atonement. The Temple had more extensive arrangements —
including provisions for singers, and a court each for the
women and for the Gentiles.

This separation and gradation had the effect of impressing
on the minds of the people the sacredness of Jehovah and the
fact that he could not be approached with the freedom with
which one approaches idols or animals, as in the Egyptian
religion. Here was the education in awe and reverence so
greatly needed at the time and, as a matter of fact, even now.
It gave a new realization of the grandeur of God.

Priesthood

The formation of the priesthood was an interesting part
of the system. The priests were the guardians of the sacred
shrines, directors of the sacrifices, and instructors of the people. Their garb was particularly striking. The priest wore an
ephod of linen with threads of gold, purple, blue, and scarlet

intertwined; a shoulder piece of gold set with onyx stones; a breastplate similar to the ephod set with twelve precious stones representing the twelve tribes; a blue robe with golden bells and pomegranates on the skirt, and a headdress mingled with gold, purple, and other colors.

This separated group, ministering at the altar, dressed in such elaborate and striking garb, stimulated curiosity and awe and had the effect of impressing on the people the importance of the work of Jehovah in a new and significant way as contrasted with the crude gods of the Egyptians and others. It helped also to prepare the way for the idea of the priesthood of Christ.

Sacrifices

The system of sacrifices was of particular educational significance. It included a variety of offerings and considerable ceremony connected with them. There were peace offerings indicative of right relations with God; sin offerings to atone for unwitting sins or errors; and also guilt offerings to make expiation to God for more serious sins. There were qualifications connected with the offering, such as being without blemish and of a specified age. Certain conditions, such as cleansing and purifying, were required of the one making the offering, and the priest had to offer it under certain conditions as to procedure and disposition of the various parts.

All of these things had tremendous value in objectively and effectively teaching a nation of people fresh from the environment of heathenism. Thus, the people learned about the nature, seriousness and consequences of sin, God's requirements of those who sin, and what was necessary to be right before God. They helped also to prepare their minds for the climax of the sacrifice of Christ in atoning for the sins of all humanity, particularly as the High Priest made the blood offering in the Holy of Holies once each year on the Day of Atonement.

In addition to these various things, there was in the Temple the reciting of Scriptures, praying, various types of singing, and discussion and explanation of the Scriptures that had great value in helping the people to understand the way of the Lord more perfectly. So the Temple was the center of the religious life of the nation.

THE SYNAGOGUE

The outstanding educational agency in the Bible is the synagogue, especially when the elementary school was attached to it. It was primarily for instruction and training. The term "synagogue" literally means a leading or gathering together and, therefore, an assembly. While the building where the people gathered came to be used as a public hall and place of worship, originally it was meant only for the exposition of the Law.[4]

Development

The synagogue seems to have had its *origin* during the Babylonian captivity when the Temple was gone and the people were in a foreign land. There a new generation was growing up without the benefits of religious instruction, and it was not feasible to have a central temple as in the homeland. So to preserve their religious heritage, they developed the synagogue.

It increased rapidly. After the return from captivity, a synagogue could be found in most of the towns of Judea, and in Gentile communities wherever there was a Jewish population. One writer says that by the time of Christ, there were at least 460 synagogues in Jerusalem — as many as there were Sunday schools in New York City in the early part of this century.

Provisions

Generally a *separate building* was provided for the purpose. This was the expectation. The poor, however, were permitted to use a room in another building. The structure was rectangular in shape, somewhat like church buildings today. Normally they were on high ground facing toward the East.

[4] Paul Levertoff, *The International Standard Bible Encyclopedia* (Grand Rapids, Mich.: Wm. B. Eerdmans Publishing Co., 1949), Vol. V, p. 2878.

A chest containing the scrolls of Scripture was kept at the back of the pulpit.

There were several *officers*, including a ruler for the organization whose duty it was to select from the congregation a leader for reading, preaching, and directing the discussion. Christ seems to have served as a reader and preacher. An interpreter was also provided to translate the Law and the Prophets from Hebrew into Aramaic, the language of the hearers.

Activities

The *services* of the synagogue were held on the Sabbath, on Monday, and on Thursday, when the country people came to market, and on feast and fast days. There were two services during the day — one mainly instructional and the other mainly devotional. This probably helps to explain the statement about Christ "teaching in their synagogues, and preaching the gospel of the kingdom" (Matt. 4:23).

The *teaching element* in the services included the general recitation of selected Scriptures; the reading and translating of the Law, a verse at a time, covering it in three years; and the reading and translating in a similar fashion of the Prophets, with three verses as a unit. This is somewhat like the Uniform Lessons in the Sunday school today. Following this minute study came a general, expository address applying the lesson to the life of the day. So the synagogue services were definitely educational.

Results

Since the synagogues were available to practically all, there was provided virtually *universal religious training* in the Law and the Prophets for those of both sexes. This was a distinct advance over the more limited and less educational activities of the Tabernacle and Temple, as well as the home. Hebrew children gradually acquired a considerable knowledge of the Old Testament.

Not only was religious training made practically universal through the synagogue, but this activity led *to the elementary schools* which came to be the outstanding school system of the world in those days. Indirectly, also, it led to the professional schools for the training of the scribes and the rabbis.

THE ELEMENTARY SCHOOL

The elementary school is the only exclusively educational institution in the Bible. It was attached to the synagogue somewhat like the parochial schools of different denominations today are attached to churches. The idea may have come from the Babylonians who had schools connected with their temples. By the time of Christ the elementary school was practically as general as the synagogue, the latter presupposing a school very much as a church today presupposes a Sunday school.

Pupils

The constituency was limited to the elementary grades. It was of course for boys only, since the formal education of girls had not yet begun. The pupils started at about six years of age and attended until about sixteen. Apparently they went every weekday. Ultimately, attendance was compulsory and even as important a matter as the rebuilding of the Temple was not sufficient to detain the children. They were graded into separate groups, according to age.

Teachers

These were men only and must be married, since the mothers might come to visit the school. For the most part the scribes were the teachers and they were God-fearing and conscientious men. A teacher was not to have more than twenty-five pupils, an assistant being employed if there were more, and two teachers if above fifty. They served without pay and made their living by other means. The Talmud said, "The true guardians of the city are the teachers." And Clarence H. Benson says: "From the time of Ezra, the Rabbi has been the man of supreme importance among the Jewish people."[5]

[5] Clarence H. Benson, *A Popular History of Christian Education* (Chicago: The Moody Press, 1943), p. 25.

Curriculum

Foundational studies, including reading, writing, and arithmetic, were taught. These were means to ends. For history they studied the life of the Hebrew people. For ethics they had the morals and manners of Proverbs. As social science they had the civil, criminal, and ceremonial law of the Jews. The Psalms constituted the basis of study in music and poetry. Scrolls were used as textbooks, and the material was adapted to the age and ability of the pupil. The course of study was thoroughly religious and moral.

Methods

The methods were not quite like those of the present day. They were more formal. *Memorization* was prominent in the system, with special emphasis on catechizing, drill, and review. Even the young children memorized portions of Leviticus and knew important scriptures by heart.

Discipline also occupied a prominent place. Punishment was freely resorted to. The leaders believed in the depravity of human nature and did not spare the rod for fear of spoiling the child. They included training as well as teaching in their program.

The *material-centered* emphasis was prominent, more regard probably being paid to the text than to the pupil. Yet, with all of its weaknesses, it seems to have been the first compulsory system of public education and the most effective of the day.

OTHER EDUCATIONAL ACTIVITIES

There were a number of other educational activities carried on in the Old Testament period besides those of the agencies already discussed. For the most part they were individual and informal efforts, usually rather temporary in nature and varying in importance. Some of these follow.

Work of Moses

During the period involved in the journey from Egypt to Palestine, Moses carried on an extensive educational activity with the Israelites. This was necessary in order to counteract the heathen influences of Egypt and prepare for citizenship and leadership in the new land. For the most part the activity was group instruction on such matters as the Ten Commandments, idolatry, and worship; memorizing the civil and ceremonial law, as given in Deuteronomy; judging disputes and explaining right conduct in connection therewith; and putting into writing the important teachings of Jehovah. These instructions touched almost every problem in personal, domestic, business, civic, and religious relationships. They prepared the people for right living with God and man. Moses left instructions for periodic and systematic instruction for the years ahead.

Joshua's Activities

Following the example of Moses, Joshua, his successor, sought to carry on definite instruction. A particular instance was that of gathering the people into two groups facing each other in front of Mount Ebal and Mount Gerizin, and rehearsing in antiphonal fashion the blessings and the curses (Josh. 8:32 f). Previously, the people had piled up a heap of stones gathered from the Jordan river to serve as a permanent reminder of their entrance into the land of promise. Special studies of the entire Law were made every seventh year during the time of rest, and also each fiftieth or jubilee year. By these means the people were informed as to what Jehovah required at their hands.

Jehoshaphat's Procedure

Another specific effort of considerable interest and effect was the teaching activity fostered by the good king, Jehoshaphat, as a means of social and moral reform. The life of the people had reached a rather sinful state, and preparatory to a reform movement he instituted a plan of popular religious instruction somewhat on the order of training classes. Sixteen priests and Levites were sent out in pairs to go from city to city throughout the land and to carry on a brief course in religious teaching (II Chron. 17:7 f). The result was far-reaching. Civic leaders today might well profit by that example.

Schools for the Prophets

Much has been said from time to time about the schools for the prophets carried on by Samuel, Elijah, and Elisha. The emphasis has been overdone as they were not schools in the sense in which we think of schools today. Rather, they were more of the nature of training institutes. They were theological institutions, only in embryo, whose purpose was to prepare the young prophets for their tasks. The locations were at Bethel, Gilgal, Jericho, and the Jordan. The older prophets visited these places and instructed the young men in the elements of learning, religious history and literature and prophetic activities.

Teaching by the Prophets

It has been well said that the prophet was a "forth-teller" quite as much as a "foreteller." Much of his task was to interpret the moral and religious significance of current events. He was, therefore, a teacher. This teaching work was done in various ways. One was by giving names to children suggestive of problems facing the people, as when Hosea named a daughter "unpitied," and Isaiah named his son "a remnant shall return." Sometimes they used dramatic illustrations to impress future events, as when Jeremiah wore a wooden yoke about his neck, and Ezekiel scattered his hair to the wind. They also spoke and wrote vigorously, using some of the most effective literary forms. They were powerful portrayers of truth.

Services of the Wise Men

Another character about whom very little is said is the wise man, or sage. These men were informal, self-appointed teachers of truth. They were usually advanced in years and were sometimes called "elders." They often sat near the gates of the city and discoursed to those who came in. Besides public discussion they gave private counsel and also trained a group of disciples, or pupils. In contrast to the prophets, who placed the emphasis on civic affairs, they dealt more with the personal graces that go to make a good citizen, homemaker, or businessman. The book of Proverbs is rather typical of their teachings and shows interesting literary forms as well as ethical instruction. They were the forerunners of the professional teachers. Job, Solomon, and others belong to this group.

Scribal Instruction

The most distinctively teaching person in the Old Testament was the scribe. The word means "man of books" and carries the idea of copyist, interpreter, or editor. They were journalists as well as teachers. At first they were chroniclers and copyists but gradually developed into a teaching group. The rabbi or master was the climax of the development. They preserved the writings, translated them into the language of the people, taught them to the masses of people by various means, and trained pupils to take their places. The rabbinical schools were somewhat after the order of normal schools. A striking individual instance of scribal activity was Ezra's open-air school in Jerusalem where the Scriptures were read to the assembled multitude. Following the reading the people were grouped according to their ability to understand, and the Scriptures were interpreted and applied by teachers who had been trained for the task. This is suggestive of the graded Sunday school.

There are other instances of educational activity in the Old Testament, but these are enough to indicate the didactic emphasis in it. The teaching element runs all the way through it and gives an idea of what should be done today. As a matter of fact, education was developed among the Hebrews to a greater extent than it probably was among any other people at the time, even though girls received little consideration. The Talmud placed great emphasis on the teacher saying: "The world continues to exist only by the breath of the children of the schools." The educational emphasis has been strong throughout the history of the Jews.

QUESTIONS FOR DISCUSSION

1. Make a survey of the Old Testament, noting the educational activities used by the people of that time.

2. Make a study of the synagogue. When was it first used? What was the reason for its inception? How was it used? Give your opinion regarding its value for Jewish people through their history.

3. Why is the home the most important institution for teaching the Bible? After listing your own reasons, refer to *Teaching for Results* by Dr. Edge. (See Part I Bibliography, p. 111.)

4. The sacrificial system was a very important part of the life of the Hebrews. Show in what way this system was a teaching agency.

CHAPTER 3

EDUCATIONAL ACTIVITIES IN NEW TESTAMENT TIMES

As prominent as is the emphasis on educational activity in the Old Testament, it is much more outstanding in the New. Particularly is this true because of the stress which the Master Teacher himself, both by precept and example, gave to teaching. In addition there are a number of other evidences of the prominence given to it in the New Testament period.

CHRIST AS A TEACHER

For a long time Christ has been considered as a revealer of God, a healer of human ills, and a redeemer from sin. Only in recent years has much thought been given to him as a teacher.

Fact of His Teaching

According to Lewis J. Sherrill:

Jesus himself was a teacher. That term, of course, does not fully describe him. For we in Christianity look to him as truly Son of man and truly Son of God, as Saviour, and as Lord of life. But that he took up the role of teacher and was commonly addressed as "Teacher" (Master) cannot be gainsaid after even a casual reading of the Gospels.[1]

[1] Lewis J. Sherrill, in Philip H. Lotz (ed.), *Orientation in Religious Education* (Nashville: Abingdon Press, 1950), p. 15.

What are the evidences for this statement? A careful study of the Gospels will prove this statement.

For one thing he was *called teacher*. While Christ was never in the Gospels called a preacher, yet forty-five times in those records he was called a teacher. Some of the times he called himself a teacher; at other times he was called that by his disciples, such as Mary or Nicodemus, and still at other times by his enemies, such as the Pharisees, Sadducees, and others. All regarded him as a teacher.[2]

Also he was regularly *engaged in teaching*. He went about teaching in the synagogues, at the Temple, by the roadside, at the seashore, in the houses, and in fact wherever he was. Teaching was his business, and he was at it constantly. He was not an official teacher but rather a self-appointed one.

He not only taught the masses, but he also *trained a group of teachers* who were to carry on when he was gone. Especially was this true in the latter part of his ministry. In this respect he became a teacher of teachers, preparing them to continue his work. This was done not only by personal instruction but also by the example of his life and by the activities he gave them to do.

Furthermore, he *commissioned his followers to teach*. When he got ready to leave the earth, he gave his parting command. All three phases of the Great Commission (Matt. 28:19 — 20) have to do with teaching — enlisting in the school of Christ, initiating through a teaching ordinance, and continuing the teaching process. The Lord's supper also is a didactic ordinance.

Controlling Aims

Undoubtedly Jesus did not go about the main business of his life without definite aims and purposes. What were these objectives? How far should they control educational aims today? The answer to these questions will give not only a better understanding of him as a teacher but also a better basis for doing what he has commanded.

---

[2] J. M. Price, *Jesus the Teacher* (rev. ed.; Nashville: The Broadman Press, 1954), chap. i.

From the *negative* point of view it is evident that the Master Teacher was not primarily concerned with inculcating a body of truth. He wrote no books nor did he present at any one place a systematic outline of all his teachings. He was not material-centered in his emphasis. He knew the impotence of mere factual knowledge. Furthermore, it is clear that he did not seek to dictate or determine the thinking of his pupils. He knew too well the effect of such a procedure on their lives and was too much concerned about free will and personality development.

On the *positive* side it may be said that he was life-centered in his approach. Findley Edge describes it:

> Jesus taught, and men's attitudes were changed; their habits were changed; their lives were changed and brought in line with the will of God. This was religious education at its best. This is the kind of results that we as Christian teachers seek today.[3]

It is interesting to notice the Master Teacher's large use of stories or parables in his teaching. In fact they have been called "the consummation of his art." About one fourth of his words as recorded by Mark and about one half as recorded by Luke are in the form of parables. The term "parable" is used about fifty times in the New Testament. If one includes under this head the maxims or germ parables, the allegory, and other illustrations, probably a hundred can be found.[4]

He sought to develop individuals so that they could face life. Therefore he dealt with life-situations and personal problems. His greatest parable, the one on the Foolish Farmer, grew out of a request made that he divide an inheritance. He was more concerned about developing religious persons than imparting religious truth. To that end he sought to stimulate and direct religious thinking, to develop right emotions and attitudes, and to lead into practical and vital Christian activity. "I came that they may have life." (John 10:10)

---

[3] Findley B. Edge, *Teaching for Results* (Nashville: The Broadman Press, 1956), p. 15.

[4] Price, *Jesus the Teacher*, pp. 101–2.

Literary Forms Used

Along with other considerations on Jesus as a teacher, it is interesting to notice something of the form in which his teaching was cast. There is artistry even in this.

Probably the most striking form is the *parable*. It is a truth taken from a familiar phase of life to make clear truth in one that is not so familiar. They vary greatly in length, some being germ parables and others long ones. They cover almost every phase of life, including inanimate things, such as soil, clothes, and food; various kinds of plants, birds, and animals, and human beings in various relationships.

Epigrams constitute another very striking form of material used by Christ in his teaching. These include short, pithy proverbs, and maxims, such as "Physician, heal thyself" (Luke 4:23), and the familiar Golden Rule. Figures of speech, including the metaphor, hyperbole, and personification, were used frequently. All of these are effective and easily remembered.

Along with the last-named come various forms of *repetition and contrast* or comparison, such as "Lead us not into temptation, but deliver us from evil" (Matt. 6:13). The various beatitudes belong here. These striking forms, as well as his personality and methods, served to drive home the truths he taught and make them easily remembered.

Methods Employed

One may go to Christ to find not only valuable truths to be taught but also the best methods to be used. His teaching is our model of method as well as of content. In fact, Squires would place him beyond us as indicated in the title of his book, *The Pedagogy of Jesus in the Twilight of Today*.

The *lecture* method had a prominent place in Christ's teaching. The so-called Sermon on the Mount is an outstanding example. It is a didactic discourse rather than a hortatory message. A number of other instances are to be found. These gave Christ an opportunity to set forth his teaching in somewhat systematic form.

Discussion is prominent and probably his most distinctive method. For the most part he did not seek to present formal material so much as to meet life problems. Even the Old Testament was presented not so much exegetically as to throw light on particular problems. Many of his discussions were with individuals, such as Nicodemus and the Samaritan woman, and were conversational in nature.

Christ also used *questions* frequently, more than one hundred being recorded. Sometimes they were for informative purposes; at other times to impress a truth; and on other occasions to provoke thought, deepen conviction, or secure response. In all cases they served to give interest and vigor to his teaching.

As previously indicated, he used the *story* often. This was usually in the form of the parable and covered a wide range of topics close to the experiences of the hearers. It usually carried its own lesson but might be used to introduce a topic or clinch a truth already stated in abstract form.

The *project* method was used to some degree. Christ gave his disciples problems to work out, took them with him on his journeys, and sent them out on missions of their own, thus teaching them through experience. Also there is the use of visual aids, such as the coin, and dramatic portrayal of truth, such as baptism.

Results Accomplished

If Christ is to be judged as a teacher according to the results accomplished, he will have to be given first place. Certainly no teacher has ever achieved so much in the life of humanity and in so short a time.

For one thing he trained a group of *leaders* that have carried his message around the world. No teacher ever trained such an effective group of workers. Yet they were from the common people, and he had only a brief time in which to develop them into such an effective leadership. This shows him to be the Master Teacher.

Also his *disciples* have come to be the largest and most significant group of followers that any teacher ever had. Including all branches, there are about 600 million Christians, which is around 80 per cent more than any other group of disciples. They number nearly a third of the population of the entire earth today.

Furthermore his *influence* has gone further than that of any other teacher. His teachings have permeated literature, influenced education, shaped governments, and accomplished many social and cultural reforms. Christ's truths have affected civilization as those of no other teacher.

PAUL AS A TEACHER

Ordinarily Paul is thought of as a foreign missionary and evangelist and seldom as a teacher. More careful study, however, reveals the fact that he was very definitely a teacher. In many ways this teaching activity stands out.

The Fact

Perhaps the strongest evidence that Paul was a teacher is the fact that he *himself says so.* In I Tim. 2:7 he says: "I was appointed a preacher, and an apostle . . . , a teacher." Evidently he knew what he was talking about. Also he refers to himself four times in his epistles as having taught. This includes teaching at Thessalonica (II Thess. 2:15), at Colossae (Col. 2:7), and in fact at all of the churches that he had established (I Cor. 4:17, Col. 1:28). This extensive teaching of young Christians was necessary, since they had recently been converted from paganism, lacked the foundation of their Jewish brethren, and in addition were cluttered up with various heathen ideas and practices.

Luke also said that Paul taught. At Antioch, for example, he remained for an entire year and "taught much people" (Acts 11:26). At Corinth he carried on his teaching work for a year and a half (Acts 18:11). At Ephesus he extended his teaching ministry to two years and three months, part of the time in the synagogue and a part of it in the school of Tyrannus (Acts 19:8-10). Even while a prisoner at Rome for two years, he taught as well as preached (Acts 18:31). From all of these statements, it is evident that much of the activity of Paul in his missionary work was that of a teacher.

His Aims

The first aim that Paul had in mind was to lay a solid *foundation for conversion* and the Christian life. His work was being done largely outside the borders of Judaism, where the theological and ethical foundations of Jewish teaching were lacking. In addition to this lack there were all the evils which in theory and practice accompany heathenism. A great many corrections had to be made and positive instruction given before an intelligent conversion could take place. It was on the same basis a little later that the catechumenate, which is discussed in the following chapter, was established. And it is because of similar conditions today in foreign lands that the missionary instructs for a period before seeking a profession of faith or church membership.

A second aim was *development* in the Christian life. Paul recognized that conversion is only the beginning of the Christian experience and that extended instruction must be carried on if satisfactory development is to take place. He was not contented, therefore, merely to secure a profession. He sought to follow it up with extended instruction "that ye may be filled with the knowledge of his will in all spiritual wisdom and understanding, to walk worthily of the Lord . . . , bearing fruit in every good work . . . , perfect in Christ" (Col. 1:9-10, 28). His ultimate objective in carrying on such an extensive teaching activity was the perfection of Christian character. Within this general aim, of course, Paul includes the specific graces that go to make a socialized, moral, and religious character and personality.

Teaching Means

In general he used two types. One was *personal contact*. Sometimes Paul taught privately, going from house to house. At other times, he taught publicly, dealing with small groups or larger crowds. Both sexes and all types of people were included. He taught at practically any time of day and any day of the week. His teaching was carried on in synagogues, schools, market-places, and by the river. He taught whenever an occasion presented itself, wherever he happened to be, and whoever came within the sphere of his influence. He was a peripatetic and perennial teacher, with much of the world as his classroom.

In addition to teaching people face to face Paul taught extensively *by letter*. It was impossible for him to be at all of the places that he desired to be all of the time to give the instruction needed. He covered too much territory, had converts in too many places, and needed to give instruction along too many lines. Therefore he instituted the epistle or didactic letter as a means of wider instructional activity. Sometimes these were written to individuals, as Philemon; sometimes to local churches, as Thessalonians; and sometimes to larger groups, as Galatians. Some were general expositions of Christianity, such as Romans, and others were largely the answers to particular problems, such as Corinthians, and were especially life-centered. These didactic epistles have been a powerful means of teaching Christianity through the centuries.

Methods and Results

Prominent in Paul's *methods*, as in that of Christ, is the lecture. There are a number of outstanding instances of such public discourse. Distinctive among them is the famous address on Mars Hill, which is a good example of pedagogical procedure in getting the point of contact, making the transition, development and conclusion (Acts 17:16-34).

The discussion method gets some consideration, particularly in Paul's writings. Romans is one example. Here he makes his arguments interspersed with assumed questions from his supposed pupils. He is strong on the logical and the argumentative.

Exposition is also prominent in Paul's didactic letters, and probably in his teaching in the synagogues. He set forth effectively in systematic, if not in outline form, the teachings of Christianity and their application to the problems of life.

The *results* of his teachings are outstanding. For one thing he secured groups of strong converts in the centers where he labored who formed the basis for church organizations. These worked out into surrounding territory and secured other converts, and other churches grew up carrying Christianity into new territory. So Christianity secured a strong footing under the leadership of this Apostle to the Gentiles.

Also through his writings Paul gave the interpretation to Christianity that has greatly shaped Christian thinking ever since his day. Present-day theology is largely the outgrowth of his interpretations. Thus through his disciples and his epistles this great Christian teacher started Christianity on its westward career and greatly shaped the course of civilization.

OTHER NEW TESTAMENT TEACHERS

Although Christ and Paul were the outstanding teachers in New Testament days, they were by no means the only ones. A number of others stand out in the life of the times, and the teaching function is given special emphasis.

Specific Individuals

The *apostles* in general were teachers. While the term "teacher" seems not to have been applied to them, the term "teach" is used two times in Acts to describe their activity. In chapter 5:25 we are told that they were "teaching the people" in the Temple. In chapter 5:42 the writer of Acts says they "ceased not to teach and to preach Jesus as the Christ." Thus their teaching seems to have been put on a par with their preaching. Furthermore the word "teaching" occurs twice in Acts (2:42 and 5:28) to describe the message of the Apostles, giving further evidence that they were looked upon as teachers.

Peter and *John* are particularly emphasized as Apostles who taught. They are referred to four times by the writer of Acts as being in the act of teaching (4:1-2, 18; 5:21, 28). Twice the reference is to teaching in the Temple or teaching the people, and twice the Sanhedrin either was troubled because they taught, or charged them not to "teach in his name." They seem to have been carrying on their teaching privately and publicly. The results would indicate that they were generally recognized as teachers and that their work was effective, at least enough so to cause the officials to be disturbed.

Another teacher referred to by name is *Barnabas*. Not very much is said regarding him, and his work is connected with that of Paul. He seems to have been one of the teachers in the church at Antioch, referred to in Acts 13:1. He was with Paul in Antioch for a year and "taught much people" (Acts 11:26). This was in connection with planting Christianity in new centers. It is possible that he continued to teach after his separation from Paul.

Still others mentioned by name are *Apollos, Priscilla,* and *Aquila*. Again the reference is rather brief. It is simply stated that Apollos "taught accurately the things concerning Jesus" (Acts 18:25). But evidently he got off the track in his doctrine since he had known only the baptism of John, for in the next verse it is said that Priscilla and Aquila expounded to him "the way of God more accurately." Leaving Ephesus, Apollos went to Achaia and taught the Scriptures there effectively. Even a teacher may sometimes be taught!

An Official Class

Along with the names of specific individuals who taught, a *teaching group* is mentioned in the New Testament. In Acts 13:1 Luke declares: "There were in the church that was at Antioch certain prophets and teachers." Among them were Barnabas and Saul. Apparently here the teacher stood alongside the prophet. It is possible that the church at Ephesus had certain elders (bishops) as official teachers, for Acts 20:17 states that there was a plurality of elders there. The post-New Testament church had a catechist or an official church teacher who apparently becomes the precedent for the educational director today.

Another emphasis which stresses the vocational idea is the reference to a *teaching function*. Says Paul: "God hath set some in the church, first apostles, second prophets, third-

ly teachers" (I Cor. 12:28). In a similar fashion in another
place mention is made of God's having given apostles, prophets, evangelists, pastors, and teachers (Eph. 4:11). Not only
for New Testament days but for all time the teacher is to be
recognized as a functionary along with the pastor, evangelist, and others. This seems to give a further basis for the
educational director or minister as a definite functionary in
the church. Instead of getting away from the Bible, churches
today are apparently getting back to its emphasis.

It is clearly emphasized in the New Testament that the
pastor should be a teacher. In scriptures already quoted
teaching was tied up with the work of the pastor. In another
place Paul definitely says: "The bishop therefore must be
. . . apt to teach" (I Tim. 3:2). Nothing could be clearer or
stronger. This is just as essential a qualification as that he
shall not be covetous, intemperate, or a bigamist, which are
referred to in the same verse. Also Paul tells Timothy: "The
things which thou hast heard of me among many witnesses,
the same commit thou to faithful men, who shall be able to
teach others also" (II Tim. 2:2). This is a fine illustration of
what a trained pastor should do for the corps of teachers
under him. Teaching his leaders is possibly his greatest opportunity as a pastor.

Volunteer Teachers

There is some emphasis on the work of the unofficial or
nonvocational teacher *in the church*. As a matter of fact
Priscilla and Aquila were largely in that class, though they
did help Paul quite a bit. Paul's exhortations to the Romans
include one for the teachers as well as for the givers and
others. He says: "He that teacheth (let him give himself) to
his teaching" (Rom 12:7). James (3:1) cautions Jewish Christians about becoming teachers too readily because of the
responsibility of the task. The author of Hebrews, however,
seems to indicate that all mature Christians ought to reach
the stage of teachers rather than having always to be taught.
Evidently in these references the nonvocational or volunteer

teacher such as is found in Sunday school and Baptist Training Union was in mind.

Similarly, unofficial teaching was done *in the home.* Apparently Christ was taught by Joseph as he went about his duties in the carpenter shop, and by his mother who yearned to see the ideals of Judaism implanted in her child. Paul was brought up by loyal Hebrew parents who observed circumcision and inculcated the strictest Pharisaical teachings. Timothy had the benefit of the teachings of his grandmother Lois and his mother Eunice, and Paul said of him, "From a babe thou hast known the sacred writings" (II Tim. 3:15). Parents were important as teachers.

EDUCATIONAL TERMINOLOGY

In addition to the examples of various teachers in the New Testament, and the emphasis on the place of the vocational and volunteer teacher, there are a number of other statements which carry a strong educational emphasis.

Methods of Work

A comparison of the terms meaning to *teach and preach* is rather revealing. C. B. Williams has pointed out that in the New Testament the noun "teacher" translated from the Greek is used 54 times as against 3 uses of the word "preacher." Also the Greek verb for "teach" is used 93 times as against 65 uses of the verb "preach."[5] The Greek noun carrying the idea of preacher emphasizes the thought of a herald or one who is hastening with a message. The one translated "teacher" emphasizes the didactic or definitely instructional idea. This is a striking emphasis on method from the viewpoint of the New Testament and the Greek.

If one were to go beyond the New Testament and take the English expressions translated from both Hebrew and Greek, he would find some more interesting facts as to the biblical emphasis on methods. The noun "teacher," used

[5] *Young's Analytical Concordance* (rev. ed.; Grand Rapids, Mich.: Wm. B. Eerdmans Publishing Co., 1955).

apart from persons addressed, is found 21 times in the Bible whereas the noun "preacher" is found only 11 times. The verb "teach" is found 222 times in both Old and New Testaments as against 123 uses of the verb "preach."[6]

In this connection it is rather significant that in the Great Commission Christ says *make disciples*. This means to instruct or cause to become learners. The Christian worker is to make disciples of the peoples of all nations, or lead them to become pupils of Christ that they may study and learn of him. This term undoubtedly involves the teaching idea more than it does the hortatory procedure. It suggests not only the method of activity but also the kind of product.

Followers of Christ

What word would most naturally be used to describe Christ's followers? Normally it would be the term *Christian*, for such would designate his sect of believers, just as "Nazarene" characterizes a follower of the Nazarene. As a matter of fact the term *Christian* is employed to designate Christ's followers. But it is only rarely used. In fact, it is found only three times in the New Testament, and in at least one of these instances as a term of derision.

Light is another expression used often. It applies not only to Christ, "the light of the world" (John 9:5), but also to the follower of Christ. He said: "Ye are the light of the world" (Matt. 5:14). And Paul said the Christian is "a light of them that are in darkness" (Rom. 2:19). Light is set over against darkness as knowledge is against ignorance. It is a symbol of instruction and understanding.

The word *disciple* is the term generally used by Jesus and others to characterize his followers. It is found 243 times in the Gospels and Acts. It means a learner or a pupil, one enlisted in a certain school of thought or life. Christianity is looked upon as a school with Christ the founder and Mas-- ter Teacher, the leaders as assistant teachers, the enlisted nations as pupils, and the Bible as the textbook. Thus the educational idea is prominent.

[6] *Ibid.*

Message of Christianity

The expression *wisdom* is used occasionally by Paul to refer to the content or body of Christian truth. This, it is evident, carries the thought of knowledge or learning, and thus suggests the school and educational ideas. The true Christian is expected to be wise, so teaching is necessary.

Light is a term often used to designate the Christian body of truth. The Psalmist said, "Thy word is . . . light unto my path" (Ps. 119:105). And Paul speaks of "the light of the gospel of the glory of God" (II Cor. 4:4). As previously indicated with regard to the Christian being designated as a light, the term emphasizes the knowledge aspect of Christianity and involves education.

The expression *mystery* is used a number of times to designate the message of Christianity. This term is more in the realm of the intellectual than it is in the emotional or volitional phase of consciousness. It suggests something hidden or difficult which has become known or understood. A mystery challenges the thought processes and is suggestive of the educational aspect of Christianity.

But the expression most commonly used to describe the content of the gospel is the word *teaching*. It carries essentially the same idea as the term doctrine, and refers to the system of thought or body of truth held by the disciple after he has been taught. It is in a sense the curriculum of Christianity. Thirty-nine times in the New Testament the different words translated "teaching" are used. So the message of Christianity is a teaching or a body of truth.

EDUCATIONAL DOCTRINES AND ORDINANCES

Not only are there many Biblical illustrations of teaching, and commands to teach, but there are also certain doctrines in which education is implied, and ordinances that are didactic in their very nature. Thus by implication and illustration education is stressed.

Doctrines

Without undertaking to be comprehensive in stating

New Testament doctrines, a few *typical ones* may be mentioned. One of the most significant is that of soul liberty and accountability. The Bible teaches that each individual is accountable not to parents or priests but to Christ alone and is free to accept or reject Christianity. "Each one of us shall give account of himself to God" (Rom. 14:12). Another vital doctrine is regeneration. Christ very definitely emphasizes that the new birth or conversion is necessary if one is to enter the kingdom of God or Christian life. "Except one be born anew, he cannot see the kingdom of God" (John 3:3). Sanctification or Christian growth is another teaching. One does not enter the Christian life full grown but is first a babe in Christ and must mature in the experience. Character has to be developed. "Work out your own salvation with fear and trembling" (Phil. 2:12). Still another vital doctrine is democracy in church government. Each individual has as much authority as another. Cooperation is the principle on which kingdom activity is carried on. "Tell it unto the church" (Matt. 18:17) is the divine command.

But what is *the significance* of these doctrines for religious education? How is education implied or involved in them? This is very easy to see. It runs all through them. They cannot be carried out without educational activity. If the individual soul is free to accept or reject God, then he must be taught in order to exercise that freedom rightly. Otherwise soul liberty may be a curse rather than a blessing. If regeneration is necessary in order to enter the Kingdom of God, then the person must understand that fact and also what is his part in the process. Otherwise he may miss the gateway. Likewise if sanctification or character development is a process rather than an instantaneous experience, instruction must be given in order to develop the proper ideals and activities. Similarly, if democracy in church government is the ideal, information must be had in order to exercise one's Christian citizenship to the proper advantage. In many Bible doctrines education is implied. In fact, had it not been for education, we would not have the Bible itself!

Ordinances

There are two ordinances in the New Testament, *baptism and the Lord's Supper*. The former is commanded in Matt. 28:19 and is the immersion of a believer in water. The latter is authorized in Luke 22:19 and is the eating of bread and drinking of wine. They are to Christianity and the New Testament something of what the Passover and other feasts were to Judaism and the Old Testament. They are to be observed by Christian people throughout all the world and to the end of time. J. B. Gambrell says they are "the two twin fortresses which safeguard the whole field of saving truth." They are objective, dramatic, and didactic.

But why the emphasis on these ordinances? What is their *significance*? The answer is they are teaching agencies rather than mere observances. The most effective means of teaching is not by the printed page or by the spoken word, but by the re-enacting or dramatizing of a truth. The most important truths to be taught are the atoning death of Christ, his resurrection which proved his deity, the believer's regeneration or resurrection to a new life, and the final resurrection of the dead. This most effective means of teaching and these most vital truths to be taught are brought together in the observance of baptism and the memorial supper. They are didactic ordinances of the most significant sort (Rom. 6:4; I Cor. 11:26, 15:29) and not mere ceremonials. In fact, if all Bibles were destroyed and the ordinances observed properly, they would still present the essential truths of the gospel.

From the example and commands of Christ, the oral and written instructions of Paul, the activities of other vocational and volunteer teachers, the use of educational terminology, the educational implications of doctrines, and the teaching through ordinances, it is evident that promoting the Kingdom of God by the educational process is prominent in the New Testament. "Without teaching, his Gospel in every probability would have been so grossly misunderstood as to defeat his mission altogether."[7]

Inspirational and mass meeting activities are not enough. There must be the more pervasive and life-conditioning activity of education if the results are to be thorough and permanent. Truly, Christians have evangelized and baptized but not taught, and out of that lack have come most of our troubles. Christianity must come back to the New Testament ideal and practice if results are to be what they should.

QUESTIONS FOR DISCUSSION

1. List the situations in which Jesus taught by example.
2. List the situations in which Jesus taught by precept.
3. Study and analyze the parables of Jesus. What main lesson was he teaching in each of them? Why was the parable used so extensively by Christ?
4. What are the values of the Lord's Supper and baptism as teaching agencies?
5. Is the human element in teaching essential or incidental? Give reasons for your answer.

[7] Lewis J. Sherrill, *The Rise of Christian Education* (New York: The Macmillan Co., 1944), p. 89.

CHAPTER 4

SOME ACHIEVEMENTS DURING CHRISTIAN HISTORY

The emphasis on education as a means of propagating religion, stressed by precept and example in both the Old and the New Testaments, found effective expression in various ways throughout the course of Christian history. It is impossible in the brief space of a chapter to discuss all of them adequately. Consequently, attention is directed only to a few of the most significant, and these will be discussed only enough to see their significance for religious education.

CATECHUMENAL AND CATECHETICAL SCHOOLS

These activities represent the first efforts in early Christianity to utilize educational means for promoting Christianity. They are significant not so much for their greatness as for the emphasis they gave to the educational method. James D. Smart says: "It was not sufficient for a man to repent and believe; he had to be led on step by step until he understood the new faith."[1]

Catechumenal Schools

In *nature*, they were more of an educational activity than

[1] From *The Teaching Ministry of the Church*, by James D. Smart. Copyright, 1954, by W. L. Jenkins, Westminster Press, Philadelphia. Used by permission.

53

a distinct agency. The catechumenate was more nearly like a communicants' class than a school. It was a kind of confirmation group, receiving preliminary instruction before being baptized or admitted to the Lord's Supper. The purpose was to prevent unprepared people from getting into the churches. It has been termed, "A bulwark of the church against unworthy members," or a bridge from the world to the church.

The *occasion* for this school grew out of the fact that Christian missions had crossed over the boundaries of Judaism into pagan lands and no longer had the foundation of the synagogue Bible school and elementary school on which to build. It was something of the same thing faced by missionaries in foreign lands today. A preliminary training had to be given before church membership could be permitted. Otherwise the churches would be flooded with unworthy members.

The *activities* included instruction in such matters as Bible history, Christian doctrines, morals, and psalmody. The first text was a little book about the size of Ephesians called "The Teaching of the Twelve Apostles." Containing in orderly form a summary of Christian teaching which would prepare for intelligent church membership, it was thus the first church manual. In early times the bishop or presbyter did the teaching, but in later days a special catechist was employed. The method was largely catechizing with much memory work by the pupils.

The *accomplishments* of the catechumenate were greater than can easily be realized now. Through it, ignorant pagans became intelligent Christians. Pupils advanced through the stages of hearers and kneelers to those approved for baptism. Sometimes they were demoted for questionable practices. When they indulged in sinful activities and persisted in them, they might be dismissed altogether. Often the process lasted as long as three years before they were finally approved for church membership. It was the chief means of religious education in the early days where synagogues did not exist.

Catechetical Schools

These were schools with specific locations and faculties and were considerably advanced beyond the simple training afforded by the catechumenate. The *situation* out of which these schools arose is best illustrated by the first one at Alexandria, in Egypt. Here was a great library. Outstanding teachers and students came together from many sections of the world. Greek philosophy predominated and a modernistic atmosphere prevailed. In this situation, new converts were overawed and skepticism arose. To meet these conditions, Pantaenus, about A.D. 180, started the first of the cathechetical schools, and the movement soon spread into Italy, Greece, and Asia Minor.

The *nature* of the institution at first was more like that of a Bible chair adjacent to the campus of a state university. The work often started in the home of the teacher without any institutional or financial backing. Gradually it expanded into the proportions of a theological college, including a faculty and a course of study. The teaching, however, proceeded from the point of view of Greek philosophy rather than that of the Bible, and therefore failed to present a pure form of Christianity. It was claimed that philosophy was "a pedagog to lead us to Christ." In their efforts to present Christianity in such a way as to appeal to cultured pagans, the teachers compromised it.

The *constituency* was a somewhat mixed group. Both men and women were admitted, and elementary as well as advanced students included. Some were new converts comparable to catechumens, taking studies preparatory to church membership. They also prepared themselves to meet the subtle attacks of Greek skeptics. Others were idolaters investigating the teaching of Christianity with a view to the possibility of accepting it. Still others were prospective religious leaders preparing for Christian service. In this way the institution came to be a sort of theological university, covering both secular and religious subjects.

Although they did not present pure Christianity, the *results* of these schools were outstanding. They helped to meet Greek philosophy on its own ground and thus to stem the tide of materialism and skepticism. Also, the leaders such as Clement and Origen led in shaping the creedal statements of Christianity even though they did cast them in a philosophical mold of thought. These schools served as missionary centers for helping to transform a pagan empire. "Alexandria became the brains of Christendom."

MONASTIC AND CATHEDRAL SCHOOLS

Pagan schools so degenerated that they were closed by official decree in A.D. 529, thus leaving religious schools in possession of the field. In the meantime Catholicism had been developing and with it different systems of education.

Monastic Schools

These schools got their main impetus from the Benedictine order which largely shaped education from the sixth to the ninth centuries as their institutions spread throughout Europe, reaching a total of 37,000.

There were three *means* of monastic education. One was through the copying of manuscripts for exchange between the monasteries in building up their libraries. It was a required part of the activity, and those doing it naturally learned a great deal about the important documents copied.

Another means of education was reading. When not busy with other things the monks were required to read. This included two or more hours per day, with additional time on Sunday and during Lent. They had someone read to them even during meals.

Formal study was of course the most effective educational method. School systems were developed which became the most effective of their day and were a great influence in the life of the times.

The *scope* of instruction in the schools was broad. There were the elementary grades composed both of children designated for the religious life and of those who came in from the outside for daily instruction, i. e., both internes and externes.

Then there were secondary grades, in which were taught more advanced subjects, including religion as well as the seven liberal arts. These also were for outsiders and those who were in training for the order.

Finally came the specialized or vocational training for those who planned to be monks. In this training special emphasis was given to the Bible, doctrines, church decrees, prayer, and music. For them, it was essentially a theological seminary. Attention was also given to the practical arts.

The *accomplishments* of monastic schools were far-reaching. In these institutions located in out-of-the-way places, there were preserved from the barbarian invaders the choice manuscripts, including the Bible, sermons, other religious materials, and the Greek and Roman classics. Also in addition to training a monastic religious leadership, they gave general training to the future princes, kings and other leaders of Europe, and through them gave a religious and moral coloring to European life for generations.

Cathedral Schools

Although not as prominent as monastic schools, the cathedral or bishops' schools played an important part in the educational life of the times.

Their *origin* was due in part to the decline of cathechetical schools and the need for some kind of school to take their place. The development of churches in large centers, together with the sending out of workers from these to the surrounding communities, also seemed to call for special training agencies. The distance between monastic schools made it needful to have other schools more readily accessible to the people. All these conditions contributed to the development of the cathedral school system.

Their *activities* were distinctively religious, probably more exclusively so than monastic schools. They were primarily vocational and intended for the training of the secular clergy as the monasteries were for the training of the religious. Likewise, the curriculum being more definitely religious and moral, was better fitted for religious leadership.

However, as time went on they broadened their activities to include other than religious leaders, thus placing stress on the rudiments of learning, as involved in elementary education, and the liberal arts, which were characteristic of secondary education.

The *results* of these schools seemed to justify amply what was put into them. Through their development of elementary and secondary education, they came to be, in a measure, the forerunners of the public schools of western Europe, at least more so than did the monasteries. Likewise, they developed more intensively the spirit of free inquiry and discussion which helped to pave the way for the Renaissance and the Reformation. From these schools came some of the greatest thinkers of the day in the realm of religion; men like Abelard, for example. The movement for universities developed more from these schools than from the monasteries. The Cathedral of Notre Dame in Paris grew into the University of Paris.

MEDIEVAL UNIVERSITIES

By the time of the Reformation, universities had grown up over a wide area and were exerting a tremendous influence over the religious life of the times. As a matter of fact, they were one of the leading forces causing the Reformation.

Rise

Several *forces* converged to bring about universities toward the close of the medieval period. One was the influence of commerce and travel which broadened contacts and stimulated thought. Particularly was this true with the Crusades which brought the West into contact with Mohammedan learning and that of the East. Another was the stimulus brought about by the rise of the professional spirit. The universities usually specialized in some one of the vocations, such as law, medicine, or theology. Still another influence was the Cathedral school with its spirit of free thinking. Some of these schools grew into universities.

Among the outstanding schools were Bologna, in Italy, specializing in law; Salerno, emphasizing medicine; Paris, stressing theology; also Oxford, Cambridge, and Heidelberg. They had such outstanding teachers as Abelard, Roger Bacon, and Thomas Aquinas.

Activities

These universities attracted large numbers of students from their own and surrounding countries. The students often lived in communities, carried on their studies, and influenced both the schools themselves and the town where they were located. The course of study included the seven liberal arts and, in addition, law, medicine, and theology. Emphasis was given to preparation for teaching. Much of the instruction was in Latin and by the lecture method. Debates were engaged in frequently.

The school life was related to religion in several ways. The majority of schools were chartered by the Pope and therefore had an obligation to foster the church. Some of them were a development from church schools and, therefore, were Christian colleges, and the others had some theology in the curriculum. Most of the teachers were outstanding church men who permeated their teaching with religion. Medieval universities were, therefore, primarily Christian, both in atmosphere and in instruction.

Achievements

These schools did much for moral and religious progress. For one thing, they stimulated *inquiry* and freedom. The investigative spirit was much more evident than it was in monasteries. Monarchs listened to what the students had to say, thus making the students influential to some degree along with the nobility and the clergy. This contributed to democracy and progress. They were one of the chief factors leading to the Reformation.

More significant, however, was the fact that they produced great *thinkers* and leaders who were independent and progressive in their activities. Among them were men like Dante, Wycliffe, Copernicus, Luther, and Calvin. These men through their translating, teaching, and writing helped to usher in the Renaissance and the Reformation. But for the universities, these movements might have been atheistic instead of religious.

THE REFORMATION

The Reformation was one of the outstanding examples of the effectiveness of education in moral and religious activity. It is one of the strongest apologetics for the value of religious education as a means of social progress.

Growth

The *beginning* of the movement which is called the revival of learning, or Renaissance, started in southern Europe as a literary reform. In Italy in the early part of the fourteenth century, under the influence of Dante and others, the study of the Latin classics was revived. As the movement spread northward into France, Germany and Holland, Hebrew and Greek were included in the studies, and it took on more of a religious nature. In England, Wycliffe translated the Bible, and the Lollards popularized its study. These educational activities were preliminary to the religious revival.

The *development* of the Reformation proper came under the leadership of Luther in Germany. After studying and translating the Bible, he broke with the Catholic church, opposed its teachings and practices, and precipitated a crisis. Almost simultaneously in Switzerland, Zwingli led in an emphasis on New Testament religion and in opposition to Catholicism. His work was followed by that of Calvin who consummated the movement and whose theological treatises have greatly shaped Christian thinking since that time. In England, Henry VIII broke with Rome and established the Anglican church, and the Puritans carried forward the reforms. Other countries in Europe took up the crusade, and the influence spread later to America, through the Puritans and others.

Causes

The *schools* stand out prominently among the originating forces leading to the Reformation. Both cathedral schools and universities played a large part. The free-thinking spirit and investigative attitude of teachers like Abelard went a long way in preparing a favorable atmosphere. The study of Hebrew and Greek helped in understanding the scriptures.

Another contributing influence was *popular Bible study*. Wycliffe's translation of the Bible in England and the Lollards' teaching it throughout the country gave a new vision. Luther's translation of the Bible in Germany and his popular presentation of its doctrines, as opposed to those taught by the Catholic church, created ideals and public sentiment. People were taught to read in order that they might read the Bible. Religion was the chief incentive for education.

Other literature helped greatly to bring on the Reformation. Luther published in pamphlet form an address delivered to the nobles and in five days five thousand were sold. His ninety-five theses nailed publicly on the door of the church at Wittenberg, with the explanations and discussions growing out of them, served in shaping public opinion. Calvin and other leaders carried on similar educational activities, all of which helped to determine the movement.

Results

The Reformation led to the instituting of extensive educational activities in the various countries where it spread. These were soon seen to be necessary if the movement was to be other than merely a temporary reform.

Strong emphasis was given to the establishment of *school systems*. Public education today is in a measure the ultimate outcome of the emphasis of Reformation leaders on education. Luther wrote the mayors of the cities of Germany: "There is no other outward offence that in the sight of God so heavily burdens the world, and deserves such heavy chastisement as the neglect to educate children." Also he said: "Next to the ministry, it [the office of school-teacher] is the most useful, greatest and best: and I am not sure which of the two is to be preferred."[2] Others made similar emphases,

[2] Clarence H. Benson, *History of Christian Education* (Chicago: The Moody Press, 1943), p. 80.

and strong Protestant school systems were established in Germany, Switzerland, England, and elsewhere.

Educational literature likewise resulted. Luther prepared a "Short Catechism" and a "Large Catechism." Zwingli wrote a treatise on *The Christian Education of Youth*. Calvin produced his famous *Institutes*. More than a score of religious texts of the nature of catechisms and handbooks appeared in a little over a decade. Some of the books were even illustrated. Portions of the Bible were printed separately. Even elementary treatises in psychology and pedagogy appeared. The Reformation not only was initiated by educational means and carried on through educational procedures but also resulted in the establishment and perpetuation of educational systems.

CATHOLIC EDUCATION

As the Reformation progressed and the Catholics saw what was being accomplished by educational means, they set out to counteract it. Schools under Protestant control were condemned, and Catholic schools were instituted. In other words, Protestants and Catholics fought each other with rival school systems. This activity by the Catholics has been termed the Counter-Reformation.

Jesuit Schools

The *organization* of Jesuits founded by Loyola in 1534 operated in the field of secondary and collegiate education. Somewhat military in form, it is headed by a general, with a graded system of officers over provinces, individual schools, and groups within the schools. Discipline stands out prominently in the system. It has been characterized as a "Catholic Salvation Army." In forty years it spread over the world and still carries on a world-wide conquest.

The *aim* is "All for God's greater glory," and the educational activity leads definitely in that direction. The aim all along has been to train the leaders rather than the masses and thus shape civilization. The priests take the threefold vow of poverty, chastity, and obedience, and devote their lives with missionary zeal to Christian education. They stand ready to go anywhere at any time at the superior officer's command, to train both those preparing for the order and those planning to go out into other activities.

The *studies* include the work of the lower school with a five- or six-year course largely literary in nature, and an upper school running seven to nine years emphasizing theological studies. A "system of studies" was worked out in 1599 to guide even in the most minute details of activity, and it has been changed very little down to the present time. Latin has been the prevailing language used. Reviews and drills are frequent, emulation is stressed, and discipline is severe.

The *results* have been significant. The Jesuits have been a power. Their effectiveness has been outstanding among school systems. For three centuries they trained most of the leaders of Europe. They carry on their work effectively throughout the world today. Will Durant pays the following tribute to the Jesuit schools:

> Through education, diplomacy, and devotion, through fervor directed by discipline, through co-ordination of purpose and skillful variations of means, the Jesuits turned back the Protestant tide, and recaptured much of Germany, most of Hungary and Bohemia, all of Christian Poland, for the church. Rarely has so small a group achieved so much so rapidly. . . . They organized their own colleges, and sought to train selected youths who would be centers of influence in the next generation. They became the greatest educators of their time.[3]

Parish Schools

The *rise* of these schools is observable through a considerable period of time. They originated long before the Reformation, received a new emphasis in the Counter-Reformation, and have had an extended history both in Europe and America. From time to time church councils authorized their establishment and decreed that youth be required to attend. Finally they were attached to almost every church, attended by millions of pupils, and constitute

[3] Will Durant, *The Reformation* (New York: Simon & Schuster, Inc., 1957), p. 915.

one of the significant educational systems — Catholicism's right arm.

The *philosophy* underlying the system is the belief that religion is promoted more effectively in childhood than later and by the educational rather than the inspirational method. They believe, furthermore, that it must permeate all of education rather than be tacked on to an educational system secular in nature. Every area of knowledge is presented from the Christian point of view as interpreted by the Catholic church.

The *characteristics* of these schools are distinctive. They are for the pupils of a church or parish, are supported by the church, and are free to the pupils. They include the elementary and, frequently, the secondary grades. The religious, and particularly the Catholic elements in geography, reading, history, civics, literature, and other subjects are definitely emphasized. In addition, a period is given each day to definite instruction in religion with graded catechisms. Additional time is given to prayer and religious exercises. Thus "the cure of souls" is central in the entire system.

Significant *results* have been achieved. By means of these schools primarily — since little attention is given to Sunday schools or to mass evangelism — the Catholics have been able to hold their ground in a time when the entire trend of the times has been away from their autocratic and authoritative system. These results are due not to superiority in doctrines or pulpit activity but rather to their capture of childhood through the educational method. In this, non-Catholics may well learn from them.

THE SUNDAY SCHOOL MOVEMENT

Probably the most far-reaching educational activity in the field of religion since the Reformation is the Sunday school movement. It has reached the largest number of people of any religious-educational organization, since it includes all ages from birth to old age.

Beginnings

Prior to Robert Raikes there were many individual activities, yet it was his efforts that gave real impetus to the movement. Raikes was a printer in Gloucester, England, and for some time had been interested in moral reform. Going one day into a poor section of the city called "Sooty Alley" to hire help, he was struck by the miserable condition of the children. He saw their needs and set out to remedy the situation. In July, 1780, he hired some women at a shilling a day each to gather the children into one of the homes and teach them for about two hours in the morning and about three in the afternoon and, in addition, to take them to church for preaching. They learned to read, and studied the Bible, the catechism, and other materials. It was not like the Sunday school of today, but did great good and transformed the community.

Growth

Raikes published the result of his activities in his paper, the *Gloucester Journal*, arousing great interest. Many schools were started as a result. For a while there was opposition to the movement; but as prominent people, including the Queen, became interested, it spread rapidly over a wide area. Promotional organizations and publishing houses were started to aid the cause. The movement spread from children to adults, poor to rich, city to country, and to other nations, and finally around the world.

In the New England and Middle colonies of the United States, schools were started early, and local organizations formed to promote the work. Later the American Sunday School Union was organized and sent missionaries into the South and West to establish schools. Gradually denominational agencies were established, more extensive promotion was carried on, and great numbers enlisted, until today the Sunday school has come to have the largest attendance of any service of the church. There are about 300 thousand schools and forty million pupils enrolled.

Improvements

As Sunday schools grew in numbers, they improved in

quality. From an unorganized institution, it has grown into a well-graded and departmentalized one. Beginning with no textbooks, it now has a variety of them for all ages. With no meeting place at first, it now has splendidly equipped buildings for classes as well as departments. Training course materials covering a wide range of subjects have been prepared. Standards have been set up, and definite aims worked out. They are real schools.

It has developed extensively in its *activities.* Originally teaching was the main function. Now it has come to include graded worship as a regular weekly activity. In many churches it is used as the main agency for developing in giving. Evangelism has become an important part of its work, until most converts come from it. In short, almost every church function is promoted through the Sunday school. This is a far reach beyond the beginnings under Raikes.

Achievements

It would be impossible to catalog the achievements of this religious-educational organization. In *enlistment* it has brought untold members in touch with the life of the church. The Sunday school has come to be the church's main outreaching agency, through its visitation and extension programs.

In *character growth* it has been most powerful. Most of those converted are converted by means of the Sunday school. Worshipful attitudes are cultivated most effectively through its departmental programs, and stewardship is likely getting its best development through the Sunday school. It is a training as well as a teaching agency.

As an agency for *moral reform* it is accomplishing more than Raikes ever dreamed of. Furthermore, the Sunday school has contributed to the development of its workers. It uses more workers than any other church agency, gives them manifold activities, and furnishes laboratory training in Christian life and service.

OTHER RELIGIOUS EDUCATION AGENCIES

Since the beginning of the Sunday school movement, developments in the field of religious education have been rapid. Many other religious educational agencies have sprung into being.

Christian Colleges

Many of those who led in settling America held degrees from Oxford and Cambridge, some even the master's degree. The ministers especially were college men. Soon after arriving, the fear arose that there would be left an illiterate ministry "when our present ministers shall lie in the dust." So Harvard was founded in 1636 to train them and to "educate Indian and American youth in knowledge and godliness." Following this came Yale, Princeton, Brown, and others. All except one founded before the Revolution were Christian, and even it had the Bible in its curriculum.

Since the Revolution most of the major denominations have established academies and junior and senior colleges for training religious leaders and Christianizing the community. Methodists have established such institutions as Boston University, Northwestern University, University of Southern California, Duke University, Emory University, and Southern Methodist University. American Baptists founded the University of Rochester, University of Chicago, and the University of Redlands; Southern Baptists, the University of Richmond, Mercer University, Baylor University, and others. Other denominations have done likewise. These institutions have been effective missionary agencies. They have served also as leavening influences in the field of higher education, and they have trained an effective religious leadership for the home and foreign lands. Without them the Kingdom of God would have suffered immeasurably.

Training Organizations

Since the middle of the past century individual churches here and there had young people's meetings for prayer, temperance study, and missionary activity; but the Young People's movement did not begin until 1881. In that year, Rev. Francis E. Clark started in his church at Portland,

Maine, an organization to help young people "pray and read the Bible every day" and "endeavor to lead the Christian life." Reports of it were published in religious papers; and the movement, taking the name of Christian Endeavor, began to spread throughout the nation, into Canada, and around the world. It was interdenominational in nature.

As the various denominations observed its activity, they became interested in establishing organizations of their own. As a result, the Epworth League was established by the Methodists in 1889, the Baptist Young People's Union of America was organized in 1891, and in 1896 Southern Baptists officially launched the B.Y.P.U., which later became the Baptist Training Union. Lutherans, Episcopalians, Catholics, Jews, and others have formed somewhat similar organizations. These societies have capitalized on youth leadership and activities, and have done much to develop church members in prayer, Bible study, temperance, stewardship, missions, and service. Especially have they created spiritual morale through their assemblies and conventions. Youth are drawn into state and national movements of their own denominations. They sometimes are tied in with the United Christian Youth Movement of the National Council of the Churches of Christ in the United States of America.

Vacation Schools

One of the moral hazards of our times, particularly in the cities, is created each year when hosts of boys and girls are released by the public schools for the vacation season. Realizing this, various organizations in different cities have sought for many years to sponsor some sort of summer activity for them. Not until 1901, however, did a definite movement get started. In that year Rev. R. G. Boville, Executive Secretary of New York City Baptist Missionary Society, having observed the school of the Reverend H. L. Jones, which had operated for three summers previously, began to promote the work in the city. Later he gave his entire time to this work, making it interdenominational and international in scope.

Gradually the different denominations took it up as a distinct part of their own programs. Presbyterians were first, beginning their activities in 1910; American Baptists were next in 1915, and Southern Baptists third in 1923. Methodists, Disciples, Congregationalists, and others have fostered vacation Bible schools. These schools which are held for two weeks in the summer with much stress on handicraft, recreation, and dramatics have been powerful agencies in counteracting the temptations of the vacation period by giving wholesome instruction and building moral character.

Weekday Schools

Closely related to the vacation church school is the weekday church school. While the former operates only during the summer, the latter carries on through the school year. It has come because of the secularization of public education to supply the deficiency through more extended instruction and closer correlation with the public schools. Some efforts have included all grades of the public schools — some the elementary grades and some the high school only. The teaching is done by the churches either separately or together. Time is given and credit is allowed by the schools. Gary, Indiana, gave impetus to the movement in 1914. It has spread widely through the nation and done much to put the missing "r" (religion) into education.[4]

Similarly there has developed a movement to provide religious instruction for *college students* through Bible chairs in state and independent schools. This is done by denominations separately or jointly. It began as early as 1893 at the University of Michigan; but most of the development, especially in the South, has come since 1925. As the proportion of students in denominational schools decreases, and that in state schools increases, it bids fair to become most far-reaching and effective as an educational activity.

[4] See Chapter 16 for a discussion of weekday church schools. Also, Philip H. Lotz (ed.), *Orientation in Religious Education* (Nashville: Abingdon Press, 1950), chaps. xxi and xxii.

Christian Day Schools

As previously indicated the Christian day school is coming to occupy an important place in religious education. The Catholics have long maintained day schools, as have the Lutherans, Dutch Reformed, and Seventh-day Adventists. In recent years, other groups, including Baptists, have fostered them. The National Association of Evangelicals has a full-time employee promoting them. Potentially both at home and on the mission fields they are the church's most effective means of promotion. They are primarily responsible for the progress of the Catholic church.

Missionary Education

Women have taken the lead in this. Prior to the Civil War little activity had been carried on. Following that conflict, came organizations for training in missions by the Congregationalists, Methodists, American Baptists, and others. *Woman's Missionary Union* of Southern Baptists was officially launched in 1888, with organizations, graded materials, and programs of activity for the various age groups. These agencies have done much to put the missionary emphasis into religious education.

Starting in 1906 as an interdenominational movement, laymen organized to develop more effectively fraternal life, stewardship ideals, and the missionary spirit among the men of the churches. The Southern Baptists Laymen's Missionary Movement was launched in 1907, and in 1926 its name was changed to the *Baptist Brotherhood*. It has helped considerably in giving religious morale to men.

Similar in purpose to the above organizations is the *Church School of Missions* started in 1923 which seeks to give vision and interest in missions to everyone in the church through special training classes for all age groups and both sexes, with texts adapted to all ages.

From this brief survey of achievements in the field of religious education by the various agencies during the period of Christian history, it is easy to see that education has played a large part in the development of Christianity. Progress in missionary achievement, moral reform, and church growth have come largely because of the emphasis placed on the educational method. These developments illustrate the striking statement of Benjamin Kidd: "Give us the young and we will create a new mind and a new earth in a single generation." And they constitute a tremendous challenge for the future.

QUESTIONS FOR DISCUSSION

1. Compare the curriculum of the medieval universities with that of your own school or college. Which gave greater emphasis to religion?

2. What was the significance of the Jesuit schools in the Counter-Reformation?

3. How would you go about setting up a church day-school program? How would you supply teachers and principals for the school? How would you secure the response and support from the parents? Would your school be recognized by the State Board of Education?

4. What should be the major objective of the Christian college?

5. Evaluate the work of your own Sunday school. Suggest ways in which your Sunday school could be improved.

CHAPTER 5

DEMANDS OF MODERN
SOCIAL CONDITIONS

The example of educational activities in the Bible and the inspiration of achievements in the course of Christian history are not the only incentives to carry on religious education today. These are positive and emphatic. But there are negative emphases just as strong. They come from the challenge of unsolved problems in the present social order which must be faced more seriously than ever before if the present chaotic conditions are to be corrected. Canon F. L. Donaldson characterized them as "policies without principles, wealth without work, pleasure without conscience, knowledge without character, industry without morality, science without humanity, worship without sacrifice."

PHYSICAL TEMPTATIONS

Some of the most serious problems pertain to the physical life and must be confronted by each individual. While every effort should be made to eradicate these evils from society, it is even more important to prepare youth to face them individually and to grow strength of character to overcome them.

Alcoholic Beverages

The use of alcohol as a beverage in the various forms of

beer, wine, and whiskey has increased in alarming proportions in recent years. According to the 1956 report of the Office of Business Economics, U. S. Department of Commerce, the estimated consumer expenditure for alcoholic beverages is $10.5 billion annually. This is a 300 per cent increase in twenty years. There are an estimated 60 million persons in the United States who drink alcoholic beverages. This is about 50 per cent of the population of drinking age — fifteen years or above. Five million of these are classed as problem drinkers, with over a million confirmed alcoholics. It is estimated that one out of every sixteen drinkers becomes an alcoholic. All of these drinkers began as moderate drinkers, 70 per cent of them in their teens.

Arrests for drunkenness and drunken driving have increased more than 100 per cent in recent years. Testifying before the American Bar Association, in 1957, Charles S. Rhyne, President-elect, said:

> More than 40,000 Americans were killed in automobile accidents in 1956. . . . the yearly number of persons injured in traffic accidents now exceeds 2,000,000. . . . The economic loss exceeds $4,500,000.00 for 1956.[1]

Using the conservative National Safety Council alcohol-caused accident figure of 26 per cent, this means that more than 10,000 persons die in traffic accidents each year because of alcoholic drinking; that another half-million have been injured; and that the economic cost of the accidents has been more than $1 billion annually. Authorities attribute from 25 to 60 per cent of all highway accidents to liquor.

Without going into detail as to the destructive effects of alcohol on the human organism, it is enough to say that alcohol affects the stomach and liver, tending to prevent rather than aid digestion of foods; the heart and blood vessels, contributing to heart disease and pneumonia; and the brain and nervous system, resulting in local paralysis and dementia. Alcohol destroys body tissue and nerve cells which cannot be restored. It retards mental perception and

[1] Clip sheet, Methodist Board of Temperance, Washington, D. C., April 12, 1957.

the higher mental processes and contributes to immorality and crime. Heavy drinkers are never good life insurance risks nor safe subjects for operations.

While there is no natural appetite for liquor, it may soon be acquired. The accessibility and respectability given to liquor, wine, and beer by its sale in grocery and drug stores; the influence of the crowds; and the widespread and pleasing publicity given to it in every medium of advertising have greatly increased its use. The most subtle educational propaganda especially aimed at youth, and even childhood, and utilizing the shrewdest sort of psychology, has been carried on extensively. Through radio and television advertising, it is even being introduced to children in their own homes.

The liquor industry is giving its advertising and merchandising a "new look" to attract more women drinkers. Since 55 per cent of all packaged beer is sold in grocery stores, they say: "If we can sell mom we can sell the whole family." The Woman's Division of Licensed Beverage Industries made this statement recently: "A long-range program to acquaint the women of America with the industry's product, its role in gracious living, its social implications and its uses. . . ." is being launched by the Division.[2]

The rapidly increasing use of alcoholic beverages is one of the most serious of all social evils.

Immorality

Another serious personal problem faced today is that of sexual immorality. It was serious in biblical times and has been ever since. All races, ages, and sexes are affected by it. From almost every community tragic instances could be mentioned. In one grammar school fifteen children between nine and twelve were found to be immoral. It is recognized as one of the most serious problems of the average city high school. In the words of a prominent physician, immorality is an evil "clutching this very minute at the throat of the nation."

[2] Baptist Sunday School Board, *The Survey Bulletin*, XII (June 10, 1957).

Immorality affects every phase of life of the social order. Physically the very blood stream of the nation is being weakened. More than a million girls are reported to have had a venereal disease; and to make bad matters worse, the second generation also suffers the consequences. Socially the harm is greater. Each year more than 50,000 unmarried mothers are registered in the United States, and thousands lose their lives by abortion. About 250,000 illegitimate children are born annually. Figures alone cannot begin to give the whole story of blighted lives and broken hearts.

Here again a type of educational publicity has greatly accentuated the problem. To be sure, the instinctive urge serves as a powerful stimulus. But this has been augmented a great deal by novels, motion pictures, salacious magazines portraying and glamorizing the improper relation of the sexes. Some radio and television programs are based on sex appeal. And of course bars, taverns, and dance halls have played their part in encouraging sexual immorality.

Tobacco

The widespread use of tobacco, particularly in the form of cigarettes, has become a constantly alarming problem. Especially is this situation accentuated since women and girls have become smokers. The increase in cigarette consumption has been 1000 per cent in the last fifty years. In spite of the cancer scare, which really cut down on the sale of cigarettes in 1954, the sales are booming again; and the industry expected 400 billion cigarettes to be sold in 1958![3]

A government survey shows that more than one-half of all the men above eighteen years of age smoke cigarettes regularly and about one-fourth of the women use them. But it also reveals that about one-third of the men never have smoked cigarettes while two-thirds of the women have not used them. The tobacco industry is spending millions of dollars each year in advertising to create new users. If there are any harmful effects in the use of tobacco, the facts should be clearly presented to the younger generation in a sane

[3] *United States News and World Report,* Washington, August 23, 1957.

educational manner. As a result of 188,000 case studies to determine the effects of smoking on cancer, the American Medical Association was told that regular cigarette smokers die from lung cancer ten times more frequently than non-smokers. And men smoking up to ten cigarettes a day had over-all death rates 34 per cent higher than nonsmokers.[4]

But what bearing on religious education have all these problems of tobacco, liquor, and immorality? If all of these evils are increasing in alarming proportions, then the people at large need to know about it, and those interested mainly in the moral aspect of education are responsible for giving out the information. If the effects produced are detrimental to the physical and moral life of the people, then these results also need to be put before the people, and those primarily interested in moral problems are the main ones to do it. And if these problems have gained their footing mainly by means of educational propaganda carried on among the young, then it is high time that religious education create a countersystem of educational propaganda to stem the tide. In other words the present situation constitutes a tremendous challenge to religious leaders of youth to bring up a generation who will use their bodies to the glory of God.

LEISURE-TIME ACTIVITIES

Closely related to the personal problems just discussed are certain forms of entertainment and recreational activities. They are very largely personal, though fostered by financially interested people, who often are more concerned with cash than with character.

Movies and Comics

The *motion picture* business is a major industry in the United States. Tremendous sums of money are invested in the big companies which foster it, and it is still one of the most popular forms of entertainment. Because of its dramatic features, its appeal to natural interests, its availability,

[4] Statistics quoted in *Newsweek*, XLIX, No. 98 (June 17, 1957), from a report to the American Medical Association in June, 1957, of a study made by E. Cuyler Hammond and Daniel Horn.

and its inexpensiveness, the motion picture house became one of the most patronized institutions in America. Far more people attend movies each week than attend Sunday schools. The motion picture is indeed the people's university. Along with it is *television*, coming to the child in the home while he is too young to discriminate.

The home is fast becoming a kindergarten of crime. The majority of families have television sets. Many homes have an extra set or two for the children, before which the child sits by the hour. According to one study,[5] children averaged more than four hours a day watching the programs. With the uncensored and the unselected shows coming into the home every day, the child is constantly subjected to gangsters and gun men. These characters have become the heroes; the models after whom boys and girls are building their lives today.

In a town in the Southwest a twelve-year-old boy accompanied by his ten-year-old brother shot and killed a merchant and his clerk and wounded a third person as they staged a supermarket "hold-up." They were only acting out what they had seen on the television screen. Three weeks later a thirteen-year-old boy in Alaska shot to death his mother, his brother, and a little sister. When an eight- and a ten-year-old boy were arrested for breaking into houses and stores, they boasted that they had learned how to do these things from the movies and television shows. Some years ago a book called *Our Movie-Made Children*[6] described the effects of the movies on immature persons; but nobody paid much attention to it.

After the movies, came the rise of *comic books*. According to Frederick Wertham, author of *The Seduction of the Innocent*, about ninety million of these so-called "comic" books are read each month by American children. While on the cover page they may appear to be quite harmless, many

[5] Cited by H. C. Brearley, "The Bible, People, and Hollywood," *Home Life* (June, 1955).

[6] Henry J. Forman, *"Our Movie-Made Children"* (New York: The Macmillan Co., 1933).

of them are actually training youthful readers in every form of mischief, vice, immorality, and crime. There has been some talk of "cleaning" them up and controlling their sales, but they still flood the market. Not only are the young affected by crime movies, pulp magazines, and comic books. Many of their most avid patrons are middle-aged or beyond.

These institutions are by no means all bad. Both the motion picture and television are providing many valuable educational features, particularly of a geographical or historical nature. Also there are many wholesome amusement elements which furnish relaxation to tired nerves and bothered minds. But along with these features there are many harmful elements. The movie industry generally disregards the Sabbath, even lobbying at legislatures to keep the day open. Worse still, they stimulate immorality and crime through the things portrayed on the screen. A study of 183 pictures revealed seduction, adultery, and other immoral features in 107; and murder, gangster activities, and other lawlessness in 81!

Dance Halls and Taverns

In some communities commercialized dance halls and beer taverns have become serious problems. Shorter working hours have given more leisure time, and good roads and automobiles have eliminated distances, so that in addition to the halls in cities, dancing places have sprung up generally out in the country — often at out-of-the-way places. In many instances high school gymnasiums are used for dancing, and the activity becomes an official affair. A study of one high school revealed that young people often learn dancing at school functions and then patronize the questionable places. Countless numbers of young people attend these places throughout the land.

While some good people patronize these institutions, the influence is generally bad. This is true for various reasons. For one thing, the dance itself is inclined to stimulate the passions. Some cannot engage in the embrace involved and not have the sex desire strongly aroused. Also the association is usually bad, these halls often being adjacent to a drinking place and cabins which are used for immoral purposes. Even if one is not personally harmed, his influence in Christian service is compromised when he patronizes such places. He sacrifices the greater for the lesser good. The apostle Paul makes this clear in the letter to the church at Corinth.[7]

Gambling

Games of chance involve the recreational and quite a bit more. In recent years the gambling spirit has spread even to children as new forms of activity have come into being. A growing practice which borders on the gambling spirit is the activity of business concerns and motion picture houses, with their punch boards, drawings, and similar methods which constitute a sort of kindergarten in gambling. Beyond these are the slot machines, marble boards, and other games of chance. In addition there is card-playing and dice-throwing for gain. Betting on horse races, and various kinds of raffles and lotteries which are sometimes national in scope, can also be included.

All of these develop the gambling spirit or the desire to get something for nothing. The fundamental principle of life is to earn an honest living by the "sweat of our brow" or to give value received for whatever is paid. Games of chance violate this principle. In fact, much of the social security emphasis does the same thing and appeals to the spirit of selfishness in man. Furthermore, gambling in its purest form develops the attitude of getting not only at the expense of, but also to the hurt of, the other fellow. Character is weakened and harm done by the gambling habit.

In the case of movies, dances, and games of chance, the question emerges again — what can religious education do about them? At least three things. One is to develop in the coming generation the kind of ideals and attitudes which will cause them to participate only in the things that will neither harm their lives nor cripple their influence for doing good. Another is to lead them not to participate even in

[7] I Cor. 8:4–13.

legitimate amusements at the expense, either in time or money of things more valuable. And a third is to create in them a desire to eliminate from society those amusements that are harmful to Christian character. These things may be done by Christian teachers in homes, churches, and schools. The best way to counteract the evil use of leisure time is for the church to provide an adequate program of leisure-time activities for all its members. This program is discussed in Chapter 20.

EDUCATIONAL DEVELOPMENTS

Turning from a somewhat negative view, a more positive problem is to be found in the contrast between the developments in secular and religious education. Probably the outstanding development in America has been its educational system — on which major emphasis has been placed during the past century. A democracy must depend upon education more than upon government. In many ways it offers a challenge to religious education.[8]

Accessibility

There was a time when school houses were few and far between, often in out-of-the-way places and with roads approaching them that were none too good. The writer remembers walking regularly nearly a mile and a half to school along a branch bottom with frequent crossings and through a muddy lane that more than once pulled his "Brogan" shoes off. Sometimes pupils had to go three and four miles. Now there are more schools, at points more nearly central, and for the most part on good highways. Besides, buses operate in most rural and village sections, enabling pupils to get to school easily.

Attendance

Growing out of the greater accessibility of schools and also their compulsory attendance laws, many *more people*

8 W. C. Bower, *Moral and Spiritual Values in Education* (Lexington: University of Kentucky Press, 1952), chap. i.

are now in the public schools. According to the report of the Bureau of Census, October, 1956, there were nearly 40,000,-000 pupils enrolled in school: 30,000,000 were in the elementary schools; 6,582,000 were in the high schools, and about 2,900,000 were in higher institutions of learning. Of the population between the ages of seven and thirteen, 99.9 per cent were reported as enrolled in schools and 88.2 per cent of those between fourteen and seventeen were similarly enrolled. It is estimated that more than one person in every four in the nation gives his time to study or teaching. Americans are a school-going people. A special committee appointed by President Eisenhower on Education Beyond the High School foresaw the enrollment of 4,000,000 young people in the colleges of the United States by 1960.[9] Federal aid has been provided to help meet this need.

Not only do more people attend school, but they attend for *a greater length of time.* Seventy-five years ago many schools ran only three to five months and the average student only completed the equivalent of a third-grade education. Now school runs from seven to ten months. The average school is open for one hundred and seventy days, and the average student completes from eight to nine years of schooling.

Efficiency

Not only are there more schools and more people attending them, but they are also more efficient. For one thing the *equipment* is much better. The writer's father attended school in a log house with split logs for seats, a dirt floor, open window, and fireplace. Now a school building can be found in many cities occupying an entire block, three stories, and a basement, with auditorium, classrooms, laboratories, gymnasium, cafeteria, and provisions for teaching not only the regular literary studies but also all phases of domestic science, mechanical arts, business, photography, journalism, and other special lines. Provision is made now for elementary

[9] President's Committee on Education Beyond the High School, *Needs and Resources* (Washington, D. C.: Government Printing Office, 1957), p. 6.

schools, junior and senior high schools, and in cities for junior and senior colleges.

The *curriculum* has broadened from the "three r's" to include all phases of literary studies, together with practical and vocational training. The course of study in the modern high school is in many cases beyond that of the college of fifty years ago, and in some cases probably equivalent to an M.A. degree then. And the end is not yet in sight, for constant improvement is being made in the direction of progressive and creative learning. Wide ranges of specialization are developing.

Furthermore, *teaching standards* have improved. At the beginning of this century, a person could teach school by making an average of 65 per cent on a special county examination with no grade below 50 per cent, whether he had ever gone to school a day in his life or not. Now the teacher must be a graduate from high school at least, usually from junior college, and frequently from a senior college before teaching school. And enough courses must be taken in the field of education to assure familiarity with pupil life and modern methods.

Results

Judging by the results of modern education, the scene is both striking and challenging. For one thing the *knowledge of the outside world* has been greatly extended. Through the microscope and the telescope man has greatly broadened his view of the universe, and this understanding constitutes a real problem unless his knowledge of God has grown at the same time. Otherwise there is a strain on the individual's faith.

But the *knowledge of the world within* has been just as amazing. The study of psychology has given us much knowledge of human life, and the understanding of sex and the mysteries of life has made a new problem morally. Junior high school pupils know more about these matters today than their grandparents did a generation or so ago. But what direction will such knowledge take? Will it uplift or degrade human life? To say the least, it constitutes a strain on the power of self-control. The outcome seems to depend on forces other than those inherent in the school system itself.

The tremendous developments in this field of secular education, whether from the standpoint of provisions made, numbers taught, or results achieved, emphasize the fact that corresponding developments have not been made in the field of religious education. If the developments made by the public school are to be matched, the church school must reach more people, have them a longer time, provide better equipment, have a more adequate curriculum, and do more effective teaching than has been done thus far. Nothing less than this will challenge American youth, provide adequately the fourth "r" in education, and so Christianize thinking as to cause students to maintain their faith in God and power of self-control in an era of widened knowledge. A prominent scientist said we should quit inventing until our self-control catches up with inventions already made.

DOMESTIC ISSUES

Prominent on the horizon of social problems today are those that have to do with the home. In many respects the most serious issues center here, for as the home goes, so goes civilization. Society can never rise much above the standards of the home. And all thinking people recognize that the life of the American home is seriously endangered.

Marriage

Too frequently when this topic is mentioned, the response is laughter. It is not looked upon as serious enough to merit thoughtful consideration. Yet more serious errors are made in the matter of selecting a life companion than in almost anything else. One needs only to observe any community for a few years to be convinced of this fact. Too often young people marry on the spur of the moment after only a brief acquaintance, and with little or no opportunity to study the background and characteristics of each other's life. Too often marriage is the outcome of mere passion or a dare rather than true love and thoughtful consideration. As a result many people are mismated and much anguish and sorrow is likely to follow in the wake of these tragic and fateful experiences.

Divorce

Growing out of mismating and hasty marriages and immature or unadjusted personalities is the divorce problem. There are more than a third of a million divorces annually, and the number is greater each year. The United States leads the world in divorces. If the ratio of increase continues, the divorces will equal or exceed the number of marriages by the end of the century. Instead of the single ground recognized by Jesus — that of adultery — there are now more than fifty legal grounds for divorce. In one or two states a residence of only sixty days qualifies one for a divorce. Without question it is one of the major social evils, and little is being done to correct it.

Parenthood

Much that has been written relative to marriage has stressed birth control and trial marriage rather than parenthood. Consequently, the attention and emphasis have been turned away from the parental idea. Marriage has been looked upon as a sort of permanent holiday affair, and the emphasis has been more on the physical than the spiritual side. The reading of questions propounded and answered by the daily columnists, as well as divorce court proceedings, is evidence of this fact. There is need for a new stress on the possibilities and advantages of parenthood today. For it has tremendous values for the parent as well as for the race.

In relation to marriage, divorce, and parenthood religious education has a large part to play. For one thing, an educational emphasis is needed both to counteract the wrong ideals and to build up wholesome ones. To this end there is an opportunity in the curricula of the various educational organizations in the church, for such discussions along these lines as will give the youth of the land the biblical concept of marriage, divorce, and parental responsibilities. Also pastors may give helpful discourses from the pulpit on these topics. And Christian colleges should offer courses to prepare for this phase of life. Fortunately, some helpful studies in this field, and regional conferences have been held. The National Council of Churches of Christ in the United States of America has a division for the study of this problem. There is a growing emphasis on the importance of the home in the total process of religious education. An increasing number of churches and denominations have set up a department of home curriculum and have begun to supply material to help parents.

Not only should instruction be given individuals away from the wrong ideals and into the right ones, but such teaching should be given as will help to crystallize public sentiment for legislation that will make it easier for youth to go right in these matters. Particularly is there a need for tightening up the laws on the conditions for marriage, such as minimum age, public notice, and medical examination. Also stricter laws are needed relative to the grounds and conditions under which divorces may be granted. These laws would need national uniformity to protect states that do try to be strict. These results will come through religious education and a public conscience.

ECONOMIC PROBLEMS

It would not require any argument to convince even the most skeptical that there are serious moral problems in the economic order. The nerve connecting with the pocketbook is a very tender and sensitive one. The problems are evident, though the cause and the cure may not be so clear, and many may not connect the problem with character. Honesty in business relationships is not merely a moral principle to be taught but a vital rule to be practiced in everyday life by men of Christian character.

Capital

Capital has been defined as man-made wealth for furthering production and distribution. It was formerly supplied by a relatively small group of individuals. Now it is furnished by millions of small stockholders. In a modern economic system such as exists in the United States of America, capital plays an important role in setting labor in motion and in increasing the material welfare of all. It has helped to raise the standard of living which is envied by most people of the world.

In recent years the degree of the concentration of wealth has been reduced, the purchasing power of the consumer has been raised, the gap between the "haves" and the "have-nots" has been narrowed, and the opportunity for education has been made available for the lower income groups. On these benefits and many others, capital has made great contributions. However, the modern machine age has resulted in a number of ills; for example, as the population is concentrated in cities, with almost unlimited purchasing power, social evils — such as drinking, divorce, juvenile delinquency, and criminality — have been mounting rapidly.

Overspecialization has reduced human beings into cogs in the wheels. Business fluctuations have enlarged the scope of unemployment. There is no final solution unless the golden rule as interpreted by Jesus is applied in the economic world. The source of most social and economic evils can be traced to the profit motive, or covetousness, which is so strongly embedded in the human personality. It is the function of religious education to refine and purify the motive and to convert it from profit-making to service-rendering.

Labor

Following the rise of capital was that of organized labor. In fact, labor almost had to organize in order to protect itself from the evils just mentioned, especially bad working conditions, long hours, and low wages. Organized labor sprang up alongside organized capital and met and solved many of the problems. But as it began to have power and realize its strength, it seemed to forget the evils done to it and to retaliate in return. Consequently there have been extreme demands for high wages and few hours, an unfair protection of inefficient union laborers, violence during strikes to those who were not members, and picketing of concerns who chose to employ nonunion labor. Organized labor can be as heartless as organized capital. Much bitterness of feeling and lack of Christian consideration have been shown. Manufacturing concerns have been unduly interfered with. Often the masses of people have suffered from high costs and scarcity of products due to the locking of the wheels of industry. These conditions have furnished fertile soil for the seeds of communism and other "isms" and have produced opportunities for the rise of dishonest labor leaders who have hurt the cause of organized labor and have seriously threatened the unity of our country.[10]

Government

During the depression years of the early thirties when so many people were out of work, it became necessary for the government to provide for them. This was done through all kinds of federal agencies which had been created to meet the economic needs of different groups. The government became the purchaser and distributor of all kinds of surplus food products. Ceiling prices were placed on nearly all consumer goods. Subsidies of farm products were provided.

All this government control, while definitely meeting a need, has added some evils to the already complicated economic situation. In some cases the government has become a competitor with business. Wages based on the changing cost of living have been fixed, and unemployment income has been guaranteed by federal bureaus. There has been a growing tendency to depend upon Uncle Sam for aid rather than upon individual initiative and free enterprise. Also there has developed a disposition to "soldier on the job" and not return a fair day's labor for the wages received. The government has plunged deeper and deeper into debt.

How far religious education can remedy the economic evils growing out of capitalism, organized labor, and govern-

[10] Verne P. Kaub, *Communist-Socialist Propaganda in our Public Schools* (Boston: Meador Publishing Co., 1953).

mental activities, it is impossible to say. Probably only a little can be done directly, for much of the solution is in the hands of these agencies themselves. A great deal may be done, however, in building right ideals and attitudes into the rising generation through the various organizations for moral and religious instruction. Something of that old-time sense of honesty, industry, and economy may be so instilled into the youth of the land that they will want to take care of their country rather than have their country take care of them. Elsie Robinson was right in saying that: "America was built by ... the sweat and pride and prayers of common citizens who paid their way as they went ... and would rather have starved than accept the hated dole of charity.... Men need work for the good of their souls as well as the good of their pocketbooks — and all the pension plans on earth won't alter that fundamental human necessity." Religious leaders in home, classroom, pulpit, and press may well join hands in one strenuous endeavor to develop the kind of character in the youth of America that will correct, both personally and collectively, the economic ills of the nation.

CIVIC EVILS

Already the civic side of life has been touched in dealing with the social problems discussed, for nearly all of them are finally rooted in the civic order. There are, however, certain immediate and evident governmental tasks that call for special attention.

Crime

It is not surprising to find that crime has been on the increase in the United States. At times it has increased four times as fast as the population and has reached alarming proportions. Organized criminal gangs might have been brought under control by the time of World War II, but according to the United States Department of Justice, "other types of organized crime are growing and are sending their poisonous tentacles into every channel of American life." The Kefauver Committee appointed by the United States Senate to investigate organized crime in interstate commerce, made an intensive study of this problem in 1950-51, and presented a list of recommendations to the Senate. The Committee pointed out that crime is largely a local problem and that basic responsibility for the conditions which nurture it rest upon the individual states and local communities. Good highways, fast automobiles, and large cities seem to give a new feeling of ability to evade the law. Hijacking is worse than Jesse James ever conceived it. Kidnapping has reached positively alarming proportions. Crime is organized with lawyers, doctors, and sometimes even policemen and judges helping. The average age of the criminal has dropped from over thirty years of age to under twenty in recent years. The president of a large life insurance company has stated: "Life was never as insecure in the United States as it is today."

Politics

Political life has always had its elements of corruption. This has been true among all peoples and under all forms of government. A more thorough knowledge of human nature and better means of handling the masses seem to have added to the problem. Citizens are not only often dominated by personal favoritism and partisan politics but also frequently sell their influence and votes during political campaigns in order to secure the election of a relative or a friend or secure a job. Politicians not only buy votes and sell their own in legislative halls, but may even be bribed in their decisions as judges or in the administration of the law as executives. The wildest kind of governmental scheme can find an advocate if it is felt that votes can be gained by it. No attention is paid to the effect of the scheme on character. Selfishness and self-interest are dominant motives today in the political life of most people.

Race Antipathy

The social inheritance of race prejudice and antipathy is readily and effectively handed on from one generation to another. While children of all races play together without antipathies, the attitude of older people soon carries over to them. In the eastern part of our country the prejudice is probably manifested most toward Greeks, Italians, and others from Central Europe. In the South it exists toward the Negroes. In the Southwest the Mexican comes in for his share of ill will. And in the Far West, Orientals are disliked. All through history, the Jew has been an object of prejudice. This attitude is contrary to the spirit of Christianity, is harmful to the person exercising it, and makes for constant trouble in the social order. It is one problem that even Christians have to reckon with constantly.

War

One of the gravest problems in civic life is the war spirit. It is very difficult for the average person to realize that there are forces deliberately working to bring about war. But such is the case. Those interested in such a way as to profit by it sometimes go to the extreme of creating public sentiment in favor of war or lobbying to bring it about. Furthermore, the ambition of self-seeking rulers to control large areas and make great names for themselves or hold on to power they would otherwise lose, contributes to fomenting the war spirit. It has been estimated that one bomber which becomes obsolete in a few years costs enough to build and equip three great universities such as the University of Michigan. More than three-fourths of the national disbursements during American history have gone for war or things related to it. And the cost in killed and crippled men is beyond calculation, for war takes "the blood of the nation." Truly has it been said: "War converts mankind into two classes: beasts of prey and beasts of burden."

If the evils of crime, political crookedness, race hatred, and war are ever eliminated from human society, it will have to be done by educators. The public school system can do much to train a generation of citizens who will be fair with their fellow-men, loyal to their country, just with all races — citizens who would constantly seek to eliminate war. The exchange of students between countries and correspondence between those of different nations will help. Our early relations with China are a good example. But if these civic evils are ever fully eliminated, it will come as the love of Christ is implanted in the lives of the coming generation. This must be done by religious education in home, church, school, and through every medium of communication. There is no greater problem today than that of undergirding and interpenetrating civilization with the ideals and spirit of Christ, and establishing, as far as it is humanly possible to do, the kingdom of God on earth. This is enough to challenge religious education to do its best to correct these conditions.

Such, then, are some of the problems in the physical, recreational, educational, domestic, economic, and civic life that call for a program of religious education adequate to meet the needs. It was out of such considerations that Woodrow Wilson was led to say: "Our civilization cannot survive materially unless it be redeemed spiritually." And Roger Babson has said: "We do not need more commerce or battleships. We need more religious education." There is no greater task confronting the citizenship of America.

QUESTIONS FOR DISCUSSION

1. Make a list of scriptures which refer to the use of strong drink. After analyzing the scriptures, write your opinion of what the Bible teaches concerning strong drink. Is your church teaching it?

2. What is meant by immorality? What is being done by the churches in your community to improve moral conditions?

3. Make a survey of the recreational facilities in your community. How many of them are good character-builders? Which tend to destroy character?

4. Do you think there is a relationship between juvenile delinquency and the family's failure to function in society today? List the reasons for your position.

5. What should be the Christian's stand on the race problem? Why is there a race problem?

CHAPTER 6

DEMANDS OF MODERN
RELIGIOUS CONDITIONS

In this chapter modern religious conditions are presented as a challenge to religious education. In some respects the problems discussed here are the most fundamental, since religious needs are seemingly the most evident and without question the most significant. Religion is at the heart of all other problems. Solve it adequately, and it will take care of all else.

ELIMINATION OF RELIGIOUS TEACHING[1]

The Puritans came to this country because of a religious motive. The Bible, therefore, was at the heart of every phase of their activity. The churches fostered it, schools taught it, business problems were settled by it, and legislation was passed in order to promote it. Gradually, however, conditions changed.

Materials

In the early days schools were established primarily to promote a knowledge of the Bible. In Connecticut in 1650

[1] For fuller discussion, see J. M. O'Neill, *Religion and Education Under the Constitution* (New York: Harper & Bros., 1949); and E. H. Rian, *Christianity and American Education* (San Antonio: The Naylor Co., 1949).

92

they resolved to establish schools, "It being the chief project of that old deluder, Satan, to keep men from the knowledge of the Scriptures." A Pennsylvania law passed in 1683 required all parents and guardians to have their children instructed in reading and writing, so that they might be able to read the Scriptures.

During the first generation of life in New England, concern for religious education remained on a high plane. The urgent need for an educated clergy is marked by the founding of Harvard University in 1636, with William and Mary, Yale, and others following soon afterward. There were nine colleges before the Revolution. It should be noted that the universities of Mexico and Lima were established at even earlier dates under Roman Catholic auspices. Religious teaching was normally a part of the regular education of the young, and parents took their responsibilities seriously.[2]

Similar reasons were given in other states for the establishment of public schools. All along, the religious motive was dominant.

Naturally, the textbooks carried a large percentage of biblical material. The hornbook, which was a sort of paddle covered with transparent material, contained the alphabet, the Lord's Prayer, the Ten Commandments, and the Apostles' Creed. The New England Primer, a small vest-pocket book, 3 million copies of which were used, had the alphabet in scripture verses, the Lord's Prayer, questions on the Bible, the Shorter Catechism, and other materials. The American ("Blue-back") Spelling Book prepared by Noah Webster, about 24 million copies of which were sold, had on 36 of the 166 pages, statements on religion, Bible facts, Bible characters, and Christian doctrines.

Due to the influences of certain liberal groups, the multiplicity of denominations, and the principle of separation of church and state, a gradual process of eliminating these materials was carried on until now the public school has practically a secular curriculum. "The Bible was not legislated out of schools; it was quietly crowded out by alien influence

[2] Randolph Crump Miller, *Education for Christian Living*, p. 25. Copyright, 1956, by Prentice-Hall, Inc., Englewood Cliffs, N. J.

and indifference."[3] M. L. Perkins investigated 1,291 readers and spellers published during our national life, and of those printed from 1776 to 1825 he found 22 per cent religious, 50 per cent moral, and 28 per cent secular. Of those published from 1826 to 1880, 12 per cent was religious, 27 per cent was moral, and 61 per cent was neither. Of those published from 1881 to 1920, 4 per cent was religious, 7 per cent was moral, and 89 per cent was of other types. During the last five years of the last period 0 per cent was religious, 3 per cent was moral, and 97 per cent was secular. Thus a secularized curriculum in the public schools has been produced.

There is a strong movement among public school leaders for including character education and moral teaching in the schools to compensate for the elimination of the Bible. The result is a humanistic form of religion, with no personal God, or Christ as Savior. The Scriptures are not studied, and moral education without religious motivation cannot be construed as real religious education. In some high schools the Bible is taught as history or as literature but not as a book on religion.

The meaning of this is clear. Pupils no longer get the Scriptures as a part of the curriculum of the public school system. Though valuable materials may be given, the Bible itself will have to be learned through other channels. Moreover, the natural tendency will be for the pupil to discount religion. James D. Smart says: "It is unhappy for the child and most confusing to find that what he learns in the one school does not agree with what he learns in the other. It is alarming for the Church if, in any degree, education in the public schools is conditioning the mind of youth to resist the Church's teaching."[4]

Teachers

In the Colonial period, the teacher was usually either the

[3] W. S. Fleming, *God in Our Public Schools* (Pittsburgh: The National Reform Association, 1944), p. 45.

[4] From *The Teaching Ministry of the Church* by James D. Smart, p. 187. Copyright, 1954, by W. L. Jenkins, The Westminster Press, Philadelphia. Used by permission.

minister of the community or some one licensed by him to teach; and even if the Bible as such had not been included, there would have been a definite religious element. In fact, the teacher was quite an ally of the pastor, often seeing that the children went to church and catechizing them on the preacher's sermon. The contract of a teacher at Flatbush, New York, called for him to help look after the church service in addition to his public school teaching. He also instructed in the Bible and the Catechism and had prayers in the school.

But this situation has changed. Now no religious obligation whatever is placed on the teacher by school authorities. In Texas, for example, trustees are not even permitted to ask about the religious life of the applicant, at least in any official capacity. The teacher may be an active Christian, negative religiously, or even antagonistic to religion. He may say things critical of Christianity but may not advocate it.

This means, of course, that church people may no longer count on the teacher officially for any assistance in the matter of Christian teaching. The influence of the public school teacher who is with the pupil five days a week may more than counteract that of the pastor or Sunday school teacher who is with him only on Sunday. He is the church's greatest ally or handicap.

Control

Formerly most of the schools themselves were under Christian auspices. Especially was this true of secondary schools and colleges. Many of the academies and other high schools were founded by religious organizations and were Christian in teachers, texts, and atmosphere. The same was true of colleges. Harvard, the first college, was thoroughly Christian in the beginning. Its seal bore the motto "Christ and the Church," and before graduation the student had to "read the originals of the Old and New Testaments into the Latin tongue." Others such as Yale, Brown, and Princeton were founded by Christian leaders, conducted under Christian auspices, and held religious services. Columbia's charter still requires a chapel on the campus open daily. Nearly all early colleges were Christian.

As time went on many Christian schools were gradually eliminated and secular institutions took their place. The modern high school has practically supplanted the denominational academy. Much the same result has come to the college. The Federal Land Grant of 1862 allotting lands to agricultural schools helped to further the wave of state colleges and normal schools, as well as A. & M. colleges. Municipal junior and senior colleges have also grown up. Denominational high schools and colleges have been pushed off the map. More than 300 such institutions founded in Texas before the Civil War have disappeared. Southern Baptists lost nearly half of their 119 schools during the depression. Four-fifths of the youth from Christian homes are now being trained in secular institutions.

The significance of this trend to eliminate religion from education is evident. Says Henry P. Van Dusen: "No longer is religion the keystone of the educational arch."[5] If Christian teachers, biblical materials, and even denominational schools themselves are set aside, a generation of youth will grow up without their values. If, therefore, religious instruction is to be provided for the coming generation comparable to that of the past, a more comprehensive system of religious education must be built. This involves religious literature, adequate educational organizations in the churches, better support of Christian colleges, and religious activity at state and independent institutions. Probably the strongest definite challenge to religious education comes from the elimination of religion from educational institutions.

ANTI-CHRISTIAN PHILOSOPHIES

Not only the elimination of the religious element from educational life, but, in addition, the promulgation of certain views that are definitely opposed to Christianity confront

---

[5] Henry P. Van Dusen, *God in Education* (New York: Charles Scribner's Sons, 1951), p. 52.

the church today. Some of this is in the field of religion and some of it relates more definitely to the moral life.

Materialism

Certain psychologists seeking to be scientific in their studies introduced the laboratory method of study. This meant that instead of introspection they resorted to observation. As usual they began with the white rat or dog. The result was that the extremists concluded there was no such thing as mind or soul and that everything could be accounted for on the basis of stimulus and response. According to this view man is merely a neural mechanism, the product of internal response to external stimuli, and therefore the result of habits rather than ideals.

The effect of such a view on religion and morals is evident. It holds that man is purely physical and not a soul. So there is no such thing as immortality and no place for God or religion. Since there is no mind or consciousness, moral accountability is left out, and one is not responsible for what he does. Thus the spiritual and the ethical are eliminated from life. This sort of teaching in some degree or other finds its place in many institutions of higher learning. Not so long ago the writer heard a professor in a nationally known teachters' college say to his class: "Do not use in your papers any more the term 'soul.' Psychology knows nothing about it." This is as dangerous a view as atheism. It is materialism of the first rank.

Naturalism

Closely related to materialism is the philosophy of naturalism which makes man his own god. According to John Brubacher, "It denies that educational philosophy in its inclusive sweep need take into account concepts of the supernatural. If there is anything hidden from man in his search for the solution of educational problems, it must lie hidden in the system of nature of which he is himself a part. . . . This philosophy omits the eternal, the timeless, from the space-time frame of reference. . . . If religion enters this philosophy . . . it is only as a deified nature; and nature is His temple of worship."[6] Naturalism needs the supplementation by the superior insight of revelation and grace. God is not recognized as a spiritual being.

Under the influence of John Dewey in particular, the field of education has been invaded by a type of humanism that not only regards Christianity and all other historical religion as antiquated superstitions from the past, but is confident that in humanism modern man finds his only intelligent approach to reality. Many representatives of this school have actually a crusading zeal to deliver mankind from its "superstitions" into the glorious freedom of the completely rational life.[7]

This philosophy underlies the emphasis of some psychologists on the unconscious. An aspect of this philosophy which has received particular attention is the complex — a group of associated ideas with a common emotional tone. These ideas may contain some natural urge that has been repressed, or natural desires that have been thwarted, so that the frustrated individual pushes his unsolved problem back into the unconscious where it is repressed. In its extreme form, this philosophy holds that the natural desires should be given free expression. The result is an emotional disturbance which often results in a nervous breakdown or some other personality maladjustment.

The cause most emphasized is sex desire. The thought is that if it is not allowed expression a dangerous complex arises. Therefore provision must be made for its free expression. The inevitable outcome of this emphasis is the giving of free rein to natural desire, which inevitably means much immoral living. Without question a great deal of the cause of the wide-spread wave of immorality is due to the emphasis on sex life in books and magazines, millions of which are printed monthly.

[6] By permission from *Modern Philosophies of Education*, by John Brubacher, pp. 322 ff. Copyright, 1939, McGraw-Hill Book Co., Inc., New York.

[7] From *The Teaching Ministry of the Church*, by James D. Smart, p. 188. Copyright, 1954, by W. L. Jenkins, The Westminster Press, Philadelphia. Used by permission.

Atheism

In the scientific and philosophical fields of thought the idea is frequently advanced that man is the product of blind forces of nature operating in the universe, and that there is no personal God at the back of the universe. This is the view of materialistic evolutionists. They seek to explain the beginning and continuation of the universe on the basis of matter and motion. When the idea of a god is mentioned at all in some educational centers, a pagan or mythological god rather than Christ is stressed. In school every pagan god in history may be the subject of the day's lesson, but not the God of the Bible.

Furthermore, certain independent organizations have been formed to promote the theory of atheism through the schools. One of these was named "The American Society for the Advancement of Atheism," with branch societies in various universities taking such names as "The Damned Souls." Similarly a Junior Atheistic League was formed with a former Christian Endeavor worker as its head, for the purpose of establishing branches in the high schools of the land. Some of these local societies have taken such names as "God's Black Sheep" and "The Society of the Godless." To be sure, such organizations have never been general and are usually short-lived, but the fact of their even getting started shows an ominous trend.

Collectivism

Just as some psychologists have stressed expressionism which may lead to license, so some sociologists have stressed a collectivism which may lead to communism. John Flynn in his radio broadcasts has quoted from educational theorists and high school text books such statements as "The age of individualism is closing and a new age of collectivism is emerging." The society of the future is to be a "planned, coordinated, and socialized economy," "America is a planless country unlike Russia," "Socialist Britain has more liberties [in 1948] than did the United States in 1920!"[8] Teachers

[8] John J. Flynn, *They War on Our Schools* (New York: America's Future, Inc., 1952), pp. 6, 10.

were urged to prepare their pupils for the new collective society.

Such statements discount democracy and play up socialism; minimize free enterprise and laud controlled economy; and tend to glorify Russia and discount the United States. All of this prepares the minds of teachers and pupils for communism. When communism comes in, Christianity goes out. In socialistic countries Christianity is on the wane; and in communistic lands, it is being crushed out. Such emphases are definitely anti-Christian in influence and effect.

The result of these antireligious tendencies does not end merely with skepticism about God, the Bible, and immortality. It carries over into everyday living. Much of today's crime, economic and political crookedness, and immorality grow out of such a background. This is natural. Eliminate God, make man a mere animal, give free rein to instincts, and the jungle life is the inevitable result. If educators are to deal with causes rather than symptoms, they must go behind the moral and religious ills to the things that inspire them.

This means that these "issues" having to do with God, the soul, and moral living, need to be met with a positive program of Christian teaching. Much of it will have to be done in the Christian college and by the teacher of the Bible in the state and independent school. Since quite a bit of the problem is related to high school, the local church can do much through organized classes, training unions, and week-day religious teaching on released time.

THE UNTAUGHT MASSES

The American home is handicapped in giving anything like thorough instruction in the Bible because of the fact that one or both parents may not be Christians, neither may be capable of effective teaching, or the time element may be lacking. Since not more than about 5 per cent of our young people get to Christian colleges, a heavy responsibility falls on the churches.

Number Unreached

One of the most tragic facts in American life is the large

number of people now remaining away from church on Sunday. The *Yearbook of American Churches* states that there are more than 100 million church members in our nation. This is wonderful, but it means there are still nearly 75 million that are not members of any church. Furthermore, there are only about 40 million enrolled in Sunday schools. This means about 135 million are not even on the rolls, to say nothing of the large number absent each Sunday. In other words, approximately 150 million people are not getting regular religious instruction in Sunday schools week by week. So accomplishing a moral reform, such as prohibition, is difficult. There are enough people who are not being taught religiously to defeat it.

Irregular Attendance

Not only are great numbers unreached for religious instruction, but of those who are reached many are absent a major portion of the time. Few Sunday schools have much more than half as many present as they have on their rolls. A survey of 1,420 Sunday school pupils in a typical small town showed 5.1 per cent attended 97 per cent of the time, 11.5 per cent came 67 per cent, 10.6 per cent were there 37 per cent, and 12.6 per cent showed up only 6 per cent of the time. Others attended at varying rates in between. In other words, not only are fewer than one-half of the youth of the land enrolled in church schools, but also fewer than two-thirds of those that are enrolled are there regularly. Of course no adequate results in religious instruction can be gained under such circumstances. The state would not think of allowing public education to be carried on under such irregular and unfavorable conditions.

Brief Time

If all of the youth were enrolled in the Sunday school and training unions on Sunday and attended every session, there would still be an unsatisfactory situation because of the brief amount of time actually given to instruction. The average Sunday school class or Training Union group does not de-

vote more than half an hour per week to a discussion of the
subject assigned. This is very meager when compared with
the 112 waking hours per week. It is also very poor in comparison, with the public schools which have almost thirty
times as much time. Roman Catholic children get on the
average approximately four times as much religious instruction as do Protestants, and Jewish children over six times as
much. To be sure much good comes from the worship periods of educational organizations, but frequently they are
not very definitely educational.

Inadequate Curriculum

If all of the youth attended church school all of the time,
there would still be an inadequate curriculum, at least so
far as the Sunday school is concerned. From 1872 through
1917 when the old Uniform Lessons were used, only 35.1
per cent of the Bible was included. In other words if a child
had entered at five years of age in 1872, attended every Sunday and studied every lesson, at fifty years of age he would
have had little more than a third of the Bible, and this mainly historical. Nine books would never have been touched.
The Improved Uniform Lessons have corrected this somewhat in that over 40 per cent of the Bible is included, but it
is still top-heavy with historical material. The Closely Graded
go considerably further and include nearly 65 per cent of the
Bible, with material much better adapted to the younger age
groups, but stop short with the Intermediates, seemingly
forgetting that Young People and Adults also need material
adapted to life problems.

If the American people are ever to handle adequately
crime and other national problems, they must face seriously
this matter of the masses of people being taught religiously,
for religion provides the stimulus for proper conduct. This
means that a more aggressive effort must be made to reach
the unenlisted for our church schools; that the enlisted must
be led to attend with more regularity, and that religious
education must be extended into the weekday so that more
time may be given to instruction and a wider range of cur-

riculum provided. To do these things there will probably have to be a closer correlation with public schools so that more may be reached, more time be available, and probably credit given. Every possible opportunity must be used to enlist the rank and file in religious instruction.

IGNORANCE OF THE BIBLE

A natural consequence of the fact that the masses are largely untaught is shown by the gross ignorance of the Scriptures. After a century and three-quarters of Sunday schools, three-quarters of a century of young people's societies, and many years of other activities, the sad fact still remains that the average person still knows very little about the Bible. Hosea's statement is about as true now as in his day, "My people are destroyed for lack of knowledge" (Hos. 4:6).

American Soldiers

During the Korean War and both World Wars, studies were made of the religious knowledge of American soldiers. A number of books were written by YMCA workers and chaplains; all are in agreement as to the widespread ignorance of the Bible and Christian doctrine by the average soldier. Statements such as these were made by these workers: "The average young American knows very little about God, Christ, prayer, and faith." "Not one in a hundred had ever heard of the kingdom of God." "The most serious failure of the church as evidenced in the army was its failure as a teacher." Since these young people come from all sections of the country and all classes of people, they represent a cross-section of the youth of the nation and give a fair picture of the effectiveness of our teaching program. Of course the number not enrolled in Bible teaching, those absent much of the time, and the failure to study and teach properly, all enter into the picture.

Woodrow Wilson, at the close of the First World War, warned that civilization could not survive materially unless it were redeemed spiritually. General MacArthur, in accepting Japan's surrender at the close of the Second World

War, defined the problem of our age as basically "theological," saying "there must be a regeneration of the spirit if we are to save the flesh." General Omar N. Bradley has declared: "Humanity is in danger of being trapped in this world by its moral adolescence. Our knowledge of science has already outstripped our capacity to control it. . . . We have grasped the mystery of the atom and rejected the Sermon on the Mount. . . . The world has achieved brilliance without wisdom, power without conscience. Ours is a world of nuclear giants and ethical infants."[9]

College Freshmen

A study was made of high school graduates who were just entering a state university. They had come from the best homes and schools throughout their state, and should have been above the average. They took the test voluntarily and naturally felt fairly capable in the biblical field. There were 139 freshmen participating. There were eight questions calling for the naming of ten books of the Old Testament, ten of the New, the divisions of the Old Testament, identifying five Bible characters, and similar matters. Twelve made as much as 75 per cent, 91 got less than 50, and the average was 40 per cent. Ten could not name a book of the Old Testament, and only 68 named ten. Old Testament books mentioned were "Hezekiah," "Phenecians," "Gentiles," and "Xerxes." Twelve could not name a New Testament book and only 46 named ten. New Testament books mentioned were "Paul," "Thelesians," "Lazarus," and "Samson Agonistes." Twenty-seven made no effort to name the "Apostle to the Gentiles," 72 replied correctly, and others mentioned "Methusaleh," "Moses," and "Judas." Twenty did not even try to name "The Beloved Disciple," sixty-eight answered correctly, and names given were "Abraham," "David," and "Peter." "Apollos" was thought to be a heathen god, and "Cana" was the promised land. And yet all of these had graduated from high school and were now in a state university!

[9] Harry C. Munro, *Protestant Nurture*, pp. 6–7. Copyright, 1956, by Prentice-Hall, Inc., Englewood Cliffs, N. J.

Religious Workers

From time to time information has been gained in various ways from those leading in various capacities in religious work. The results have been rather startling. One is reminded of the biblical emphasis concerning the blind leading the blind. A businessman who was Sunday school superintendent asked the writer in a training class one night if it was definitely known *who* Genesis was. A farmer who was also a Sunday school superintendent in answering a question in a training course examination as to what the Book of Judges told about said, "the General Judgment." A public school superintendent and Sunday school teacher who had graduated from a Christian college did not know whether the book of Ephesians was in the Old Testament or the New. Many pastors have shown ignorance of the Bible just about as great as the above. The spiritual illiteracy in the land is indeed appalling. It is of more consequence than literary illiteracy, though it arouses much less excitement.

The widespread ignorance of the Bible not only among the masses but also in the ranks of college students and even voluntary and vocational religious leaders obviously reveals that a new crusade is needed. If the generation now in college, including vocational and nonvocational workers, will set themselves to the task of remedying the situation, the problem can be relieved almost in a generation. It will require creating public sentiment, setting up organizations, enlisting the people, and consistently teaching them. Therefore, urges Ligon, "Let us teach as much of the Bible to our children as we can. But let us teach it so that it becomes a part of their lives, not merely as inspiring phrases to be repeated on solemn occasions. Let us hope that the Church will feel the challenge to make the Bible live in the lives of our children and not be satisfied to have them gain only a superficial familiarity with its passages."[10] An aroused church, a nationwide program of religious education, and trained leadership will remove the menace of spiritual il-

[10] Ernest M. Ligon, *A Greater Generation* (New York: The Macmillan Co., 1948), p. 86. Used by permission.

literacy that now threatens the life both of church and state.

UNDEVELOPED CHRISTIANS

Too often in the zealous effort to reach the last unconverted person and "evangelize the world in this generation," proper attention is not given to those who have made professions. Consequently they fail to develop. One prominent evangelist has emphasized "the ministry of conservation" along with "the ministry of rescue" saying: "Two hundred new members are two hundred new liabilities until they are properly lined up in their respective places in the church." A few years after the famous Northampton revival, Jonathan Edwards said: "Multitudes of fair and high professors have backslidden. . . ." Harry C. Munro warns against a shallow evangelism which does not result in changed lives:

> Many of our church membership drives which are called evangelism overlook this spiritual nature of church membership. Persons are urged to join the church on the assumption that somehow this will bring them into right relationship with Christ. The evangelistic policy that says, "The first thing is to get them into the church so that the church's program can help them find Christ" ignores this prerequisite to real church membership. To be sure, many people do join the church and then actually find Christ afterward. But a much larger number merely join the church assuming that is all there is to it. When statistical goals cause evangelism to press from discovery directly to church membership, by-passing fellowship cultivation, preparation, and conversion or genuine spiritual commitment, such goals and procedures become spiritually hazardous to all concerned.[11]

In Attendance

It is a noticeable fact that many who make professions of faith during an annual revival meeting do not show up again until the next revival, if even then. The average church, and particularly the large one, will do well to have one-third as many present at the Sunday morning services as it has members. At the Sunday night services probably one-sixth will be a good percentage for the big church. What about the other two-thirds or five-sixths? They are becoming

[11] Harry C. Munro, *Protestant Nurture*, p. 151. Copyright, 1956, by Prentice-Hall, Inc., Englewood Cliffs, N. J.

a matter of increasing concern in many sections of the country. This derelict group has been referred to by John R. Sampey as the "lost sheep of the house of Israel." (Matt. 10:6). The situation has become so serious in some places that the churches have set up special organizations and put on special campaigns to get their own members back to church. In at least one instance the churches of one denomination of an entire state have taken that as their primary task.

In Giving

Just as noticeable as the matter of failing to attend church is that of failing to support it and its work with one's means. In fact, the latter naturally grows out of the former. It is proverbial that about one-third of the church membership carry practically all of the financial burdens. Many never give anything at all for religious purposes either for work at home or in foreign lands. Many others who contribute some, do it meagerly and spasmodically, when they "feel like it." Southern Baptists have given less than a dollar per capita per week to all purposes. Less than one-fourth of them give as much as a tithe of their income, when this should be the starting point rather than the stopping place. Only two of a Training Union membership of more than twenty, after giving a splendid program on tithing, were found to be tithers. Often religious leaders are short in their giving. Many of the poorest people spend more on soft drinks, shows, and tobacco than they do on the church and its work. And not only does the Kingdom of God suffer thereby, but their own characters are dwarfed, for they live in God's world, enjoy his blessings, owe him a part of their income, and cannot short-cut a moral obligation without suffering the consequences in character.

In Service

When one considers the matter of religious leadership in church life, the problem is still more serious. Even in cultured centers and large churches it is extremely difficult to find enough people to carry on all of the responsibilities of church life without greatly overworking a few. Many who will promise to teach a class in Sunday school or lead a group in the Training Union soon quit or are irregular in their attendance. Often those who are prominent in other phases of community life are incapable or undependable in church work. Many who can teach in public school or speak in political life cannot or will not perform similar duties in church. Few, comparatively, can intelligently guide an inquiring soul to Christ. Many cannot even lead in public prayer. Some are still so ignorant or prejudiced as to be opposed to some of the educational activities of the church and missionary enterprises on the foreign field. Either the church has brought too many people into its membership or failed to do for them what should be done.

It is almost needless to say that the great host of undeveloped church people, whether as to attendance, giving, or service, has created a situation that calls for a new emphasis on the educational method. Probably it should begin by following a sounder psychology in leading people to make professions of faith, promise to give sums of money, or to undertake leadership responsibility. Possibly these results should be sought more through individual conviction than crowd pressure. But whatever may be true as to that activity, greater effort should be put forth to develop those who do get into our churches. Without question, it is true that most of our troubles come out of a lack of training. The ministry of conservation must follow that of rescue to have converts who are substantial.

LAPSES IN FAITH

Going still further in consideration of the challenge of religious conditions, the church is confronted with the problem of the large number of people who go back on their professions completely or switch their alignment to an entirely alien group. Sometimes the defection is even to the point of skepticism or atheism.

Backsliding

Many who make professions simply ease out of religious

activity altogether, or perhaps it would be more nearly correct to say that they never get started in it. The fact is that many who attend revivals and are baptized into church membership never show up later with any degree of regularity. As an example of such defection, consider Southern Baptists. In a twenty-year period, 32.5 per cent of those baptized were lost to the churches by other means than death. This was twice the percentage of deaths and nearly a third of the total number. Such a loss in the educational or business world would be counted very serious. The country boy was about right who told the writer that in his church "about a third of the ones that profess in the revival one summer have to refess the next." Either a great many unconverted people are getting into churches, or the churches are failing to develop young converts. At any rate, the church has certainly failed to introduce control into conduct, as education is supposed to do. There is entirely too much dead wood in the churches.

Heresies

Not only do many drop out of evangelical church life, but others go off into groups that are far from scriptural in their Christian beliefs. One illustration is the number that go over to the Russellites or the Jehovah's Witnesses, for most of their gains come from the ranks of the churches rather than from the ranks of the lost. By means of their highly advertised lectures and wide circulation of inexpensive, many-colored books, they have made tremendous gains in recent years. Similarly the Christian Scientists through their newspapers, lectures, and distribution of free tracts in hotels, depots, and on trains have drawn many from the ranks of evangelical Christianity. But perhaps the most noted instance is in the case of the Mormons. Undoubtedly their house-to-house distribution of free literature and carrying on of weekday schools of religion adjacent to the public high schools in Utah, as well as regular Sunday instruction, help to account for the gains. Increases in the ranks of the Spiritualists and Buddhists are other instances.

If these lapses in faith, particularly backsliding and the inroads of heretical groups, are to be counteracted, it must be done not only by sound instruction prior to profession in order that a sane experience may be had, but also by continued efforts at teaching and training that the new life may become intelligent and the individual habituated to the Christian faith. Especially should more attention be given to teaching the fundamental doctrines. As much attention should be given to the converts already made as to those yet to be won. W. E. Hatcher was eminently right when he said: "It is at least as important to save what we have as to save the lost." And this definitely involves religious education.

If in this chapter on the challenge of religious conditions the picture has been made a bit darker than some feel it is, let it be emphasized that it has not been done pessimistically nor to criticize what has been accomplished but rather to make emphatic the need for more thorough training in religious matters. If the public schools are not to be depended upon to teach Christianity, but instead often present things opposed to it; if, after what the churches have done, the majority are still untaught religiously and are ignorant of the Bible; and if undevelopment is common and lapses from the faith frequent, then without question the supreme religious task of America is a program of religious education in Sunday church schools, weekday church schools, Christian day schools, Christian colleges, and state universities sufficient to correct these conditions.

QUESTIONS FOR DISCUSSION

1. Canvass the members of your class at school and at the church to determine what kind of books and magazines they buy and read. How much time do they spend reading the Bible and religious literature? How much time do they spend reading other literature?

2. What is meant by the terms "pantheism," "humanism," "agnosticism," "materialism," and "communism"?

3. Investigate the provisions being made to reach the untaught masses in your community. Make the study more valuable by in-

terviewing pastors and religious education directors from other denominations.

4. Many of the people who do not attend Sunday school are prevented from doing so by sickness or employment. What provisions have been made or are being made to teach these people about God?

5. Consider what changes should be made in the Sunday schools to insure a more thorough knowledge of God's word among those who attend.

6. What percentage of the number baptized by your church last year failed to continue in the church. What reasons can you find for their lapse in faith?

Part I

BIBLIOGRAPHY

BENSON, C. H. *A Popular History of Christian Education*. Chicago: The Moody Press, 1943.

BOWER, WILLIAM C. *Moral and Spiritual Values in Education*. Lexington: University of Kentucky Press, 1952.

BOWER, WILLIAM C., and HAYWARD, PERCY R. *Protestantism Faces Its Educational Task Together*. New York: National Council of the Churches of Christ in the United States of America, 1950.

EAKIN, FRANK, and EAKIN, MILDRED M. *Let's Think About Our Religion*. New York: The Macmillan Co., 1944.

EBY, FREDERICK, and ARROWOOD, CHARLES. *The History and Philosophy of Education, Ancient and Medieval*. Englewood Cliffs, N. J.: Prentice-Hall, Inc., 1940.

EDGE, FINDLEY B. *Teaching for Results*. Nashville: The Broadman Press, 1956.

GAEBELEIN, FRANK E. *Christian Education in a Democracy*. New York: Oxford University Press, 1951.

HACKMAN, GEORGE G., and OTHERS. *Religion in Modern Life*. New York: The Macmillan Co., 1957.

HOOVER, J. EDGAR. "Why Crime Is Dropping," *U. S. News and World Report*. 39:45, September 30, 1955.

————. "You Can Help Stop Juvenile Crime," *American Magazine* 159:15, January, 1955.

LIGON, ERNEST M. *A Greater Generation*. New York: The Macmillan Co., 1948.

LOTZ, PHILIP H. (ed.). *Orientation in Religious Education*. Nashville: Abingdon Press, 1950.

MASON, HAROLD C. *Abiding Values in Christian Education*. Westwood, N. J.: Fleming H. Revell Co., 1955.

MILLER, RANDOLPH CRUMP. *Education for Christian Living*. Englewood Cliffs, N. J.: Prentice-Hall, Inc., 1956.

MUNRO, HARRY C. *Protestant Nurture*. Englewood Cliffs, N. J.: Prentice-Hall, Inc., 1956.

PRICE, J. M. *Jesus the Teacher*. Rev. ed. Nashville: Convention Press, 1954.

SHERRILL, LEWIS J. *The Rise of Christian Education*. New York: The Macmillan Co., 1944.

SMART, JAMES D. *The Teaching Ministry of the Church*. Philadelphia: Westminster Press, 1954.

SMITH, H. SHELTON. *Faith and Nurture*. New York: Charles Scribner's Sons, 1941.

WERTHAM, FREDERIC. *The Seduction of the Innocent*. (The effects of comics on children.) New York: Rinehart & Co., Inc., 1957.

Part II

PRINCIPLES OF
RELIGIOUS EDUCATION

CHAPTER 7

PSYCHOLOGY

The problem of the religious educator is that of translating ideas into conduct, and transmuting conduct into character. The average teacher, on the contrary, has assumed that there is a separation between the idea presented and the conduct expected. He thinks in terms of two processes, one of imparting truth and the other of building character. Experience has demonstrated that the habits and attitudes of growing youth are actually being shaped by every experience in the lesson process and by his associates in the throbbing atmosphere of life itself. It has been well demonstrated that the ideas of the lesson will more likely control conduct when definitely linked with the experiences of the lesson period and with practice in living these ideas with associates whose approval he values. The task of a religious educator in achieving a character result embraces the utilization of the lesson material, the teacher himself, and community approval of the conduct proposed.

THE LEARNING PROCESS

Learning, as suggested by the statement of the problem, is largely adjustment to the conditions of life. This learning may be secured through a trial-and-error process in which the successful reactions are linked together in a unity of experience. Likewise learning may be secured by the use of ideas growing out of the experiences of others and accepted by the individual as experience. This enables one to gain practice in the absence of the situation. It is also true that the learner may acquire certain skills by observation. By watching others perform he may abridge the trial-and-error process to a noticeable degree. In any case the individual learns the reactions which he makes in his adjustment to the conditions of life.

The process of learning looks to four achievements — changes in the pupil's knowledge, skill, attitudes, and appreciations. Knowledge has been defined as "familiarity with facts, events and principles with an understanding of their meaning." Skill has been defined as "an ability to do some act with ease and accuracy." An attitude has been defined as "a habitual way of thinking and feeling about persons, relations and things." Appreciation has been defined as "the ability to assign values."[1] The concern of the teacher is primarily that of the development of skills, attitudes, and appreciations. The human organism, however, approaches these results through knowledge.

In the process of translating knowledge into skills, attitudes, and appreciations, certain well-known principles of teaching have been established and laws formulated by which the mind functions. A brief statement of these principles will clarify the general laws of learning and will be a guide to more effective teaching.

Action Urges

These urges reside in the individual by inheritance. These are needed for the protection of the individual, and when they act it is for the satisfaction of a particular need. It appears to be true that man's behavior is a reflection of his striving for various forms of satisfaction. Man has certain

[1] J. L. Corzine, *Looking at Learning* (rev. ed.; Nashville: Convention Press, 1957), pp. 17-18.

legitimate wants or needs which give direction to his actions.

Situation Response

The situation response is the testing ground of an urge. Trial and error is the timid advance on an environment, and the first learning. When an urge arises, the child responds with one of these unlearned responses. The world is not always friendly to the way in which the mechanism responds. For this reason the child early in life discovers that his innate modes of behavior have to be modified, if they are to find satisfaction in the environment. This modification to secure satisfaction constitutes learning. Social tradition is the tested pattern by which an urge should act for the sake of the fullest benefit to the future self. The responses to a situation may consist of a split reaction — one being called primary learning, and the other incidental. All learning arises from a local situation, and its effects are associated in the mind with the local situation. The incidental learning may be in the nature of a maladjustment and result in unseemly behavior. It is in this area that attitudes are formed.

Motivation of Urges

The motivation of urges is the dynamic step in learning. Purposeful guidance of learning requires the locating of the fundamental urges responsible for activity, or that actuate the individual to get on in life. One who would control another must adapt himself to the interests of the individual. The most potent motives have their roots in the dominant urges. For the purposes of learning the urges within the social bracket are of most value. Achievement of one's self, or of beating a record, or of competing with another, or of securing the approval of others is based on human urges. Stated differently, the major control motives are fear or blame, rewards or approval, duty, and love. Man responds favorably to that which has the greatest appeal to him. The key to controlling behavior is knowing what the pupil's interests are at a given moment. Change of response results from establishing within the individual a sense of higher values in the proposed conduct. The desirable conduct must be made appealing to the individual. Among these incentives are the will to live, health, hunger, perpetuation of the race, companionship, social approval, power of control. Every failure in an attempt to win an individual to an ideal behavior is an indication that adequate incentives have not been discovered or applied.

Effects

The effects resulting from activity of these urges are definitely educational. An act of learning takes place only when the individual is motivated. When the organism acts simply, satisfaction results unless some element is introduced into the experience which sets up dissatisfaction. In order to regain satisfaction, repeated efforts at adaptation are undertaken until a satisfactory result is obtained. This process is learning.

Guidance stimulates the reactions that tend toward right conduct, and suppresses those that tend toward wrong conduct. The problem of profitable instruction is largely that of correctly motivating the study so as to secure a satisfying outcome. Repetition of the act will depend on the previous satisfaction in performing that act. Specific habit depends upon that repetition with satisfaction.

General Habit

General habit, or an ideal covering all situations, results from the application of specific habits in various situations. The specific habit must be learned in the process of reacting repeatedly to a specific situation. Virtues and vices are specific, not general. They become general as their repetition under widely different conditions gives them a set as an ideal of conduct. The principle involved in the process is known as transfer of training. Unless the individual is directed to the conscious adoption of a general ideal there is no assurance of a transfer of training.

On the basis of these general facts there are certain laws that have been formulated:

The Law of Readiness

The principle of motivation may be stated in terms of a law as follows: "When an individual is ready to act in a certain way, for him to act in that way is satisfying and for him not to act is annoying. Conversely, when an individual is not ready to act in a certain way, for him to act in that way is annoying."[2] An individual acts when action is desired. One will learn when the learning is related to his felt needs. When there is no felt need efforts to learn are drudgery.

The Law of Effect

The principle of satisfaction may be stated in terms of a law as follows: "Those experiences which are satisfying we tend to repeat and those that are not satisfying we tend to avoid. Learning is stimulated by a satisfying outcome and is hindered by an unsatisfying outcome."[3] Whether one wishes this result or not, the result is present. There is something about the effect which accompanies the act that determines future attitudes. The more satisfying the result, the more certain is the reaction to be repeated. Incidental learning, which may be the opposite to the lesson, often has its origin in the satisfier or in the annoyer.

The Law of Use

The principle of activity may be stated in terms of a law as follows: "Those elements in our environment to which we make response are learned, and those to which we do not make response are not learned. Those learnings which are put to use are retained and strengthened; while those which are not put to use are weakened or lost."[4] An act that is once performed is more easily repeated whether good or bad. William James' laws of habit formation rest on this law. "Launch a habit with zest." "Never allow an exception."

Two corollaries to the law of use and disuse are the law of frequency and the law of recency. The law of frequency as generally stated is: "Other things being equal, the more

2 *Ibid.*, p. 69.   3 *Ibid.*, p. 70.   4 *Ibid.*, pp. 60, 61.

frequently a connection has been exercised the stronger the connection." The law of recency as generally stated is: "Other things being equal, the more recent the exercise, the stronger the connection between the situation and response." The more frequently and intensely a learning is put to use the more permanent it becomes.

NATIVE URGES AND CHARACTER

Education must begin somewhere. The body is the gateway to the self. Personality is reached through the native endowment, which Hocking calls "the permanent ingredients of our being." Each child has inborn responses to environment, corresponding to the oak tree that dwells in the acorn. These are called instincts or urges, reflexes, and capacities.

Nature

Instincts are the starting point in education. They are urges, drives, or stings to action and hence dynamic in nature. They are the unlearned tendencies to act in certain ways. Their recurrence results in habits, and habits are basic in educational procedure. These self-starters naturally react upon themselves and aid in accelerating the work of learning. All learning is based on conditioning of these basic urges.

Kinds

The grouping of instincts or urges is a mechanical aid in handling these impulses. A simple classification would consist of individualistic, perpetuative, social, and projective urges. The first group includes the protective tendency to feed, fear, and fight. The second group has reference to the sex or racial urges. The third group includes tendencies to flock together, to compete, to seek approval, and to communicate. The fourth group embraces those tendencies to establish standards of conduct and to regulate interests that effect the utmost expansion of the self. This includes efforts to reach and prevail with the Determiner of Destiny.

Modification of Tendencies

The directing of instincts is the problem of the trainer of character. Unmodified, these pure impulses trail to the wild man. Modified, they lend themselves just as freely to the constructive program of society. It satisfies them just as well to help as to hinder. Learning is possible through the modifiability of urges. This is true for three reasons. First, modification means basic plasticity. Heredity does proportionately less for man than for the animal. It provides him with the raw materials and challenges him to complete the work. Second, modification means a tendency to act. Like cement it is ready to conform. Instincts are not snobs, they accept the first influence as correct. This is the teacher's challenge. Third, modification means responsiveness to guidance. Like cement it is ready to set. Because of this willing impulse it is comparatively easy to establish control. The danger and the strength lie in power developed by auxiliary forces.

The character outcome of handling urges lies in the understanding by the religious educator of these potentialities. These tendencies are willing to enter into an alliance with the teacher for moral and spiritual ends. They yield readily to a process of pattern weaves which are called habits. They lend their power to modes of thought which are called ideas. They conform to socially approved standards of action which are called ideals. The builder of character uses this wealth of urges in introducing social patterns into the life of the individual.

In building character the skillful teacher knows the need for control of these urges. Some tendencies need to be confirmed, others redirected. Confirmation is achieved by associating some satisfaction with the instinctive act. Pleasurable results lead to repetition of the act. Elimination is achieved by so managing the child's environment that the impulse will disappear through disuse. The association of dissatisfaction with the wrong response tends to weaken its recurrence. The boy jeered by his mate for showing "yellow" will face fire rather than be rebuked again for fear.

In redirecting these innate tendencies, "instinct, as a

guide, shows a fatal lack of sense of direction." Real guidance for these "urges" is sought outside of the tendency itself. The method is to find a better outlet for the impulse than is being sought. Psychology names these: "sublimation," "compensation," and "identification." Sublimation is the term used by psychologists to refer to the process whereby an unsocialized impulse comes to take on the form of a socially approved goal. The process of making up for personal failure, or feeling of inadequacy, in one line of activity by changing to another in which success is achieved is called compensation. Identification is the ability of the individual to identify himself with circumstances and persons outside of his immediate environment.

THE INTEGRATION OF PERSONALITY

The task of the Christian teacher is to so direct the innate urges that they will result in a unified person. It is the object of Christian education to introduce control into the experiences of living in such a way as to lead to responses in the direction of Christian faith and life. When these are rightly guided they will build up a system of habits, attitudes, motives, and knowledge which will integrate into character. This total way in which one thinks, feels, and acts constitutes his personality. The Christian teacher is primarily concerned that this personality be Christian, that the moral decisions of the individual be in harmony with his Christian ideals.

The Art of Personality Building

Personality has been defined by Bernhardt as: "the day-by-day experiences of the individual, the kinds of environment in which he has developed, and the opportunities for all kinds of learning that have made him what he is today."[5] It provides a balanced realization of the fundamental urges. The quest is for human happiness, and it is acquired by a legitimate realization of these life needs. Failure to provide

[5] Karl S. Bernhardt, *Practical Psychology* (New York: McGraw-Hill Book Co., Inc., 1953), p. 159.

legitimate satisfactions for these needs produces maladjust-ments of personality through the thwarting of the satisfactions to which the urge is entitled. Disciplining of these maladjust-ments would consist of seeking for the causes of the unseemly behavior and the finding of more acceptable outlets for one's interests. The critical concern in personality develop-ment is, therefore, the type of attitude that the particular discipline would produce.

Types of Personality

Personality types are classified in terms of the extent and nature of their integration. First, is the psychopathic per-sonality, one that tries to satisfy each instinctive urge upon its appearance. There is a lack of purpose, a resulting un-happiness, and a conflict with society which withholds ap-proval. A second type is the inhibited personality, resulting often when the child is taught that some of his instinctive urges are sinful. Although he banishes these appetites from his immediate consciousness, he cannot banish them from his personality. They emerge in some malignant fashion. Certain sources of power seem to be extracted from that personality. The third type is the integrated personality, the individual who succeeds "in forming such a harmony of healthy emotional attitudes, that all of his energy is united into one common purpose, moving in one direction. It is he who has developed the strongest personality for which his native endowments fit him."

When the wrong methods of satisfaction are used, the result is disintegration. The theory of child training which concerns itself with the future development of the child rather than with the immediate behavior is most important. Of greatest importance in childhood years is not so much external behavior, but the emotions that are developed. Ab-stract ethical principles are not so significant in the early years. Temperament, on the other hand, is formed during these years. The child may not learn from punishment that a certain course is wrong, but he may have instilled within him a fear which will contribute toward his becoming a weakling in his maturity. If he is forced to be generous toward one whom he dislikes, he will not learn generosity, but he may learn to resent discipline. To the religious educator, then, the future development of the child is the important concern in childhood experiences. Bernhardt says:

> The happy, well-adjusted, efficient person has found or built for himself a meaningful philosophy of life or religion. . . . A religion which emphasized unselfish consideration for others has been shown to be a powerful force for mental health in the lives of individuals.[6]

The integration of personality is determined by the basic philosophy of life adopted by the individual.

Based on Faith

The integration of the personality requires the development of faith in an invincible cause and with that a sense of dependence which is a faith in parent and in God to help achieve the results. This faith releases all one's power for the achievement of his vision without a hampering fear of defeat. This faith rests ultimately upon the belief that the ideal which will give the best personality is Jesus. The person who accepts Jesus as the guiding ideal of his life and identifies himself with him can hope to stand against overwhelming forces of life.

DEVELOPMENTAL PSYCHOLOGY

Not all of the instinctive tendencies are manifested in infancy. Some of them make their appearance at different age levels. Their unfoldment covers every period of life. Only a few urges are native or "inborn." Some appear during the periods of childhood and adolescence. Some may be developed in the early adult years. Education for character, and in religion, is most effective as it recognizes and works in accordance with these periods of development. According to Jersild,

> All through childhood years the organism is constantly establishing developments that become visible to the eye at a future time.

[6] *Ibid.*, p. 312.

There is a great carry-over of habits and attitudes, strengths and weaknesses from earlier years of development into adolescence.[7]

and on into the years of maturity.

Growth of personality is a continuous process. This means that there is a relationship in terms of growth between what is taking place now with what has happened in the earlier years of life; and what is learned now will affect the knowledge, attitudes, and behavior of the individual in the years ahead. Nor is growth saltatory. This means that the changes are not sudden but gradual for the individual or the group as a whole. Habits and attitudes, whether good or evil, are results of long-continued and gradual growth. They may appear at certain periods of development, but they have not been suddenly formed. They are the result of gradual and continuous responses of the individual to new social situations as the child grows.[8]

Periods of Development

For purposes of study of the unfolding life it has been the general practice of psychologists to divide people by ages into groups. This does not mean that each individual person attains a specific stage of development upon reaching a fixed chronological age; but that usually at some time in the span of three or four years, the characteristic change appears gradually in some and suddenly in others. The teacher or parent who understands and used the principles of developmental psychology will be able to guide the pupils into stronger and happier personal growth.

Infancy is the term which covers the first two years of life. The infant experiences the love of parents and develops attitudes of security and happiness from them. A mother who adequately and systematically meets the needs of the baby and little child is unconsciously interpreting God and laying the foundation for religion. Jesus must have meant some-

[7] Arthur J. Jersild, *The Psychology of Adolescence* (New York: The Macmillan Co., 1957), p. 15.

[8] R. G. Kuhlen, *The Psychology of Adolescent Development* (New York: Harper & Bros., 1952), pp. 5, 8.

thing like this when He said, "Verily I say unto you, Whosoever shall not receive the kingdom of God as a little child, he shall in no wise enter therein." (Luke 18:17) The child's first acquaintance with love comes from the parents. In recent years the church's program for the toddlers and two-year old children supplements and guides the parents' part in the child's growth.

Early childhood is the period which describes the third, fourth, and fifth years. It is called the preschool group by some. Learning during these years is largely determined by the satisfaction of basic needs. The deeper emotions are not experienced. The child is mentally active, inquisitive, very suggestible, and largely imitative. During these years the child is more responsive to the influence of teachers than to what they say.[9] In the fifth year the consciousness of right and wrong may be shaped by the attitude of the parents and teachers.

Middle childhood begins with school life at six and includes the seven- and eight-year-olds. These years cover a period of rapid advancement. During this period the child comes to recognize himself as a member of society. While the influence of the home is still dominant, the school becomes the new center of interest, and the authority of the schoolmates and teachers becomes increasingly strong. The church and the church school likewise play an important part in the enlarged environment. A growing independence of the home upon his initiation into school means an expanding social nature. These years constitute the primary department of the church school.

Later childhood begins in the ninth year and extends through the eleventh or twelfth year. Boys and girls of this period are called juniors. The development of the earlier period is continued. Not many new powers and few new interests arise during this period. It is a time for mastering the tools of learning and for the development of habits and skills needed in using them. Verbal memory is at its height

---

[9] Randolph C. Miller, *Education for Christian Living* (Englewood Cliffs, N. J.: Prentice-Hall, Inc., 1956), p. 79.

and lends itself to drill in those matters that need to become a part of his life and character. The junior is developing social needs and is concerned with the rights of others. He has a keen sense of justice and fair play. He resents any form of behavior which is "unfair," either to himself or to others, regardless of racial, religious, or economic status. This is the time of growing independence. A certain willfulness is replacing the plasticity of earlier years. He is increasingly rebellious against force, although he respects true authority. This is the time for a fuller social life. The child is more intensely cultivating a group of chums. He is becoming a hero worshipper. The responsibility of the church school teacher is to present the Christian religion as a heroic experience.

Parents and teachers will select those forms around which habit shall gather its skills. Religious habits, moral habits, personal habits of thrift, punctuality, and the like will be formed at this age. They will also recognize the need for authority but will guard against the ultra-arbitrary type that lacks the undergirding of reason and leaves wrong attitudes in the child. They will, further, give attention to the friends of the child, both immature and mature, and surround him with persons who will challenge the heroic in the child.

Early adolescence begins about the twelfth year and continues through the fourteenth year. It is approximately the same age group enrolled in junior high school. Whatever else early adolescence is, it is first and foremost a time of physical changes and can best be recognized by a spurt of physical growth.[10] First comes growth in height; then in weight, and then a filling out and strengthening of the muscles. The most marked change is the arrival of puberty. It usually takes place a year earlier in girls than in boys. Not all parts of the body grow at the same rate either in an individual or in the group as a whole. This unevenness of growth causes the adolescent to be self-conscious and sensitive. He appears to be awkward but is only having difficul-

[10] W. C. Morse and G. Max Wingo, *Psychology and Teaching* (Chicago: Scott-Foresman & Co., 1955), chap. vii.

ty of coordinating the rapidly growing parts of his body. His personal appearance, based on his interest in the opposite sex, becomes his chief concern as he nears the end of early adolescence.

Boys and girls at this age are more likely to have emotional religious experiences of conversion and dedication. Many surrender their lives as preachers, missionaries, or other religious workers. Often their feeling for the divine exceeds their understanding of God. Many fail to keep their vows because parents and church school leaders have not helped them to understand the true meaning of their experience. It is most imperative that workers with the early teen-agers understand their chief needs and problems and know how to guide them as they seek their own solutions.

Middle adolescence corresponds with the last three years of high school. It usually consists of fifteen-, sixteen-, and seventeen-year-olds — the middle teens. It is a time of intensely emotional extremes. Everything is described in superlatives. They have a vocabulary of their own which is constantly being revised. Many of their elders think of them as irresponsible. This is because parents and teachers have not made the right approach to understanding them.

The emotional life of the adolescent at this period has a more determinative effect on his behavior than does his intellectual development. This is the peak of religious idealism and the high tide of personal commitment to Christ. If the church does not provide for the wholesome expression of emotional experience, the youth will leave the church and search for it in some of the nondenominational movements which do not provide the permanent values of a Christian institution such as the church.

Later adolescence begins in the seventeenth or eighteenth year and continues until the individual reaches maturity. It usually ends with the acceptance of adult responsibilities. For some it is about twenty-one, and for others it is twenty-four or even later. It includes youth of college age and may extend a few years beyond graduation. It has been called the period of mental adjustment. For it is during this period that the most important decisions of life are made. They are: the choice of a vocation, the choice of a life partner and marriage, and the acceptance of a philosophy of life. The personality is developing full power of mastery over self and over environment. Action is less dominated by emotions and is more often the outcome of thoughtful deliberation. If a well-balanced personality is not developed during this period, it is due to some mental or physical defect; or to ignorant, if not vicious, emotional experiences during earlier periods of development; and there are many such maladjusted persons. The task of the teacher is to help personality "find itself" and, progressively, "to develop itself toward its highest conceivable form."

Younger adults are those who are from twenty-five to forty or forty-five years of age. They are the people who are establishing themselves in the business world; buying homes and household furnishings; and raising a family. In large communities, they may even be divided into two groups of ten years each. During these years they should be led to active participation in the life of the church if they are to be reached.

The theory that learning ability ends at physical maturity has been discarded. The processes of learning are as real at this stage as earlier in spite of excessive practical demands on the individual. The maturing adult is a product of all the influences, experiences, and attitudes of the preceding periods of growth.

Middle adults, ages forty-five to sixty-five, are those who have attained success or have become adjusted to their social and economic status. They are enjoying the fruits of their labors. These, too, might be divided into two groups of ten years each. Men and women of this age group have more time for church work and should be kept busy in all its activities.

Older adults are those who have passed their sixty-fifth anniversary. This is fast becoming one of the largest groups. In 1900 those above sixty-five years of age comprised 4.1 per cent of the total population. Now the percentage has reached 8.5. Then there were 3,100,000 people sixty-five and above; now they number above 15,000,000, and they are increasing at the rate of 1,000 each day. Statisticians predict that by 1970 one of every eight persons living in the United States will be above sixty-five. They are facing retirement with all its problems. Their economic security has been provided for by their own savings, by a pension plan of their employers, or by the Social Security plan of the government. Suddenly they become aware of much extra time for doing the things they have long wanted to do. Happiness is found in discovering new interests or in resuming earlier interests which had been postponed. The church should plan a program to meet their needs just as for any other age group.

IMPLICATIONS FOR RELIGIOUS EDUCATION

Unfolding of new life means hope for religious educators. It is not the number of criminals, but the number of respectable persons who are morally unenlightened and religiously orphaned that inspires pessimism in moral and religious leaders. In the new generation there is hope. For practical purposes, the surface implications of the unfolding life may be listed:

For Grading

To experience social values in education, children must be graded and will group themselves. Developmental psychology implies that certain general principles should be observed in grouping.

1. The unit in grading should be a group of pupils drawn together around basic needs and common interests. Unfolding brings certain interests to the fore, and character building grows faster by using the central areas of interests as motivation. It is common knowledge that in spite of individual variation, certain years are conspicuous for their uniqueness. The principle would be to take these years as representing the approximate stage of development and would urge the importance of grouping pupils by age. It would be convenient if each pupil were uniform in degree of aptitudes

and ability in all areas to grade them on basis of knowledge and skills. But such is not the case. The one common denominator of social experience is age. Accordingly the church school is in line with modern educational practice to group and promote pupils by age.[11]

2. Developmental psychology has taught that the unlearned responses of the child should be guided from early infancy through each period of growth for the sake of the fullest individual development. The application of this principle would mean an early effort at influencing the child as his nature demands. Provision must be made for the arriving of new interests and for the training of leaders for each age group. This would suggest the transfer of twelve-year-old children from junior to the intermediate grouping.

3. Developmental psychology teaches that the need of the child is the primary determinant in grouping. Two cases will illustrate the point. In the control of children, autocratic authority prevails largely with junior ages. Early adolescents are rapidly growing into inner control and resent the earlier authority. Wisdom would recognize the change and place the latter under the control of ideas. Again, precocious or mentally retarded children should be grouped, with their finest adjustment in mind, with persons of their own age. This will give them better opportunity for personality growth under normal social conditions.

For Method

Growing a person is like farming. The farmer plants and cultivates. The growth comes from the inside. The religious educator simply offers favorable conditions for growth that the life within sends forth. He must provide the environment that will bring the proper response. This is called method.

Psychology has parted with the method of selection of materials and procedure by individual judgment. Psychology through experimentation will present those phases of

[11] H. L. Kingsley and Ralph Garry, *The Nature and Conditions of Learning* (Englewood Cliffs, N. J.: Prentice-Hall, Inc., 1957), pp. 280-82.

knowledge that are within the comprehension of the child
and in harmony with the mental stages through which the
child is passing. The approaches to his interest and control
centers are a matter of method, and their laws are fairly
definitely formulated. A discussion of method appears later
in this book.

For Conduct Control

The introduction of control into experience in terms of
religious ideals is the theory of religious education as defined
by the late President W. S. Athearn. Three forces for control are at the disposal of the teacher of religion; namely,
habit, ideals, and religion.

1. *Habit* means that the tendency to act has been encouraged to act in ways that have been pleasant. The teacher will use methods of habit formation for setting up the
skills of moral living that make for character. The habit of
prayer, for example, is a distinct control. Church attendance
habits become controls. Training conscience is training a
control. The more widely and deeply constructive habits are
cultivated, the more promise there is for control in personality.

2. *Ideals* control when conduct is governed by self-
approved standards. Conduct becomes amenable to ideals by
stages. Instinctive behavior is first modified by pain and
pleasure. Behavior is controlled by anticipation of the praise
or blame of society. Behavior is controlled by an ideal of
right or wrong without regard to the mandates of society
which is the control desired by religious educators. Control
was established in the full when Luther stood and said: "I
cannot do otherwise."

3. *Religion* as conduct control transcends all other motives. Religion lifts habits and ideals into the control of a
person. Belief that certain conduct is according to the will of
God is strong undergirding for control. Conscience rests
upon a feeling of obligation to that Being above man. The
projective instincts find no satisfaction short of their completeness in that Person. His will and favor are final for con-

trol. The religious educator must impart knowledge of that Person directly and effectively and completely.

For Conversion

The unfolding life offers the religious educator a supreme concern at the point of personal relation to the Supreme Being. It seems that man does not become capable of religion at any specific age, for he is always capable. His response to the divine manifests itself differently as the personality develops. Christian conversion is usually described as an adolescent experience. But in the religious sphere, as in every other area of life, the young person's religious decisions and convictions must be built upon what he has already learned and accepted. His impressions of early childhood, even in infancy, will have significant bearing on his religious behavior through adolescence and into adulthood. For example, in childhood he learns the meaning of love and trust which are necessary foundations for building a Christian life. Other basic religious facts are acquired in the primary and junior years. The personal commitment of the teenager to Christ as Lord is usually the climax of a steady religious growth, even though the emotional elements seem to overshadow what has been happening through the years. Conversion of the individual becomes much more difficult as the person enters the adult level of experience.

There are different types of conversion experience. The differences in type are due psychologically to differences in temperament, in childhood training, and in the life that they have lived. The way of the religious educator is plain in view of these facts. He must utilize every contact between the youth and the finest Christian men and women for reaching the central objective, a personal surrender of his powers to God.

For Worship

The attainment of full Christian personality requires power and vision. These come through worship as mystical union with God. The church at Jerusalem first met for spiritual renewal and experience, then a revival broke out. Personal power in the Christian life has come only as men have found reality in their devotional life.

Religious educators will find the implication of unfolding for worship to mean: first, that there is but one way to God and that is by experience. Second, that experience of God is possible for every age in terms of its own development. Third, that the media of worship must be adapted to the stage of experience of the worshiper. This includes hymns, Scripture, prayers, and ceremonies. Fourth, since worship is the meeting point of God and men, worship is a matter for Christian leaders to safeguard by capitalizing its power and by tabooing slovenliness in its conduct.

QUESTIONS FOR DISCUSSION

1. Discuss the problem of the religious educator — that is the minister, Sunday school teacher, youth director, and others — in translating Bible knowledge into character.

2. Discuss learning — when it takes place, what it is, etc.

3. Discuss the three types of personality — psychopathic, inhibited, and integrated. How may the religious educator guide in the development of personality?

4. Discuss the factors that influence personality development.

5. How does the unfolding of life mean hope for religious educators?

6. What is your church doing for people who have reached retirement age? Outline a practical program for this age group.

CHAPTER 8

OBJECTIVES

The educational process includes objectives, curriculum, and method. Objectives are the results to be achieved in the lives of the pupils. The curriculum is the subject matter and planned activities offered as the vehicle for reaching the objectives. The method is the way in which the curriculum is manipulated. An objective without a vehicle is a dream. An objective without a method is a hazard. A curriculum and a method without an objective is folly. The process is like a tailor cutting out cloth by a pattern but without a customer. Such a process is wasteful. A tailor with a pattern and a customer but lacking cloth is useless. A tailor with cloth and a customer but with no pattern would waste his material and disappoint his customer. In the religious educational process, these three elements are so interrelated that one without the other is useless.

An objective has been defined by Edge as a "statement of that which the teacher hopes to accomplish."[1] Objectives are the "statements of desired outcomes to be achieved through the process of education."[2] They are to education what orders

[1] Findley B. Edge, *Teaching for Results* (Nashville: The Broadman Press, 1956), p. 91.

are to a transport convoy sailing without lights or signals to a predetermined port; what the blueprint is to a builder; the pattern to the dressmaker; or the recipe to the cook.

FUNCTION OF OBJECTIVES

It is most important to blaze the trail for childhood by the poles of the Christian compass. Supreme values lie in the purposes and ends of religion. Waste and aimlessness in religion are economically and spiritually vicious. To avoid these evils, it is imperative that leaders should understand something of the functions of objectives.

Pattern for Building the Curriculum

The objectives furnish the pattern for building the curriculum. The formation of the curriculum is determined by the product desired. For example, the instructions of Jesus assign definite objectives as "making disciples" and "teaching them to observe." The master passion for the Christ was that all men might see and love God as he saw and loved Him. To this end the curriculum is formed.

Guide in the Choice of Method

Method is the technique of the process. Its function is to approach every problem with an open mind for the discovery of truth. Its function is to ferret out the meanings of the truth in human relations and problems. Its function is to achieve the task of carrying over into deeds and changed conduct the ideals of the curriculum. An objective functions when it employs method to give meaning to subject matter that may be requisite to the knowledge, attitudes, and skills needed in a Christian society.

Pattern for Leadership Training

Insurance men train their salesmen in a different manner than asparagus growers or watch manufacturers. Neither group would be effective in the other fields. The materials

2 Paul H. Vieth, *Objectives in Religion* (New York: Harper & Bros., 1930), p. 18.

handled, the processes, and the purposes are different; training takes these into account. The leader in the teaching of religion must be trained so to interpret religion that men may be won to Christ and so to motivate religion that men may apply his principles to daily life. Training for public school teaching does not suffice for this service. The objectives of the two types of teachers have much in common, but much more that is distinctive. The leader in religion has his pattern of training implied in his objective.

Motivates Christian Endeavor

Tests made among average Sunday school teachers disclose an inadequate or indefinite sense of direction in the teaching function. Lack of interest, absence of enthusiasm, lifeless performance, weariness of the work, carelessness in preparation and attendance, and discouragement in outcome usually result from failure to set out objectives. A tangible and real goal stimulates effort and encourages endurance. The workman who sees a cathedral in a pile of stones is more fortunate than the fellow-laborer who sees only an opportunity to earn his bread. The Christian teacher who senses in the life of the boy in his class a potential prophet of a new day or a spiritual workman in the daily toil knows no bounds to his zeal.

Conserves Energy, Spirit, and Life

The tragedy of life is its wastes. Confusion, uncertainty, destruction of materials, and loss of efforts are rare where men know what they are doing. Courts have sometimes confirmed youths in criminality by inadequate and incorrect ideas of the reason for law and of the meaning of justice. Likewise many parents and perhaps many Sunday school teachers have aided and abetted malformation of character through lack of understanding of the nature of the child and of the objectives of teaching activity. Artillery practice may produce noise, satisfy the powder manufacturers, and give a type of pleasure to the gunners as they train their guns toward open space in night target shooting, but the purpose of practice is defeated and the procedure wasteful because they do not see a target, or know its location. Likewise much Sunday school teaching is as prodigal of effort as night target practice because there are no visible objectives. A religious objective avoids waste of energy of teacher and pupil, and possibly a waste of human life.

Provides a Measuring Instrument

In making an automobile trip to a distant city in a limited time, the driver checks his daily mileage against his total mileage and the allotted time. In college a degree at the end of four years enables the youth to know his daily progress. A failure at one point may defeat the end. The whole course moves forward with certainty as it is checked daily by its objective. Sunday schools set up standards of excellence as objectives in administration, organization, and teaching. These register good or poor performance. Of more vital concern is the setting up of objectives for the classroom and the home. The determination of such aims as conversion, change of habits, reshaping of maladjusted personality, knowledge of Bible facts, decision for Christian life-callings, will provide measurements of progress. The more definite these objectives the greater will be the satisfaction in checking results. Without these objectives there is no valid basis for choosing or evaluating much of the curriculum material and procedure. Without them attempts at directing class instruction are likely to lean toward lesson learning rather than growth in understanding.

DETERMINATION OF OBJECTIVES

Three methods have been used in arriving at objectives. In the past curriculum construction was left to tradition, hit-or-miss efforts, and the whims of lesson writers. Rather glibly these individuals discoursed on "knowing the Bible," "character building," and other general terms whose only virtue was indefiniteness. The objectives that used to be set up certainly have the appearance of being a kind of "New Year resolution," conforming to the spirit of the occasion but not to be taken seriously under any condition. Today, educators are concerned with determining specific objectives which bring education into more vital relation with life.

The first method for discovering objectives has been called the *consensus of opinion method.* It is a kind of questionnaire procedure. This is the practice of asking equally perplexed friends who have given little thought to the matter to help solve problems. Out of "collective ignorance" a solution is attempted. The judgment of thoughtful men, however, may help to formulate a philosophy and aid progress. Its value in determining objectives will depend upon the training of the men and the nature of the product sought.

The second method may be called *analysis of life experiences,* or *the scientific method.* Sociologists refer to such a plan as "job analysis" which will show the abilities, attitudes, habits, appreciations, and forms of knowledge that men need. The educational sociologist, by a more systematic study of everyday life, has discovered social needs and educational values. Each educational activity must prepare for some situation that will likely be faced by the pupil. To meet these requirements impersonal scientific investigations of the needs of society must be made.

The church has done little in this area. Hartshorne and May opened a new approach to character education through their "Studies in Deceit." They turned trial and error into a prescribed method. Vieth enriched the field of religion by his scientifically conducted study of the writings of approved religious leaders, the results of which were submitted as comprehensive objectives. No doubt there are values for religion awaiting further careful investigation. It is in the minds of some that the Christian college should be specifically entrusted with investigations in the field of religion that would yield superior values to the church. One college, for example, undertook a limited study of biblical material with a view to determining certain values for citizenship building. Another test based on recognition of a quoted passage, location of passage, memorization of passage, and personal observance as a philosophy of life, established the priority of certain passages as lesson materials. Another investigation covered a study of specific hymns in a selected group of churches over a period of weeks. The results became a basis for a possible re-education of those congregations in hymn usage. These unpretentious experiments suggest the possibilities of church colleges in applying scientific methods to religious uses. Out of such study valuable sets of objectives might be produced.

A third method of determining objectives may be called the *philosophical method*. Philosophy has been referred to as "the attempt to think consistently about the meaning of life as a whole," or "an answer to the problem of human values." Vieth[3] maintains that the ultimate aims of education can only be determined by philosophy. Education and life are more than scholarship. The development of a program to meet this need of social, ethical, moral, and religious living is an undertaking in philosophy. It furnishes a guide by which the immediate objectives, in terms of factual knowledge, may be determined. All of this means that the objectives determine the kind of facts which are to be taught.

What are life's supreme values? What is the ultimate purpose of life? The philosophy which correctly answers the questions is theistic, not humanistic. It believes in a controlling personal deity, concerned about human values, and requiring certain ethical conduct after a Divine pattern, dwelling within the spirit of man, accessible to the spirit of man, yet transcending human reach. Humanism leaves God out of life, or identifies him with human ideals. The objectives growing out of such philosophies differ widely. Theistic objectives involve an acceptance of the fact of God, an experience of God, a committal to God's way, religious ideals of living, and an intelligent knowledge of the Book of God. They recognize the existence of a soul and of a destiny known as personal immortality. The Christian faith proclaims a living Christ, offers comfort in bereavement, ennobles the present life, and plants the conviction that the crown of life is the wealth of eternity. Naturalism and humanism have offered no adequate substitute. The Christian faith further believes that man can

[3] *Ibid.*, p. 45.

choose between good and evil and that every individual is accountable for his conduct. The Christian philosophy based on that of Jesus exalts the good life, accepting the doctrine that losing one's life is the way to find it.

Ultimate objectives must be determined by Christian living. The choice among the many values contending for primacy in life will be made in the light of one's philosophy of life. The scientific method is useful in the defining of immediate and specific objectives in religious education, but the determination of the ultimate ends can be made only through philosophy. It is probably true that the best results are obtained through a careful integration of the results of the three methods.

TYPES OF OBJECTIVES

A road trip to a distant city is not so difficult today because the objective has been anticipated by experienced travelers. A certain marked route is recommended, and the road map will provide all further information as to intersecting roads, cities en route, points of special interest, and definite mileage. Reaching the destination depends upon taking, and keeping on, the right road. Along the way further planning is necessary — setting daily distances to match the total time allowance, reaching hotels at the end of the day, stopping at points of interest along the way. In terms of objectives the first would be called *ultimate*, while the second would be *specific* objectives. The attainment of the first depends upon the second. The validity of the second depends upon the reality of the first. Neither is complete without the other. Yet the words "ultimate" and "immediate" do not define objectives. They simply indicate the order in which a goal is reached. Other groupings are more definitely purposive.

The term "ultimate" does not mean final but long range. Ultimate objectives are aims that cannot be achieved in the present. Possibly they are never completely achieved. Christian character and good citizenship are of this type. Ultimate objectives are difficult to locate, because they are intangible. They are like the Kingdom of God that men search for widely, only to find it within themselves. They are life's perspective. Compared with the immediate objectives they are the ideal as contrasted with the active objectives. They mark out the direction of life, while the specific aims mark out the daily efforts. They are the teacher aims while the latter are the pupil purposes. They are the curriculum concern while the latter are the method concern.

The areas of ultimate objectives, as defined by the scientific method, were formulated in 1930 by Paul H. Vieth after studies of the writings of the foremost leaders in the church field in America. While prepared primarily to meet a graduate school requirement, and then published under the title, *Objectives of Religious Education*, his statement of aims has been accepted by various church bodies as the general basis of the curriculum. Their general acceptance and value have been demonstrated by the fact that they have been repeatedly used by the International Council of Religious Education in all publications for many years. They were used without revision, except for the addition of a statement of the place of the family in the program of Christian religious education.[4] The objectives as set forth by the International Council, now the Division of Christian Education of the National Council of Churches of Christ in the U.S.A., are given here.

1. Christian religious education seeks to foster in growing persons a consciousness of God as a reality in human experience, and a sense of personal relationship to Him.

2. Christian religious education seeks to develop in growing persons such an understanding and appreciation of the personality, life, and teachings of Jesus as will lead to experience of him as Savior and Lord, loyalty to him and his cause, and manifest itself in daily life and conduct.

3. Christian religious education seeks to foster in growing persons a progressive and continuous development of Christlike character.

4. Christian religious education seeks to develop in growing persons the ability and disposition to participate in and contribute constructively to the building of a social order throughout the world, embodying the ideal of the Fatherhood of God and the brotherhood of man.

[4] Randolph C. Miller, *Education for Christian Living* (Englewood Cliffs, N. J., Prentice-Hall, Inc., 1956), p. 57-59.

5. Christian religious education seeks to develop in growing persons the ability and disposition to participate in the organized society of Christians — the church.

6. Christian religious education seeks to develop in growing persons an appreciation of the meaning and importance of the Christian family, and the ability and disposition to participate in and contribute constructively to the life of this primary social group.[5]

7. Christion religious education seeks to lead growing persons into a Christian interpretation of life and the universe; the ability to see in it God's purpose and plan; a life philosophy built on this interpretation.

8. Christian religious education seeks to effect in growing persons the assimilation of the best religious experience of the race, preeminently that recorded in the Bible, as effective guidance to present experience.[6]

The areas of ultimate objectives, as determined largely by a Christian philosophy, will cover in general the same needs. They are grouped naturally under the divine relationship, the social relationship, and the personal growth. The first covers the Creator, the Redeemer, and the revelation of divine will. The second group covers the institutional relations of men of brotherliness in a church fellowship and of men of good will in a human society. The third group covers the character traits and the integration of personality in a philosophy of life that guides to the ideal destiny.

DIVINE RELATIONSHIP OBJECTIVES

The Creator Aim

"Thou shalt love the Lord thy God with all thy heart." Religion meant for Jesus the assurance of God as Father, of God's will as the law of life, and the ability to see Him everywhere. The objective of the religious educator is to bring the individual into the confidence that we live in "a reasonable world; that we are a part of a just and moral order." The teacher seeks to create a sense of need for what religion has to offer as well as to show how religion meets that need.

[5] This objective was added in *Christian Education Today* (Chicago: International Council of Religious Education, 1940).

[6] *A Guide for Curriculum in Christian Education* (Chicago: Division of Christian Education, National Council of Churches of Christ, 1955.) Used by permission.

The Redeemer Aim

"Believe on the Lord Jesus Christ, and thou shalt be saved." These words express the faith of church people. The teacher of religion sets as his dominant purpose the winning of the pupil to Christ, not only as personal Savior but also as Lord of his life. To leave the living Christ out of instruction is to destroy every reason for the Christian movement.

The Revelation or Bible Aim

"The sower soweth the word." The word is God's revelation of Himself to man as recorded in the Bible. Religious experience has produced its philosophy and has well tested its right to claim the loyalty of men to the spiritual control of life which it proclaims. The teacher's objective is to plant the Bible truths in the mind and affections of the youngest and of the most seasoned veteran, to teach the meaning of these truths, and to lead men to test every act and every thought by their precepts.

INSTITUTIONAL RELATIONSHIPS

The Christian Family Aim

The family is the oldest social institution. According to Genesis, it was established by the Creator and given its responsibilities by God Himself. The obligation of the parents to teach religion stems from the beginning of Hebrew history. Abraham was called for that purpose (Gen. 18:19). When the nation was established, Moses commanded it (Deut. 6:1-9). The church must give specific help to the family in the development and use of objectives which will result in Christian living in the normal situations of homelife. Co-operation between teachers and parents will produce the strongest Christian character. Failure at this point will undo much of the work of church school leaders.

The Church Aim

"In whom ye also are builded together for a habitation of God in the spirit." Jesus did not make the church an end in itself. It finds its meaning as a means to the end in the building of the Kingdom of God. It is the Master's great missionary society. The objective of the religious educator is to enlist every disciple of Christ in the church, and to develop every member into an efficient apostle. The teacher regards every pupil as potentially a missionary and sets about training him to assume maximum responsibility.

The Kingdom Aim

"Thou shalt love thy neighbor as thyself." The first-century Gnostics branded all matter as evil. The only two escapes from the flesh, which was matter and therefore evil, were through withdrawal from life, or through utter disregard of the flesh. Contrary to the teachings of this sect Jesus ordered his followers, "Go ye into all the world," for "ye are the salt of the earth." A better understanding of the meaning of Jesus will reveal to men a closer correlation between the Kingdom of God and the good society. Men grow in Christian virtues as they mingle with society rather than as they withdraw from society. The objective of the teacher is so to guide the child in the midst of his daily experiences that he will come to discover God in the streets, and to find the purposes of God increasingly effective in human relations.

THE PERSONAL GROUP

The Character Aim

"Be ye therefore perfect, even as your Father which is in heaven is perfect." Christ thus concluded instructions touching human relations. Christianity entrusts its adherents with a spirit of life. Character consists of socially approved attitudes, habits, and appreciations; but Christian character consists of the same characteristics and traits fashioned after the Christian pattern and governed by the Christian motive. The objective of the religious educator is to bring the individual to govern his conduct and thoughts by the Christian ideal.

The Personality Aim

"Abide in me, and I in you." The Christian philosophy of

life grows out of this Christ-centered outlook. The pattern of life which a man accepts gives shape to his personality. The materialist thinks of life as a treasure-house for him to possess; get it as he can. He crowns might king and accepts the spoils as belonging to the victor. The Christian looks at life as God's greatest value and has learned that its highest riches are obtained through love. The objective of the teacher is to build a philosophy of life which discovers its meaning and value and opens human eyes to see spiritual reality.

In general ultimate aims should satisfy the following demands: (1) They should dovetail into practical, daily life. (2) They should cover religious, social, and personal needs of the individual. (3) They should be true to the accepted revelation of Divine truth. (4) They should be true to the best ideals of human experience. (5) They should mould changing society by the pattern of the society that wisdom decrees should exist.

SPECIFIC OBJECTIVES

After determining the direction of education the function of the teacher is to locate specific or immediate aims. These constitute the objectives for each lesson period and for each unit of work. They are selected on the basis of their fitness for implanting useful knowledge, developing abilities, and creating right attitudes that are required for building the ultimate objective. These aims are within the reach of a day or a recitation period. They seek to meet today's problems today. Their educational value lies in their direct relation to and contribution to the more remote purposes. Mastery in teaching consists in ability to see the ultimate objective through the specific aim.

Nature of Specific Objectives

The nature of specific objectives appears when one remembers that there is a reason for performing every act. In every life situation there is a goal which the individual desires to achieve. That goal is a Christian objective when it rests upon the ideals of the Christian religion. The religious educator recognizes this fact and seeks to arouse a motive for doing the specific act in a Christian manner. The specific Christian act becomes a specific objective.

There are specific objectives for each learning situation. They are peculiar to each situation and may be as numerous as the persons who share in the experience. Calling learning situations "episodes," Butler finds that upon achievement they always give way to new episodes different from the ones passed. "Every consummation of a learning episode is a means to new learnings which find their consummation in succeeding experiences."[7] In religious education the ultimate aims give direction to the specific, or immediate, aims. This forces the teacher to select an objective, either in knowledge, attitudes, or conduct, and to use a method that will carry over into life the specific aim of each unit of learning. The specific objective may be thought of as the immediate change to be brought about in the ideas, attitudes, or behavior of each pupil as a result of the learning experience.

Assuming that ultimate aims are the general direction of educational processes, the educator knows that their realization depends upon the successful attainment of the immediate aims. Formerly the pupil listened; now he participates. Formerly the pupil assented to the instruction; now he thinks. Formerly the pupil received only the spiritual facts of the lesson, with a pious word of application; now he discovers the solution of his personal problems at the heart of the lesson. Formerly the pupil left his personal responsibility in the class room; now he carries his solutions into his personal life throughout the week.

The range of objectives extends beyond adolescence into the years of maturity. Under the urge of specific objectives there should be groups of adult churchmen moving out into the social, the industrial, the governmental, the economic activities of men. Religion should permeate every area of modern life.

[7] James D. Butler, *Four Philosophies* (New York: Harper & Bros., 1952), p. 462.

The Knowledge Aim

Purposeful Bible study is essential to Christian growth. Translating the Sunday school lesson into life is the original purpose of the Scripture. To know the purposes and plan of God for the individual and for the human race throughout the Old Testament are teaching objectives; to find the teachings of Jesus in New Testament times are specific objectives; to discover the purposes and the providences of God in modern times are objectives of teaching. The teacher must become skilled in these fields if he is to make Bible study stir the motives of his pupils. Daily objectives become vital when pupils discover the need for God in comfort, in guidance, in forgiveness of sins, and in strength for meeting life issues. "Pep" rallies will no longer be thought of as worship when young Christians discover the spirit of Isaiah's temple experience (Isa. 6:1-8). Such an experience can only come as a result of the knowledge of the nature of God. Further, Bible study leads to a sense of sin and a vision of salvation. The convert enters upon a new life as day by day he discovers new meanings in being God's child and new enrichments in growing into His likeness.

Conduct Aim

The tragedy of Christendom has been the morally undependable Christian. Contrary to expectation of some, conversion does not automatically guarantee the development of Christian social virtues. They must be learned. Teaching a Christian is relatively easy but necessary to growth in Christian habits. Courtesy, for example, may not be considered an essential Christian virtue by some, but it assumes shape under Jesus' words, "In honor preferring one another." Honesty is usually an approved virtue, but its range is so wide that gaps appear even among reputedly Christian students. Moral dependability is a product of specific objectives in moral behavior.

Beyond personal habits of the usually named types, the church school teacher will select as specific objectives the practice of the various functions of the church: evangelism, stewardship, personal responsibility in leadership, the world-wide ministries of the congregation. Many church members lack a sense of responsibility in such matters. Specific objectives may be realized every Sunday and daily in observation, in participation, in conferences, in aiding the program of other departments. Choir members, ushers, group leaders, and many other forms of service facilitate the task of building dependable Christians. Character in action is a potential achievement for every youth under carefully guided specific objectives.

Attitudes Aim

Specific objectives reach beyond personal habits and church loyalty to individual attitudes. The individual becomes aware of God's rule as real in the present. He becomes a "living epistle," revealing love, sincerity, humility, forgiving with forgetting, respecting the personality of others, seeking good even for enemies. Individuals learn by such methods to think without prejudice, to overcome deeply rooted prejudices, to weigh values in terms of eternal standards. They develop service motives in youth organizations and classroom ministries. They overcome anxiety as they practice daily trust in God. Religious emphasis weeks, conferences, retreats, and camping foster the spirit of dedication. They fear not unforeseen events when taught the values of their lives under the providence of God. Even death for a dedicated youth, loses its terrors. Experiences of trust in God surpass volumes of lesson materials taught as mere knowledge to be listened to, even to be memorized.

If the human race is to operate on a Christian rather than secular basis, the church must sponsor the achievement. If the church is to prevail over the secular world, it must study the power of specific objectives in an individual life. The world is giving hourly practice in forming manners and morals in human relations. Fast cars, crowds, and sales events cultivate selfish attitudes. The world is selling its "specific" objectives to youth and reaping its benefits in adults. Church education is called upon to counteract such with objectives that effectively offset the power of the world by forming socially constructive ideals in modern youth and mature Christians.

Social Action

Social action stems from the adult membership of the church. It is the fruit-bearing stage of the sowing and tilling in the childhood and adolescent years. An experienced educator, William Clayton Bower, has observed that adults are "deeply involved in the complex processes and problems of economic, civic, and international life," that "it is adults who make decisions and formulate and execute policies," and that "the power of social control lies in their hands."[8] This group of undeniable facts gives impetus to majoring on specific objectives for adults in church school education.

The new frontier is challenging adults to project Christian ideals into all human relations. Current campaigning for adult departments has usually stressed numerical growth. Activities for men and women have consisted mainly in class recruiting service, in lecturing on the uniform lesson, in enlisting the few "unsaved" persons in church life, and in personal faith in Christ. Every adult utilized becomes a link in the chain of anchoring society to the Kingdom of God. A major activity of every church should be the expansion of adult education. Specific objectives for adult achievement are legion and bristle with vigor and potential realization. The Kingdom of God is functional. Adults are responsible for bringing the Kingdom to reality .

Valid objectives assume the infiltration of homes, industry, the professions, community social life, and governmental agencies with Christian values as they are studied, adapted, and consecrated in the church sanctuary. Capitalist and laborer, lawyer and client, doctor and patient, merchant and customer, neighbor and neighbor, face each other in the spotlight of Divine truth in the adult school of the church. Learning in experience is transferred by grace. Jesus aimed at nothing less than every man loving his neighbor as himself and every man

---

[8] W. C. Bower, *Religious Education*, Sept.-Oct., 1953, p. 299.

loving God with all of his heart, and his mind, and his strength.

TEST OF OBJECTIVES

When the teacher has determined the specific objectives of each unit of learning, he should write it in a complete grammatical statement. This helps make clear just what change he seeks to bring about in the pupil's knowledge, attitudes, or conduct.

How may a teacher know whether his specific aims are good or poor? How may they be tested? Findley B. Edge gives three qualities which are the essentials of a good objective.

It ought to be brief enough to be remembered. When the teacher does state an aim, too many times it is long, involved, and complex. The aim is the statement of what the teacher wants a class (his pupils) to learn or do. If the statement is so long that the teacher cannot remember it, how can he expect the class to practice it? Therefore it should be brief enough to be remembered, and the teacher should be able to repeat it without difficulty.

It ought to be clear enough to be written down. Another difficulty that teachers often have as they try to give a statement or aim is to make it clear. The teacher feels that he has the aim clearly in his own mind; but when he tries to state it, he finds that he is confused. . . . Many times we may think an aim is clear until we try to write it. Then we find it exceedingly difficult to express exactly what we mean. We must conclude that it is not a good aim unless it is clear enough to be written down (in a complete grammatical statement).

It ought to be specific enough to be achieved. One of the major weaknesses in this problem is that our aims have been too vague and too general. The teacher must recognize that on a given Sunday he will have only thirty minutes in which to teach. In stating an aim for that lesson, he ought to try to make it specific enough to achieve within the time limits of the class session.[9]

QUESTIONS FOR DISCUSSION

1. What are the ultimate objectives of the program of religious education in your church?

2. Is the educational program determined by reasonable objectives? Give reasons for your answer.

[9] Findley B. Edge, *Teaching for Results* (Nashville: The Broadman Press, 1956), pp. 92–93. Used by permission.

3. Are the curriculum materials published by your denominational publication agency determined by objectives?

4. Discuss the relationship between ultimate and specific objectives.

5. Examine the Sunday School Quarterly you are now using to see if the lesson writer's objectives meet the tests of a good objective.

CHAPTER 9

CURRICULUM

Traditionally the curriculum has been thought of as an organized body of knowledge. It has more recently been defined by the Special Committee of the National Council of Churches on Curriculum Guide as:

experience under guidance toward the fulfillment of the purposes of Christian education. Whereas the total experience of the individual is certainly educative in the sense that he is learning from life at every moment, all of this complex of situations is not thought of as curriculum. In other words, the curriculum is not the entire social situation within which the person acts and with which he is interacting, but rather that part of it which is consciously planned to attain certain objectives, to realize certain purposes of Christian education.[1]

According to Randolph C. Miller, the curriculum is defined thus:

"Curriculum," which originally meant a race course, is the path traversed by pupil and teacher in reaching a desired objective. It may be a pathway over which many others have traveled, or it may be the opening of a road through new terrain. It may be going somewhere, or it may be aimless as it wanders through a maze toward an undefined goal. It has a heirarchy of values that is open to constant re-evaluation, and it has a theory of knowledge that stands or falls on the basis of an adequate philosophy.[2]

[1] Quoted from *A Guide for Curriculum in Christian Education*, p. 25. Copyright, 1955, by the National Council of Churches. Used with permission.

[2] Randolph Crump Miller, *Education for Christian Living*, pp. 43–44. Copyright, Prentice-Hall, Inc., Englewood Cliffs, N. J., 1956.

In an earlier definition given by Betts, it is all of the "organized educative influences brought to bear upon the child through the agency of the school."[3] The scope of the curriculum is therefore made to include instruction, worship, expression, and all the planned activities that take place in the church school, whether in the classroom or in some real life situation which is planned by the group.

In the field of morals and religion such a curriculum occupies the place of importance next to the child and consists of the posting by mature society of markers along life's highway for the guidance of the immature. It is hoped that this knowledge of life based upon human experience will enable younger members of society to make safe and happy human adjustments. Experience comes out of life. The curriculum proposed to return it to life and that with interest.

THEORIES OF THE CURRICULUM

Discipline

The first theory to take form was that of education as discipline. The thousand years before Luther were characterized by authority and discipline. This was the order in church and state. The few imposed their wills upon the masses, and demanded obedience and submission. The teachers of Luther and Ignatius Loyola encouraged the performance of hard or distasteful things in order to achieve victory over sinful natures. Any personal satisfaction was felt to be of the Devil, hence to be avoided. Naturally these conceptions colored educational theory and set disciplinary materials at the center of education. The more difficult a subject the more value it held for education. Individuals who had been subjected to rigorous mental processes of memorization or reasoning in one area were by virtue of that discipline likewise capable in all other fields. The educated man was one who had applied himself to the disciplinary subjects, and submitted himself to the repressive measures of the authorities.

[3] George H. Betts, *The Curriculum of Religious Education* (Nashville: Abingdon Press, 1921), p. 239.

Knowledge

A second theory stressed instruction or knowledge as the foundation of education. Herbart came to the conclusion that there is not an intellectual and a moral education: there is only one education, and that founded upon instruction. There is no education apart from instruction. Knowledge is not an ornament but a builder of mind. Feeling and willing, or moral and spiritual states spring from objects of knowledge.

The cumulative experiences of the race have crystallized into customs, and their violations into taboos. Thus these have grown into a treasured body of knowledge. The protective urge of maturity has prompted the parent to teach these facts to the child, as the Shema of the Hebrews so well illustrates. This organized body of knowledge therefore becomes society's curriculum. It follows that the preparation of every child for later responsibilities requires that this subject matter of learning be imparted by instruction. Fixing knowledge in the mind, this theory holds, is the open door to character and faith. "Knowledge is power" has been an honored motto in many a schoolhouse.

This theory had its effect on the curriculum in religion. Men must know the doctrines. The gravest error consisted of ignoring or refusing sound doctrine. Creeds must be planted in the minds of men. The catechism was an attempt to break down these massive doctrines into child-mind portions. Subject matter presented with interest and thoroughness was depended upon to produce character. The fallacy of the theory, so Bower points out, lay in the forcing of education to the patterns of race inheritance, with an adjustment to the past rather than to ongoing life. The curriculum became Bible centered, with the courses limited to the history, biography, and theology of the Book, the purpose of instruction in religion being to transmit the recorded inheritance of the past.

The Child at the Center

A third theory of the curriculum puts the child at the center. Begun by Froebel in an unhappy childhood, his philosophy of education discovered the child. In his "cosmic evolution" "creation is not an act performed once and for all; it is rather a continuous process of productive activity." Education becomes "an element in the process of cosmic evolution." The Herbartians developed this theory under the title "culture epoch." In biology it was called the "recapitulation theory." Froebel's educational system was a protest against the idea that learning could be imposed upon the child from without.

The curriculum in this theory rests on the belief that the child learns by doing and through doing, and that learning is the result of his self-expression. The object of learning is not knowledge but the building of habits, skills, attitudes. The material to be used in education must be drawn from the ideas, customs, and institutions at the culture level experienced by the child. Boys' clubs at one time projected their programs largely on the "culture-epoch" theory. Little "savages" were let loose to tear apart the household furnishings of a civilized father and mother. To correct them would be to impound the pent-up savagery that must at some time be released. The difficulty arising from this approach to the curriculum is that it anchors its material in the past, and fails to anticipate progress.

Maximum Development of the Individual

A fourth theory places the maximum person at the center of education. The interest of education is not so much in the child as an immature human being, but in what the child may become. The objective is the achievement of the maximum development of the individual. The educator sees the integration of the self taking place, as Bower advocates, through purposeful experience, in the midst of an environing society. The teacher's part is to help the child find meaning in his experience, and guide him in recognizing a purpose in it all.

The curriculum aims to provide for such a person an opportunity to find experience in contacts with ultimate value, but accepts the tested experience of the race as to the direction of ultimate achievement. Society guides as the individual ascends, and society has fulfilled its end when the individual has arrived at fullest self-realization.

Religion is vastly concerned with this theory. The teacher must keep in mind the fact that if morality and religion are to function as effective controls in experience, they must be taught as a part of the experience. The habits and attitudes of the growing child are being shaped by experiences with his associates in his play and social life, and by the actual practices which he observes in the community. The pupil learns what he practices and not necessarily what he is told. When instruction in the Sunday school consists of words, such as "be good," what the child learns is to listen to words. Physicians, lawyers, and skilled workmen in many arts, have attained superior performance through practice under trained supervision. This is no new fact, yet many teachers forget that mere knowledge of facts of the Bible will not insure Christian conduct. This theory of the curriculum is exceedingly valuable because it assumes the necessity of guided experience in producing a maximum Christian person.

BACKGROUNDS

In answering the question "How are we to get children to want to do what they ought to do but what they do not want to do?" various devices have been proposed from "spare the rod and spoil the child" to cramming his mind with Bible verses. The early Sunday school movement inherited the religious convictions of the Reformation, which placed the Bible at the center of the church and of life. Luther taught the Bible to the masses. From his day to the present the curriculum has been constructed with varying relations to the Bible. Some leaders look upon the Bible as the text book of religion, and question the validity of any type of lesson material drawn from any other source. Others go even further than allowing Bible centered lessons, and demand "the Bible only" for instruction.

The Bible alone has never remained for long periods the sole curriculum. In order to understand and enrich its meaning organized courses of study have come into existence. At least four steps have been taken in the development of the traditional lesson courses.

1. Before the American Revolution the churches were bent on destroying heresy. Since correct doctrine was so important, the Bible must be interpreted in terms of accepted statements of truth. The "catechism" arose as the instrument of instruction in doctrine.

2. When the movement for general education in America became widespread, the schools dropped religion from their curriculum because of the separation of church and state. Likewise, the secular element was dropped from the Sunday school course, and the Bible again became the sole textbook.

3. The first attempt at organization of Bible study took the form of Bible verse memory contests. The discovery was soon made that the memory was tricky, and that there was no great instructional value in this recital of Scripture. Churches keeping careful records reported a falling off in moral and spiritual conduct. To meet the practical need of bridging between the Scripture and the child a "question book" was prepared for the purpose of stimulating explorations into the Bible.

4. Prior to the middle of the last century it dawned upon the leaders that the wide use of catechisms and question books was evidence of a definite need that the Bible be organized into lesson plans, and be adapted to individual differences. As early as 1823 certain passages of Scripture were selected as the basis of a course of Biblical "lessons." Their value was apparent, and the selected lesson has remained popular for over a century.

TYPES

Confusion arose in the early experiments with an organized study of the Bible because no aims had been devised, and no leaders were trained in the principles of curriculum making. The acceptance of the Bible as the sole subject matter of the Sunday school limited any attempts at the formation of a curriculum. It soon became obvious that some thread of purpose must be run through the Bible to give the serial studies uniformity of length, sequence, and usefulness. Truman Parmelee, as early as 1823, offered the churches of Utica, New York, a group of lessons based on the historical portions of the New Testament. The earliest permanent effort at an organized curriculum was made by the American Sunday School Union in 1825, by enlarging their two-year course based on biblical materials to a five-year cycle. The school year of nine months seems to have determined the number of lessons given annually.

There followed a number of similar or improved courses which are more or less familiar to the present Sunday school worker. They may be grouped as the Uniform Lessons, the Graded Lessons, and the Elective Courses.

The Uniform Lesson

By 1872 Sunday school associations, denominational promoters, and private publishers brought to maturity the "uniform lesson." In the same year the National Sunday School Association met in Indianapolis. B. F. Jacobs, a Baptist layman of Chicago, offered the resolution that formed the International Lesson Committee. The resolution provided for the appointment of a committee of five clergymen and five laymen, to select a course of Bible Lessons for a series of years not to exceed seven. Alternation between the Old and New Testaments was to occur semi-annually or quarterly. The Convention by this resolution recommended the adoption of these lessons by the Sunday schools of the whole country. The function of the committee was limited to the selection of the lesson title, the Scripture passage, and the memory verse. The materials thus selected were sent to each denomination wishing to use the uniform lesson, and each publishing board prepared the lessons with comments for distribution in "quarterlies."

Advantages and disadvantages cluster around the uniform lessons. During its more than eighty years of existence the plan has increasingly sold the world on the value of systematized instruction in religion. It has made the world Sunday school conscious but the limitations of the plan in this day of public school enlightenment make its continuance questionable. Its disconnected order, "hop-skip-and-jump" method will never unfold the maximum of spiritual facts of the Bible. The Book so taught, in the words of a devoted Sunday school teacher, "will remain too largely a source book for moralizing and preaching. No one would undertake to teach any other great literature by such a scrappy method."

The Graded Lesson

A few years later William Rainey Harper prepared his Hebrew texts on the inductive study plan. His method was transferred to general Bible study. Through his pupils the plan spread in popularity. The public schools gradually added strength to the idea by their experiments in a graded course of study. Many public school teachers were teaching in the Sunday schools, and trying out in the Sunday schools principles employed by them for five days a week. These forces operated to create a definite demand for lessons more suitable to child needs.

Conservative leaders objected to grading the materials of the Bible. A late pastor of great wisdom contended that the Bible was the same for seven-year-old Mary as it was for seventy-year-old great-grandmother. But public school leaders, disillusioned teachers of primary children who had seen the harm of uniformity to younger pupils, and educationally minded parents, directly and indirectly forced an issue on a graded Sunday school curriculum. "If graded lessons about the Bible are necessary," objected a prominent Sunday school superintendent, "then why not graded lessons in the Bible?" The International Graded Lessons resulted.

The Closely Graded Lessons consisted of a separate unit of subject matter prepared for each year, to be used as textbooks are used in the public school. These lessons were pupil-centered rather than material-centered. Their aim was determined by the needs of the child rather than with the thought of covering any particular section of the subject matter. In plan the lessons are intended to be consecutive and cumulative; that is to say, the lessons of each succeeding age group presuppose the training afforded by those of the preceding grades. Thus was created a continuous series of steps upward through the curriculum.

These closely graded lessons are planned for church schools which desire a curriculum correlated to the experience and needs of pupils, paralleling their year-by-year growth and religious development. A separate lesson is prepared for each year for church schools graded by age from the three-year-olds to the sixteen- or seventeen-year-olds, or from kindergarten through senior high school age.

Cycle Graded Lessons were prepared for Sunday church schools which desire a course of lessons graded on a two- or three-year cycle. They were departmentally graded; that is, each department of the school had a different lesson, but all classes in one department studied the same lesson. For the beginners (kindergarten) a two-year cycle was planned. Three-year cycles were planned for the primary, junior, intermediate (junior high), and senior age groups.[4]

The Elective System

The former rigidly organized curriculum has suffered severely in public school circles of late. Larger liberties are granted local groups for the determination of content and arrangement of curriculum. The introduction to a state bulletin begins: "The school must give a larger place to realities; it must develop in youth, through actual experience, greater initiative, greater willingness to accept responsibility and to face reality; greater powers of leadership, of organization, and of dealing with problems on the basis of data and objective interpretation. The curriculum must provide for individual pupils, as well as groups, upon the basis of inborn capacities, background of experience, present needs, and predictable future needs." (Alabama Department of Education, Curriculum Bulletin No. 5, 1938, p.v.)

The church must develop a type of curriculum in addi-

[4] *Introduction, Cycle Graded Lessons* (Chicago: Division of Christian Education, National Council of Churches, 1954–55).

tion to the uniform lessons to meet the needs of men today. The Bible is a closed book to many, except as familiar writings yield select passages for moralizing. The increasingly higher level of intelligence in many churches would warrant the use of background studies, and correlative courses as illuminators of the Bible. Studies in religions of the world, Greek philosophy, the development of Christian churches, philosophy of religion, are within the grasp of many church members today, and would enrich their lives. Such human variables can be provided for only through a system of the electives supplementing the regular courses.

The range of electives beyond the Uniform Lesson, or the strictly Biblical studies, covers such areas as missions, church history, Christian apologetics, Christian hymnody, Christian biography, Christian industrialism, Christian parent guidance. A case in point is described by Grace H. Patton in "Character" (Vol. I, No. 2). The curriculum for parent education in Riverside church, New York City, was the experiment reported. The aim of this school is "to find a satisfactory approach to every moral and ethical problem which the average parent of today has to face in dealing with children. It aims to lead them to some practical and helpful conclusions regarding these problems." In this way parents with wide ranges of problems become beneficiaries of the contributions of religion to every day living.

Certain secondary values are also attached to elective courses. One thoughtful teacher believes that their introduction will improve the quality of teaching, just as specialization has improved the quality of teaching in the high schools and colleges. Further, it is believed that the use of textbooks will result in an improved scholarship over the requirements of the lesson leaflets or quarterlies.

DEMANDS ON THE CURRICULUM

A curriculum of religious education means more today than the subject matter of the Sunday school. Every spiritually cultural contact falls within the scope of the curriculum. "As culture materials have sprung out of life and arisen out of the processes of everyday experience," Betts declares, "so they must be built back into the life of each succeeding generation if culture is to persist."[5] The church receives a steady-moving stream of fresh blood into its body from year to year. The processes of orientation, of absorption, of idealization, of spiritualization are entrusted to the curriculum.

The Individual

The individual makes the first demand. The child of the race needs his potential self developed and nurtured. He has a right to the religion that has controlled human conduct through the ages. He needs to know of the faith that steadied his forefathers in peace and strife. He has a right to be led into the way of God. He has a right to a working knowledge of the time-approved and tested human values.

Society

Society makes demands on the curriculum of religion. Betts[6] says that the contribution which society has made to each of us is not meant "as an out-and-out gift, but as a loan." The individual must pay back, not only the original principal, but this with interest." The curriculum must cultivate the sense of social responsibility. It must cure the desire to get without giving in return. Society therefore expects the curriculum to Christianize the institutions of society. The spirit of service in public office, national and international peace, respect for law, justice in human relations, are some of the products expected of the curriculum.

The Church

The church, likewise, looks to the curriculum as the chief agency through which it fulfills its teaching function among men. Jesus commissioned this institution above all others to "make disciples," and to "teach them to observe whatsoever things I have commanded you." The accomplishment of

[5] Betts, *The Curriculum*, p. 203.
[6] *Ibid.*, p. 281.

these tasks is the result of the church school curriculum in action. The church expects every member to know its meaning and message. Christian zeal, mission-mindedness, loyalty, evangelism, training workers for local leadership and for world service, are entrusted to the curriculum. The interlocking relations with the school and the home involve the church in a responsibility for an integrated curriculum which builds up to and into the Christian college curriculum in religion, into and along with the home, and into the life of the public school.

PRINCIPLES OF CURRICULUM CONSTRUCTION

The race moves forward on the shoulders of the father generation. No set of youths begin and move on in their own right. There is the inheritance of yesterday to thank or to recognize. To forget the past is impossible, and to ignore it is suicidal. Yet that generation which accepts the conventions of yesterday without testing their validity for today has played traitor to God's plan of discovery. A curriculum in the making, therefore, should be governed by the principles of adjustment to the present, adaptation to the individual, validity of past experiences, varied application, and a consciousness that a definite end must be approached.

Adjusted to Life

The effective curriculum will consist of materials that apply the pattern objectives to actual life experiences. The curriculum is the agent of the objectives, and must be patterned by the objectives. Objectives to be valid must be stated in terms of life situations. Parents usually succeed in establishing desirable habits by training the children in the habit patterns of daily living. Table manners are learned at the table. Peaceable attitudes are formed on the ball field. Regularity in churchgoing is formed in the practice of going to church. In their moral and religious life the changes to be expected will be realized as training takes place in the midst of, or in terms of, real situations.

Thus the curriculum becomes and must be increasingly

creative by drawing from real life the patterns for experience. The problems for religion come from real life. Abraham learned the value of faith in Jehovah in the midst of the famine, and at the improvised altar on Mt. Moriah. The early Christian church learned the meaning of the risen Christ as they faced the taunts of an unbelieving Judaism, producing the prophets and the gift of the Holy Spirit as evidence of their faith. Virtue is born in the midst of temptation, and temptation is real when virtue is challenged. The curriculum will set forth clearly the moral and religious experiences that await every man.

Such an experimental curriculum seeks a "center of interest" as the controlling purpose. This interest is developed through units of work, which are major experiences taken from the life of the child or the community arranged into extended lessons that may require two or three months for completion. The center of interest, for example, may be some principle of Christian living. The unit of work may be a study of the personal and official practices of men in public trusts who are observing or violating that principle. The study would lead to an understanding of Jesus' standard for the practice of men. Whether or not the curriculum in a particular church or denomination can be adapted to the unit plan, the fact remains that the selection of subject matter should be determined on the basis of its fitting into the present needs of the pupils.

Adapted to the Development of the Child

Students of child life say that at each new level of development "the problems of life are reset in different forms and upon a larger scale." If the curriculum is to enrich the child, it should reach the child through his interests. One is seldom interested in ideas outside his experience. Many studies have confirmed the claim that the child is not a miniature man. He is in the process of becoming a man. His ability to maintain control in experience will depend upon the instruction falling within his experience. These variables include age, social experience, the attitudes of association groups, and the individual capacities.

The most effective curriculum is the graded curriculum adapted to the capacities, needs, and experiences of the learner. Paul fed his "babes in Christ" on "milk," and not "meat." The whole Bible is the Word of God, but some of its meanings are beyond the child's understanding. The effective curriculum avoids the unintelligible materials and adapts the Bible's content to the age and experience of the child.

The experimental curriculum admits that it was made for the child and not the child for the curriculum. Every new section of experience begins where the earlier section ended, but it is not mechanical joining. When there is forcing of application too far in advance of the child's interests, or out of the ranges of interest, or the use of materials foreign to the needs of the child, the educational process fails. The harm that results in disinterestedness may permanently injure a sensitive nature. Middle-aged persons who have suffered in Sunday school at this point reflect sadly, "I never learned anything in Sunday school." The child does not begin with principles and work to problems as an adult might but begins with his problems and works to the principles needful for his age. A modern, progressive educator challenges the curriculum builder thus:

A new curriculum based upon problem-solving situations appears much more appropriate to the needs of contemporary youth. The learner can best develop those competencies with which to adjust satisfactorily to new situations that he meets now, and to the unknown ones that he must face in the future, as he multiplies his experiences in successfully meeting problem situations that are significant and vital to him today. To provide an experience curriculum based upon problem-situation learning is the task and the challenge of the modern school.[7]

Tested by Race Experience

The theory is current that it does not matter greatly what

[7] Roland C. Faunce and Nelson L. Bossing, *Developing the Core Curriculum*, p. 36. Copyright, 1951, by Prentice-Hall, Inc., Englewood Cliffs, N. J.

facts the pupil learns as long as he becomes forward-looking. Such a doctrine may be good for trial and error procedure, but it may be expensively wasteful. One may grant the right to others to explore in morals and religion, but he wants his own son to follow the approved trails to clean, honest, upright living. In ministering to life, the curriculum must check its offerings by the tested and accepted experience of the race.

The effective curriculum is thus the guided curriculum. The race has looked to its religious books for authoritative guidance. Christians have found their Bible to be a sufficient and approved guide. Their confidence rests back on the nature of God so strikingly proclaimed by Isaiah. Isaiah proclaimed for Jehovah, "My word shall not return unto me void." Isaiah's confidence in the validity of his word to man did not rest on a conception of God as a dictator but on this superior knowledge of the hearts of men, and of their needs. Isaiah interprets God as wishing to guide men not by His will, but by His infinite wisdom. This reflects the spirit of the Bible and gives it an irrefutable claim to acceptance by men. A guided experience, then, means an experience patterned by the superior wisdom of God.

A curriculum, therefore, that enters into individual experience must recognize the race experience in the setting up of codes of ethical conduct, and in the giving of form to faith. Ethical neutrality negates even the most artistic life, for less than the Biblically approved code will lead us by its own fruition to defeat, disillusionment, disgust, and death. Ethical conformity leads naturally into richer life. Optional faith or belief in God disqualifies the most profound philosophy, and confusion marks humanistic lessons as lacking in spiritual dynamic, and as confusion of sense of direction. Intelligent faith enheartens and glorifies life. A curriculum tested by the experience of the race will incorporate materials of faith and worship which the race has "practiced and prized." The experiences that have established a right to govern undoubtedly arose out of situations that have "common elements with the present situation." No better code of conduct or of faith has been devised than that contained in the Book.

Many-sidedness of Application

The outcome of a specific lesson depends on the way it is taught. Careful surveys and wide observation have destroyed the notion that "telling" guarantees doing. Psychologists have pointed out that there is no transfer of training where there are no common elements of content in the two types of activity, and a clear understanding of the universal element in the activity that is to be carried over.

The effective curriculum will provide for many-sidedness in the application of its truth. When honesty, for example, is taught the teacher naturally expects the child to live honestly. In teaching honesty the stress might be placed on theft, and the commandment "Thou shalt not steal" well impressed. It might happen that the same pupil would cheat on an examination the following day without thought of having violated the lesson, or later he might be elected to public office and rob the public treasury "as everybody does," or in official position he might "shave" the salaries or wages of dependents in his employ without the slightest sting of conscience. The principle of varied application would lead the teacher to show how the truth should be applied to several possible situations. Naturally the process would not be complete until it had been tested by the sanction of Jesus, and measured by the character of the Kingdom of God.

The experimental curriculum, therefore, will connect the instruction with definite experiences of the individual. The use of parallel areas of life will afford an opportunity for the application of the principle to other life experiences. The whole of life's relations, personal honesty, intellectual honesty, social honesty, honesty with God, must be canvassed in connection with the lesson taught before there can be reasonable certainty of transfer. The question asked of every curriculum might be, "How far into the various areas of life does the subject matter reach?"

The Content Patterned by the Objectives

A well defined goal makes possible the selection of suitable instruments for the attainment of the end. The effective curriculum will contain subject matter selected with a view to maximum suitability to the objectives. The average church has set conversion, church membership, stewardship, training for leadership, recruiting for professional leadership, as definite objectives. The lesson content should reflect these purposes.

QUESTIONS FOR DISCUSSION

1. What are the values of each of the theories of curriculum? What are its weaknesses?

2. Discuss the types of curricula now being prepared by your denominational publishing house. Compare them with those of other publishers.

3. Should graded materials be prepared for classes in the young people's and adult departments?

4. What are the materials and leadership required for building a curriculum to meet the needs of your local church?

5. If the curriculum materials published by your denomination are inadequate, where else might you find suitable materials? What basic principles would guide you in their selection?

CHAPTER 10

METHODS

Educational science has shown that growth takes place through experience, and that experience will develop most satisfactorily under a set of tried conditions. Educational art is simply good method in providing opportunities for these conditions to be realized. It will be observed that this conception of method commits teaching, preaching, and worship to the one task of guiding the experience of the individual toward the objectives of the Christian religion. Method is the way by which the objectives are attained.

CONTROLLING FACTORS

From the teacher's standpoint there are four controlling factors in the educational process. The pupil, the objective toward which he is to be guided, and the curriculum by means of which the objective is to be gained, are the major factors, equipment entering as the fourth. There must be a way of connecting up the curriculum and the individual. This is method, and when it is in harmony with the laws of growth it may be called educational.

The Pupil Factor

To be efficient, method must involve understanding the

pupil. His development results from experience. Experience is built out of his reaction to environment. Through reacting to life he learns the ways that are better for him, and the ways that are worse for him. Attitudes, skills, and appreciations are formed, and these aid him in making later responses. The educator must so understand the pupil that he may be able to direct these growth processes toward the Christian objectives.

The primary challenge of the pupil to method lies in individual differences. These differences are due to age, sex, and psychological variations. Age differences definitely change method. Differences in capacity, interest, and needs of individuals call for an adaptation of method.

Method in dealing with individual differences must recognize the fact that learning is the purpose of teaching, and is an individual experience. The transfer type, the lesson learner, and the direct learner type must be dealt with differently. This means a rethinking of the old lesson-hearing method of teaching, and the substitution therefore of direct teaching of the ends to be learned. The old tests, instead of measuring knowledge, will be used for checking effectiveness of teaching, and for correction of method. These differences in capacity are to be met by variations in the rate of progress, in the quantity of material, and in the quality employed. Differences in interest are to be met by variations in strength of motives, and in the type of reward. Differences in need are to be met by offering incentives that will satisfy those needs.

The Objective Factor

Method is not a free agent. It is under compulsion to find the way to the objectives. The teacher with an objective is teaching for results. His methods may be varied, individual, or peculiar, but they are methods when they produce the desired change. Having determined what kind of training the subject proposes, method determines the kind of training the pupil should get from the subject.

The objective will vitally affect method in that it is the determinant of the worth of a process. The objective no longer serves as inspirer to renewed effort, but admonishes, "if at first you don't succeed find out why your method has failed." Since the aim or objective is not knowledge so much as a change in conduct and ideals, it is apparent that definite aims must be met by definite methods.

The type of objective will definitely affect method. (1) One objective, for example, might be a mastery of biblical facts. Outline texts might be memorized, scrap books made, work books developing the main teachings of the Bible might be followed; tests and the like would be a part of this method. (2) If the objective is the application of Bible messages to men of today the method might include a discussion of current philosophies, national and social questions; scanning of the daily press for challenges to religious education; visits to the welfare agencies, juvenile courts, and other institutions of dependency and correction; correspondence with selected groups of children of other nationalities; and further pursuits of some project. (3) If the objective is concerned with committing individuals to Christian decisions, the method might include guided conversations with vital Christians about their experiences, talking to older persons who have failed to commit themselves and are grieved because of it, collecting figures on "conversion probabilities" for various ages, the assignment of Christian service "in the name of Christ."

The Curriculum Factor

Method cannot ignore materials. Since the modern curriculum includes in addition to textbooks "all the agencies within the school organization which combine to produce the educational results," the sources of religious materials are as broad and rich as the experience of the race. Biblical material is varied in its rich treasures, and varied in its forms. Here lie historical backgrounds, ethical and moral precepts, and a philosophy of Hebrew monotheism and Christian trinitarianism. In addition to biblical materials there is a rich heritage of extra-biblical materials, covering Christian biography so powerful for ideals, Christian art expressing the conflict of the ideal with the elemental forces of life, and Christian music reflecting spiritual release from enslaving passions and powers. These materials are available for religious instruction, but can be handled in different ways and lend themselves to distinctive techniques.

Subject matter definitely determines method. Where the objective is competence in the individual, habits of courtesy, promptness, respect for the rights of others, devotion to truth, love of the church and the like, there is a general goal for teaching regardless of the subject matter. Where the objective is the adjusting of the instruction to the goal of the Christian church and to the atmosphere of the Christian religion, there is a function calling for specific subject matter methods. Training for church membership, for example, calls for training in the purposes, values, responsibilities, and philosophy of church life and function. Such training should develop a love for the ideal, and for the fellowship of its wider ministry in a world fellowship. The materials used for the acquiring of these ideals, beliefs, skills, and attitudes, are largely printed matter for the representation of facts. The method varies with the materials used.

Method is the way the pupil learns subject matter, and not the way the teacher teaches it; yet the way the teacher teaches it helps the way the pupil learns. Consequently there are principles implicit in the process that are serviceable. (1) Subject matter should be taught in the spirit of its content. Geography is intended to interpret the physical environment of people, and not their faith. History is intended to explain the manners, customs and ideals of a people, and not their faith. Religion as the philosophy of a race is intended to account for their faith and their aspirations. Each of these subjects requires a different method, though the purpose of each converges in the other. (2) Subject matter should be taught by a method that will develop its underlying purpose. Biography is not taught as art, but to teach religion. Biblical material grew out of an experience of concrete truth, for the purpose of imparting spiritual values, of inspiring Christian ideals, and of stimulating religious faith. The methods used should discover these purposes and follow a technique that will replant them in current life. (3) Subject matter should be adapted to pupil experience. Unless the curriculum fits into the experience of the learner it loses effectiveness. Things that belong together should be learned together. Bible experiences that fit the present experience inspire a sense of truth and reality of the Bible experience. (4) Subject matter incorporated into a unit of work should offer manysidedness of application. Materials draw to themselves wide ranges of related truth, and reach out to widely expanding experiences of life. Through weeks of study and application the truth of the unit comes to a richer and wider dominance in the pupil's life.

The Equipment Factor

The traditional classroom is a place for hearing lessons. As such it is a bare sort of place. Under the hearing-recitation plan the desk and the chair were enough. Under the firsthand experience plan of teaching the pupil needs a workroom in which are collected the materials essential to the immediate study. Equipment for research, handwork, visual aids, graphic implements, auditory mechanisms, are regarded as essential and often indispensable appurtenances to effective education.

Method will be changed to utilize the available equipment. Instead of question and answer, or drill or other verbal procedures, the lesson will be conducted by studying maps, graphs, models, concordances, and reference books, by making scrapbooks, preparing reports, and observing pictures of scenes or incidents. In each case a method will be used that will fit the teaching situation.

TYPES OF METHODS

While dependence should not be placed upon one method to the neglect of another, there are several types of methods which have a place in the practice of the church. In general these may be classified in terms of the technique employed. (1) Individualized methods are those in which the teacher alone participates. (2) Socialized methods are those in which the teacher and the pupils cooperate. (3) Laboratory methods are those that utilize direct expression by the pupil.

Individualized Methods

The usual methods so classified are the lecture, the sermon, and the story. They are more or less vicarious, and lack the values of firsthand pupil experience. Learning takes place through experience. Experience may be had through direct activity, through witnessing the activity of another person, or through hearing from another the experience of himself or of some other individual. The experience of hearing becomes educative only in so far as the facts related become associated in the mind of the hearer with some experience in his own life. This is the most remote process of learning but is not lacking in value. For persons of wide contacts, and of long exposures to life, the best results often obtain from the use of these methods.

The *lecture* or "telling" method is adapted to certain instructional situations. Experience advises a sparing use of the formal lecture for the early adolescent ages, though lecturing for short periods is often desirable, provided the pupils are getting what the teacher expects of them. Interest and attention may not always mean understanding and learning. To be effective the lecture must "stimulate activity, raise problems, and lead pupils to ask questions." Certain subjects depend more upon the lecture method than others. Languages depend upon telling. History, geography, manners and customs, require much illumination through the lecture and the story. The introduction of any subject, even of a project or unit of work, requires certain types of lecturing.

Success in the use of the lecture method will depend upon the ability of the lecturer to explore the experience centers of his hearers. Before he can claim effective speech he must discover responsive areas in which past experience approves and accepts the new. The lecturer seeks to arouse interest in new situations, or to impart new knowledge. The story teller, whose process is one of telling, seeks to illumine truth by dramatized lecturing. The preacher through his sermon seeks to inform his hearers of vital truth, and by reviving emotional experience under a new direction to lead to decision and action. These are the characteristic lecture forms. The teacher of religion often combines the three forms, imparting exegetically the truth of the lesson, telling a story for illustration, and using the homiletical art for securing decision.

The development of a sound lecturing technique is imperative. Experienced lecturers advise several practices: Think through your message and how you are to say it. Speak to your hearers and not at them. Start the lecture with a problem, and keep the class in a watchful state of mind. Allow pauses occasionally for pupils to think through the presentation. Visual aids help to hold attention, and fix truth. The lighter moods interspersed will lift the heavier periods. The summary should gather up the threads into a compact message.

The *story* should not be rated as a separate method. It holds a dependent position. As an illustration of a truth, as an "appetizer," or to motivate, the story serves with tremendous effect. As a unit of instruction it lacks purpose.

The general rules for the selection of stories have been variously stated. The first requisite is adaptability. Since small children are more responsive to stories their needs should receive first attention. Primary pupils usually care for a narrative filled with mystery, a part of which may be produced in the telling. They also wish an element of fancy. They live in the world of make believe. Fancy stretches their imagination, and imagination later makes faith possible. They also delight in a story that will bear repetition. A second requisite is action, for younger children particularly. A third requisite is that the story should be permanently useful to the child. The universally known stories are more interesting and constitute a bond of social cohesion necessary for developing human understanding and sympathy. A fourth requisite is that the central figure of the story should embody positive moral or religious values. Negative virtues in the hero do not seem to produce positive effects. A fifth requisite is that the story should reflect the highest ideals in plot, and in literary form. An effort to "step down" exalted imagery to the level of the child is tragic.

The sources of story material are usually listed as tradition, heroics, and nature. Legends, fables, parables, and well known fairy tales have come from many quarters and many ages. They bear their message of the conflict of good with evil, of the quests of men for the good. Lowell's "The Vision of Sir Launfal" and Tennyson's "Idylls of the King" represent a very usable group of this type. The heroics are numerous. Stories of poor boys who achieved fame, of heroes of mission field and frontier, are full of human interest. History and current literature abound in such stories. No stories excel those of the heroic period of Israel. Nature stories are numerous and lend themselves admirably to religious instruction. Jesus undoubtedly found inspiration and spiritual insight through watching the sparrows and the lilies. Interpreters of the animals, the plants, the rocks, and the stars have opened a treasure house of materials for the teacher of religion. The Bible contains materials taken from all of the experiences of life. Bible stories lend themselves admirably to narration, and can be used with abiding satisfaction. Denominational publishers should be consulted for suggestions as to books of Bible stories.

Suggestions for telling the story are better made in larger studies. In general, however, the theory of story telling embodies these principles: (1) Know the pupil. The narrator and the pupil should understand each other for best results. Preparation for telling includes an advance fitting of all the narrative to the mind of the hearer, and an advance answering of all questions likely to arise. (2) Know the story. Failures are often due to the fact that the narrator does not know "where he is going." The story should be so well known that it becomes a part of the experience of the narrator. (3) Know good technique. A well modulated voice, a natural poise, an easy manner, suitable facial or other gestures, imitation and impersonation especially with children, avoidance of gaps, explanations and stops, are essential to good effect. (4) Know when the message is felt. It is only when the hearers feel the message of the story that the story teller has succeeded. If the story has been well chosen, and well told, it will teach its own moral.

Socialized or Group Methods

Since method is the way of making the materials of instruction accomplish the desired end in guiding the experience of the learner, it is natural that the socialized processes should be more effective than the lecture method. In the latter the responsibility of each pupil is to the teacher, and not to the group. There is no group aim, no cooperative attitude, no pupil responsibility, no sense of ownership in the enterprise, and no group recognition of common problems. In bringing the learner to think, to plan and to cooperate, these experiences are important. Personal responsibility for progress and for the subject builds up within the pupil a permanent interest in the procedure. It develops initiative, skill in clear thinking, ability to use freedom profitably, consideration for others, and skill in cooperation.

The *question and answer* method is commonly practiced, coming next in use to the lecture method. It is largely an individual pupil-teacher performance, lacking in group stimulus. It aims at impressing the memory with subject matter, and is concerned only remotely with thinking and acting. It centers in reciting to the satisfaction of the teacher, or in substituting the teacher for the subject matter, or in a memorizer learning.

The values of the question have been universally recognized. The first and widest use that the question has been put to is that of testing knowledge. A second function is to develop correct habits of response. A third function is to arouse interests and to discover tastes. A fourth function is to interpret and evaluate facts. A fifth is to stimulate pupils to think, which is the most important function. To this end great care should be exercised in asking questions and great wisdom in interpreting the answers.

Admitting the abuse and misuse of the question and

answer, there is no method so frequently employed by even the best of teachers. It supplements the discussion, by correcting error in understanding, and emphasizes important points. It follows the story, the drama, the lecture, the assignment, the project, making sure that the learning has been experienced.

The discussion method is more difficult, but is one of the most effective methods when used by a well-trained group leader. The socialized procedure in teaching has developed into two general types, often referred to as the formal type and the informal type. The formal plan organizes the class after the scheme of some adult organization, like a mission board, denominational state convention, church session, directors' round table for gathering group conclusions, and court "panel" for considering the fate of a given topic. The group operates under the leadership of representatives, with guidance of the teacher; the entire group assumes responsibility for its work. The other type is informal group discussion. This plan involves no special organization. Discussion is encouraged, with the teacher accepting a less conspicuous position in the class. Common goals are prominent. In reality, the informal type is the discussion or the seminar method of teaching.

The discussion method consists of free interchange of thought by members of a class upon some problem more or less common to the class. The instructor simply guides the discussion by making clear the problem, by keeping on the main issue and avoiding fruitless digressions, and by keeping participation by members of the class in proper balance. Instead of asking questions, the teacher raises problems and then stimulates the discussion. Pupils talk to the group rather than to the teacher. The ordinary courtesies of debate are observed, such as avoiding interruption of the speaker, respecting the time of others, and avoiding the trivial. Success in discussion requires a certain amount of subject matter, a diversity of points of view, and a well distributed time allotment.

According to Randolph C. Miller, ". . . the discussion method is the most successful method with all who have enough intellectual background to participate in it!"[1] Although discussions are notably unpredictable, if the leader is willing to let the real issues come up, a class session may have these divisions:

1. The problem should be launched in such a way that the students will desire to participate. The problem must seem significant to the members of the class. . . .

2. Everyone should come to an understanding of the problem. . . . The right kind of questions lead to a redefining of the problem on the religious level.

3. Group participation may be obtained at any point. . . . It must always be present in the defining and then in the redefining on the deeper level. . . . The task of the leader is to keep certain pupils from monopolizing the discussion, to make sure that everyone participates, and to guide the discussion.

4. Some discussions will come to clear decisions, and the group will follow through with a plan of action. . . . But there are some problems that cannot be solved within the framework of discussion and need to be rephrased in terms of how to live with our unanswered problems. . . . Careful planning is essential for a good discussion.[2]

Laboratory or Experimental Methods

In the laboratory plan the students learn from original sources, or from secondary ones where necessary. The object is to relive the part or period studied. The teacher gives direction to the activities through "laboratory manuals," or prepared written assignments. The assignments may cover collecting objects pertinent to the subject, scrap books, paper-pulp models, pageants and drama. The advantages of the method are the realistic approach, and the opportunity to create activity and purposeful effort on the part of the pupil. Experiments testing the value of the laboratory as compared with the daily recitation procedure in citizenship studies, as reported by Reed, show that laboratory procedures earned as

[1] Randolph Crump Miller, *Education for Christian Living*, p. 213. Copyright, 1956, by Prentice-Hall, Inc., Englewood Cliffs, N. J.

[2] *Ibid.*, p. 214.

much as twenty per cent more points than did the daily assignment plan.[3]

The use of experimental processes is as valuable in moral and religious education as in other fields. In this field, however, it is a method of learning more than a method of discovery. It is a method of reinforcing data that are already available. It provides for the pupil the experience at first hand, and in this manner makes more vivid and more accurate the impression than would reading or hearing the data. Experimentation becomes a method of observing, and a method of problem solving. Through these processes the individual does make discoveries in relationships that lie dormant in lectures or reading.

Practical observations on the experimental method show its values to lie in handling qualities, events, and relations, as well as things. Its essence consists in the spirit of investigation. Its purpose is to make vivid through sensuous data the meaning of events or relations in terms of general principles. Its expectation is the solution of a problem which has arisen in the class, and which is conducted parallel to the work of the class. Its results should become a basis for class discussion.

The church is discovering that *manual arts* is not simply "busy" work. Often handwork has been introduced to keep children interested. The aim of handwork is far more than making things. The director seeks to get back of the object fashioned, to the urges that produced it. Such a director will feel that he has failed if he seeks only to work off a child's surplus energy through the hands. His real purpose is to provide an opportunity for expressing concretely a truth already acquired, for the sake of enriched appreciation. Certain incidental learning values lie in the development of neatness and accuracy. The cultivation of the habits of economy, orderliness, and cleanliness are particularly valuable in manual arts in teaching religion.

[3] Homer B. Reed, *Psychology and Teachings of Secondary School Subjects* (Englewood Cliffs, N. J.: Prentice-Hall, Inc., 1939), p. 379.

The manual arts are used for purposes of illustration, and for construction. Drawing is sometimes a better vehicle for understanding than words. There is less demand on imagination where lines and colors are employed for concreteness. A single mark on the blackboard will symbolize a man far better than the word "man" alone. Posters provide for a vivid presentation of the subject under study, and train the makers in arranging advantageously the materials employed. Scrapbooks have educational value when they are made for a purpose, such as portraying the life of a missionary, or creating interest in a local welfare project. Arranging the Gospels in harmony form, or a pictorial life of Christ, are worthy uses of the scrapbook. Mapmaking fits into the geography ages of the Sunday school. For studying the contour of the Bible lands, or the changing borders of changing kingdoms, or the historical connections with important places it is valuable. Construction includes paper cutting, clay modeling, and wood working. Special books on these subjects are available.

Certain principles have been found valuable in governing the use of manual arts for religious development. (1) Of chief importance is that the teacher must know the psychological reasons for using handwork in teaching religion, else the activity is mere busy work, and a waste of time. (2) The manual work must be connected with the lesson being studied or the educational value is lost. (3) Grading of the activity is as important as grading the lesson material. (4) The best results come from a service motive, especially when that service is personal and challenging. Making things for a needy family in the community will greatly impress the lesson on "being a good neighbor." (5) The incidental learning, neatness and the like, must be carefully safeguarded, or the loss will offset the gain.

Dramatization is one of the most effective means for conveying a sense of reality to the pupil. It makes a strong visual and auditory appeal. In this way identification of the actor with the situation becomes a reality. The ultimate effect of the drama is a more vivid understanding of the episode. Through dramatization the pupil sees and lives the life of the period under study. The aim of dramatization is to make the past so real and vivid to the learner that he will sense it and relive it as if it were a part of the present.

"Dramatic play . . . is a mode of expression whereby individuals identify themselves with persons and objects they have studied in various units of work; it is stimulated activity in which children act out what they have experienced."[4]

The value of presenting religious truth in the form of drama is generally recognized. Much ritual in religious observances is the dramatic expression of an earlier faith. The more ancient Christian churches continue the use of the dramatic method of presenting truth. The interest of the church in dramatization is chiefly educational. The old miracle plays, and the Oberammergau Passion Play, were produced as acts of devotion, but modern uses are limited almost entirely to educational purposes. Truth is made vivid when so presented. Dramatization utilizes the urge to activity, imitation, and play. It has educational value in that it releases the individual from his environment, and through his imagination enables him to experience the feeling of new attitudes, ideas, and powers.

To obtain lasting educational value certain principles are to be observed. (1) Dramatization must be made an integral part of the educational work of the church. The effort on the part of an unskilled teacher to "give a play" for the purpose of bolstering up lagging interest is pointless. Betts and Hawthorne have observed that "only those forms of dramatics have educational value which call for spontaneous interpretation and action on the part of the players," and that "by studying and producing prepared materials these same values and still others are developed." (2) Every pupil must be included in the production in one capacity or another. The purpose is to develop the imagination, the emotions, and to provide an avenue for self-expression. Every pupil must have this opportunity to visualize the teaching and subject matter. (3) The informal dramatization is of chief value. The stage setting and

<hr />

[4] John U. Michaelis, *Social Studies for Children in a Democracy* (Englewood Cliffs, N. J.,: Prentice-Hall, Inc., 1956), p. 369.

costumes are not necessary for an educational effect. The presence of an audience defeats the primary purpose. (4) Dramatization must be purposeful, else it becomes undesirable for church purposes. Its purpose is to "reveal to them moral and religious values in action." Betts and Hawthorne interpret its function to be to "crystallize principles of noble living, set up worthy ideals and character made real in great personalities."[5] (5) The materials of dramatization must be chosen for their permanent value to the developing lives of the pupils. The content must be usable, positive in moral and religious values, and adapted to the needs and capacities of the pupils. (6) The class discussion following the play is the most important feature. Questions will arise that should open wide discussion.

The sources of materials for dramatization include the Bible, especially the narrative portions of the Old Testament, the expansion of the church through missions, mission fields, hymns and other great music, home life, industrial relations, international relations, neighborliness and the like. The leading publishers among the denominations will gladly furnish information as to the best available materials for the use of the teacher.

Teaching Aids

The *value of pictures* has been found to be so great that some of the nation's most influential journals tell their story of social change in pictorial form. Pictures tell briefly the contents of many words, and the impression produced is more lasting. History told through pictures is far more vivid than when told through the printed page. Other subject matter carries over better by this means for the reason that pictorial is less variable than written or spoken imagery. It has the additional value of vividness, and of greater permanence of retention.

Visual aid is the suitable term for the service of concrete materials to instruction. The most satisfactory learning takes

[5] George H. Betts and Marion O. Hawthorne, *Method in Teaching Religion* (Nashville: Abingdon Press, 1925), p. 354.

place when accurate imagery accompanies the verbal symbols. Only to the extent that the learner forms a clear picture of the character, the scene, or the process, does he really learn. Much learning is wasted because the abstract idea presented does not take definite form in the mind. Those who have little apperceptive background are severely handicapped under verbal instruction. Visual aids supply that lack as they show what the idea is like or how it operates. Real things are more interesting than verbal symbols. Next to studying the thing itself the best approach is through studying a picture or representation of the thing. Pictures, drawings, diagrams, and films will provide this approach.

Not all subjects can be presented visually. Nor does all visual instruction have equal value. Where the material is not well adapted to the instruction the effect may be undesirable. Where the explanatory message is lacking, or the picture or film poorly selected, the effect will be disappointing. Good thinking cannot be aided by confused images. New images cannot be well formed from those that have not been directly experienced.

Types of *visual aids* include films, slides, charts, maps, stereographic views, pictures, relics, diagrams, and graphs. The type to be used will depend upon the teaching situation. Geography will call for maps, globes, slides, and stereographic views. Where social conditions or customs are to be taught films, charts, pictures, field trips will be of value. Pictures are particularly helpful in teaching the life of Christ. Many prints of the great paintings are available in inexpensive form. Collections of these should be available, and properly filed for ready use. Slides also are easily secured and at small expense. The film strip has come into use, and has certain advantages over the glass slide. Motion pictures exert greater influence on the emotional side of education. They have a place, provided there is careful preparation before, and careful follow-up work after, the showing of the film. Full information regarding these materials may be had from the denominational publishing houses.

Certain common *procedures* apply to the use of these

various types of visual aids. (1) The use of any type of visual material should be for some definite teaching purpose. There should be a definite function for it to perform. The need for such usually arises from the lack of adequate conception of the person, or place, or event, and the aid should supply just enough of the concrete for that need. Where the pupil can visualize such background there is little need of visual materials. (2) Visual materials are appropriately used when the subject presented is beyond the experience of the child to imagine, or where an interest in a problem can be aroused quickly through vivid material. (3) Visual materials are especially helpful in reviews and summaries, or where the shortness of the period of instruction makes adequate oral presentation difficult. Such materials may be used profitably to illustrate or to impress the content of a lecture. (4) With the possible exception of the blackboard, experience dictates that careful preparation should be made for the use of these aids. Pupils should be told what to look for in the picture, and what they are to retain. They should find that the aid supplies the needed information. (5) Follow-up work is the best procedure where the visual aids consist of more than illustrations of points in the lesson. Where pictures or other aids make up a definite part of the teaching, there should follow a careful checkup to determine whether they have served their purpose.

UNIT OF WORK

Definition

A unit of work has been defined as a series of valuable experiences bound together around some central theme which is of interest to the pupil. The unit of work method of teaching is based upon the principles (1) that in the end, learning must be direct learning and not lesson learning; (2) that the child's interests, his past experience, his present needs, determine what his school activities will be; (3) that pupils can learn together better than individually; (4) that a procedure involving firsthand experience, plus discussion in the group, is the most effective; (5) that in the process of adjustment to environment learning is most effective when a complete adjustment has been secured. Education is not a divided experience. In the process of education each adjustment is called a unit of learning.

Content

The curriculum is composed of materials of learning which help the pupil to adjust himself properly to the wide range of contacts that he must make in life. Certain situations must be planned which will give the pupil the opportunity for the adjustment needed. The situations are the units. The facts, the activities, the discussion, and the events make up the experience. What the pupil does about these constitutes the adjustment. To become a unit these facts and activities must be related to each other with a view to facilitating a useful adjustment to life and must be mastered by the pupil with full knowledge of the results to be obtained. The total of the units regarded as necessary to meet the requirement of the objectives is the curriculum. A good curriculum will of necessity require a carefully planned organization of all the teaching materials.

The unit may be in terms of over-all themes for certain periods of time or in effectively arranged groups of lessons. "A satisfactory curriculum," according to the Special Committee on Curriculum, "does not consist of a mere collection of lessons or courses. Fragmentation is avoided and adequacy secured through careful interrelatedness of each part of the total plan. An organization of the curriculum in terms of units provides purposefulness and relatedness in a way which is not possible when each lesson is considered as complete in itself. Organization by units prevents individual lessons being taught as separate, unrelated entities. A unit provides for the development of experiences in a specific area over a number of sessions (meetings of the class)."[6] The teacher must learn the technique of teaching in units of experience.

[6] Quoted from *Special Committee on Curriculum Guide*, p. 48. Copyright, 1955, by the Division of Christian Education, National Council of Churches.

The selection of a unit will begin with a search of an area of life for the comprehensive and significant aspects of its environment. By "comprehensive" is meant that such aspects of the environment as may be found will explain satisfactorily the demands of that environment. By "significant" is meant that the aspects selected will possess intrinsic importance and prove essential in the life of the adjusted personality. The unit selected should be worthy of making such a modification. Of all institutions the Christian church stands first in breadth of opportunity in the matter of selection of units. The Christian must be adjusted in the home, in the school, in society, in the Kingdom of God. A Christian home life and its radiations offer a vast field for exploration. The church in its worship, its literature, its history, its leaders, its ministries offers a field for study by intelligent Christians. The social environment, causes of social ills, delinquency, crime, and their correctives lead into the purposes of Jesus. These areas suggest the possibilities of units.

The *techniques* of the unit of learning consist of principles successfully employed by Reed:[7] (1) the organization of the facts into a meaningful pattern, (2) practice for the sake of improvement by means of repeated efforts to do better, (3) recognition of individual variations as to capacity, interest and needs, and (4) motivation growing out of a felt need, with a movement toward the satisfying object. The location of a unit of interest will mean the building of materials around it for interpretation and meaning. Practice brings facility and often comprehension. Individual differences are cared for in grading, promotion, individual case guidance, and special classes for creating opportunity for meeting individual needs. Motives for increasing the speed of learning are effective as a goal is definitely set and its attainment made desirable.

Advantages of the unit of work plan lie in the focusing of significant materials on important experience areas. It results in learning Bible truths and human relations vitally. It safeguards the truth by requiring a mastery of the whole, rather than parts. It makes more certain the retention of the mate-

---

[7] Reed, *Psychology and Teachings.*

rials of the lessons and a carrying over of the precepts into a wider life. On the other hand it does not promise to solve all of the educational problems. Its purpose is to develop understanding and not to give information. If information is the objective, other methods should be used.

QUESTIONS FOR DISCUSSION

1. Study the recorded examples of the teaching of Jesus and select the best example you can find in the use of each method described in this chapter.

2. Explain the controlling factors in choice of method from the teacher's standpoint. Can you name some other factors in the teaching process?

3. Make a list of the advantages and disadvantages in the use of each method.

4. Divide the present quarter's uniform lessons into units of learning suited to the needs of your Sunday school class.

5. What methods do you consider the most valuable for your use as a teacher? Give reasons for your answer.

CHAPTER 11

RELIGIOUS EDUCATIONAL ACTIVITIES

The responsibility of Christian churches for meeting the issues where human values are involved has led to the promotion of activities for the achievement of specific ends. Schools have been conducted to instruct men in the ways of righteousness. Evangelism has been utilized for enlisting individuals in the Kingdom of God. Worship has been encouraged for deepening in Christians a sense of fellowship with and power from God. Stewardship has been fostered for training men in the habit of Christian living. Through these activities religious education seeks to achieve moral and spiritual results.

INSTRUCTION

Religious education and instruction are not identical. Religious education is essentially a moral and spiritual process which consists of the operation of all the influences that shape character and faith. Instruction is one of the means of religious education for intellectual, emotional, and volitional training in the building of character and in the integration of Christian personality. Instruction is concerned primarily with the intellectual aspects of the process of helping persons master essential facts that cannot be left to chance.

Objectives of Instruction

Since the preservation of these spiritual facts and their interpretation are central in the objectives of instruction, the tangible aims may be stated as the preservation of the spiritual heritage, the formation of character, and the commitment of the individual to the will of God. The first is the transmissive act of teaching the literature and ideals of Christianity; the second is the creative process of building character, and the third is the evangelical aim of conversion.

Transmitting Christian teaching is a humanitarian as well as a church objective. God made the world for love and for unselfishness. The social order will not run harmoniously except in the Christian way. Discord and destruction follow the tilting of society off the Christian center. The constitution and by-laws of a good society are embodied in the literature of Christianity. The Christian centuries have charged these writings with impractical idealism, but have demonstrated the futility of ignoring their teachings. The Bible is the perfect pattern of life, the standard of human measurements and values, the story of God's conquest of the heart. Planting the Bible facts for fruitage both for today and after many days is a Christian purpose of instruction.

Creative character building is a more intricate process. Instruction in religion and character training are not synonymous. Instruction in religion is thought of as instruction in the Bible, the catechism, Christian ethics, and philosophy. Instruction in character is thought of as the impartation of certain traits, such as honesty, truthfulness, and sobriety. The public school emphasis on character development centers largely in trait development. Religious education accepts responsibility for specific traits, but assumes further the task of organizing personality around Christian purposes. The reason for emphasis on specific character education in the Christian sense rests upon the fact that tests have shown a lack of essential correlation between biblical information and phases of conduct. Thoroughgoing tests have revealed the fact that correlations between knowledge of right and wrong and the expected conduct are the result of the human equation in teaching more often than of subject matter. Hartshorne and May found that the relative influence of parent, public school teacher, and Sunday school teacher, in affecting character, stands in this order, .545, .028, and .002 respectively. Such facts challenge religious educators to undertake purposive character education on the Christian basis.

The evangelistic objective surpasses in importance knowledge of the Bible and well ordered habits of conduct. When one hears great Christian leaders say, "I never saw the world until I saw Christ," the reason is clear. Instruction in religion encourages and aims at a public avowal of Christian faith and discipleship. Every church leader will confirm the fact that two persons, otherwise alike, will differ at the point of the possession of a great purpose. The dedication to a great cause, commitment to a program like the Kingdom of God, are secret keys to a different life. Conversion, commitment, and dedication, become central in the teaching objective of Christian education.

Contents of Instruction

What the church wishes to put into the lives of its members must first be put into the curriculum. The curriculum is in the main a complete cycle of subject matter and other content so arranged as to give to the pupil a correct approach and setting for instruction. It will consist of all the experiences that pupils have as they occur under the direction of the teacher.

The materials of the curriculum fall into three functional groups. The first group seeks to achieve solidarity of the group, and consists of confessions of faith, creeds, doctrines and church polity. Solidarity depends upon bringing about proper adjustments within the group. The second group seeks to provide Christian culture and enrichment, and consists of a division covering knowledge about Christianity, another covering Christian teachings on human relations, a third on cultural aspects of faith, and a fourth on source materials of faith. Included under these divisions are the life of Christ; church history; missions; Christian social relations like race, industry, international, and personal; Christian biographies; Christian art and hymnology; history of the Hebrews and neighboring peoples; oriental life and literature. The third group seeks to transform potentially efficient persons into persons of effective Christian living and consists of inspirational literature and practical helps in personal development.

Guided experience is educational and is a part of the curriculum. Expressional activity in its psychological meaning is a term long used for the term "guided experience." Its underlying philosophy holds that knowledge unrelated to life experiences has never been learned. Biblical knowledge, for example, unapplied affects no conduct, but may remain as an ungerminated seed in the mind until some later experience gives it life. Knowing the process, current education seeks through guidance to carry the pattern of experience in the material over into real experience. Three areas of experience split knowledge up into attitude patterns, skill patterns, and appreciation patterns. The first may be called the "core" curriculum, and includes those common experiences which all pupils are to have under the guidance of the teacher, without respect to individual differences. These are the basic learnings, such as respect for life and property, a right regard for the human body, the making of a living, and committing the life to the Christian Way. These are the attitudes of Christian culture. The second area may be called the skills curriculum, and includes experience in the use of tools of learning, and the development of techniques necessary for the achievement of the first group. The third area may be called the individual interest or appreciation area, and includes those experiences connected with the making of life choices. Chief among these choices will be the committment to Christ and the decision as to a life work.

Method in Instruction

Method is the way the materials and the setting are handled to bring about the educational aims. The best method as stated by the International Curriculum Guide Book is "that which efficiently brings about guidance of the learner's experience toward conduct centering in Christian ideals." This implies two principles in method; first, that all materials must be pupil directed; second, that effective learning grows out of specific life situations.

Pupil direction means that the Bible is taught for the sake of the child. Through it God is proclaiming his quest for that life. The method aims at the creation of a motive Godward, and Christian traits manward. Guidance of the learner's experience may be sought through the initiation of the learner into the experiences that the material used has preserved in its record. The manner of achieving this end belongs to methods.

"Specific life situations" means the experiencing of the lessons in daily conduct. The principles to be followed are: First, it must be realistic, not necessarily an actual situation, but one that is either real or imagined; second, it must be a situation offering two courses of action; third, the situation must be one in which the pupils will apply the teacher's lesson aim in making the choice.[2] In applying these laws several facts are of value. In the practice of the character traits the teacher should use all constructive agencies of society to make contribution to the training. The home, camps and character organizations get the finest results. Group activity is a powerful determinant in behavior. Closely knit groups, like gangs, clubs, troups, provide and utilize activity, and offer opportunity for democratic and Christian expression. Program making by the group is more effective than the standardized programs made for the group. The reason for this is that this method calls out initiative and cooperation, produces natural situations, and better enables the individual

[2] Findley B. Edge, *Teaching for Results* (Nashville: The Broadman Press, 1956), pp. 138-39.

to adjust to new situations. It is of special importance that the individual experience a sense of social adjustment in association with others. In such situations the learner faces problems in Christian life and faith, and determines a course of conduct.

EVANGELISM

Evangelism is the heart of the church. As popularly conceived it is often more of a theory than a necessity, perhaps a fetish more than a fact. Actually it is the core of the Christian faith and the most beautiful of Christian practices. Evangelism is a *purpose*. All teaching and guidance is toward a decision for Christ and the rule of Christ for character and conduct. It is a *spirit*. It is a spirit of continuing love to Christ, and wishing his love for others. Without being conscious of the set of the heart, it is governed daily by a passion for winning men to Christ. It is a *method*. The teacher, parent or minister simply needs some occasion or stimulus "to bring to a focus the impressions and crystallize the convictions" that yield consent.

Purpose of Evangelism

"There is a shallow evangelism," Dobbins observes, "that would seek primarily to add numbers to the membership of a church. Then there is an evangelism that stirs the emotions and leads to outward profession, but fails to anchor to Christ and his church. Again, there is dry-eyed intellectual evangelism that presents a system of doctrine and a standard of morals, but lacks power to translate creed and ethic into life. More common is warm-hearted, sensible, doctrinally sound evangelism that is inadequate because it is confined to a brief season of revival, and is not sufficiently preceded and followed by enlistment in service and nurture of the implanted life. We need for our day a vital evangelism — the living testimony of convincing Christians that Christ is able to save and keep and make strong and useful and happy all who come to God through him."[3] It is such an objective that the religious educator makes central in the program of the church. At least three phases of the purpose stand out as objectives in the program of evangelism.

First in the process of evangelism is implanting an understanding of the nature and purposes of God. "How shall they believe in him whom they have not heard?" (Rom. 10:14). In light of God's nature, sin, which is the root of all problems, stands revealed as uncleanness of life, as neglect of the source of thought and life, as dominant selfishness, as currently and ultimately spiritual death. All sin means suffering for God. In light of God's purposes the present day difficulties become channels of strength for turning difficulties into triumphs. Spiritually sensitive men discover a passion for teaching others the beauty and the joy of a life committed to Christ.

Second in the process of evangelism is the expectation of a decision by the individual to accept Christ as Savior. The aim of evangelism is not acquiring knowledge or opinion, but life. A spiritual awakening follows in the course of the "seasons of the soul." As such it is seldom experienced before full instinctive development has been attained, and its peak occurs in the period of maturing emotions. These conversion experiences differ with the mental experiences of the individual, depending upon the temperament of the individual, his childhood training, and the period of life. The church teacher or parent seeks to understand these conditions that he may secure a personal commitment of the life to God.

Third in the process of evangelism is the training to make Christ Lord in the life. This is the easiest and yet the most difficult; easy because there is a new and powerful motive for learning, and difficult because it must register in conduct and habit. Salvation cannot be a negative experience. It does not rest in belief or in going to church but in losing one's life in an absorbing cause. To forsake a pupil at conversion

[3] G. S. Dobbins, *A Winning Witness* (Nashville: Baptist Sunday School Board, 1938), p. 12.

is to offer God a dwarfed life. Full evangelism follows through to the full grown stature.

Content of Evangelism

Evangelism is a spirit, an attitude, a passion. It consists of sharing Christian convictions, of mastering the art of living, and of loving our neighbors with a Christlike devotion. Christian conviction is more than assent to a statement, it is a personal commitment to a person. Mastering the art of living is more than a good character, it is falling in love with God for life. Loving one's neighbors is more than sharing in the goods of life, it is an unquenchable and ceaseless concern for the neighbor himself.

The Christian convictions to be shared are that life's deepest needs have an answer, that human weakness has available an adequate strength, that life has a meaning, and that when understood this faith will be desired by our fellowmen. The answer is that captives of sin may be set free, that the gospel is for those who lack will power to master life except through Christ their dynamic, that men need not perish since God has provided abundance of life. Men who know these things, and pass them on will hear men answering back, "That is what I want."

Mastering the art of living is a Christian secret. The balanced life is Christ governed. Like the great flywheel of a factory that runs perfectly when on center, the Christian life runs smoothly and powerfully with Christ as center. It is when men regard the Christ as secondary that disaster ensues. Evangelism puts Christ in whom "all things hold together," at the heart of its message but its mission is not over until it has brought men to attain unto "the measure of the stature of the fulness of Christ."

Loving one's neighbors is evangelism. One of the strong proofs of the continuing life and presence of Christ is the Christlike life of his followers. When his disciples love one another they proclaim a living Lord. Loving one's neighbors is more than sentiment, it is a transforming force. It is a ceaseless concern for the neighbor that strengthens his weakness, rebukes his oppressors, protects him from his unsuspecting worst self, and interprets to him his highest values. Jesus commanded this love, and commended its accomplishments. "Inasmuch as ye did it unto one of these my brethren, even these least, ye did it unto me" (Matt. 25:40). A social gospel does not run ahead of a personal gospel, but it must follow after. Evangelism begins first as a brotherhood of religion, but its evangel spreads to include a religion of brotherhood.

Method of Evangelism

Method is the way the pupil learns the subject matter and not the way the teacher teaches it. That principle of instruction is applicable to evangelism. Method of evangelism then is the way the individual comes to accept Christ, and not the way some think he should accept him. The vital consideration is that the full evangelistic message shall be proclaimed, and that men shall be changed by what takes place in their lives.

The educational approach to evangelism seems to oppose revival evangelism to educational evangelism. On the contrary the whole of the program of the church has the evangelistic aim. Any apparent difference is in emphasis, educational evangelism emphasizing method, while revival evangelism emphasizes results. Educational evangelism and revival evangelism must recognize a mutual task. "There is no Christian education that leaves evangelism out," is Dobbins' way of declaring them inseparable. "It is foolish," he continues, "to put evangelism over against Christian education as if they were opposites. Evangelism is the end, Christian education is the means. — As well try to separate the seed from the soil and expect a crop as to separate evangelism from Christian education and expect a gospel harvest. Where Christian education has done its work well evangelism is made easier and its results more permanent."[4]

The continuous ministry of evangelism seeks in every way to win men to Christ. In the spirit of Paul who would

[4] *Ibid.*, p. 114.

be all things to all men that he might win some, the program of evangelism would use all spiritual methods with all men that it might win some. It would promote mass evangelism for the wider reaches of Christian influence, seasons of revival for the church school, units on evangelism for the class, and personal evangelism for individuals. One purpose runs through them all.

Mass Evangelism

Within the community mass evangelism would arrest and enlist the attention of the indifferent. Through advertising, bulletin boards, and posters the church would appeal to the worth of religion; to a consciousness of personal needs; to a desire to be a better parent and citizen. One church carries this message on a highway bulletin board, "It costs much to follow Christ, but it costs more not to follow him." In this way, and by the confidence churchmen inspire in the unchurched, by their unselfish community service, as well as by individual appeals to the Christian decision, pastor and people prepare for a season of intensive ingathering.

Seasons of Revival

Within the church seasons of revival will occur periodically as "decision" days, "win one" campaigns, as may be fitting. The pastor and the teacher have been doing the work of the evangelist. When the spirit of the Christ moves strongly in the hearts of the teachers and the pupils a season of revival will be set apart for the ingathering. The later childhood and earlier adolescent years will be particularly responsive to this method.

Units of Evangelism

Within the class units on evangelism may produce finest results among middle and later adolescents. The unit consists of a series of worthwhile experiences brought together around some interest. The principles of the unit stress direct learning rather than lesson learning, activities determined by present needs, the superiority of learning together rather

than individually, the value of first hand experience followed
by group discussion, and the securing of a complete adjustment to the environment. Jesus' experience with the woman
at the well (John 4) can become the basis of a unit on evangelism. Its ending is significant, "Many of the Samaritans
believed on him because of the word of the woman . . . and
many more believed because of his word" (John 4:39,41).
This method should prove most effective with the unchurched within the group.

Personal Evangelism

Personal evangelism is the method of Andrew who "find-
eth first his own brother Simon, and saith unto him, We have
found the Messiah" (John 1:41). Underlying all methods is
the man-to-man approach. Within the Church the Sunday
school teachers should be a select group to whom this service is committed as a special interest. No method will avail
apart from an evangelistic passion.

WORSHIP

Worship is not an opening exercise which permits any
procedure observing fair decorum. It is not good-fellowship
which requires only one test, that of good feeling and a spirit
of brotherliness. It is not preparation for a specific lesson,
which merely uses related hymns and scripture to introduce
the lesson facts, and express a spiritual sentiment. Worship
is spiritual reality. The hymns and prayers and scripture are
to produce a feeling of the presence of God. The place becomes a sanctuary. In this atmosphere the lesson becomes
the word of God.

Purpose of Worship

Historically worship re-enacts a drama of man's ways
and means of approaching God. Seeking the will of God,
propitiating an unsympathetic God, expressing gratitude for
favors, and endeavoring to discover any unity with God,
called for prescribed forms approved of God. Christ's answer to inquiring disciples removed feasts and ceremonies

for subjective worship. The hymns, and the sacred writings, and the prayers supplant the objective acts. The great liturgies have been called "the sifted devotions of the centuries." Their litanies "rehearse timeless perils and voice unescapable needs for deliverance."

Escape from reality is a major purpose of worship. Men are seeking a plain road away from the daily life to God. They are confused by the impotence of moral achievement. They are abashed by human pessimism. They are baffled by human problems. They seek escape from the toils and cares of life. They cry out from a sense of sin. Worship offers the answer to the human hungers. "My steps had well-nigh slipped . . . until I went into the sanctuary of God" (Ps. 73:2, 17a).

A sense of direction is another purpose of worship. Men are seeking the meaning of life, the purpose of existence. They plummet the depths of life to discover that only through the worship of a Supreme Being can the mystery of man be accounted for. The only answer to man's quest of direction lies in identification with the purposes of God.

Socialization is an objective of worship within the meaning of the Christian faith. Genuine worship is a school for mutual edification. "Forsake not the assembling of yourselves together" is more than a principle of congregation building. Churches that truly worship create and keep alive a beautiful spirit of fellowship. Fellowship in worship sets the spiritual pitch of brotherhood. Singing, praying, and working together in a sacred union nourishes a corporate sense in a congregation.

Vitalization as an objective in worship is suggested in Paul's experience, "I can do all things through Christ which strengthened me." One hour spent in worship does something to the spiritually sensitive akin to lifting one from a street level to the top of a high building. It gives vision and stirs a sense of power to achieve.

Communion is the highest objective of worship. Isaiah "saw the Lord, high and lifted up." His vision of God brought a confession of sinfulness. Confession brought fitness for service, and a commission to go in the Lord's name (Isa. 6).

That form or ceremony which does not eventuate in some sense of communion with God is a desecration.

Content of Worship

Worship is intended to be experienced. The media of worship — hymns, scripture, and prayer — are used because they are effective in producing experience. They are most effective when they have been born in experience. Hymns of greatest power were so born. Scripture came from hearts and hands that God had inspired with a sense of His reality. Effective prayer is made by men who know that God is real. Offerings that are worshipful outwardly express an inward acceptance of God's Lordship over all of life. No worship is complete that fails through these media to effect spiritual experience.

Scripture reading that suits the hearer's imagination must first stir the reader. Selections for public reading must possess qualities generally regarded as essential for effective reading. The reader must identify himself in spirit with the spirit of the passage and must read it as nearly as possible as it was originally read or spoken. The passage came out of intense life and worshipful reading will return it to intense listeners.

Prayer is the most intimate part of worship. In prayer the human spirit comes closest to the spirit of God. Prayer opens the mind to new insight into the will of God. It confesses sin and failure. It voices praise. It utters petitions. It bridges the gap between earth and heaven. In prayer a man is not spiritual as distinguished from intellectual and physical; he is all there is of him. He is offering to God all there is to give.

Music is a vitalizing part of worship. Paul advised the church at Corinth to check their growing coldness by singing psalms and hymns and spiritual songs. Hymns create an atmosphere of spiritual reality. They arouse congregational interest in the common faith, and enhearten Christians in the midst of suffering and disappointment. They stir a passion for the Christian conquest against fear and iniquity.

They teach men the staunch doctrines of faith more truly than through instruction. Worshippers sing the hymns of experience to reproduce a kindred faith.

The *offering* or giving as an act of worship has been neglected. The Corinthians thought of it as practical rather than spiritual. The tragedy of the churches is the travesty of cajoling church people into giving and presenting it as a duty rather than a spiritual exercise. Correct conceptions of stewardship will make the act of giving an act of worship. It is an act of consecration, and consecration is the final step in worship. "Here am I Lord, send me."

Method in Worship

The problem in worship is to help people in their quest for God, and to work with God in approaching the individual. Certain processes have been found invaluable in establishing this contact. There must be spiritual motivation; there must be spiritual sensitiveness; there must be creative experience, as men are brought into a sense of communion with God. Method must find the way. Method must not only tell men to pray, but must tell them how to pray.

The technique employed in securing a sense of reality in worship seeks three experiences in the individual — release, union, and power. Release means consent or the shaking off of a theoretical will, a subduing of the mind into a channel of contemplation. No one can come into a mystical union with God who reserves his will for wandering or for criticism. This consent comes on at least two conditions, first that the truth of the media for worship conforms to the truth of the worshiper's experience, and second that the agent in worship shall be thoroughly sincere in his ministrations. The second experience is union or communion, which becomes so after release, provided the power of suggestion of the media and of the ministrant continues uninterruptedly to a climax. A third experience is power, which follows a sense of communion with the Divine. It is a sense of confidence or victory that comes to one who knows that the strength of God fills out his own strength. "I have seen the Lord," and "I can do all things through Him which strengtheneth me" express the sequence that inspires invincible power.

STEWARDSHIP

Great religious programs can never be realized until churchmen develop some greatness in their own souls. To this end the churches stress the training of men in the habit of Christian living. Training in church membership and leadership are but phases of the larger activity which the church fosters as stewardship.

Stewardship has meant to many the securing of money rather than the meaning and use of money. Church officials too often have looked at the pledge rather than at the pledger. Church offerings too often have been forced collections, sometimes accompanied with ribald buffoonery and the implication, "We need the money." Canvassers for church expenses have measured their success by the total money raised. Church societies have been judged and praised by the money they can produce. Little concern seems to be felt for the growth of each member in the grace of giving.

The new stewardship emphasis goes deeper than the legalistic accounting to God in Malachi and the motive of "proving God." Stewardship was made by Christ a spiritual principle. Living beneath a stewardship life is poverty of spirit. Stewardship is a way of life that finds its deepest meaning in "the potentialities of human personality." "I came that ye might have life and have it more abundantly." A steward is a new type of person.

Objectives of Stewardship

While stewardship of time, of influence, of talents, and of possessions are specific practice areas for individual development, the real issue in stewardship lies in the relation of the individual to the material things of life. The work of religious education must come vitally to grips with the Christian's relationship to material things.

Practical objectives of stewardship have been well stated

by J. E. Dillard: "(1) The acknowledgment of God's ownership of all things; (2) the acceptance of what we are and have as a trust from God; and (3) the administration of the same according to the will of God for the good of mankind."[5]

Stewardship of Money

The motives of stewardship appear to be a trustee recognition of God's ownership, a duty to support the Kingdom of God, a sharing for the sake of human personality, and a corrective for spiritual poverty. The first emphasizes God's right to exact a portion as man's debt for the use of materials with which he makes a living. The second emphasizes the human regard for a proportionate part in maintaining a corporate organization working to establish the Kingdom of God. The third emphasizes the love born of Christ which prompts the relief of human suffering and want. They emphasize the value to the individual of sharing as a counteractive to covetousness, through which man comes into self-identification with the needs of the world and with the purposes of God.

Tithing, with all of its values, may not do more than pay a debt without recognizing all that is implied in God's ownership. The motive for tithing may be merely a profit motive, against which the church is educating. The motive for generous giving of substance and of self is the love of God. This motive causes men to suffer in the face of human suffering because it causes God to suffer. Depravity causes them to agonize, and covetousness causes them to grieve because they cause God agony and grief. In this spirit tithing may be stewardship and not legalism.

Supporting the work of the church with money is stewardship. Selling things "for the church" destroys self-respect and beggars Christ. A disproportionate budget between the local church and outside causes dishonors stewardship. The building of character in its expanding interests is the object of proportionate giving for church support. System in the

[5] J. E. Dillard, *Building a Stewardship Church* (Nashville: The Broadman Press, 1946), pp. 16–17.

Christian life, an understanding of the objects of support and the reason for supporting them, broaden the Christian horizon. That is stewardship.

Stewardship of Life

Sharing possessions because of the worth of human personality is stewardship. Christ went to the cross to give the fullest and the richest life to every man. When Christians share this purpose with him the worth of human life becomes spiritual. The tragedy of the church is the poverty of the budget for those without a chance, and the generosity of the budget for selfish interests. Christians will share when they care, and they will care when they see human life through the eyes of Jesus. This will be stewardship.

Full and complete Christian living is stewardship. As long as the main drive in the life of a man is economic he cannot experience the full spirit of Christ. "My business is serving the Lord," said a successful shoe manufacturer, "I make shoes for a living." He knew its meaning. Paulsen[6] summed up this truth pungently, "know one's attitude toward the meaning and use of money, you need not be told about his manner of life." He explains that "until money, economic power, property, things, are regarded solely in the light of the worth of human personality and administered for the upbuilding of the life of the individual and society, we are not and cannot be Christlike."

Method of Stewardship

Stewardship is brought about through building attitudes, ideals, and habits of life. The main concern is what the gift does to the Christian. That is a matter of diligent training. Along with educational practice three methods have been suggested by Christian workers — participation in program making, group discussion, and worshipful giving.

Participation in program making becomes a motive in Christian living when it is related to a life need, or comes within the range of individual experience. Lack of concern

[6] Irwin G. Paulsen, *It Is To Share* (Cincinnati: Methodist Book Concern, 1931).

about the financial support of the church occurs when the member does not know where the money goes or how it is spent. Educational method in stewardship training suggests that the individual supports objects within his interest; that he be given full knowledge of what the object is and why it is supported; and that he might be given some part in making out the budget for the sake of developing loyalty to the obligations that have no glamor. By this method the budget grows, but better still the individual increases in the spirit of liberality as his knowledge of need widens.

Group discussion shares ideas and experiences. Facts gleaned by one member will stimulate the thinking and purpose of others. For young people and adults a series of discussions in the pulpit or at the round table on the philosophy and activities of stewardship will be helpful. Investigations of local community, church or mission needs, followed by discussions of the findings would stimulate the budget and the member.

Worshipful giving brings the experience of meeting human needs into the purposes of God. To pray about an object of stewardship enables each person to see it from God's point of view. It may reveal a Christian in caricature. What the offering does for the giver is far more important than what it is used for. Training to give to God, with full knowledge of the human need relieved, will make for "abundant life on the Christian basis."

QUESTIONS FOR DISCUSSION

1. Why are activities an essential part of the religious educational process? Why is instruction necessary?

2. What are some basic theological facts which must be included in the instructional activities?

3. Give a complete definition of evangelism. What are the character-building values of evangelism to the soul-winner?

4. Describe some sane methods of evangelism.

5. Observe assembly programs in three different age groups. Was there an adequate element of worshipful response? Was there participation by the group?

6. Discuss tithing as the minimum expression of Christian stewardship.

CHAPTER 12

LEADERSHIP

However important it may be to select efficient personnel for the rank and file of any organization it is far more important to place excellent men and women in positions of high authority. An efficient executive can produce good results from the work of mediocre associates, but an incompetent executive will nullify the ability of the best of men. Objectives and curriculum may be ever so good but they fail to achieve their ends in the hands of a leader who has no skill in translating them into human faith and conduct.

The strategic importance of leadership is most evident when a change of officers occurs in an organization. A triennial turnover of 400,000 teachers in one large denomination, for example, contains serious implications. Every department suffers in function and spirit. Every removal from leadership means that "production" suffers until a successor is found. Time is lost in securing a successor. Efficiency in other workers is reduced by the extra load. Loss results in the time consumed in training a new man. Lacking experience or being incompetent the new man fails in production results. The new worker is an experiment and if he proves totally unfit for the place, may thus force a repetition of the whole process.

Change and inefficiency are hindrances to the Kingdom of God.

DEFINITION

Ask three persons for a definition of leadership and there may be three different answers. One associates leadership with power. He has discovered in himself an unusual capacity for imposing his will upon others and prides himself upon his ability to bend the wills of his fellows. Another associates leadership with position. He has discovered his ability to govern men by his control over their economic status, by his social or industrial position, or by other connections. He finds satisfaction in using his advantage for securing desired ends. Still another identifies leadership with ability to inspire men. He finds within himself a conviction as to some course in life and knows the way to its achievement. He discovers that the earnestness of his faith in the value of the venture arouses in others a similar passion. When great crises confront men and heroic action is the way out, true leadership becomes the privilege of men who can inspire a movement.

A leader is one who has an answer to the problems of human need. He is able to show people how they are benefited by a specific course, and convinces them that they want that end. His integrity and ability to perform elicit their allegiance. Leadership consists of putting into operation a plan for the solution of a problem, and that through inspiring the group who must undertake and achieve the specific objective. Ordway Tead defines leadership as "the activity of influencing people to cooperate toward some goal which they come to find desirable."[1] Leadership is interested in how people can be brought to work together effectively and happily for a common end. Such a leader is not only interested in the result, but also in the process by which the result is attained.

The latter conception of leadership prevails in the work of the church. The intimacy of the relationship in a church, the

[1] Ordway Tead, *The Art of Leadership* (New York: McGraw-Hill Book Co., Inc., 1935), p. 20.

delicacy of the process of education in morals and religion, and the voluntary nature of the service makes it imperative that the leader understand this meaning of leadership. The selection, training, and support of every leader in the church field presupposes this conception of his task.

NATURE

There is a difference between an executive and a leader. The executive may be successful as a producer or organizer but a failure as a leader. Organizations need an executive who can plan and define policies and procedures, who can organize the activities of others, and who can coordinate the efforts of a large number of workers. In more recent times it is being discovered that organizations need another phase of direction, that of stimulating and vitalizing the individuals who make up the organization. Human energies can be combined in ways which create personal harmony in working together, and which can be tuned up to develop multiplied power in production. The attainment of this result is the function of leadership.

Experience justifies the leader type of executive. In spite of the method of elevation to leadership, whether by democratic selection, selection by those in power, or by individual energy and self-reliance, permanence in leading will depend upon the recognition of the human element in the process. The leader must be accepted before he can lead effectively. He must inspire confidence in himself and in the direction of his efforts. He must recognize his dependence upon those who are led, for Jesus taught men that those who would lead must be servants of all. The leadership of the general is proved when the war is won. The leadership of teachers of youth is proved when boys and girls grow into strong Christian men and women.

This type of leadership is particularly important in religion and its educational processes. Unfortunately untrained men sometimes come into executive positions and in their lack of training for leadership resort to domination or subterfuge. They assume that the end justifies the means and do not hesitate to use any method necessary to obtain their ends. In so doing they destroy personality and suffer other results that come from broken laws. When the appeal is made to fear, hate, anger, greed, suspicion, the personality is integrated outside the circle drawn by Jesus, who made love central. The real leader, however, stands out in front and calls the crowd to follow in a noble cause. To achieve moral ends, the desires and the motives of the followers must be aroused, directed, and released. It is the challenge to do something important which the good leader brings.

In describing the task of educational leadership in the church school, Nevin C. Harner sets forth the following educational functions for the leader:

1. He will interpret the privilege and task of religious education to the entire congregation. . . . One test of his success at the end of five or ten years is whether or not the members of this religious community are more alive now than they were when he came.

2. He will vitalize the congregation's program of religious education as a whole, and organize it as a unit.

3. He will vitalize the major educational agencies within the congregation. . . . He is a fertile source of suggestions for curriculums, programs and plans. . . . In a meeting of lay-workers he is the catalytic agent. . . .

4. He will procure, train and inspire leaders . . . because in the final analysis the better day in religious education waits so much upon equipment or programs as upon people.

5. He will participate directly at necessary and strategic places in the program of religious education . . . and without being labeled as such, they [his public appearances] can become useful demonstrations of materials and methods to the advantage of the lay leadership of the congregation.[2]

ART OF LEADERSHIP

The task of influencing others requires consummate skill in creating desires, in stirring motives, and in guiding action. There is an art in bringing people to work together. It has been called "the fine art of living together." There is an art in producing generated power. There is an art in making

[2] Nevin C. Warner, in Philip H. Lotz (ed.), *Orientation in Religious Education* (Nashville: Abingdon Press, 1950), pp. 387-89.

people want to do something creative and doing it because they love the task. There is an art in building an *esprit de corps* in a church group whose intellectual, economic, and social levels differ widely. Like other arts leadership in religion has well established techniques, which are available for the Christian leaders.

Rules of Leadership

There is no excuse for church leaders to stumble over barriers when the problem is merely one of applying the rules of an art. A few of the accepted rules may be of help.

The leader must win the confidence of his followers. This means confidence in his character, his honesty of purpose, his sincerity of life, his knowledge of the task, and his ability to achieve. Lack of confidence in him at any point destroys his usefulness as a leader, particularly of one in church activities.

The leader must convince the followers that his objectives are reasonable and attainable. The leader achieves "only as he is in a situation where those he leads can achieve." A hopeless quest arouses no enthusiasm.

The leader will seek to arouse from within impulses and efforts which the follower accepts as "self-creative self-expression." There is a human resource in a sense of unity of personality and performance in which men realize themselves. The proof of leadership is in the group of those who are led. The individual must discover that the leader has done something to him rather than for him. The leader is an inspirer of men.

The leader who would continue to lead must help a group "to get what it wants with the least friction and the most sense of unity and self-realization." Aims have an appeal when they help people to attain something they deeply desire. The leader must know human nature. Everyone wishes to be somebody and objectives based on this motive will produce action. The self of each follower must be served in some way. The skill required to secure social action of a group will include sharing in control and sharing in results.

The leader should be a comrade, not a boss. The power of leadership is not the leader's alone. It is his power to line up others with him to get a project put through. Arrogance, pride of place, or selfish grasping of power defeats the leader. Humility of spirit takes the helper into the task, as together they labor for a common end. All the things that have any meaning for life keep their inner secret for the shared vision. There is a penalty back of the law which we break at our peril. The resources for creative living are conditioned by, and dependent upon, our right relations with others. The outstanding "lag" is in the region of human relationship.

The leader who is undaunted in inspiring faith in others should practice the presence of God. In every age the men who have lead great religious movements have been mystics. They have had definite fellowship with God. They are convinced of God's leadership and of their part in His plans.

SELECTING LEADERS

It makes a tremendous difference in personality as to who associates with the child and gives him his social inheritance during the early years. If unworthy leaders are followed it is very likely that their followers will have the same characteristics. Good leaders will produce good fruit, evil leaders will produce bad fruit. Personality is formed early in life from the ideals present. The person who seems to the child to be strongest in every way is his ideal. Likewise the child's ideal is the person who develops in him the greatest admiration and affection. It is therefore of great concern that the leader meets certain personal qualifications.

Characteristics

Qualities expected in a leader in the church are those expected of leaders in other relations, plus the added quality of spiritual awareness. Old Testament heroes revealed definite traits of physical prowess, a strong sense of direction, a contagious enthusiasm, personal integrity, and an unconquerable faith in their God. The New Testament leaders, Peter and Paul, were cast in the same heroic mould. Outstanding qualities essential in a church leader of the immature are physical attractiveness, intelligence, temperament, and character. The teacher's temperament and his character occupy the chief place.

Physical attractiveness is primary, though not indispensable. One person vitalizes another. Something happens to another when such a person enters his presence. A leader's energy passes over to his followers. Physical vitality is basic in getting work done. The effect of a strong or weak teacher's mood in a school room is instantaneous. Nervous disorders, irritability, weariness for example defeat the work of a teacher. Christians who have tried to impress their religiosity upon others by their long-faced attitudes have failed. Jesus advised those who fasted against acquiring a sad countenance. Good health, zest, affection, on the other hand, are immediately reflected in the behavior of the room. Their presence at the beginning of the day assures a happy day. Their absence torments teacher and child alike.

Intelligence is important, but not indispensable. Some of the finest results have been achieved by uneducated men who were sincere and possessed practical common sense. The selection of leaders must give attention to more than intelligence. The ultimate test of a teacher is the character development of the pupil. Many Sunday school workers have possessed personal and spiritual qualities which have overcome any lack of technical and professional preparation. This quality, however, is to be sought as important.

Temperament is more important than intelligence. An even disposition, a sympathetic nature, an optimistic outlook, are requisites of successful leadership. One type of teacher exalts knowledge of the subject matter. The other type loves the child supremely. The old idea that a mastery of subject matter insures good teaching has been exploded. But it will ever be true that the teacher who loves the child and possesses these qualities will secure large spiritual results in spite of technique. Other things being equal, choose the man of heart.

Character stands above the other qualifications for leadership. Men of unethical character often appear more attractive than some who are ethically correct. Men of strong endowment and great energy often break the commandments and yet appear more attractive than some who keep all the commandments. Yet the stability of society depends upon moral integrity. There is much false thinking at this point. The gentler type is often strong in his resources of life, and most of the immoral are far from admirable. Character consists not so much in external behavior as in strength and unselfishness of life. Paul climaxes the demand of character, "be strong in the Lord, and in the strength of his might" (Eph. 6:10). No character is complete that lacks a strong undergirding of faith in God.

Willingness to train is the final major demand. In general the ideal is a culture as broad as Christian truth, an attitude toward the social order that is thoroughly Christian, and a training that provides for adequate leadership. Training includes an understanding of religious objectives, a fair knowledge of the content of instruction, knowledge of human nature and the processes of learning, familiarity with the principles of administration, and the techniques involved. Since these needs will not be found ready made, it becomes a duty to train for the job. If one has a willingness to learn he will follow the outlines proposed for the training of lay and professional leaders.

TRAINING LEADERS

The fate of Christianity does not depend on the priesthood but on the laity. The genius of the Christian churches is the mobilization of vast armies of volunteer leaders. Professional leadership is necessarily limited by the prohibitive cost. Laymen must be depended upon for the bulk of leadership. The training of professional leaders will be cared for largely by the graduate universities and seminaries. The task of the churches is the provision for an adequate training of the associates in service.

H. G. Wells has well said that devices for making good teachers out of mediocre individuals will have to be multiplied. The churches have recognized this need and are supplying the devices. Three plans for training leaders are offered: the apprentice plan, the in-service or "shop" plan, and the collegiate plan.

The *apprentice plan* embraces a combination of study and practice. Study covers a period beginning preferably with entrance into the young people's department of the church. The need for maturity in the delicate process of religious education makes it desirable to spend these later adolescent years in study, with occasional practice, rather than on assignment to teaching posts. Elective courses may be introduced in the department for prospective teachers. Such courses would include the history and objectives of the church, the source materials of our religion, the Bible, hymns, biographies of ancient and modern leaders. During the apprenticeship stage the individual will study, observe, help, and occasionally practice under supervision. The aim will be to keep a fair balance between technical mastery and the personal fitting of the individual for effective leadership. This method requires careful selection of apprentices and opportunities to practice. The promotion to assistant positions will come naturally and full responsibility will eventually arrive.

The teacher *in service* requires a distinct plan of training. The rapid development of knowledge of human nature and techniques in teaching makes a static policy tragic. Children are subjected to skillful learning processes in their grammar or high schools. The disparity in methods used by the two schools registers against their Sunday school teacher and against their church. Their loyalties become uneven. An unfavorable incidental learning has been harmful. To correct this situation definite planning must be done. State schools pursue such a course with great satisfaction. Churches are meeting with good results through their teacher training schools, institutes, conferences, assemblies, professional teachers' organizations, summer courses, local church surveys, visitations, self-rating scales, reading courses, and the use of departmental supervisors. The most difficult problem of the "shop" plan is that of reaching the "top leadership" of the church.

The *collegiate plan* rests on the fundamental assumption that modern churches wish to lift their leadership above mediocrity. Experience in public schools, agriculture, pharmacy, medicine, and other areas of interest has established the value of college training for their leaders. Public school men have urged for many years that Sunday school teachers "should have all the general scholarship and professional training required of public school teachers." The curriculum in the Christian college should definitely accept responsibility for preparing students for church leadership as well as for civic leadership, to teach in church schools as well as in public schools.

Advanced teacher training should be a definite feature of a Christian college. The cream of the church's potential leadership is in the colleges. Students are leadership conscious and responsive to college guidance. The college years provide time for unhurried and thorough courses. A certain degree of supervision is possible during the college years. The place of the teacher takes on a new dignity when the college handles the training. There is a broader training possible through wider contacts and varied observational privileges. Utilizing the college years in this way ties the student to his church purposes and returns him ready to lead. Churches look to the "new crop" of college students graduating into their communities to fill the teaching and leadership ranks of the churches and the community welfare agencies. The collegiate plan saves them disappointment. This is the chief function of the department of religious education in the Christian college.

DEMAND FOR TRAINED LEADERS

Churches, like industry and government, are awaking to the superiority of skilled workmen. In one of the larger Southern cities several of the strong churches are combing the city for men and women whose training qualifies them for teaching positions. Sunday school superintendents are as rare as church organists and strong churches will bring to bear all pressure possible for securing the congregational affiliation of a desirable prospect. City religious organizations seeking to

offer parallel instruction to city school children are faced with
the problem of enlisting qualified teachers.

Reasons for the Demand

Men are discovering that a properly trained leader secures better response and cooperation of fellow-workers. A
sense of unity of purpose in a common enterprise produces a
community of action. Even the Jerusalem church discovered
that the laying down of dogmatic schedules for the control of
their Gentile members was producing discord and disunion.
The policy of conference and cooperation saved Christianity
for Europe and the New World. This is supremely true in
conducting a modern church.

The demand further arises out of the current philosophy
that personality results are superior to the material output.
Industry is magnifying the spirit of the worker, the human
element, as the inescapable mark of a good business. Their
vital problem is "how to make group activity a happy and
satisfying experience for people." For such management only
those skilled in the personalistic philosophy of leadership
need apply. From industry the church is taking its cue as it
recognizes in its objective the personal spiritual values to be
sought in every organization within the church, in every
class, and in every lesson. None but the trained leader can
weave the pattern into the fabric.

A still further demand for trained leaders has arisen as a
result of the use of large numbers of untrained workers. They
lack basic knowledge of subject matter and correct ways of
procedure. They have no experience in interpreting even their
own faith and they certainly have no experience in aiding
another to arrive at satisfying experiences. The scar left by
such malpractice on a human personality is ineradicable. But
the fact remains that the teacher recruit must be used. The
church lives under a moral obligation to develop them into
more skillful leaders.

It is likewise true that the personal needs of the recruited
leader demand a trained leadership. Young Christians may be
made or marred in their initial effort in serving the Kingdom

of God. A wise superintendent of a county high school confided to a friend that his heaviest duties concerned the adjustment and guidance of beginning teachers. Permitting defeats to occur, or wrong teaching habits to be formed during the first weeks in the schoolroom, would mean the fixation of inferiority complexes and in some cases the utter ruin of a teacher. The church can do no less for its recruits than offer the same encouragement, counsel, and instruction that this superintendent gave daily to his staff. Love for the church, love for the people, love for guidance of youth in character and in faith, a more intense love for God, may be at stake in their initial effort in Christian service. There is a growing demand by churches for leaders whose training qualifies them for this exalted ministry.

Supplying the Demand

Long time planning for leaders will begin with teaching men the spiritual value of their vocation. Any clash between one's vocation and his spiritual self-expression ends in a hollow, unreal, spiritual life. Through one's vocation there should be the fullest expression of his personality. The business or profession should be a means of helping fulfill God's purpose of creating a happier world.

Long time planning for leadership will impress upon Christian laymen the urgency of training for service. A frightful waste in Kingdom economy results from the fallacious reasoning of innumerable young people that any preparation for Christian leadership is only for ministers and missionaries. A young student hesitated to enter a college Bible class with scholarly aims on the ground that he did not need more than a general knowledge about the Bible, comparable to a cultured person's knowledge of Shakespeare. Since these youths plan to study medicine or law or business they think that spending a few hours in religious study is more than a waste of time. Sensing this situation, the Latter Day Saints require of their young converts an internship in Christian service. Christian churches are allowing their "acres of diamonds" to lie undiscovered and permit vast power to go unharnessed when they permit the impression to continue that only professional workers need training.

Training for lay leadership implies a twofold obligation. The first is the obligation of the church to impress upon Christian youth the logic of placing the Kingdom of God first in one's life work. The other consists of teaching them. No medically minded youth should leave his church or his college without having settled the question that his practice of medicine is a ministry for Christ. Likewise the other professions and businesses should be so interpreted. The second objective of parent and pastor, and of college authorities, should be the completion of, or some achievement in, training for Christian leadership. Until the Christian colleges consciously accept this as a major function the work of Christianizing the world will go forward haltingly.

The church must revise its recruiting tactics. Efforts are usually limited to filling up the ranks of the salaried vocations in church organizations. The mission of the church does not preclude a call for dedication to Christian medicine or law. The traditional emphasis on the ministry or mission fields only has implied a release of church concern from the other vocations and possibly justified the impression that all other callings, professions, and businesses belonged to the world, and should be conducted by the rules of the world. The test of a spiritual ministry in a church rests in the number of men and women who have carried into their business life a conviction that their business is their witness to the reality of religion.

Vocational guidance is a church and college responsibility. Pastors should prepare themselves to advise youth in the selection of callings congenial to the Christian life. They need a ready knowledge of the general principles underlying the various professions and life callings. The rapid multiplication of vocations confuses youth and opens the way for a helpful ministry. The Christian college offers a major opportunity to pastor and professor. Pastors will be serving well when they encourage the young people from their churches to pursue training in religious education as a preparation for leadership. No student should be graduated from such a college who has not faced two decisions, namely, to make his vocation Christian, and to devote his service to the organized work of the church. Understanding the demands of the ministry and other Christian agencies he will know whether his best service can be directed through any of these channels.

Employing the Workers

Remuneration is a determining factor in deciding one's life work. Many capable youths are willing to forego the social prestige afforded by more lucrative employment and undergo necessary training for the church if they know that a living wage can be had. Many graduates have trained for public school positions who wished to devote themselves to religious leadership because the church offers no employment while the state does. The number of "pay jobs" appears disconcertingly small. The church needs trained leaders in every department and is now employing many kinds of trained workers. In view of this situation the church must enlarge the scope of its salaried positions. Under present institutional conditions this is right and necessary. The church must view such service as a ministry. Such a ministry is as truly related to the ultimate purpose of the church as is the preaching ministry. For such service the church and the individual must urge the necessity of adequate training. Anything less than adequacy will incur the reproach of every other human organization which has magnified a trained leadership.

The church job puzzles the youth. What is there to do within the church? Diverse types of service in religious organization may be classified as the ministry, missions, educational, promotional, secretarial, character forming, literary, and social service.

The Ministry

This service to which men traditionally have been called will continue its function of awakening the consciences of men. Intelligent young men of prophetic mind and passionate souls will find an uncrowded field. The broader the culture and the deeper the scholarship, the wider the opportunity for service.

The Mission Fields

Since Jesus commissioned his disciples to cover the earth with his gospel there has never lacked either opportunity or resource for men and women who have capacity for interpreting one cult to another. Pauline capacities would be welcomed. To interpret Christ to pagan and nonevangelical life, to interpret Christ to internationalism, to interpret Christ to questing minds and hearts, places the foreign missionary in a strategic position. The channels of service are many: evangelism, teaching, medicine, social service, character-building agencies, physical education, literature. The home fields open service to foreigners, negroes, underprivileged, unevangelized, rural life, industrial life. "The harvest is white and the laborers are few."

Educational Ministry

All education is technically a mission service. Educational directors and ministers of music are in demand by an increasingly large number of strong churches. Combinations of smaller churches form a "field" as in the ministry. Cities employ directors for denominations or for cooperating denominations. Colleges will continue to employ professors of Bible and religious education, with a staff of field workers as advisors and extension service men. Professorships in related fields are open to trained men in religion, and all Christian college professors should possess a background of such preparation. Denominations employ highly trained men and women for teaching and for student leadership positions in state and privately controlled colleges and universities.

Promotional Agencies

These include denominational and other boards, field staffs, survey agencies, clinicians, financial canvassing. Most of the positions require highly technical skill.

Secretarial Work

Secretarial work offers service opportunities to persons of administrative talents. Many boards and many churches employ executives of differing degrees of capacity. While widely different in type they are classified together for convenience.

Character Forming Agencies

Character forming agencies employ vast numbers of more or less technically trained men and women. The Young Men's and the Young Women's Christian Associations, the Boy and the Girl Scouts, Sunday School Councils, employ a wide range of talents to care for their management, physical, educational, health, camping, community center, and foreign work. Specialized training is required for the important positions.

Literary Positions

Editorial work in preparing lesson materials, denominational newspapers, the writing of books, open important positions to qualified individuals. Some of the literary work is produced in related professions, but there is a demand for permanent employment in certain departments.

Social Service

Social service is a growing profession. Within and without the church there are influential and far-reaching positions open to qualified persons. Welfare and uplift agencies, governmentally supervised work with underprivileged groups, relief workers, playground and recreational centers, employ large numbers of individuals, but favor the trained applicants.

Leadership lies at the base of the whole structure of a Christian society and of the Kingdom of God. Purposeful planning of the churches will include a program of recruiting which begins with the child and continues through the college. Scotch Presbyterians have helped predestination by holding constantly before their sons the ideal of the Christian ministry. The ideal of Christian service needs prominence in every household and in every church. The college is the harvesting floor. Jesus set the example as he struck conviction into their souls with his invitation, "Follow me, and I will make you fishers of men." Jesus pointed out the way as he trained with care the twelve, and at the end bade them, "Go ye into all the world — preach — teach — and lo I am with you." An intelligent passion for the reign of God among men will assure the needed leadership for tomorrow.

QUESTIONS FOR DISCUSSION

1. Make a study of the changes in leadership in your Sunday school. What percentage of your teachers and officers have served in their present capacity more than one year? Less than one year? How many teachers has each class in the Intermediate Department had during the past year?

2. Describe the program for teacher improvement in your local church.

3. What percentage of this year's graduating class of your college have credit for at least one course in religious education in addition to the Bible requirements?

4. How many courses in religious education are offered by your college?

Part II
BIBLIOGRAPHY

BERNHARDT, KARL S. *Practical Psychology.* New York: McGraw-Hill Book Co., Inc., 1953.

BETTS, GEORGE H., and HAWTHORNE, MARION O. *Methods in Teaching Religion.* Nashville: Abingdon Press, 1925.

BRECKENRIDGE, MARIAN E. and VINCENT, E. LEE. *Child Development.* Philadelphia: W. B. Saunders Co., 1955.

CHAVE, ERNEST J. *A Functional Approach to Religious Education.* Chicago: University of Chicago Press, 1947.

CROW, LESTER D. and ALICE. *Understanding Our Behavior.* New York: Alfred A. Knopf, Inc., 1956.

Curriculum Committee, Division of Christian Education. *A Guide for Curriculum in Christian Education.* New York: National Council of Churches in the U.S.A., 1955.

DALE, EDGAR. *Audio-Visual Methods in Teaching.* New York: Dryden Press, rev. ed. 1954.

EDGE, FINDLEY B. *Teaching for Results.* Nashville: The Broadman Press, 1956.

FAUNCE, ROLAND C. and BOSSING, NELSON L. *Developing the Core Curriculum.* New York: Prentice-Hall, Inc., 1951.

GWYNN, J. M. *Curriculum Principles and Social Trends.* New York: The Macmillan Co., rev. ed. 1957.

GWYNN, PRICE H., JR. *Leadership Education in the Local Church*. Philadelphia: Westminster Press, 1952.

JAARSMA, C. R. *Fundamentals in Christian Education*. Grand Rapids: Eerdmans Publishing Co., 1953.

JENKINS, GLADYS G. and OTHERS. *These Are Your Children*. Chicago: Scott, Foresman & Co., rev. ed. 1953.

JERSILD, ARTHUR T. *Child Psychology*, 4th edition. Englewood Cliffs, N. J.: Prentice-Hall, Inc., 1954.

_____. *The Psychology of Adolescence*. New York: The Macmillan Co., 1957.

JOHNSON, PAUL E. *Personality and Religion*. Nashville: Abingdon Press, 1957.

_____. *Psychology of Religion*. Nashville: Abingdon Press, 1945.

KINGSLEY, HOWARD R. and GARRY, RALPH. *The Nature and Conditions of Learning*. 2nd edition. Englewood Cliffs, N. J.: Prentice-Hall, Inc., 1957.

KUHLEN, RAYMOND B. *The Psychology of Adolescent Development*. New York: Harper and Bros., 1952.

LOTZ, PHILIP H. (ed.). *Orientation in Religious Education*. Nashville: Abingdon Press, 1950.

MILLER, RANDOLPH CRUMP. *Education for Christian Living*. Englewood Cliffs, N. J.: Prentice-Hall, Inc., 1956.

MORSE, W. C. and WINGO, G. MAX. *Psychology and Teaching*. Chicago: Scott Foresman & Co., 1955.

OATES, WAYNE E. *Religious Dimensions of Personality*. New York: Association Press, 1957.

SCHORLING, RALEIGH and BATCHELDER, HOWARD T. *Student Teaching in Secondary Schools*. New York: McGraw-Hill Book Co., Inc., 1956.

STONE, L. JOSEPH and CHURCH, JOSEPH. *Childhood and Adolescence*. New York: Random House, 1957.

TEAD, ORDWAY. *The Art of Leadership*. New York: McGraw-Hill Book Co., Inc., 1935.

WITHERINGTON, H. C. *Psychology of Religion*. (A Christian Interpretation.) Grand Rapids, Mich.: Wm. A. Eerdmans Publishing Co., 1955.

Part III

RELIGIOUS EDUCATION IN THE CHURCH

CHAPTER 13

THE SUNDAY SCHOOL

The complex patterns of modern life have created situations which call for the practice of Christian principles in every area of life. Not since the Protestant Reformation has there been such widespread intellectual, moral, and religious unrest. Customs, beliefs, and all social institutions are being critically examined for their values in the solution of present-day problems. Some institutions are being discarded. New ideas of the world, of God, of man, and of life's values are being widely disseminated by press, radio, and television. Today's world makes it imperative that the church arise and meet the needs of the changing times with the challenging truth of God's Word.

Now more than ever it is being realized that the Sunday school is a most valuable channel of righteous living. Its value in teaching the way of life has been described in these statements by leaders in many fields:

J. Edgar Hoover, Director of the Federal Bureau of Investigation of the United States Government, says: "I urge our people to place their children in Sunday school as a preventive of crime."

Roger Babson, noted statistician and economist, says, "There never was a time in the history of our nation when the Sunday school was so much needed."

Calvin Coolidge said: "The Sunday school is of inestimable benefit in providing a higher type of citizenship."

Theodore Roosevelt said: "When I was a young man I not only attended but taught in a Sunday school. I hope the pupils I taught were helped. I know it helped me."

Religious instruction now depends more largely on the Sunday school than any other agency of the church. Few homes give their children any vital religious teaching today. The Bible has been eliminated from the public schools. The Sunday school reaches more than twice as many people as any other agency for teaching religion. The churches in America have depended largely upon the Sunday school, which in great measure has been responsible for their very existence. The multiple and varied interests of life make it necessary for the churches to promote the Sunday school as the chief agency for reaching the untaught multitudes and guiding them in practical Christian living.

Now is the time to re-examine the Sunday school. Is it worth while? What is it actually doing for the building of character and life? Is it reaching the multitudes? Is it really changing the lives of those enrolled? Or, on the other hand, is it producing pharisaical religious snobs, narrow sectarian bigots, or worse, pious hypocrites? Are the administrative leaders more concerned with the organization and operation of the machine than the product as measured in terms of changed lives and attitudes? Are teachers more eager to build classes than to build Christian personalities in their pupils?

Some critics of the Sunday school have even suggested the advisability of keeping the child at home on Sunday and giving him religious instruction. But would parents know how to do it? Other critics have condemned the Sunday school as inefficient if not actually contributing to the formation of bad habits of living. Whatever its faults may be, the Sunday school remains, with the exception of the Christian home, the most aggressive force for moral and religious education. It must be made more effective as a character-building agency.

More progress has been made in the last decade in science, medicine, economics, communication, and transportation than in all the past. In this new world of nuclear fission, automation, and space travel, nothing seems impossible. Man can destroy the human race if not the world itself. Such a world needs men of character who can control its newly discovered forces and direct its power into constructive channels. The church has this responsibility. It should utilize every possible resource in developing a pattern of religious education which will produce the right sort of men. Can the church make of the Sunday school such an agency? The possibilities loom large! Just what are the basic functions that the Sunday school must perform if it is to become such a force in this new world?

BASIC FUNCTIONS

Developing Healthful Personality

One of the advantages of Sunday school work, though often overlooked, is the opportunity for the individual to develop his sense of importance. There are four or more native human drives which are basic in the well-rounded life, and the urge to be important is one of these. In religious circles so much has been said about the need for self-effacement and humility that it has almost resulted in repressing the urge to achieve — to be victorious. This drive is quite necessary in the development of a symmetrical and successful life. This is just another way of saying, in the field of Christianity, that the development of Christian selfhood — of happy and healthful personality — is basic with the church. Jesus grounds love for one's neighbor in a sound love for one's self.

The Sunday school, through its classroom procedures, its various expressional activities, and its official functions, provides outlets and inlets, actual and potential, for a happy growth of the individual. The more officers, functions, and offices there are, provided they are vital and properly correlated with the work of other agencies inside and outside the church, the better it is for those who make up its constituency. From this angle there is no such thing as over-organization. A modern writer, with discerning insight, very happily speaks of this process as "aeration" — adequate exposure of the most surface in religion to the sunshine and fresh air of normal functioning.[1]

Fostering Social Growth

Next, the Sunday school helps the individual to achieve normal adulthood by way of creative functioning at the social level. Through democratic procedures, social interaction goes on, and numbers of people learn to work together. The meeting may be in an instructional situation where guided group discussion proceeds. It may be on the tennis court or in the recreation hall where a number of young people meet, under the guidance of a recreational leader, for regular exercise and fellowship. It may be in leadership situations of an organizational nature where attitudes of healthful domination and submission are at play. In other words, there are many opportunities, potential and actual, which the Sunday school offers for the social development of individuals. These should not be regarded lightly, even though they may occasionally bring to the surface problems of acute maladjustment in the area of personal relations.

Building Christian Character

A third function of the Sunday school is that of character building. Some have raised questions as to the ethical values of this institution in cases where improper management and poor character-conditioning prevail. But, in the absence of scientific surveys dealing with the total situation, it is not amiss to note the tools of morality that lie at hand and to point out the potentialities for ethical development. Also, the

[1] H. Paul Douglass, *Church and Community: Oxford Conference Book*, (New York: Willett, Clark & Co., 1938), p. 251.

testimonies of many people to the effect that the Bible and the Sunday school have meant much in the shaping of their character may not be overlooked.

Roughly, the moral problems of human life may be grouped according to three stages of chronological development — childhood, youth, and adulthood. Very broadly, there are certain persistent moral problems which every child, every adolescent, and every adult seems to face. For example, after allowing for some oversimplification in analysis, the three major problems with which youth is wrestling today are, when framed as questions, the following: What shall I do for my life's work? How shall I manage my sex life? What recreation shall I take up? Of course, many other vital problems stem out from these and take on rich colorings according to the landscape of particular situations, but the three major problems within this cycle are certainly crucial. Just here the *forte* of the Sunday school shows itself. By grading its constituency according to age and shaping its teaching tools and methods to fit chronological groups, as well as through providing buildings and equipment in terms of age needs, it is, to that extent, prepared to deal with the moral problems of these ages.

Grouping according to intellectual attainment, and not according to physical and emotional growth, as pertains in the public school, is not sufficient to take care of life's moral problems. However, ethical conditioning is much deeper than schemes for grouping people and details of buildings and equipment. It also lies beyond all current plans and theories of character education. Hence, a word about the highest function of the Sunday school is in order.

Giving the Right Philosophy of Life

Lastly, and above all, this institution helps to build the right philosophy of life. By establishing right attitudes toward the total environment and by facilitating the individual's adjustment to the will of God, the Sunday school makes its most far-reaching and profound contribution. Many people are unhappy today because they have no basic purpose to guide them in their living. There is no unity and harmony of activities. Banality blights their days. By giving direction to living and by generating an enthusiasm for life at its best, the Sunday school can be a blessing and a permanent hope.

As a sort of summary, then, it may be said that the basic functions of the Sunday school are of a psychological, sociological, ethical, and religious nature. Little has been said about organizational and promotional matters. It is agreed that "the Sunday school ought to grow," but there should be greater interest in *what* it grows than in the mere fact of expansion. The levels of growth are quite significant and may not be ignored with impunity.

ORIGIN AND DEVELOPMENT

One can realize more definitely the precise nature of the Sunday school today if he sees how it has changed through the years in keeping with changing social and individual needs. Such a study will throw into relief its true functions and make more specific what has just been said above. The Sunday school was started by Robert Raikes, of Gloucester, England, in 1780. From it has developed the modern Sunday school, supported by the church. Raikes's school furnished the model for similar schools in England and Scotland and on the continent. In America considerable modifications were made. Inasmuch as illiteracy and low morals were rather common on this side of the Atlantic, too, Raikes's ideas prevailed here in general.

The *second phase* of development in the life of the Sunday school, as far as the United States is concerned, was the organization and promotion of Sunday schools by churches. With the establishment of the United States and the adoption of the Constitution, public sentiment came to be so crystallized on the subject of the separation of church and state that most religious and moral instruction was taken out of the public school classrooms and put into the hands of the church. The church did not want the Sunday school at first, particularly on account of its lay leadership. But it was in dire need of an organization to do the job which the public school was relinquishing. Furthermore, the church saw that the Sunday school was going to succeed in spite of opposition. Consequently, there was every reason to adopt and utilize it. Its program and activities changed. Catechisms and church doctrines now appeared in the curriculum. Consequently, the Sunday school became quite definitely a school of religion, and an agency whose policies were those of the church.

The Protestant Sunday school, as it exists today in the United States, had its real beginning December 19, 1790, at Philadelphia when a group of twelve people decided to begin the work. In January, 1791, the Philadelphia Sunday School Union was organized to promote organization of Sunday schools. Sunday School Associations were formed in other large cities, such as Boston and New York. These all combined their resources and formed the American Sunday School Union in 1824. The purpose of this organization was to plant a Sunday school wherever there was a population. Being nondenominational, it was supported by givers of several denominations. The first and oldest denominational Sunday school in America was organized by the Broadway Baptist Church, Baltimore, Maryland, in 1804.[2]

About 1830 a *third change* in emphasis took place, though it had been gradually coming for some time. This new development was characterized chiefly by the fact that the Bible was put at the center of the curriculum, as distinguished from catechisms, doctrines, and ecclesiastical emphases as such. The reason for this was that most Protestant churches came to see that the Bible is their chief authority on matters of faith and practice. Denominational publishing houses began to appear. Each prepared and published lessons of its own choice. There was such a great confusion in the matter of curriculum materials that this period is often described as the "Babel" period. Finally, unity was brought about by the

[2] Clarence A. Benson, *History of Christian Education* (Chicago: Moody Press, 1943), p. 133.

adoption of "The International Uniform Lessons," in 1872. But the emphasis continued to be on material-centered lessons.

The *fourth cycle* of growth came about the turn of the century when the shift was made from the material-centered curriculum to what is now known as the organized curriculum with the needs of the pupil at the center. The demand for this development began about the middle of the nineteenth century and was well on its way by the 1880's and 1890's. It was temporarily set back by the adoption of the International Uniform Lessons, but graded lessons made their appearance in the early years of the twentieth century. An effort was made to train the teachers in their use. The lessons were adapted to the needs of the pupil. General improvement in secular education and vast social changes also came to be reflected in the life of the Sunday school. Interest in missions, evangelism, and community life were very noticeable. Even pronounced changes in internal structure appeared. For example, new members were added at the top, in the instance of adults and shut-ins, and the organization grew beyond the bounds of a children's agency. Today it is the one distinctive organization for all ages and all people in the community, whether or not they belong to any religious denomination. And the growth of the Protestant churches is largely dependent upon its development, both as to breadth of interest and as to aggressiveness in contacts.

METHODS AND ACTIVITIES

It is well to examine next, the activities of the modern Sunday school. Such procedures as teaching, grading, worshipping, evangelizing, and character conditioning come in here. However, for educational reasons they are customarily grouped under the broad divisions of instruction, worship, and activities.

Instruction: Learning Through Guidance

Broadly speaking, the oldest and most prevalent procedure in Sunday school methodology is that of instruction. It is the one clear thing for which the institution exists and without which it would cease to exist today. But a further fact needs stressing also; the usefulness of the Sunday school at the present hour is more particularly grounded in the purpose and quality of the teaching than ever before. To be specific, educators are convinced these days that the once prevalent practice of formal and mechanical instruction must be relegated to the past. Guided learning and purposive activity, with healthy growth for both guide and pupil, are necessary for effective Christian teaching. This means that instructors should have the best possible preparation in order to work with their pupils and guide their experiences. Accordingly, teacher training schools of the highest character are required. Furthermore, pupils have to be grouped according to age units, and life needs have to be met in the atmosphere of adequate buildings and equipment.

At this juncture the old question always arises: What, then should be taught? the Bible? church doctrines? denominational history? practical moral truths? Now, broadly speaking, the answer comes in the form of another question: Should the program be centered about subject matter, as of old, or should it be student-centered and have the warm blood of life in it? If the last is what is really needed, and many religious educators definitely think so, then a very difficult and complex problem is confronted; namely, that of constantly finding what pupil needs are and then setting about vigorously, persistently, and honestly to meet them. The Bible will have a big place here, and the teacher will certainly need to know how to use it to best advantage. But, in the main, the reason so little has been done for pupils is not because the Bible or church doctrines have been forgotten. Such criticism carries too simple an analysis. The real reason lies in the fact that few adults are qualified for the job of being good teachers or guides. In short, the leaders themselves stand in need of guidance.

Evangelism

In the early days of the modern Sunday school movement, the winning of the lost to Christ was one of the chief activities. It was the theme of the great international Sunday school conventions during the last third of the nineteenth century. Today in some quarters, there has been a strong effort to substitute religious education for evangelism, which has resulted in serious neglect of the emphasis on a personal experience of spiritual salvation and definite personal commitment of life to God.

The process of Christian teaching is never complete until the pupil has accepted Christ as Savior and Lord. Individual Christianity is a personal and spiritual experience. Each pupil must be confronted with the claims of Jesus and led individually to a personal belief in him as Savior and commitment of life to him as Lord. Nor is the work of evangelism complete until the individual believer has become a personal witness, able and willing to share his experience with others. The evangelized one must become an evangel. Each teacher should not only have assurance of his own salvation, but should be adept in the art of leading his pupils to Christ and guiding them as they seek to share their experience with others.

The fact that evangelism is an important activity of the Sunday school does not mean that every meeting may be set apart for special evangelistic effort. As an agency of the local church, the school should work in closest harmony with the revival. Each teacher should maintain a prayer list and pray daily for the salvation of their pupils and the lost members of their families. Sunday school teachers are usually the best personal soul-winners in the church.

Creative Worship

Another consciously chosen activity of the Sunday school for personal self-direction and spiritual conditioning is worship. To be sure, this is not absolutely separate from instruction, inasmuch as guidance in classroom activities ought to be carried on in an atmosphere of reverence. But it is treated separately for the sake of emphasis. There are planned exercises and periods of worship labeled as such. These are structural forms of a program and tend to be regarded as the only worship moments in the Sunday school. This is not a good practice. Furthermore, where worship is formal and is largely confined to opening and closing periods, some Sunday school departments build up elaborate programs at these places and copy the church services. Special music, the taking of a collection as in church, and even sermonettes at the instructional period are promoted. The result is that the members of such classes do not desire to attend preaching later, because they have already gotten emotional satisfaction from the church service in replica at Sunday school.

This is just another illustration of the need to practice the new teaching procedures. May not the discovery of a new spiritual truth be an act of worship? And should not a moment of inspiration, in which one experiences a purging of life purposes, be divine? Such values as come from creative learning — may they not strike one's heart down before God? Furthermore, spontaneous worship and spontaneous prayer, such as are sometimes experienced in the Beginner's Department or in the Christian home, are eminently desirable. Opening and closing worship periods have their functions, of course, but real worship as Christ has taught His followers to practice it must not be neglected.

Service Activities

Sometimes these are called "expressional activities," though such terminology is not precise, for there is a sense in which all activities are expressional. Furthermore, instruction and worship are themselves forms of activity. So the term is not meaningful, either way it is taken. However, it does have some value as applied by educators. The emphasis seems to be on aggressive action as against passive impression.

But an illustration or so tells the story better. All efforts such as visiting sick people, sharing in recreational projects, helping the needs in a cooperative manner, and promoting extension work of a distinctively religious nature (evangelism, for example) are classed as activities. Also, Vacation

Bible School work and many week-day religious educational projects belong in this category.

Right here, therefore, is where the question arises as to a better name for the Sunday school. For the simple reason that there are program procedures which are worked out almost exclusively during the week, while there are others which are confined to Sunday, educators and churches are coming more and more to speak of the former as week-day religious education and the week-day church school, in contradistinction to what is promoted on Sunday. In this case, the term "Sunday Church School" is reserved by some denominations for the latter.

IMPLEMENTAL GROWTH

Buildings and Equipment

It is a long way from the "pioneer" days of the one-room "meeting house" to the modern church building with its complement of educational buildings. In almost every large city one may find churches with multiple departments. This means a separate departmental assembly room for each age group from the one-year-olds up through the seventeen-year-olds. Also there will probably be three or more young people's departments and from three to eight separate adult departments. Each department above the primary will have from six to ten or more separate classrooms. This growth can best be understood in the light of changed ideas of teaching. Small departments and small classrooms with proper age grouping are generally agreed to be much more favorable for effective teaching than large classes.

Even rural pastors are devising ways and means of reconstructing auditoriums so as to get separate walled-in classrooms for each age group. In some instances they are adding rooms from outside; in other places they are constructing a separate educational building. Facilities are also being provided for recreational and social needs, not only of the church, but also for the whole community. In other words, equipment needs must be seen in the light of all educational agencies and functions of the church.

Standards

Any Sunday school can become a great Sunday school if its leaders will follow the Standard of Excellence as a guide. It sets forth clearly the essentials of a good Sunday school and the plans for building a great school. It is a program which any Sunday school, regardless of size, may use. It is just as easily reached by a small Sunday school as a large one if the pastor and superintendent understand its ten requirements and realize its value as an implement of growth. Any Sunday school can be a standard school if its leadership determines to follow the plan and is willing to make the effort. Standard Sunday schools are not only bigger but also are better than those which are not. Standard schools reach more people for Bible study and win more lost people to Christ than nonstandard schools. The ten essentials of the *First Standard of Excellence* erected by Southern Baptists are:

I. *Church Relationship.* 1. The church shall elect the officers and teachers. 2. The school shall make monthly or quarterly reports to the church.

II. *Enlargement.* 1. The enrollment of the school shall at least equal the number of resident church members as recognized by the church. 2. The school shall promote a program of visitation.

III. *Grading.* The school shall be graded as follows: Cradle Roll, birth through 3; Beginners, 4-5; Primaries, 6-8; Juniors, 9-12; Intermediates, 13-16; Young People, 17-24; Adults, 25 and above; and an Extension Department for those who cannot attend. (NOTE — if possible, a Nursery should be provided for children, birth through three.)

IV. *Baptist Literature.* Southern Baptist Sunday school literature prepared for the teachers and pupils in the various age groups shall be used throughout the school.

V. *Bibles.* 1. The Bible shall be used as the textbook of the school. 2. The officers and teachers shall provide opportunities for the pupils to use their Bibles in the school. 3. The officers and teachers shall encourage the pupils and their parents to engage in daily family Bible reading and prayer.

VI. *Preaching Attendance.* 1. An average of at least 70 per cent of the officers, teachers, and pupils above eight years of age attending the school shall remain for the preaching services. 2. The Beginners and Primaries shall be encouraged to remain for the preaching services.

VII. *Evangelism.* 1. The school shall be positively evangelistic. 2. The teachers shall earnestly seek to lead their pupils who are not Christians to a personal acceptance of Christ as Saviour and Lord. 3. The superintendent and pastor shall give frequent opportunities for the pupils who are not Christians to confess Christ publicly, and urge them to do so.

VIII. *Meetings, Equipment, and Records.* 1. The school shall maintain a weekly officers and teachers' meeting or a monthly workers' conference. 2. The Sunday sessions of the school shall be at least one hour in length, preferably one hour and fifteen minutes. 3. Each age group below the Intermediates shall be separated from the remainder of the school at least for the class sessions by walls, movable partitions, screens, or curtains. 4. At least 50 per cent of the classes above the Juniors shall be separated from the remainder of the school for the class sessions by walls, movable partitions, screens, or curtains. 5. The school shall use the Six Point Record System.

IX. *Training.* 1. The school shall conduct at least one training school each year completing at least one book in the Sunday School Training Course. 2. At least 50 per cent of the officers and teachers, including the pastor or superintendent, shall hold an award for either BUILDING A STANDARD SUNDAY SCHOOL or A CHURCH USING ITS SUNDAY SCHOOL. 3. At least 50 per cent of the officers and teachers, including the pastor or superintendent, shall hold an award for at least one other book in the Sunday School Training Course.

X. *Stewardship and Missions.* 1. The school shall support the church program and promote the general missionary, educational, and benevolent causes fostered by the denomination. 2. The school shall present educationally each year at least four denominational causes, and shall provide opportunities for the members to contribute to each of these causes in accordance with the policy of the church.[3]

For schools which are organized on the departmental basis and are blessed with good equipment and large educational buildings, there is the Advanced Standard, although many of them continue to use the First Standard with excellent results. Also departmental and class standards are available and should be followed as "blue-prints" for building better Sunday schools. They may be secured from the Bap-

---

[3] Revised copies of the *Standard* may be secured from the Southern Baptist Sunday School Board, Department of Sunday School, Nashville, Tennessee.

tist State Sunday School Secretary in any state which co-operates with the Southern Baptist Convention.

Lesson Helps and Teaching Materials

One of the greatest changes which has come with newer teaching methods is to be seen in the field of literature and teaching aids. As a matter of fact, in some instances the newer materials have been objected to; largely because teachers have not been trained to use them. Here obviously, change has put too great a strain upon the leadership of the churches. But educators have anticipated this and have created lesson materials to fit all situations.

First, there are the *Improved Uniform Lessons.* These lessons are well adapted to meet the needs of the smaller, non-departmentalized Sunday school, which must use un-trained teachers. They use the same lesson passages, daily Bible readings, and "golden text" for all classes in the school; but whenever a text is beyond the experience and under-standing of the younger pupils in Beginner and Primary classes a simpler lesson text is substituted. A different lesson topic is selected for each department. In most Sunday schools the Uniform Lessons are used in Young People's and Adult classes and departments.

Then there are the *Closely Graded Lessons.* These lessons are prepared to meet the needs of the growing person year by year. There is a different lesson for each year from the three-year-old child to the sixteen-year-old boys and girls. The scripture text, lesson topic, memory verse, and lesson discussion are all selected to meet the needs of the actual life situations of the pupils. The lessons are organized around units of learning. But many teachers, who have not learned to use the graded lessons, revert to the old subject-matter approach, and fail to guide their pupils in applying the les-sons to life. By frequent revision and diligent effort to im-prove the skills of the teachers, graded lessons may be kept in line with the newest emphases of educational procedure. These lessons are best suited for use in the department Sun-day school.

Lastly, there are the *Group Graded Lessons*, used by some denominations. They are written for Sunday schools which have only three classes or grades to a department. A different lesson series is made up for each department, and yet the lessons are the same for all classes in the department. Emphasis is placed on life's needs, and the Bible is used creatively. Much extra-biblical material is to be found in group graded lessons, so those denominations which hold to the Bible as the Word of God and the primary textbook of the Sunday school are reluctant to use them.

Enlargement

From the time of Robert Raikes to the middle of the twentieth century it has been found that the best way to get people into the Sunday school is to go after them. Arthur Flake has given Sunday school workers the most successful method of enrolling great numbers. It has been tried and proven many times with equal success in both small and large churches. It is briefly this:

1. The constituency (membership responsibilities) of the Sunday school should be known, graded, and tabulated;
2. The organization should be enlarged (new classes and departments);
3. A suitable place for each class and department should be provided;
4. A program of visitation should be maintained.[4]

The most efficient way to *know the possibilities* is to take a religious census of the area served by the church. Every one who is not enrolled in another Sunday school is considered a possibility. Once discovered he becomes a responsibility. The responsibilities thus located are graded by age and sex and divided into classes or groups of ten.

The second step is to *enlarge the organization*. This means to form enough new classes and departments to reach all responsibilities. Two or three pupils already enrolled may

---

[4] Arthur Flake, *Building A Standard Sunday School* (rev. ed.; Nashville: Convention Press, 1952), pp. 29–48.

be assigned to the new class to help the new teacher build it. These newly enlisted teachers must be trained by the educational leadership of the church as they begin their new task; it might be called "on-the-job" or "in-service" training.

One of the most difficult problems is to *provide a place* for each class to meet. This requires ingenuity, initiative, and courage. Old classrooms may have to be given up; partitions must be erected; and new buildings must eventually be constructed. But temporary provision must be made for each class even if the space can only be separated by curtains. Some churches have located vacant buildings near by, and have arranged for their use. Some have bought residential property adjoining the church property and have remodeled the houses for temporary use. One church in a Texas town is reported to have secured the use of a synagogue which was located on the same block but was not used on Sunday by the Jewish congregation. Churches are known to have used movie theaters, school houses, and even funeral homes. Before the responsibilities can be reached, a place for each class to meet must be provided, though only a bench.

The final step in building a large Sunday school is to set up a program of *continuous visitation*. Not only will each teacher visit his own responsibilities repeatedly, but a weekly visitation day should be observed. On whatever day of the week thus designated, all visitors come to the church to receive assignments. The visit is made on the family by one visitor who seeks to enlist the whole family in the total church program. Some men's classes go visiting at night. When visits are properly made, new pupils keep coming. The slogan "When we go, they come" has proved over and over again to be true.

NEEDS

Trained Workers

The greatest need of the Sunday school is trained teachers and officers. Teachers who can change the lives of their pupils by sharing meaningful experiences with them are not easily found. Each church must discover and train its own workers. This training must include Bible study, doctrines, missions, and evangelism as well as teaching method and psychology. The teacher must not only know what he is teaching, what constitutes real teaching, how to teach; but above all else know the pupils' interests and needs. The weakest point in the Sunday school today is the ineffective teacher. At this point the next step of progress must be made.

Each church should set up its own program of training for its teachers and officers. An associate superintendent of teacher training should be elected by the church. In large departmentalized schools there might well be such an officer in each department. This officer should keep a close check on the past training and present needs of all workers in the organization as well as to secure and train future teachers. All teacher-training work done by every member of the church should be on file in the church office or in the superintendent's records.

There are three widely used courses of teacher training. They are: (1) The International Standard Leadership Course, promoted by the Division of Christian Education, National Council of Churches of Christ (interdenominational); (2) The Evangelical Teacher Training Association (nondenominational); and (3) The Workers Training Course of the Southern Baptist Convention (denominational). In evaluating these training courses C. H. Benson, one of the leading spirits in the Evangelical Teacher Training Association, has described the Southern Baptist program in the following words:

> The success of the Southern Baptist program — and it must be recognized as a success from the far-reaching results it has obtained — lies in the simplicity of its requirements and in the enthusiasm of its promotion. Instructors made their appeal to the heart as well as to the head. . . . While this course lacked the scholastic standards that were to be attained by other teacher training agencies . . . yet the larger enlistment that this course commanded more than made up for the lack of scholastic standards.[5]

[5] Benson, *Christian Education*, p. 240.

While it may possibly be true that the books do not measure up to academic standards of some other courses they have, nevertheless, been the guiding principles by which Southern Baptists have built more large Sunday schools and have enrolled in one year more new pupils than all other denominations combined. But these results do not mean the teacher-training books cannot be improved. They are constantly being revised, and the new books on teaching procedure are setting forth the more progressive methods of education. (For the latest list of Sunday school worker training books of Southern Baptists, write to the state Baptist Sunday school secretary, Baptist state convention in your state.)

Supervisional Management

In the past the details of organization and promotion have been the chief concern of the leadership. The manner in which instruction, worship, and service activities have been performed has not been given enough consideration. These were the pioneer days of clearing the forests and preparing the soil for sowing the seed. But now the religious frontier has shifted. The land has been prepared. The method of reaching people for Sunday school enrollment has been proved. It is now time to improve the effectiveness of teaching. This requires some form of supervisional technique. The pastor's cabinet for building a meaningful calendar of activities, the supervisor's schedule for improving instruction, correlational planning to aid all agencies of the church to avoid overlapping of activities, but, above all, an integrated curriculum are the chief needs to be met by supervisional management. The enthusiasm for mere numbers is not sufficient. There must be an equally keen desire to guide large numbers of people to grow through right motivation into full-grown Christian characters.

LIMITATIONS AND WEAKNESSES

Next, attention must be directed to another side of the Sunday school, if the whole picture is to be seen. When one objectively views this organization as definitely tied into highly socialized modern life, he becomes acutely aware of its limitations. For one thing, it gets the pupil, whether young or old, as a whole pupil, already highly conditioned by home, school, and play group. It does not get him simply for what he is religiously or what he can be. This makes the job of Sunday school a very complex affair, if taken seriously; and few Sunday schools are prepared for so complex a task.

Then, at best, the Sunday school has the pupil for about an hour a week or for only fifty-two hours a year. The facts are that the movies and television will take him through their paces much more frequently than this. What can the Sunday school do with such odds against it? The only answer comes in terms of making the time spent in the Sunday school the most meaningful and challenging of any similar span in the life of the pupil — allowing, of course, for other religious agencies and activities. Can it honestly be said that the Sunday school has always done this?

However, there are more culpable weaknesses than these more or less necessary limitations. Broadly speaking, they may be grouped under two heads. First, *defects in interpretation of function* exist, and rather generally. Secondly, *mistakes are constantly being perpetuated in methodology*. By defects in interpretation is meant inadequate or wrong conceptions as to the purpose of the Sunday school. For instance, so many approaches tilt the scales of interpretation in favor of the institution instead of the individual — not consciously, but none the less tragically. The Sunday school in such instances becomes an end in itself, and its goals are defined in terms of organizational proficiency or institutional growth. A complete roster of officers, teachers, and committees, along with a good statistical showing of people in attendance, becomes the *summum bonum*. Obviously, where affairs have taken this turn a general overhauling is needed. Let it be remembered that the primary purpose of the Sunday school is to assist the individual toward well-rounded and successful Christian living.

The second area of rectifiable weaknesses is that of methodology. Frequently, procedures of organization and standardization go on without consideration for the local situation, and without reference either to other organizations in the church or in the community. Consequently, there is overlapping of function and duplication in curriculum, as well as doubling back in administrative duties.

Furthermore, the instruments of tests and measurements have not been used sufficiently to see how the Sunday school may proceed. For example, achievement tests, information tests, and attitude tests would show more about the needs of individuals in the Sunday school and pave the way to better methods in helping them.

FUTURE POSSIBILITIES

In the main, three rather clear-cut conceptions prevail as to what may be expected of the Sunday school in the future. One is that of *complacency*, and runs something like this: Why raise any question about the outlook of the Sunday school; has it not succeeded in the past? The second view is characterized by mild *cynicism* and takes this form in thought: Inasmuch as many representative leaders are absorbed with perpetuating what they have found and as they have found it, there is little chance of necessary changes being worked into the structure of the Sunday school. The third and most vital wing of thought sees reassuring *signs of progress* here and there. Experiments in creative administrative revisions are cited as tokens of hope. Also, in the churches where educational purposes and methods are understood, progress is being made.

Educational leaders entertain no serious doubt about the Sunday school; but they realize that the kind of structural form which the institution will have in the future is beyond human prediction and may be of little moment if damage is done to individuals in personality and morality. On the other hand, they are definitely committed to a more vital and serviceable functioning of its activities, so that the fullest Christian life and the most well-rounded character may result for each one connected with it. What more could be desired?

QUESTIONS FOR DISCUSSION

1. What changes should be made in the Sunday school methods in your community to better meet the needs of a rapidly changing society? Evaluate the use of audio-visual aids, extension departments, teacher training programs, counseling, and guidance.

2. Interview some of the teachers in the Sunday school to find out what plans they use to secure a follow-up of their Sunday school lesson.

3. Offer some specific suggestions for increasing the amount of time for weekly Bible study. What value would there be in a week-day or week-night Bible class? Consider those who work on Sunday.

4. From your own observation, what vital functions does the Sunday school perform in your church?

5. What is the most important factor in the Sunday school? Consider these: pupil, teacher, material, attitudes, class spirit, and interest.

CHAPTER 14

THE TRAINING PROGRAM
OF THE CHURCH

The Baptist Training Union originated as a youth program, but has now been extended to include in its membership all adult church members as well as the youngest children. The emphasis is placed on "learning by doing." The Training Union is essentially an activities program. As such it makes its strongest appeal to youth. If it continues to serve its original purpose, young people must be permitted to share more largely in planning its activities as well as in presenting its weekly programs.

Every institution in organized society is making its bid for youth. Fraternal orders, realizing the need for recruitment, have set up programs for transmitting their values to the sons and daughters of their members. Political parties organize youth groups. It has been said, "The world moves forward on the feet of little children." It may equally well be said, "The world is moved forward on the feet of marching youth." Charles A. Wells tells of seeing thousands of youth in Russia marching through the snow, barefooted and in rags, chanting, "We may be hungry, and we may be cold; but we'll change the world." Communism has demonstrated the value of training youth. If the churches are to project their mission into the future, youth must be trained in all essential church activities and loyalties.

ORIGIN AND GROWTH OF YOUTH WORK

Before 1800 there were no large-scale youth organizations in America, nor any concerted efforts to utilize the youth power of the land. However, during the nineteenth century numerous organizations sprang up which had some sort of program to appeal to young people. For example, there were singing schools which were composed almost entirely of adolescents, and were devoted largely to religious music. Also, temperance societies arose to draw within their circles a large youth group. Then, there was the senior class movement in the Sunday school which took in those above fourteen. In addition to this, various missionary and devotional societies became very prominent, and many young people joined them.

The first Young Men's Christian Association was established in England in 1844, and the Young Women's Christian Association in 1855. Both of these organizations later took America by storm. However, distinctively religious organizations for young people in the local church trace their origin to the work of Theodore L. Cuyler, of Brooklyn, New York. He organized a young people's association in his church and used for a motto "Young people for young people," a modification of the Y.M.C.A. motto. Young people of both sexes belonged to the association. Also, a pledge was adopted, a weekly devotional meeting was planned, and the society functioned through committees. Later, Francis E. Clark, of Portland, Maine, organized the Christian Endeavor Society in his church. From this the Young People's Society of Christian Endeavor, embracing all denominations and having a national and international reach, was formed in 1881.

The next cycle of growth was largely in terms of denominational organizations. Within fifteen years at least nine of the major Protestant denominations had formed organizations for training youth. They were: Brotherhood of St. Andrew (Episcopal), 1883; Epworth League (Methodist), 1889; Baptist Young People's Union of America, 1891; Walther League (Lutheran), 1893; Baptist Young People's Union, Auxiliary to Southern Baptist Convention, 1895; Luther League of America, 1895; Young People's Religious Union (Unitarian), 1896; Junior Daughters of the King (Episcopal), 1896. Presbyterians and Congregationalists continued to use the Christian Endeavor Societies.[1] At this stage the denominational structures more or less displaced the interdenominational work.

The Baptist Young People's Union of the Southern Baptist Convention followed the organization of the Baptist Young People's Union of America by five years, and had the benefit of the experience of its sister organization in the North. It was launched at Atlanta, 1895, and was declared independent of all interdenominational connections. As a matter of fact, it functioned as an auxiliary unit of work even in the South until experimentation had established it solidly in the minds of the people.[2] By 1918 the Southern Baptist Convention felt sufficiently assured of its value to entrust promotion of it wholly to the Sunday School Board as a part of the denominational program.

TYPES OF YOUTH ORGANIZATIONS

Southern Presbyterian Church

The youth program of the Presbyterian Church is built around the "Fellowship concept" — the concept that all activities of the church constitute the program for that age group, and that all persons participating in any phase of the program constitute the membership of the fellowship. It is part of the church's total program, and an excellent example of an integrated curriculum.

The Presbyterian Youth Fellowship is composed of all the

[1] For a more complete description of the historical development of B.Y.P.U. see William W. Barnes, *The Southern Baptist Convention 1845–1953* (Nashville: The Broadman Press, 1954), pp. 183-91.

[2] J. M. Price, L. L. Carpenter, and A. E. Tibbs, *A Program of Religious Education* (New York: Fleming H. Revell, 1937).

young people of the church from the time they enter the seventh grade until they finish college. There are normally three groups: the Pioneer Fellowship for those in grades seven, eight, and nine; the Senior High Fellowship for young people in grades ten, eleven, and twelve; and the Westminster Fellowship for students in college. High school graduates not attending college are considered a part of the church's young adult organization.

The *Pioneer Fellowship* is for boys and girls as they meet for Sunday or any week-day activities, whether they are worshipping, studying, playing, or singing in the choir, or participating in any form of church activity.

"The purpose of the *Senior High Fellowship* is to lead the young people of the church and congregation to grow in effective Christian living by knowing Jesus, accepting him as Lord and Savior, following his principles in daily living, and leading others to know and follow him; to bring the way of Christ to bear on needs in society; to develop Christian fellowship among the members in their relationship to each other and to the community; and to train them and give them opportunities for Christian service both at home and abroad."[3] This is done by dividing the membership into commissions. The areas of concern included in these five commissions — Christian Faith, Christian Witness, Christian Outreach, Christian Citizenship, Christian Fellowship — are the bases on which the program of most of the denominational youth fellowships are built.

The *Westminster Fellowship* exists because the church "sees the college campus as a mission field, where all students — Christian and non-Christian alike — must be confronted with the saving Gospel of Jesus Christ. It seeks to bring these students to a fuller knowledge of the Gospel and an allegiance to Christ, and to help them become loyal, intelligent members of Christ's church."[4]

---

3 Bettie Currie (ed.), *Senior High Fellowship Handbook* (rev. ed.; Richmond: John Knox Press, 1957), p. iv. Used by permission.

4 *Campus Christian Life Manual* (Richmond: Board of Christian Education, 1953), p. 13. Used by permission.

All the activities for each age group are planned and promoted by a council for each fellowship. This council is composed of the elected officers, the adult leaders, and commission chairmen. This plan provides opportunity for training the youth for leadership in the Christian movement.

Methodist Church

The Methodist Youth Fellowship was formally installed at the watch night service in Methodist congregations throughout the United States, December 31, 1941. It represents the merger of the youth groups of the Methodist Protestant Church, the Methodist Episcopal Church (South), and the Methodist Episcopal Church, which were joined together in 1939. At the time of unification a Youth Commission was set up to make recommendations for unifying the youth programs, which were the Epworth League and Christian Endeavor. After careful study, and in accordance with the results of a churchwide poll of Methodist youth, the Methodist Youth Fellowship was formed.

It is composed of all the youth of the church from twelve years of age through twenty-three. The statement of purpose becomes the declaration of faith of those who join it. It is: "to live clean lives . . .; to give our loyalty and service through the Methodist Church . . .; to hold the ideals of unselfish service ever before us . . .; and in simple trust, to follow Jesus as our Savior and Lord."[5]

The program areas of the Methodist Youth Fellowship are: Christian Faith, Christian Witness, Christian Outreach, Christian Citizenship, Christian Fellowship. In smaller churches these areas may be combined and all youth organized into the one fellowship. In larger churches the fellowship is graded into three departments: Intermediate, twelve, thirteen, fourteen; Senior, fifteen, sixteen, seventeen; and Older Youth Fellowship, eighteen to twenty-three. Short term committees have replaced the older form of

[5] *The Handbook of the Methodist Youth Fellowship* (Nashville: Youth Department, General Board of Education, the Methodist Church), p. 14. Used by permission.

commissions for each area. Each fellowship is governed by a youth council composed of elected officers. Adult leaders meet with the council and participate in discussion, but only the youth vote upon the questions.

These program areas and council plan of organization are used by most of the thirty-nine denominations in the United Christian Youth Movement, the organization through which the denominational fellowships cooperate.

THE SOUTHERN BAPTIST PLAN

Southern Baptists have what may be called the *group-committee* plan of organization for the individual units. The separate units are graded according to age and are called unions. When grouped together under the general organization, which is a universal practice among Southern Baptists, this plan of cooperation and leadership training is known as the Baptist Training Union. The membership of each union, in turn, is divided into two, three, or four groups and placed under group captains. Under this plan not more than six or eight members are enrolled in a group, in order to provide maximum individual development and to stimulate competitive interest and wholesome rivalry.

The plan provides for each of the elected officers to be chairman of a committee in addition to serving as an officer. The officers and the committee of which each is chairman are: president, program committee; vice-president, membership committee; Bible readers leader, devotional committee; social leader, fellowship committee; and stewardship leader, stewardship committee. Furthermore, each committee has one member from each group. Definite responsibility for promoting the work of each committee within the group is placed upon this one person. In this way, development in some form of cooperative activity is planned for every member of the Baptist Training Union. Also, the structure of the organization does not render its use impracticable in a church limited in numbers and leadership ability, as would be the case were the chairman of the committees named in addition to the officers. Each person, therefore, is working

with one set of people on his group, and with a different set
on the committee. This plan trains in the art of cooperation
as well as in the development and growth of the individual.

Finally, the Baptist Training Union is not the former
young people's society. It is not a loosely organized unit of
religious education, such as a youth prayer service; nor a
mixture of various ages; nor an interdenominational service
agency; nor a make-shift of totally different church organizations. It has a distinctive task from which it is not to be
turned aside. But this leads to consideration of the development and growth of the Baptist Training Union.

DEVELOPMENT OF THE BAPTIST TRAINING UNION

A few facts on the structural growth of the Training
Union are important, as they show how this general organization came to be built up and how it differs from the
youth work of the other denominations. At first the Baptist
Young People's Union was planned for young people of both
sexes seventeen years and above. Then, the Junior B.Y.P.U.
was formed to take care of those below seventeen years of
age. By 1922 further expansion took place. In keeping with
the grading by age which had proven so valuable in the
Sunday school, a general organization was formed, with
unions for juniors, intermediates, and seniors. A little later
the need for the adult union was evident, so that by 1932
the adult union was included in the general organization.
This necessitated the grading of seniors (now called Young
People) from seventeen to twenty-four, and adults, all above
twenty-four. The story-hour was first provided to care for
the children below nine years of age who came to the Training Union with their parents. Graded lessons for Nursery,
Beginners, and Primary ages are now provided. The term
"story-hour" was discontinued in 1950, and now there is a
department for each age corresponding with the age grouping of the Sunday school. Many churches now have multiple
departments, or separate departments for each year, from
the nursery through the sixteen-year-olds. Also, in larger
churches, there are from three to six young people's depart-

ments and as many adult departments. Thus Southern Baptists now have the completed general organization, the Baptist Training Union, with a fully graded system of unions, set up to train and develop the entire membership of the church.

THE STANDARD OF EXCELLENCE

The Standard of Excellence is a guide to be followed in organizing the training program of the church. It presents a practical plan of work. The church should adopt it as a plan of procedure and use it as a measuring device for checking the effectiveness of its Training Union. There are separate standards for the general organization — the Training Union — and each of the departments. There is also a standard for the union within each department. All are built along the same general plan, but each has its separate departmental requirements to meet the needs of the different age groups. The standards outline in simple steps the essentials of a worthy church training program. Copies of all of the standards — general, departmental, and unit — may be secured without cost from the Baptist Training Union Secretary, State Baptist Headquarters, in any of the states cooperating with the Southern Baptist Convention. The standard for the general organization in a church is presented here.

THE STANDARD OF EXCELLENCE

ORGANIZATION

1. *Officers.* — (1) Pastor, director, associate director, secretary, chorister, and pianist. (2) One half of the general officers shall hold or earn during the quarter an award on THE BAPTIST TRAINING UNION MANUAL or BUILDING A CHURCH TRAINING PROGRAM.

2. *Committees.* — (1) Executive, composed of general and department officers, or in nondepartment Training Unions, the heads of all units of the Training Union. (2) Efficiency, composed of secretaries. (3) Membership, composed of associate director, department associate directors in department Training Unions, and vice-presidents.

3. *Grading.* — The Training Union shall be graded as follows:

Nursery, ages 3 and under; Beginner, ages 4-5; Primary, ages 6-8; Junior, ages 9-12; Intermediate, ages 13-16; Young People, ages 17-24; Adult, ages 25 and above. If the church does not have all of these age groups in its prospect list for the Training Union, Standard rating is given if it provides for such groups as it has. (Each age group, Junior and above, having possibilities for two or more unions should be organized into at least one department with a department director. In all Training Unions each age group, Primary and under, should be organized into one or more departments.)

4. *Church Control.* — All general and department officers, leaders, sponsors, and counselors shall be elected by the church, and all other officers approved by the church.

5. *Enrollment.* — One fourth of the resident church membership shall be enrolled in the Training Union.

MEETINGS

1. *General Assembly.* — The Training Union shall hold weekly a general assembly of the unions, with a report by the general secretary. All unions shall co-operate in this assembly. This assembly may be integrated with the preaching service.

2. *Department Assemblies.* — In Training Unions having department organization, the departments shall hold assemblies, preferably before the union meetings. All age groups under the Junior department may count their regular procedures as meeting this requirement.

3. *Executive Committee Meeting.* — The executive committee (composed of general and department officers in department Training Unions, and general officers and heads of units in nondepartment Training Unions) shall hold a monthly meeting to plan Training Union events and activities, consider problems, and determine policies. (1) General officers and department heads in department Training Unions, and general officers and heads of units in nondepartment Training Unions, shall make monthly written reports to the executive committee. (2) The director shall make monthly and annual written reports to the church.

4. *Officers' Council.* — (1) The officers' council (composed of general officers, department officers in department Training Unions, officers of all unions above the Junior department, and the adult workers of the Junior, Primary, Beginner, and Nursery departments) shall meet monthly to review the work of the past month and plan all of the work of the unit organizations of the Training Union for the next month. (2) All departments shall be represented in the officers' council each month.

5. *Associational Meetings.* — The Training Union shall send representatives to the associational meetings and training schools, if association is organized and holds these meetings.

6. *State Meetings.* — The Training Union shall send one or more representatives to the state or district Training Union convention or assembly.

ACTIVITIES

1. *Study.* — (1) *Lesson Courses* — The Training Union shall follow the lesson courses for all departments in the periodicals published by the Baptist Sunday School Board. (2) *Textbook Study Course* — The Training Union shall conduct a study course for all departments at least once every twelve months, using the books of the Graded Training Union Study Course of the Baptist Sunday School Board.

2. *Daily Bible Reading.* — The Training Union shall follow the Daily Bible Readers' Course for individual reading and daily devotions as published in the Training Union quarterlies.

3. *Worship.* — (1) The Training Union shall promote attendance upon the evening preaching service. (2) The Training Union shall promote attendance upon the church prayer meeting. (3) The Training Union shall promote daily family worship in every home represented, using the daily readings of the Uniform Sunday School Lessons.

4. *Stewardship and Missions.* — (1) The Training Union shall promote education in stewardship, tithing, and systematic giving by all members to church expenses, benevolences, and missions, according to the church plan. (2) The Training Union shall encourage the enlistment of all of its members in active service in other church activities and organizations. (3) The Training Union shall participate at least once each quarter in some practical missionary activity. (4) The Training Union shall seek to enlist all of its active members in praying for and witnessing daily to lost people.

5. *Social Life.* — The Training Union shall promote a program of Christian social life for all unions and departments as required in the Standards of the unions and the departments.

6. *Visitation.* — Regular visitation of all absentees and prospects shall be sponsored.

ACHIEVEMENT

At least one fourth of the total number of unit organizations of the Training Union (representing at least two departments or age groups) shall qualify as Standard for the quarter.

Each union and each department should have a large copy of its Standard on the wall of the room in which it meets. At least once a month the union should check itself by its standard and plan to reach specific goals each month until it has completed all requirements and received the standard award.

AIM AND VALUES OF THE TRAINING UNION

Aim

The avowed purpose of the Baptist Training Union is *training in church membership*. When the Baptist Young People's Union of the Southern Baptist Convention withdrew from the Baptist Young People's Union of America, one of the most significant changes was set forth in the statement of the aim. That of the earlier organization was "training in Christian service." It was the desire of the Southern Baptist leaders to integrate the training program into the denominational structure of which the local church or congregation is the basic unit. Hence the aim was changed to give a sense of direction. This proved a wise choice and since its origin, the control of the organization has rested in the local church. The constituency includes the whole membership of the church. A well-rounded plan for the training of each individual in the entire church membership is its distinctive purpose. To such an end the organization is set up and the program of activities is laid out.

Values

One of the most evident values has been the *development of loyalties to the local church*. In churches which have an effective Training Union, year-round Sunday evening preaching services are easily maintained; tithing and stewardship goals are readily reached; revivals are more enthusiastically supported; mid-week prayer services are better attended; young church members will publicly lead in prayer and participate more readily in all the activities of the church; and leaders are discovered and developed for every phase of church work.

A most worthwhile value to the denomination has been the *development of the Training Union curriculum*. There are three parts of the curriculum; they are (1) Training

Union Lesson Courses; (2) the Daily Bible Reader's Course; and (3) the Graded Training Union Textbook Study Course. The lesson course provides effective graded materials for the planning of the weekly programs. The Bible reader's course is a five-year cycle. Its highest value has been the enlistment of many thousands as daily readers of the Bible.

The graded textbook study course, consisting of more than seventy-five books, meets the need of all church members for additional knowledge, which is not provided for the average church member in any other way. The course is definitely denominational and provides a comprehensive, though simple, course in Christian education which cannot be secured in any place short of a theological seminary. A more detailed description of the curriculum will be given in a subsequent paragraph.

A third value of the Training Union is the *deepening of the spiritual lives* of countless numbers of church members. Of course there are many who are only temporarily enlisted, but in this age of reckless living, there is often found in a local church a nucleus of sincere young people who have yielded their lives to the Lord and are happily serving Him in their church and community. There is also a similar group made up of young adults. The Training Union affords the most effective place for growth in these spiritual relationships. It helps to make spiritual living real and practical. It guides the individual into the growth of a Christlike personality.

Another value is the increased *understanding of the meaning of Bible doctrines, and greater loyalty to the denominational program.* The great majority of preachers and missionaries received their first impressions of a divine call while active in Training Union. Many multiplied thousands, who have not been led to choose a religious vocation, have dedicated their lives to the service of God as lay members with deep love for their church and denomination and are able to give intelligent reasons for their beliefs. The monthly missionary program and the study course books on missions, stewardship, and denominational life have helped to build strong and intelligent loyalties to the denomination and its world-wide mission.

TRAINING UNION CURRICULUM

When the Southern Baptist Convention organized the Sunday School Board in 1891, its chief function was to provide literature for Sunday schools. Two years later the convention authorized the board "to provide literature suitable for the purposes" of the young people's societies in Southern Baptist churches. These societies were the forerunners of the Baptist Training Union. So for more than half a century the development of curriculum materials has been the responsibility of the Sunday School Board. As indicated above, there are three principal types of curriculum materials.

Lesson Courses

These are published in the form of quarterlies and furnish materials needed for presentation of the programs at the weekly meetings. The first periodical to make its appearance was the *Young People's Leader*, in January, 1894. At the meeting of the convention in 1895, the Board reported, "We have published the *Leader* and have been holding it as the nucleus of a larger literature . . . should such be demanded." As the Training Union has developed, the "larger literature" has been created. The *Leader* was replaced by the *B.Y.P.U. Quarterly* in 1900. From this single quarterly, which is still being published for the young people's programs, early in the century there arose a need for a separate quarterly for boys and girls below the age of sixteen who were attending B.Y.P.U. Known first as *Junior B.Y.P.U. Quarterly*, this periodical made its appearance in 1908. Later, in the early twenties, its name was changed to *Intermediate B.Y.P.U. Quarterly*, for ages thirteen through sixteen; and the *Junior B.Y.P.U. Quarterly*, for ages nine through twelve, was added.

By 1956 the graded training union program had developed to the extent that a more closely graded curriculum was demanded. New quarterlies have been added through the years until now there are fifteen quarterly publications being used to present the weekly programs. They are: *Baptist Adults*, for members of unions composed of adults older than twenty-five and members of ungraded adult unions; *Baptist Young Adults*, for members of adult unions from twenty-five to approximately thirty-five years of age; *Baptist Married Young People*, for members of unions composed exclusively of married young people, ages seventeen to approximately twenty-five; *Baptist Young People*, for unions composed of young people, ages seventeen to twenty-five; *Baptist Intermediate Union Quarterly I*, for intermediates ages thirteen and fourteen; *Baptist Intermediate Quarterly II*, for intermediates ages fifteen and sixteen; *Baptist Junior Union Quarterly I*, for boys and girls nine and ten years of age; *Baptist Junior Union Quarterly II*, for boys and girls eleven and twelve years of age; *The Intermediate Leader*, for adult leaders and sponsors of intermediates; *The Junior Leader*, for adult leaders of juniors; *The Primary Leader*, for adult leaders of primary unions; *The Beginner Leader*, for leaders of unions composed of four- and five-year-olds; *The Church Nursery Guide*, for workers with children under four.

In addition to the lesson periodicals there also were introduced four new quarterly magazines designed to help parents understand the experiences their child is having in Training Union and to build upon those experiences in guiding the child's religious growth in the home. These magazines are to be distributed to the parents before the first Sunday of each quarter. They are: *Living with Children*, for parents of children ages birth to three; *Every Day with Beginners*, for parents of children ages four and five; *Every Day with Primaries*, for parents with children ages six through eight. Additional quarterlies will be added on each departmental level until there will be a complete closely graded Training Union curriculum, with a different lesson provided for each year from the beginners up through the intermediates and possibly a course of lessons for older adults. The construction of this program of study is the task of the Training Union Department of the Baptist Sunday School Board.

Bible Readers' Course

Systematic daily Bible reading has been a major emphasis since the beginning of the training program. This course was originated by Landrum P. Leavell, the first South-wide secretary of B.Y.P.U. work for Southern Baptists, and has blessed the lives of hundreds of thousands who have used it since its first appearance. At first the readings were related to the weekly program materials. In 1905 a two-year course of reading the Bible by books was introduced. The plan provided for the reading of Old Testament books during the first two months of each quarter, and of a New Testament book during the third month. In 1918 a two-year topical course was added along with devotional comments, thus giving a four-year plan. It was made a five-year cycle in 1924 when a year was devoted to reading through the New Testament. Daily prayer suggestions and the missionary calendar of prayer were added in 1935. Since January 1, 1955, new references and comments have been used.

Graded Textbook Study Course

From the appearance in 1907 of the first study course book, *The B.Y.P.U. Manual,* to the course as it now stands, the history of the graded study course is a remarkable story. To Jerry E. Lambdin goes the credit for the development of the graded study course. He had the vision of such a course when he became associate secretary of B.Y.P.U. work in 1925. It was his purpose to arrange the course for each of the four departments by subjects, with one or more books under each division. The Young People's and Adult books were for the first time divided into ten classifications in 1932. Shortly afterwards, the Junior books appeared under seven classifications, and the Intermediate books were divided into ten categories. By 1949 the books for all four departments appeared for the first time under the same classifications.

There are from two to six books in each division. The divisional subjects are:

I — Principles and Methods
II — The Church
III — The Christian Life
IV — The Bible
V — Doctrine
VI — The Home
VII — Missions
VIII — Stewardship
IX — Soul winning
X — The Denomination

These textbooks usually are written to be taught in two forty-five minute periods each night for five nights. There are some deviations from the plan, but the most popular and effective method is the one-week study course. A step of further progress is the integration of this course with the correlated study course plan now used in the Southern Baptist Churches. By this means the Training Union course has become a part of the church's program and is offered to the total church membership even though they are not members of the Training Union. Every member of every Baptist church should be enlisted in the study of these books and should have no less than one award for at least one book out of each division and on each departmental level. (For complete description of the course, write the Baptist Training Union Secretary in your state.)

SPECIAL YOUTH ACTIVITIES

Annual Contests

In the transformation from the B.Y.P.U. to the fully graded Baptist Training Union, certain distinctive youth training projects have been developed and are actively promoted. Among these are the *Bible Memory Drill*, the *Sword Drill*, and the *Better Speakers' Tournament*. The primary purpose of the memory contest and word drill is to teach juniors and intermediates how to handle the Bible as an effective implement in Christian service. The purposes of the speakers' tournament are to familiarize young people with distinct denominational emphases and vital principles of Christian living and to develop skill in speaking on religious subjects. A church conducts a competitive contest in each of the three departments. The winners enter the associational contest. The winners in each association compete at the state Training Union conventions in the spring. Each summer the state winners, Intermediate and Young People, meet the finalists at Glorieta or Ridgecrest during one of the convention-wide Training Union assembly weeks.

Youth Week

This is a plan to place young people in all the official positions in the local church for one full week. The actual work of serving in the capacity of pastor, deacons, Sunday school teachers and officers, W.M.U. and Brotherhood officers, Training Union director and officers, is an experience which no young person will ever forget. Hundreds of churches now observe this plan for increased appreciation and understanding of the work of the church. Youth week has demonstrated its value and has become an annual affair in most churches which have tried it.

Youth Night

This project was launched in April, 1955. It is a night set apart in the month of April for associational youth rallies throughout the Southern Baptist Convention territory. The meeting is planned, promoted, and presided over by the youth of each association. It is held under the auspices of the associational training union, but for youth only.

Military Service Membership Plan

With the realization that practically every young man must take some form of military training, it was evident that something should be done to help them during their term of service. Accordingly, the military service plan has been set up in conjunction with the Sunday school Young People's Department, and the Home Mission Board. The objectives are to "help the young person or adult in uniform to maintain continuity in his relationship with his church and to utilize the experiences of military service as opportunities for Christian growth." Upon entering the service the member is transferred to the Military Service Group of the Training Union. He is sent quarterlies and a special report form for keeping in step with the church at home. He can maintain his daily devotional life by following the Daily Bible Reader's Course. He may complete Study Course books by the individual study plan; be promoted into the next department; mailed the church bulletin; and receive special correspondence from his home church. Its promotion will help the absentee member to keep on growing in his spiritual life, and he may be more easily led to resume his place in church life upon his separation from the service.

The Baptist Training Union is doing a great work in articulating and deepening beliefs in youth; in teaching young people how to perform church offices; in helping to round off character building; in providing opportunities for fellowship and social life; in affording outlets to talent in public speaking, music, and religious art; in making some efforts to give guidance in choosing a vocation, developing church leadership, and establishing a Christian home. But looking to the future, what has been done is only to get a vision of greater possibilities ahead. As the churches and denominations face the moral issues and social problems of modern society, might not the Training Union be more effectively utilized for presenting the truth and enlisting church members in vigorous combat against the forces of evil which threaten to destroy the nation and the world?

LIMITATIONS OF THE TRAINING UNION

Before going too far in bringing in social service activities for the Baptist Training Union to take over, it should be noted carefully that all public-serving institutions today are threatened with carrying excess baggage of burdens thrust upon them by a society with problems too great and complex to be handled by traditional means. In other words, an individual agency can be forced to assume responsibilities which ought to be taken up elsewhere, and can to that extent depart from its distinctive purposes. Furthermore, vital energies will be dissipated, and the loss may be fatal. Therefore, it is well for the Training Union to recognize its limitations.

First of all, the Baptist Training Union, while doing its part to foster vocational guidance in the atmosphere of Christianity, nevertheless cannot be an employment agency or a vocational guidance clinic. Much can be done to help Christian youth make this most important choice by considering every honorable vocation as an opportunity to serve God and mankind. It is not primarily the responsibility of the church to find jobs for its members. A new aid available for the church in this task is *Career News*, a monthly publication of the Education Commission of the Southern Baptist Convention, which the church should provide for each high school junior and senior.

Secondly, the Training Union is not to be thought of as the recreational agency of the church. It cannot be expected to care for all the leisure activities of its members. A reasonable amount of time and money may be spent to provide some much-needed social life on the Christian level; but responsibilities for meeting all recreational needs of the membership of the church should not be placed on the Training Union. There should be the closest cooperation with all the agencies of the church at this point, and the Training Union is expected to assume its share but not to carry the whole program of recreation and leisure-time activities.

Thirdly, the Training Union cannot serve as a marriage agency for youth; nor can it solve all problems of courtship, love, and the family. Nevertheless, it can be informed in this field. It certainly has a responsibility to discharge towards the home.

Lastly, the Training Union even in its strongest territory of creative contribution, that is, in religion, cannot shoulder all the burdens of young people's religious needs. The Sunday school must do its part; Woman's Missionary Union and the home must cooperate also. In other words, there should be an integration of efforts of home, church, school, and community in all the matters mentioned above. But may the church not lead out in more cooperative, organic, and personality-building efforts? It is time for religious pioneering in this field.

Statistical growth has been steady, the curriculum is undergoing constant revision, the leadership is learning more about sound educational techniques, and most churches are forward-looking. In any event, the forces of evil are working too hard for the Baptist Training Union to slow up. Social movement may be baffling, and procedures may need renewing, but the vision remains. Spiritual pioneers are needed. Training Union leaders will not fail youth nor surrender them to defeat.

QUESTIONS FOR DISCUSSION

1. Compare your youth program with those of other denominations.

2. Evaluate as objectively as possible the influence which the Training Union has had on your own spiritual development.

3. Explain in your own words what is meant by the statement "The avowed purpose of the Baptist Training Union is that of training in church membership." Make a list of the activities in which church members need training.

4. Offer some specific suggestions for increasing the interest in the Baptist Training Union in your church.

5. Do you think it would help in the development of church members if the material in the Sunday school lesson and the Training Union quarterly were correlated? Support your position.

6. Make a list of the youth organizations in your community, including those of other denominations and those sponsored by other community organizations.

CHAPTER 15

THE WORK OF THE WOMEN:
WOMAN'S MISSIONARY UNION

If one reads the New Testament with an eye for the part women played in the new movement of Christianity, he will find that their contribution was conditioned unconsciously by the position of women in New Testament community life. This is in line with the dictum of theology that historical revelation is poured into the vessels of human instrumentation and — though eternal — has its position in time and place. The finest illustrations of this are found in St. Paul's instructions to the women of the church at Corinth, which we now interpret in the light of the peculiar Corinthian situation.

The same approach should be made to the place and work of women in present-day Christianity. That is, the separate and supreme importance of women in church life both as individuals and groups, must be understood in the light of current growth in the recognition of women's rights and the modern conception of their destiny. For example, as recently as 1885 the constitution of the Southern Baptist Convention was deliberately changed in order that the word "member" could be construed to mean only *brother*, and the two women messengers from Arkansas were thereby automatically eliminated from representation in the convention.[1] In other words, until quite recently there have been cultural handicaps lying across the pathway of service, hindering the progress of women and compelling them to follow circuitous detours. Also, unfortunately disturbing emotions have been impounded by these devious ways and have colored unconsciously the specialized meetings of women. As a matter of fact, sociologists look upon the phenomenal growth of women's groups as due in part to an unconscious reaction to the circumscription imposed by men. This is just another way of saying that the age-old struggle of the sexes is reflected in religion, though on the whole it is sublimated and may be vitally useful, flowing forth as a stream of idealized and enriched missionary work.

HISTORY AND GROWTH

History

In the home of Mrs. Beeby Wallis, a widow living in Kettering, England, was organized the first "Missionary Society for the Propagation of the Gospel Among the Heathen." William Carey was sent out by this society to India in 1792. There were monthly concerts of prayer which grew up in this connection in both England and America, and they brought on a great spiritual revival.

A missionary periodical was published, many of Carey's letters were printed, and newly awakened missionary interest bubbled over everywhere. Among these were the Wadmalaw and Edisto Female Mite Societies of Charleston, South Carolina, and the Hyco Female Cent Society of North Carolina. The chief objectives were prayer and giving, with a view to supporting mission work. However, the honor goes to Miss Mary Webb, a cripple, for organizing the first woman's missionary society of modern times. This was in 1800.

[1] William W. Barnes, The Southern Baptist Convention, 1845–1953 (Nashville: The Broadman Press, 1954), p. 149.

It was called "The Boston Female Society for Missionary Purposes."[2]

During the next two decades, however, the work expanded greatly. Phenomenal growth began with Luther Rice and the Judsons. In 1812 they went out to India under the Congregational Board, became Baptists, and gave the Baptists of the United States a real vision and incentive to promote missions. To Luther Rice, especially, goes the credit for this, for he came back to America to plead the cause of missions in person. Within eight months of his return to America, the Triennial Convention was formed by the thirty-three delegates who met in Philadelphia in May, 1814. There were two boards; one to promote home missions, and the other foreign missions. Adoniram Judson and Ann Haseltine Judson were accepted as missionaries, and India became the first mission field for American Baptists.

Growth

So rapidly were missionary societies growing, that by 1817, or the second meeting of the Triennial Convention, there were reported 110 women's societies. By 1840, there were from one to fifteen units in eleven of the eighteen states of the Union. In 1833 the Triennial Convention sent its first missionaries to China, John Lewis Shuck and Henrietta Hall Shuck. A sewing society of Beulah Church in Virginia aided Shuck when he was a student in Richmond Seminary and outfitted him with clothes when he sailed for China.

In 1860 an interdenominational organization for women was formed, the Woman's Union Missionary Society. Mrs. Doremus of New York was the guiding spirit. In 1868 the Congregational women set up their own organization; the Methodist Episcopal followed in 1869; the Northern Presbyterians in 1870; and the American Baptists in 1871.

In 1868, when the Southern Baptist Convention met in Baltimore, Mrs. Ann Graves gathered together the women

[2] Kathleen Mallory, *The Manual of WMU* (rev. ed.; Nashville: The Broadman Press, 1953), pp. 10–11.

who were attending the convention to pray for the Kingdom interests. From this meeting came the call for organized mission activities by the women. At the next convention, 1871, the work of organization was begun; a central committee was appointed; and a committee in each state for the purpose of mission study and prayer. At the convention in 1888, at Richmond, Virginia, thirty-two women delegates from twelve states who were denied admission to the Southern Baptist Convention as messengers, met in the basement of the Broad Street Methodist Church to complete the general organization. Ten states voted for the organization of the Executive Committee of Woman's Missionary Societies, Auxiliary to the Southern Baptist Convention.[3] In 1890 the name was changed to Woman's Missionary Union, Auxiliary to the Southern Baptist Convention, and Miss Annie Armstrong was elected its Corresponding Secretary. Thus Woman's Missionary Union was born.

ITS EDUCATIONAL FUNCTION

A brief definition of Woman's Missionary Union should precede a discussion of the plan of organization. "Woman's Missionary Union is a graded system of organization for women and young people in Baptist Churches for the purpose of promoting Southern Baptist mission work the world around."[4] The basic principles of Christian living color and suffuse its objectives. These are "Bible and Mission study, prayer, and personal service, enlistment and soul winning, and Christian stewardship." This definition describes a religious educational unit which in its structure and function, has arisen to satisfy a very definite need in church life. That is, like the Sunday school and the Baptist Training Union, Woman's Missionary Union originated in response to a social and religious demand.

However, like other social institutions it has grown into a highly centralized organizational structure. One may pic-

[3] Barnes, *Southern Baptist Convention*, p. 155.
[4] Wilma Bucy Stockton, *Woman's Missionary Union At Work* (Nashville: Baptist Sunday School Board, 1948), p. 44.

ture it in an outward and formal way as an ever-widening series of circles. Beginning with the local church, which has the primal and pre-eminently personal organization, a second circle may be drawn to represent the association; a third, the state, though there are usually districts within the state; and the fourth circle, the South-wide organization. Most manuals, however, list the South-wide organization first, due perhaps to its size and the further fact that promotional work begins at the top and works its way down to the local church. Then, too, missionary Baptists are cooperative in the support of their leaders.

The most obvious reason, though, is the traditional one, which sociologists have explored for us, namely, the tendency of all organizations to grow alike, beginning locally and expanding in an ever-widening, as well as in a more or less impersonal, way, until the state, the nation, and other nations are involved in a sort of "geographical hierarchy of administration."

FORM OF ORGANIZATION IN THE LOCAL CHURCH

While it is not necessary here to describe the structure of Woman's Missionary Union in its totality — associational, state-wide, convention-wide, and world-wide[5] — it is essential to understand the plan of organization in the local unit, especially where the program is built up from the point of view of the local situation and not from the angle of an absolute or arbitrary standard.

Plan of Organization

First, there is the *general organization* which is called Woman's Missionary Union, embracing all the organized women's mission work of the church, graded down through the auxiliaries. When there are two or more of the organizations in a church, it is recognized as a Woman's Missionary Union. When all the auxiliaries are to be found in a church, it is called a graded Woman's Missionary Union. Secondly, there are the *graded organizations*. Woman's Missionary

[5] Mallory, *Manual of WMU*, chap. i.

Society is designed for all the women of the church above twenty-four years of age, its purpose being "to promote Christian missions and to stimulate the grace of giving among women." For all young women between the ages of sixteen and twenty-four, there is the Young Woman's Auxiliary. The Intermediate Girl's Auxiliary is for girls ages thirteen to sixteen; and Junior Girl's Auxiliary for girls from nine through twelve. The Sunbeam Band is for girls and boys four through eight, divided into beginner and primary bands, four and five years, and six through eight, respectively.

In addition to the graded organizations in each church, there are *two special units* to meet the needs of young women away from home for educational purposes. One of these is the Ann Haseltine YWA for those in colleges and universities. The other is the Grace McBride YWA for those working in hospitals and schools of nursing. Separate "Aims of Advancement" are set forth which permit each organization to function better in its particular institution.

In 1908 Woman's Missionary Union started the order of Royal Ambassadors for Junior and Intermediate boys, ages nine to twelve and thirteen to sixteen, respectively. The real value of this organization was emphasized when the Missionary Education Committee of the Northern (American) Baptist Convention selected the Order of Royal Ambassadors as "best fitted for real world mission endeavor." In 1939 Woman's Missionary Union "projected the idea that Baptist Brotherhoods could help with Royal Ambassadors by studying their program of work and by helping train men as counselors."[6] The Southern Baptist Convention meeting in St. Louis, in 1954, voted the transfer of the Order of Royal Ambassadors from Woman's Missionary Union to the Brotherhood Commission. The plan was to make the transfer gradually over a period of three years. Culmination of this action was set to take place at the end of 1957. For the three-year period the work was promoted by a joint committee, composed of the presidents and executive secretaries of

[6] *WMU Yearbook, 1955–56* (Birmingham, Ala.: Woman's Missionary Union), p. 74.

Woman's Missionary Union and the Brotherhood Commission with three additional members of each organization appointed by the respective body. In churches where the Brotherhood is not functioning, it would be advisable for the Order of Royal Ambassadors to be promoted by the women until the Brotherhood can be organized. In assuming promotion of the Royal Ambassadors by the Brotherhood, it was definitely agreed that the missionary emphasis should be continued as a feature of the permanent program.

It is important to call attention to the need for considering the type and condition of the local church as determining whether it is best to start out with the idea of setting up a graded Union. Furthermore, the promotion of any religious educational unit ought to be planned with the total educational program of the local church in mind; that is, in terms of coordination and unification of religious activities so as to eliminate petty jealousies and duplication of efforts.

The Officers of the Union

The local situation again will be determinative. In some cases not only is a complete roster of officers unnecessary, but the local church does not have available members. Where this is the situation, those which can be had will be elected, and the local union should not feel any less important for it. As Woman's Missionary Union grows, more officers may be added. In some small urban, community, and rural churches, a good wide-awake president and secretary-treasurer will be depended on almost entirely as the minimum staff. In some cases offices may be combined. It is necessary that each activity be assigned to some officer. No reasonable excuse exists for saying the church cannot have a Woman's Missionary Union, or at least a Woman's Missionary Society. If the women live long distances from each other and there is preaching only once or twice a month, successful work can be done by one or two leaders keeping the women busy by telephone and through the mail, so that they are prepared when they do come together, if only once or twice a month. *Royal Service* furnishes good material for programs, and as many members as possible should subscribe for it. If there are only a few who take it, parts may be copied, and written suggestions made by letter. Wise pastors of small churches are making the above approach and are laying stress on the particular situation as the final court of appeal in handling the structure of any church organization. There are and ever will be various types of churches — urban, rural, large, medium-sized, small, etc. Also, there are peculiar local conditions which must be considered in every instance. Thus and only thus may personality growth and development of the women be given pre-eminence.

The Duties of the Officers

The duties are not unlike those of other church organizations. The president plans for the monthly business meetings and presides over them. Also she exercises supervision over all Woman's Missionary Union work of the local church; presides at the executive committee meeting; knows the duties of all officers; and supplies the necessary enthusiasm to give the work an optimistic and aggressive flavor. The first vice-president should understand the duties of the president and act in her absence; also, she is chairman of the enlistment committee. The second vice-president takes charge in the absence of the two officers above her. In addition she is chairman of the program committee and sets the pace in all program building. The director of youth leads in fostering the auxiliaries, and helps the counselors. The corresponding secretary writes the letters which are authorized by the society and publicizes Woman's Missionary Union through the usual avenues of church bulletins, local papers, posters, etc. She may also be chairman of the literature committee. The recording secretary sends out notices of meetings and keeps accurate minutes. She also sees to the promotion of the "Aims for Advancement" as a plan of work. The treasurer supervises and reports all receipts and disbursements of money. She may, in addition, be chairman of the stewardship committee, where the church and the local society are small.

Qualifications of the Officers

Generally speaking, the personal qualities and aptitudes, such as should characterize the various officers, are hard to describe since they are intangible traits and are enmeshed with environmental situations. Furthermore, on the theoretical side at least, they belong in the realm of the psychology of leadership as well as in the field of social psychology.[7] All of this means that the local situation and the circumstantial training of the leader or leaders will color the official and executive functioning of the local Woman's Missionary Union.

Certainly all who are chosen should be sincere Christians, loyal to their church, and devoted to the cause of world missions. They should be willing so to plan all their other activities that adequate time may be given to their Woman's Missionary Union work. Each Woman's Missionary Union should search out the best ones available and willing and put them to work. Improvement will come with added responsibility, new opportunities to develop talent, and experience. Here is where Woman's Missionary Union, as well as other organizations, make a great contribution — though personality development is often overlooked in the effort to promote a program.

MISSIONARY FUNDAMENTALS

According to the *WMU Year Book* (1955-56) "The object of Woman's Missionary Union shall be to emulate the spirit of our Lord and Savior Jesus Christ; to promote Christian missions and to stimulate the grace of giving among women and young people." To carry out this objective each society is expected to enlist and develop the women and young people in missionary fundamentals, which are: prayer, mission study, stewardship of possessions, and community missions.

Prayer

From the earliest days this has been the first and foremost

[7] See R. T. LaPiere and Paul R. Farnsworth, *Social Psychology* (New York: McGraw-Hill Book Co., Inc., 1936); also Ordway Tead, *The Art of Leadership* (New York: McGraw-Hill Book Co., Inc., 1935).

activity of the organization. Individual daily use of the calendar of prayer, which is found in the departmental publications, is urged not only in Woman's Missionary Society but also in the auxiliaries. Family prayers are promoted in the homes. A major prayer emphasis is the observance of special weeks of prayer. These are: week of prayer for foreign missions with Lottie Moon Christmas Offering, usually held the first week in December; the week of prayer for home missions with Annie Armstrong offering for home missions, usually held in March; the season of prayer with offering for state missions, date to be set by Woman's Missionary Union in each state.

The history of the weeks of prayer parallels that of Woman's Missionary Union, for the two were begun in the same year. In China, Lottie Moon, sick and due for a furlough, wrote a stirring letter to the three-month-old organization. She urged the societies to make a special Christmas offering for sending two new missionaries to China. Annie Armstrong, the corresponding secretary of the new organization, believed they could, and letters were written by hand to the fifteen hundred societies. The response was thrilling. In 1918 the name of the special "week of prayer and offering" was changed to the "Lottie Moon Christmas Offering for Foreign Missions." The Home Missions Week of Prayer and offering for home missions was begun in 1895. In 1933 it became known as the Annie Armstrong Offering, in memory of the first corresponding secretary of Woman's Missionary Union. Each of the states names its state mission offering as it so desires.

In 1955 the total offerings received for these three weeks of prayer was $6,814,548, more than two-thirds of which was used for foreign missions.[8] Every dollar of these offerings is used for direct missionary activity and is turned over to the various Boards to be used according to previously prepared budgets. The achievement of these weeks of prayer is truly phenomenal.

[8] *WMU Yearbook 1956–57* (Birmingham, Ala.: Woman's Missionary Union), p. 121.

Mission Study

Mission study has been the distinctive work of the women. The missionary emphasis of the Bible is given first place. World missions is studied and mission program material is given in the mission magazines *Royal Service, The Window of YWA, Tell,* and *Sunbeam Activities.* Mission study books play a most important part. Titles of all books to be used in these classes and for missionary reading are found in the current WMU catalog, *World in Books.* Helps and supplementary materials for teachers are also listed. Woman's Missionary Union also sponsors Mission Study Institutes and encourages participation in correlated church study courses and church schools of missions. Individual reading is further encouraged by the Woman's Missionary Society Round Table and the Young Woman's Auxiliary Book Club. These are organized in their respective units to promote the reading of books, which, though not strictly missionary in nature, will give the reader a broad background knowledge, enabling her to better understand and interpret mission movements. Prescribed titles for such reading are found in the book lists published annually. Every possible opportunity is seized for guiding its members in mission study.

Stewardship of Possessions

A slogan of the women is "Every member of Woman's Missionary Union a faithful steward." The purpose of this activity is to win tithers, to increase missionary giving beyond the tithe, and to lead in the faithful stewardship of all possessions. The means used are the distribution of literature; the study of books on stewardship; the use of covenant cards; cooperation with the church in subscribing its budget; promotion of the special mission offerings as over and above the tithe or subscription to unified budget of the church. The women are encouraged to teach the children, by example as well as precept, to become good stewards of that which God has entrusted to them.

Community Missions

The chief purpose of this activity is to win souls to

Christ and to meet the other spiritual needs in the community. This is accomplished by individual efforts in personal soul winning; prayer meetings in homes; working in mission Sunday schools, vacation schools for unchurched groups and in Good Will Centers; visiting in jails, hospitals, and other institutions; and the distribution of Bibles and evangelistic tracts. High Christian standards for community life are upheld. The means used for strengthening these standards are: Christian living in the home; alcohol and narcotic education; removal of centers and influences detrimental to the moral and spiritual welfare of the community; providing wholesome recreation for youth; working against racial discrimination; and promoting Christian use of the ballot. Through these activities the women of the church may make articulate their opposition to the evil forces of the community and thereby wield a mighty influence for social righteousness and Christian morality.

AIMS FOR ADVANCEMENT

As in all educational activities found in Southern Baptist churches, Woman's Missionary Union has its distinctive pattern of work clearly set forth in a standard. Replacing the former standards of excellence, "Aims for Advancement" became the program of work and measuring device for all WMU organizations as of October 1, 1956. Two features are in these aims which will encourage organizations of every size. First, there is a choice of basic objectives, which enables a society missing one month's activity to have another chance to receive recognition. The second encouraging feature is a graduation of advancement, permitting a society fulfilling eighteen of the basic objectives to be recognized as an "Approved Society." One which achieves eighteen basic requirements and nine electives is recognized as an "Advanced Society." A society which meets eighteen basic objectives and eighteen electives becomes an "Honor Society." The same plan in general applies to the youth organizations with slight variations in the number of requirements.

Taking the place of old high-standard recognition known

as a Full-Graded A-1 Union is the Honor Woman's Missionary Union. This recognition is awarded to the WMU which has an Honor Society, one or more Honor YWA's, one or more Honor G.A.'s, and one or more Honor Sunbeam Bands.

Space does not permit the inclusion of all these aims in this book; but, in order to set forth their practical values, the Aims for Advancement of the Woman's Missionary Society are given below.[9]

WOMAN'S MISSIONARY SOCIETY
AIMS FOR ADVANCEMENT

Basic Objectives For Approved Society	Electives for Advanced And Honor Society
I. WORLD AWARENESS	
General Missionary program meeting of society each month except those months in which the Weeks of Prayer for foreign Missions and Home Missions are observed	
Subscriptions to *Royal Service* equalling one half of membership	Every member receiving *Royal Service*
	Subscriptions to *The Commission* and *Home Missions* totaling one half of membership
Teaching of two books listed for Mission study classes in *The World in Books*	Teaching of additional book(s) listed for mission study classes in *The World in Books*
	Functioning WMS Round Table(s)
	Qualifying for recognition on the Mission Study Achievement Chart
II. SPIRITUAL LIFE DEVELOPMENT	
Observance of Weeks of Prayer for Foreign Missions and Home Missions, and Season of Prayer for State Missions	Definite promotion of use of calendar of prayer in *Royal Service* in homes and in meetings
	Intercessory Prayer League maintained

[9] Copies of the Aims for Advancement for WMU and all the auxiliaries may be secured free of cost from the State WMU Secretary in each state or from WMU Headquarters in Birmingham, Alabama.

WOMAN'S MISSIONARY SOCIETY
AIMS FOR ADVANCEMENT — *continued*

Basic Objectives   *Electives for Advanced*
For Approved Society   *And Honor Society*

III. CHRISTIAN WITNESSING

Participation of members in planned community missions throughout the year

A survey to determine spiritual needs in the community

Regular soul-winning visitation

Organized efforts to activate one or more of the Christian standards named in the WMU Plan of Work

IV. SHARING POSSESSIONS

Quarterly emphasis on stewardship of possessions

One third of the members tithing

One half or more of the members tithing

Three fourths of the members giving through the Cooperative Program

All members giving through the Cooperative Program

Gifts to the Lottie Moon Christmas Offering for Foreign Missions, Annie Armstrong Offering for Home Missions, and WMU State Mission Offering

V. EDUCATING YOUTH IN MISSIONS

Adequate fostering of three WMU youth organizations, leadership selected by the WMU nominating committee and elected by WMS

A graded WMU providing for all age groups in the church

New WMU youth organization(s) formed during the year

Assistant youth leaders for each youth organization as recommended in the WMU Year Book

Functioning committee on WMU youth work

Division of membership of existing youth organizations at the close of the year as recommended in the WMU Year Book

Basic Objectives For Approved Society	Electives for Advanced And Honor Society

VI. ENLISTMENT FOR MISSIONS

Definite program of visitation throughout the year in the interest of WMU enlistment	Organization of new circle(s)
One third of the resident women members of the church enlisted	One half of the resident women members of the church enlisted
An average attendance for the year of one third of the members at the ten general missionary program meetings of the society	An average attendance for the year of one third of the members of each circle at the ten general missionary program meetings of the society
	WMS Focus Week observed

VII. LEADERSHIP TRAINING

Officers, committees, and counselors studying together the current WMU Year Book	Youth director, counselors, and Sunbeam Band leaders each holding current leadership card of accreditation, WMU, SBC, or studying the respective leadership course offered by Woman's Missionary Union, SBC
Regular executive committee meetings throughout the year	
Regular, planned meetings of all committees throughout the year	
Representation at associational WMU meetings	Representation at state or convention-wide gathering of Woman's Missionary Union

VIII. REPORTING ADVANCEMENT

Quarterly Woman's Missionary Union reports to associational Woman's Missionary Union	Officers and committees reporting plans and activities to the Woman's Missionary Society regularly[10]

[10] *WMU Yearbook, 1956–57* (Birmingham, Ala.: Woman's Missionary Union), pp. 30–32.

WORTHY PROJECTS

In addition to the effective program of mission study and enlistment in stewardship as promoted in the local church, there are some general missionary projects of Woman's Missionary Union of Southern Baptist Convention which have made a distinct and valuable contribution to the world mission program.

Carver School of Missions and Social Work

One of the unique convention-wide projects of Woman's Missionary Union is the Carver School of Missions and Social Work located at Louisville, Kentucky. This school was established primarily for the purpose of training young women for all kinds of mission work. At the beginning of the twentieth century there was little or no opportunity for women who felt the call of God to receive professional training for Christian service. A few young ladies attended classes in the Southern Baptist Theological Seminary but were not allowed academic credit for the courses. In 1904 the Baptist women of Louisville opened a boarding home which in a short time proved inadequate. The Baptist women of the South came to the aid of the Louisville women and adopted the school in 1907. It was called Woman's Missionary Union Training School for Christian Workers. So for the first time in their history, Southern Baptists had an institution for training young women in Christian service.

Since its organization more than four thousand students have enrolled in the school; 1769 of whom have completed the two-year course and are listed as graduates. Since the primary purpose of the school is missionary training, it is especially gratifying to note that more than three hundred and fifty former students have gone as foreign missionaries to twenty-nine countries. Hundreds of others have worked as missionaries under home, state, and city mission boards. Many have served as field workers, local church workers, and Good Will Center workers. In 1953 the name was changed to Carver School of Missions and Social Welfare, thus honoring Dr. W. O. Carver, one of the greatest missionary statesmen of Southern Baptists. At the meeting of the Southern Baptist Convention in Kansas City, 1956, after forty-nine years of distinctive missionary training, the school property was transferred by Woman's Missionary Union to the Convention. It continues its missionary training emphasis. Its curriculum and physical resources will be expanded on the graduate level to permit advanced study in missions and social work. The most significant change which was authorized by the trustees is the opening of the school to both men and women with no restriction for admission because of race or nationality. Woman's Missionary Union will continue to direct the school, although the trustees will be elected by Southern Baptist Convention.

The Margaret Fund

Another notable achievement of Woman's Missionary Union is the Margaret Fund. This fund originated as a memorial fund in 1904. The initial gift of $10,000 was made by Mrs. Frank Chambers of New York and Alabama. The purpose of the fund is to provide college scholarships for sons and daughters of regular missionaries of the Home and Foreign Mission Boards in schools of their own choice, subject to the approval of Woman's Missionary Union. During the first fifty years of its operation, scholarships were granted to 752 students, to the amount of $807,666.93. The amount needed for these scholarships is obtained each year from the Lottie Moon and the Annie Armstrong offerings.

During the scholastic year each year approximately $50,000 is paid for scholarships for more than 100 students, 60 percent of whom are sons and daughters of foreign missionaries and 40 per cent of whom are children of home missionaries. In addition to the scholarships which pay for tuition, room, and board, societies in the different states maintain personal relationships with the Margaret Fund students through the Burney Gifts Fund. This fund provides three additional checks each year for students to use for personal expenses. Each state gathers the money for this fund according to its own plan. During the year 1954 the Burney

Gifts from the states amounted to $11,378.06. By providing this help to our missionaries in the education of their children, Woman's Missionary Union has richly blessed the families and relieved the parents of much anxiety. Many of these young people have responded to the call of God and have dedicated their lives to the continuation of the missionary work which was begun by their worthy parents.

Publications

Through its Department of Publications, Woman's Missionary Union has made a distinctive contribution to mission literature. Among its publications are three interesting monthly magazines. They are *Royal Service*, for all members of the Woman's Missionary Society; *The Window of YWA*, for all members of Young Woman's Auxiliary; *Tell*, for all Girl's Auxiliary members. *Ambassador Life*, for all Royal Ambassadors, was first published by WMU, but is now the responsibility of the Brotherhood. There is also a quarterly for all Sunbeam Band leaders called *Sunbeam Activities*. These provide material for program discussion and special articles on missions. The Publications Committee of each WMU secures subscribers for all these magazines and also for the general mission journals: *The Commission*, monthly, Southern Baptist Foreign Mission Board, and *Southern Baptist Home Missions*, monthly, Southern Baptist Home Mission Board. The *Year Book* which gives the annual calendar of activities is commendable. There are five booklet manuals which describe the work among young people; and separate books are published on mission work. The *Woman's Missionary Union Annual Report* gives a record of the annual South-wide meeting. The monthly magazines, leaflets, prayer-season programs, etc., continue to come from the press. But there is room for creative and fresh materials, and a great need for original writers. The same condition, of course, exists with other church organizations among the Baptists of the South.

QUESTIONS FOR DISCUSSION

1. What proportion of women church members belong to Woman's Missionary Union in your own church? What proportion attend regularly?

2. Compare the Aims for Achievement of Woman's Missionary Union with the standards of the Sunday school and the Training Union.

3. What was the dollar value of all gifts and work of the women in your church for the past year?

4. In what way does your Sunday school teach missions? What suggestions can you offer for correlation with the missionary organizations?

5. What provisions does your young peoples' program make for the study of missions?

6. What has your Vacation Bible School done to teach missions?

7. Does your church library cooperate with WMU by securing books listed in *World in Books?*

CHAPTER 16

USING THE WEEK DAY FOR RELIGIOUS EDUCATION

During the first half of the twentieth century two of the more progressive forms of church school education have been developed. They are the Vacation Bible School and the Week-day Church School. Educators in the field of religion are particularly interested, because in them they see the educational work of the church being seriously maintained for the first time on a week-day basis. Also, there is seen in these activities a widening and deepening of religion, wherein the church seeks more realistically than ever before to help the individual adjust to his world through moral and spiritual guidance.

It is hoped that a new type of community citizenship, national loyalty, and world cooperation may result from this new design for teaching religion. As ever, the test of its continued usefulness depends on the type of leadership and support which the churches can furnish. Each of these types of week-day religious instruction has proven its worth to the children, the church, and the community.

VACATION BIBLE SCHOOL

Nature

The school is *held in the vacation period* when the public schools are closed. It is usually conducted during the early summer for two or three weeks, depending on local conditions, for three hours daily, Monday through Friday. The courses of study are planned for three weeks. Many schools meet for only two weeks. Membership is open to all boys and girls of the community from the nursery, for children under age four, to the intermediate department, through age sixteen. Provision is being made to include those below four years old and also to provide additional Bible study for young people and adults. Grading is by age on the same basis as in the other educational agencies of the church.

The ideal arrangement would be to enroll every member of the Sunday school and training union up through the intermediate department in the corresponding departments in the vacation school. It really should be considered as the summer session of the church school using Sunday school teachers and training union workers as much as possible in the same departments of the vacation church school.

The school is *authorized and supported by the local church,* and not by one of its agencies. All expenses should be paid by the church and no tuition charged, although a free-will offering may be taken at the commencement at the close of the school, for use in paying the cost of the school. The church provides the teachers, buys the supplies, furnishes the place to meet and all the teaching aids and equipment. Each summer in mission centers, where an intensive program is promoted for the summer, and financial assistance is necessary, several hundred paid summer workers are employed and sent to these places by various mission boards. In the summer of 1955 the Home Mission Board of the Southern Baptist Convention sent out 388 college students as special summer workers. Many of these conducted vacation schools, in which were enrolled more than one hundred thousand.

Textbooks are not used by the pupils but are for the teachers only. Since the school is held during vacation time, the pupils are not required to study. Notebooks or workbooks are used, but the work is done by the pupil himself at the church under the guidance of the teacher or group leader. At first it was planned for the pupils to make their own notebooks under the direction of the leaders. But in response to increasing demands, workbooks, based on the departmental lesson courses, have been provided for churches desiring them. The workbooks are more practical than the notebooks.

So the vacation Bible School might be defined as a school held by the church three hours daily, two or three weeks during vacation time for all boys and girls of the community from three to seventeen years of age with departments or classes graded on the same age basis as other organizations of the church.

Types

There are four types of vacation schools: the individual church school, the denominational cooperative, the interdenominational, and the community type. The *individual church type* is authorized, supported, and controlled by a local congregation. This type is most popular among Southern Baptists. In one summer, Southern Baptists reported 26,033 schools with an enrollment of 2,733,990. When several churches of the same denomination combine their resources and cooperate in the promotion of the school, it is called the *denominational cooperative type*. The *interdenominational type* is set up by churches of several denominations joining together for promotion of the school. This type is quite popular throughout the United States and is recommended by the Division of Religious Education of the National Council of Churches. The *community type* is rare. It is a Vacation Bible School which is conducted by some agency of the community without any church or denominational supervision or control.

Origin

During the summer of 1898, Mrs. Walter A. Hawes, a member of the Epiphany Baptist Church, New York City, being deeply interested in the throngs of children of the tenements on the East Side, conducted a "summer Bible school" for them. In fact, she planned and led such a school each summer for seven years (1898-1904) for four hours daily. Dr. Robert G. Boville, Baptist city missionary, became interested in her project and began promoting similar Bible schools in 1901, when five schools were held in five mission churches on the East Side. The first two, directed by Mrs. Hawes, were held in a beer garden behind a saloon on East Seventy-first Street, New York City. The rental was twenty-five dollars a month for "the use of Hoffman Hall and an up-stairs room from July 12 to August 12, 1899," according to the original receipt issued to Mrs. Hawes.[1]

In 1902 there were ten schools and in 1903 there were seventeen, with an enrollment of four thousand. Dr. Boville prepared the first lessons which were taught in these schools. He used on his faculty thirty-one college and seminary students, seventeen of whom were men. He named the schools Daily Vacation Bible Schools, by which name they were popularly called. The word "daily" has been dropped and now most of the promotional agencies use the name "Vacation Bible School" or "Vacation Church School." Among the children the tendency is to use the shorter "Bible school" or "vacation school."

In 1904 Dr. Boville resigned as secretary of the Baptist City Mission Society and gave his full time to the promotion of Daily Vacation Bible Schools for the New York Federation of Churches. He organized the Daily Vacation Bible School Association in 1911 which became international in 1916. He was secretary of the association from 1917 until 1922 when he formed the World Association of Daily Vacation Bible Schools which he served until his death in 1937 at the age of eighty-three. The International Association of Daily Vacation Bible Schools is now incorporated in the Division of Education, National Council of Churches of Christ in America. Vacation Bible schools of today are the logical outgrowth of Dr. Boville's work. He initiated and

---

[1] Homer L. Grice, "How Vacation Schools Began," *The Baptist Leader,* February, 1951, p. 5.

promoted the movement and directed the development of the curriculum and publication of textbooks in the early days of the movement. "Except for Dr. Boville's vision, insight, and dynamic personality," according to Dr. Homer L. Grice, "there would have been no movement."

Denominational Promotion

The Presbyterian Church in the U.S.A. (Northern) was the first denomination to recognize the values of the movement. In 1910 this work was begun by their Board of Home Missions as a missionary project. The Northern Baptists began its promotion through the American Baptist Publication Society in 1915 under the leadership of Dr. Charles H. Sears. In 1920 they published a cycle of eight books for beginner, primary, and junior age groups, and in 1925 three intermediate books were added to the cycle. Most of the other denominations have also promoted these schools, including Roman Catholics.

Southern Baptists began to be interested in Vacation Bible School work as early as 1918. That year the First Baptist Church, Bessemer, Alabama, held such a school. In 1919 Miss Lilian Forbes, within a year after she became the first secretary of the Elementary Department of the Baptist Sunday School Board, was in correspondence with Dr. Boville concerning the movement. In 1923 she and her state elementary workers group recommended to Dr. I. J. Van Ness, Executive Secretary of the Sunday School Board, the active promotion of Daily Vacation Bible School.[2] In 1923 the work was formally begun when a special worker was employed to give part time to its promotion and part time to Sunday school work.

In 1924 a separate department was created. On September 1, Dr. Homer L. Grice, then pastor at Washington, Georgia, where he had conducted schools in 1922 and 1923, became the first secretary of the Vacation Bible School Department of the Baptist Sunday School Board. This marks

[2] Homer L. Grice, "Southern Baptists and the Vacation Bible School," *The Quarterly Review*, XIII, 2 (1953), p. 3.

the beginning of active promotion of the work by Southern Baptists. In the following summer two hundred and nine schools were reported with an enrollment of less than four thousand.[3] For the last summer before Dr. Grice retired, after thirty years of service, there were in the Southern Baptist Convention 21,741 schools with a total enrollment of 2,059,163. For this remarkable growth much credit is due to the tireless energy and enthusiasm of Dr. Grice.

MEETING NEEDS

Organizational Needs

The times demand a unified church educational program. The vacation school is well adapted to such a need. It should be correlated with the Sunday school of the local church. In fact, since 1935 the recommendation of the Vacation Bible School Department of the Board has been that the church vote in conference to make the vacation school a division of the Sunday school; so that now it has become a part of the Sunday school, with a permanent associate superintendent responsible for planning and promoting the vacation school all through the year as well as during the summer.

When a church takes this action, the pastor, the general superintendent of the Sunday school, and the departmental superintendents whose divisions are involved, are charged with selecting a time, securing a principal, and assisting him in the selection and training of a faculty. They should assist in promoting the school and conserving its results. Thus they help to correlate the Sunday school and the church more closely. The training course books for the Vacation Bible School workers are now correlated with the new training course for Sunday school workers; and the vacation school is promoted by the state, associational, and local Sunday school leadership. Therefore, when the movement for unification and integration becomes fully realized in the local church, the vacation school will more easily fall into the plans for coordination.

[3] *Ibid.*

Needs of Society

Next, and perhaps more important, social needs enter into the definition and articulation of the Vacation Bible School. The emphasis of progressive education on growth through social interaction is wholesome. But a sound educational philosophy should underlie the opportunities for socialized experience; in short, the community situation surrounding the particular local church should be realistically visualized. Some churches have tried to do this, and with some success, but there is yet much to be done in educating the oncoming generation for adequate practice of the social implications of Christianity.

Needs of the Children

As an opportunity for leading boys and girls to accept Jesus as Savior and Lord, the Vacation Bible School is unsurpassed. It may well be considered the best means of reaching the 17,000,000 boys and girls in the United States under the age of sixteen who have no relationship to Christ or the church. There are upwards of 8,000,000 boys and girls living in the South over five and under seventeen years of age. About half of these are not enrolled in any Sunday school and are not getting any form of religious instruction. The annual increase in birth rate and population is rapidly rising. This constantly increases the constituency. If these newcomers are ever to know Christianity, it will be necessary to go after them. Since so many are not being enlisted on Sundays through other church organizations, obviously some new organization which meets on week days will have to be used to reach them. In the ten year period from 1940 to 1950 approximately one million children were enrolled in Southern Baptist vacation schools who were not enrolled in any Sunday school. The number of such pupils in Southern Baptist vacation schools in 1955 was 198,572, and is increasing each year.

Furthermore, there are many dangers which come to boys and girls in vacation time. During one-fourth of the year, approximately ninety days, children are turned loose and are allowed to shift for themselves, except as careful home supervision, vacation play schools, or summer camps take them in charge; and comparatively few come within these groups. The results of so much idle time are the rapid increase of juvenile delinquency, more traffic fatalities among children, and waste of valuable human energies during the summer. The general hazards of vacation time are beginning to be realized, and the vacation school has grown up as an institution which partially meets this need. This means that play life is now being supervised. Purposeful guidance and creative experience through worship, discussion, music, drama, handwork, and directed play are necessary. They are not looked on merely as activities to keep children busy, but as most valuable situations for guidance of boys and girls in habits which result in Christian character.

Needs of Church

Finally, the church needs such a helper as the Vacation Bible School to increase its effectiveness in religious education. At its best the Sunday school has the pupil about sixty-five hours a year for distinctively religious instruction; the Training Union, only fifty-two; while the public school has him over eight hundred hours. Something should be done to improve this condition. The Sunday school and Training Union together cannot do it. There must be reinforcements. When the Vacation Bible School meets for three weeks, it will add forty-five hours to the time used, thus giving the church one hundred and sixty-two hours for religious instruction.

Furthermore, the vacation school furnishes the church with one of its finest opportunities *for training future workers* for its entire educational program. Of the workers used in the Southern Baptist vacation schools in one summer, some 25,000 who did their first teaching work in the church were enlisted as Sunday school teachers. New faculty members will be secured and trained each year. From these recruits new teachers may be found for the Sunday school and workers for all the other educational activities of the church.

The value of such a teacher-training agency cannot be overestimated. Not only will the local church profit from the schools, but the pastor and the church at large, as well as the community and the nation, will receive rich benefits. One of the greatest values is the understanding and fellowship between the pastor and the children of his church. It will also bring to the summer program of the church a new vitality and will be a means of enlisting new families in the church.

ORGANIZATION AND FINANCING

If the Vacation Bible School is to succeed, thorough preparation is absolutely essential. A last-minute public announcement before the church, a hurriedly thrown-together faculty, and an unplanned program will destroy the educational value of the school. Oversimplifying the problems, and too careless a regard for the significance of the school also make for failure. Where an occasional church dreads promoting a second or a third school, the dissatisfaction can usually be traced to improper preparation and poor management in the organization of the first and second schools.

Preliminary Steps

Proper preliminary steps leading to organization are necessary. For the first school, usually the pastor has to take the initiative in making the church feel the need and value of a school. He will not do this by springing the proposition on uninformed officers and deacons. Nor should he appoint a committee to begin with, because they may be ignorant of vacation schools generally and therefore may manifest indifference or even hostility. On the other hand, the pastor may begin by thoroughly informing himself of the plan and purpose of the school. He must show the church what happens to boys and girls during vacation time. He may explain, at the proper time, that the vacation school is an agency set up to minister to the spiritual, moral, physical, and group needs of children in a creative and happy way. Thus, interest will be aroused and the proper mind-set provided for the project. Only thereby may the pastor hope for the maximum of success.

Next, the one who is promoting the school will launch out into a campaign of more direct publicity. The boys and girls will be contacted during the Sunday school hour. Short speeches may be made before the various departments. After this the pastor should preach a sermon on vacation school work though he will tactfully announce it beforehand as a special message which vitally concerns the interests of the home. By now, perhaps, church action may be secured. The last step in publicizing the school is advertising. County and city papers may be utilized for announcements. Short news sketches will be made all along concerning special features, picnics, enrollment items, etc. Bulletins, painted signs, posters, a mimeographed letter to parents, and special tags and buttons are also helpful. No matter how many times the church has had a vacation school, advertising is needed each year.

Preparation Day

This is a part of the advertising, though it will appear to be a joyous recreational outing. A parade is often promoted on the Friday before the school opens on Monday. However, this usually takes place after a general faculty meeting, a departmental faculty meeting, and a registration session are held. In other words, after everything has been discussed in detail covering the first day in school, and after as many pupils as possible have been registered, there is a parade. A well-executed preparation day is one of the best guarantees of a successful opening day.

The Organizational Structure

The Vacation Bible School faculty should be formed as far as possible in a nonmechanical and vital way, where organization is not an end in itself. As Blair suggests, it is "organization and administration which make for creative individual and group living."[4] That is, the needs of the

[4] W. Dyer Blair, *The New Vacation Church School* (New York: Harper & Bros., 1934), chap. vii.

pupil are to be properly considered and personal guidance with proper spirit or classroom procedure, are to be deliberately chosen. Personality and Christlike character are the ultimate aims of the school. The *pastor* can serve profitably as principal of the school. When he is not the principal, he may set aside a part of his time each day to help as needed in the school. His presence and moral support are most helpful. Getting someone else to run the school, going away for a revival,or taking a vacation deliberately to avoid being in the vacation school show limitations in training, interest, and vision. Of course, where there is a very large church, it may be nearly impossible for the pastor to be of great direct assistance. Such a church will most likely have an educational director who can relieve him of much detailed work, but the pastor should be there each day.

The *faculty* required will be determined by the local situation and the type of school promoted. It will vary in different communities, but for the average-sized church the following will be sufficient:

Pastor
Principal
Assistant to the Principal
Departmental Superintendents, one for each department
Three teachers for each department
Pianists, one for each department
Group leaders, one for each 6-8 children.

The work of the principal is largely supervisory and administrative. His assistant may be a dependable high school boy or a college student. He takes over such tasks as icing water, running errands, and taking care of emergencies which are sure to arise. Five department superintendents are needed when there are Nursery, Beginner, Primary, Junior, and Intermediate Departments. When there are more than twenty beginners, forty primaries, eighty juniors, or eighty intermediates, there should be multiple departments, or two for each age group. The assistant departmental superintendent may serve as doorkeeper and department secretary. He should not serve as a group leader but be ready at all times to help the superintendent. When a piano is available for the department, the pianist should not be a teacher or group leader but should at all times be near the piano ready to play when needed.

At least three teachers are needed for each department as a general rule — one teacher for storytelling and dramatization; one music teacher; and a handwork teacher. These three divisions of activities are arranged to insure cooperative, creative, and meaningful pupil-centered work. In each department below the intermediate, there should be one group leader for each six or eight children. This leader should be above sixteen years of age. The leader should be with his group at every period of the daily schedule, from the processional to the close of the handwork period. There should be no classes. The pupils are taught by departments, not by classes. The group leaders are not teachers in the formal meaning of the word but are helpers who guide the pupils in group activities under supervision of the teachers. Students home from college make excellent workers and group leaders. Many thousands of them now gladly serve on the faculties of their own and other schools. Each summer more than 12,500 college students work in vacation schools of Southern Baptists on a voluntary basis.

Financing the School

The church should pay the expenses just as it does for Sunday school and Training Union. A careful budget should be worked out. The school need not be expensive, but there should be enough money available to provide workers with all necessary books and supplies. Usually the milk and crackers used daily in the nursery and beginner departments will be donated by interested individuals as are also the weekly treats for the Primary, Junior, and Intermediate Departments. When the cost of the school is not included in the church budget, as is usually the case in the church's first school, it is wise to secure from five to ten persons who will underwrite the cost. In some parts of the United States the faculty is frequently paid, but in the South this is not necessary. From the beginning the work has been projected on a voluntary and sacrificial basis. In determining the cost a safe plan is to allow one dollar for each child enrolled. Many schools use only one-half that amount or less. An offering may be taken at commencement to help pay the costs of the school. If it is not enough to settle all bills, the underwriters pay the difference on a pro-rata basis. All purchases should be made by the principal in accordance with the purchasing plan of the church and all bills paid through the church. Never should tuition be charged; nor should a daily offering be taken for the school's expenses. Some schools take a mission offering, but it should be clearly understood that none of the offering is used for the expenses of the school. For the past few years the mission offering of Southern Baptist vacation schools has been given to the cooperative mission program of the denomination. Each year this offering exceeds $250,000.[5]

CURRICULUM MATERIALS

When Dr. Grice began in 1924 there were no textbooks for Southern Baptists. Only a few pamphlets describing the needs had been printed, but nine months later he had written or edited three complete textbooks, one each for Beginner, Primary, and Junior Departments. These were not mere outlines of programs but complete textbooks, containing all the materials needed for each department. All these books were edited by Dr. Grice in harmony with his original purpose — to be used by volunteer workers, trained and untrained, for every type of school, in every community. This made it posssible for a faculty secured within the membership of a local church to plan and conduct a vacation school without need of extensive library facilities and extra supplementary books or the employment of outside workers. The books were nontechnical, and free from psychological or theological terminology, although based on a sound philos-

[5] Southern Baptist Convention, 1956 Annual, *Sunday School Board Report* (Nashville: Executive Committee, S. B. C.), p. 238.

ophy of education. They can be used in any church, large or small.

When these books were revised, the first four new superintendent's books made their appearance in 1938. The second series consisting of thirteen departmental books was complete within four years. The first edition of the *Junior-Intermediate Joint Service Book*, which is for use of the principal in worship services, was published in 1938; and a new volume followed each year until 1943. The book has been revised each year. It now includes a worship service with all the needed music, character stories, suggestions for evangelistic opportunities and missionary activities. The Nursery Book and pupil's notebooks were first made available in 1952.

The departmental superintendent's books published by Southern Baptists are the most complete and practical guides on the market. They give the daily schedule, the elements of the program, and practical helps for all procedures. Busy teachers will find almost everything they need in these books and the principal's package.[6] Vacation schools of other denominations should consult their own publishing house for literature and supplies. The Scripture Press, Chicago, also publishes an excellent set of graded vacation school textbooks, which are nondenominational.

Generally speaking, there are eight types of activities in the vacation Bible school. These vary according to departments, development of pupils, and local situations. They are: worship, music, storytelling, dramatization, handwork, notebooks, Bible memory work, and supervised play. Missions and evangelism are included in most schools. While everything is planned and graded in keeping with the latest methods in education, room is left for spontaneous activities and self-directed projects by the pupils. However, the extent and the nature of such activities are conditioned by the abilities of the leaders and the development of pupils enrolled in a particular school.

[6] For list of supplies write the state Baptist Book Store or Vacation Bible School Department, Baptist Sunday School Board, Nashville, Tenn.

THE WEEK-DAY CHURCH SCHOOL

Types

The week-day church school is a school for the religious instruction of boys and girls attending public school, held by the churches of the city or community in cooperation with the local public school. Two general plans have been followed. One plan is called *released time*. The children are released from school to go to the church school for one hour a week during the regular school hours. Only those students who bring a written request from parents are released. Usually the classes at the church school are taught on a staggered schedule, so that only one or two grades are released during the same hour. Special activities or supervised study is provided by the public school teacher for children who do not have parent-request for released time from the public school.

The other plan is called *dismissed time*. The classes are held at an hour when all pupils are dismissed from public school one hour early, or school work does not open until an hour later on the day the church school meets. In some places the church school meets two days for forty-five minutes each, preceding the opening of school. Of the two, released time is much more desirable than dismissed time; because it makes religion a part of the educational experience of the child and it reaches a greater number.

Facing a Tradition

One of the finest traditions of American life is the separation of church and state. By keeping the state and the church free from each other administratively and financially, there has been preserved in America a distinctive form of government and a new form of religion. This has encouraged vitality of church life and independence of government. The unique Baptist position on this point has been repeatedly emphasized in denominational gatherings and most recently in the Baptist World Alliance.

Some have feared that the cooperation between the

churches and the public schools in promoting week-day church schools might lead to the violation of the spirit of this time-honored American tradition. But such is not necessarily the case. The tradition of our forefathers is not being violated. What they were seeking to do was to prevent the state from establishing a state church and to prevent any one religious sect from dominating the state. It was not their purpose to rule out all religion and make public education non-religious or antireligious. As a matter of fact, all education in early days of American history had a distinctly religious flavor, and those who wrote the Constitution and the First Amendment certainly did not foresee the time when the public schools would be completely secularized as they are today. The founding fathers were not trying to separate religion and government, but were seeking to prevent an unholy alliance between any one denomination or religious sect and a free state. A free church in a free state was the ideal.

It would seem that the week-day church schools are in principle a further elaboration of the spirit of our forefathers in that negatively they do not violate the principle of separation of church and state, because they do not set up any religious sect as dominant in the school system; and positively in that they definitely build a higher standard of morality and citizenship which furnishes a firm foundation for law and government — municipal, state, and federal.

Origin and Development

Although some earlier efforts were made to provide religious instruction on week days, it is generally agreed that the week-day church school is the result of the planning of William Wirt, superintendent of the Gary, Indiana, school system. He believed that the public school was but one of the educational agencies affecting the life of the child. In the fall of 1913 he offered to release pupils during school hours to the churches for religious instruction. The pastors promptly accepted the offer, and in the year 1914 the Gary plan of week-day church schools was inaugurated. For the first five years the schools were denominational, but in 1918

five Protestant denominations united to form a community
Board of Religious Education and to organize a community
system of week-day church schools on an interdenominational basis. This resulted in an increased efficiency and a
corresponding reduction of expenses. The chief significance
of the Gary plan of week-day religious education lies in the
fact that religious instruction was considered a part of the
child's complete educational experience and that the churches were asked to provide for it during school hours as an
integral part of his education. This type of week-day school
is recommended by the Department of Week-day Religious
Education, National Council of the Churches of Christ in
America.

A similar school was begun by a rural community at Van
Wert, Indiana, in 1918. It was an adaptation of the Gary
plan to the ordinary public school system. A teacher was
employed to go from room to room to give religious instruction as the music teacher did in those days. The school property and public school time was used for teaching religion.
This plan permits a trained teacher to devote her full time
to the work and eliminates the problem of supervision of
teachers and transferring the pupils to another building.

In 1919 at Batavia, Illinois, a denominational school was
instituted. Each pastor, or someone chosen by him, instructed the children of his particular church. The classes met at
the church building every Thursday of the school year for
an hour of religious instruction. The children were released
from the public school, two grades at a time. The reports
showed as many as 97 per cent of the pupils attended the
church school classes. In small towns the denominational
plan usually reaches a larger number of children than the
interdenominational plan. For Southern Baptists in the larger
cities the denominational type is suggested as the most suitable.

From these early beginnings the movement has become
nation-wide, until now week-day church schools are operating in nearly 2,000 communities and enrolling about two million children. This new kind of school has certain distin-

guishing characteristics. It meets on school days when the child is giving his attention to learning. It makes religion a part of his learning experience. The fact that the public school shares its time with the church school causes the pupil to regard religion as a vital part of his life.

Need

Week-day religious schools have come into existence because public school educators have felt that public school education has needed more moral and spiritual ballast. The church schools have followed in the tracks of the character education movement in the public schools and are the logical outcome of a more liberalized curriculum. Juvenile delinquency and criminal acts among young people have created the demand for week-day religious education as a foundation for moral living. Also, church leaders have become aroused and have welcomed the opportunity to have additional time for religious instruction. Furthermore, the week-day schools have dealt with religious fundamentals and have not reverted to secularism. Another need for the schools is the twenty-five million youth of school age in America who are not enrolled in any kind of church school. If the week-day school were fully used, it could reach multitudes of these unenlisted and could minister to their religious needs. Figures gathered over the years indicate that, on the average, 25 per cent of the pupils enrolled in week-day schools are not enrolled by any church or Sunday school.

Organization

The steps in organizing the school will be determined by the local situation, though there are some things which have to be definite and fixed. Convictions should be aroused and cooperation secured. The kind of program to be used must be thought out carefully. Adequate plans for financing must be made. A Board of Religious Education must be formed to make arrangements with the public schools; secure a supervisor and teachers; provide adequate meeting places, courses of study, and equipment; and act as a liaison group between the church schools and the public schools.

Any churches or communities planning to organize week-day church schools would do well to follow the *Ten Point Platform for Week-day Church Schools* which has been set forth by the Department of Week-day Religious Education, National Council of the Churches of Christ in America:

1. A year of planning before launching the program.
2. All religious groups working closely together.
3. Parents accepting their responsibility for the school and supporting it in every way.
4. Cooperation with the public school system without using its building or machinery.
5. A representative and reliable week-day church school board continuously on the job.
6. A course of education in religion as well planned and implemented to its purpose as the courses in the public schools are to theirs.
7. Teachers as well trained for teaching religion as the public school teachers are for their work.
8. A supervisor — trained, experienced, and religious — working with every school.
9. An expenditure per pupil (in proportion to the teaching time) equal to that for his public school education.
10. The spirit as well as the letter of the law preserved in all relationships.[7]

Week-day religious education, institutionalized in separate classes, may not be the solution to our problems of juvenile delinquency, crime waves among the young, and degeneracy in public morals — perhaps no one institution can do the job. But at least it is worth trying.

THE CHRISTIAN DAY SCHOOL

The present emphasis upon the use of week days for religious education is not a new experiment. Roman Catholics and Lutherans have maintained parochial schools most diligently since the time of the Protestant Reformation. The revival of interest in Christian day schools simply marks a return to the practice of an earlier period of church history.

[7] Erwin L. Shaver, *Remember the Weekday to Teach Religion Thereon,* a pamphlet (Chicago: International Council of Religious Education, 1949). Used by permission.

In New York City an excellent system of Jewish day schools has been inaugurated. The plan provides for two years' kindergarten work and three grades of elementary school which is strikingly suggestive of the elementary schools which prevailed among the Jewish people at the beginning of the Christian era. The basic purpose of these schools is to give the Jewish child a better understanding of his religious heritage and a stronger loyalty to the religion of Israel. According to the United States Office of Education, there are 5,408,000 pupils in the nonpublic schools of the United States, compared with 2,546,000 in 1943-44. About 90 per cent of the schools are under Roman Catholic auspices. The number of pupils enrolled in nonpublic elementary and high schools has more than doubled in the past fourteen years — a much greater percentage rise than in the public schools.

A few Baptist churches have established Baptist elementary schools for children of grade-school age. One of the first was the Lakeview Baptist Church, San Antonio, Texas. This school held its first session in September, 1946, with an enrollment of eighty-five students and four teachers. Ten years later it had 155 pupils and seven teachers. Its course of study is the same as prescribed by the Texas Education Agency, and the school is accredited by the State Department of Education. In addition to the regular course of study, Bible is taught daily for forty-five minutes in each of the six grades. The school is sponsored by the Lakeview Baptist Church. It has an annual budget of $22,000. The church pays two-thirds of the cost of operation. The other third comes from tuition. At present three other churches in San Antonio have opened day schools and another is planning a Baptist high school. In 1955 eleven Baptist day schools were found to be operating in six states of Southern Baptist Convention territory. There is a strong feeling on the part of some that Christian education should begin in the formative years of a child's life, and that churches should go into the school business. But many oppose the idea as undemocratic and an unnecessary expense in duplicating the public school system.

There may be some communities where such schools are needed and should be established, but the need for a general system of Protestant parochial schools does not seem necessary at the present. If churches are to continue to maintain and promote Christian day school work, more knowledge upon which to build should be obtained, and a better understanding of its values set forth.

KINDERGARTEN AND DAY NURSERY

The Situation

In most cities the kindergarten facilities are inadequate, and here is a community need which many churches can meet. Usually the Beginners' Department facilities in the newer educational buildings can easily be adapted to kindergarten activities. An increasingly large number of mothers are finding it necessary to seek employment, and many are leaving their pre-school children with incompetent caretakers or in poorly equipped nurseries and kindergartens.

If the churches can employ skilled Christian kindergarten teachers, such as are being trained in seminaries, it would be a distinctive service to many people. Already a number of churches have begun this ministry. Kindergarten is a place where children grow and learn through play, creative activities, listening to and sharing stories, conversation, rest, health, and safety education. It is planned for five-year-olds. Of course, a church-sponsored kindergarten, conducted by a genuine, radiant, happy Christian will provide religious instruction through Bible stories, religious songs, and prayers — all on the pre-school level. Securing the right kind of teacher, who is a qualified kindergarten worker, is the most important factor in setting up such a program.

A kindergarten committee or board may be named to work with the teacher in setting up objectives; securing equipment and supplies; adapting the building; determining tuition to be charged, salaries of workers, provision for children unable to pay tuition; and all other problems of administration. The pastor and educational director of the church should serve on this committee. There should also be some public school leaders who are familiar with kindergarten techniques and some interested parents on the committee or board.

The Support

A tuition fee is desirable for its effect on the parents. People value more highly what they have to pay for. Then, too, the money collected will help to defray the expenses of the school. The tuition should be the same as that charged by private kindergartens. The church should pay all costs of the school out of the church budget and collect the tuition through the church office. Usually the income from tuition will almost pay the teachers' salaries, but this should not be a determining factor. The kindergarten teacher might also be expected to serve as a supervisor in the *Beginners' Departments* of the church school on Sunday.

When children under five are admitted, there should be a separate teacher and meeting place for them. The class for four-year-olds is called a junior kindergarten. When children under age four are cared for, the church is operating a day nursery. For such service the same charges should be made by the church as that of similar agencies in the community.

Now that churches are providing adequate educational buildings and equipment at such great expense, there is no reason why they should stand idle for six days in the week and be used on Sunday only. Whether the church conducts a vacation school, a week-day church school, or any other form of mid-week religious education, it is encouraging to see them utilizing the week day for religious instruction.

QUESTIONS FOR DISCUSSION

1. From your own Vacation Bible School experience or by talking with your pastor or whoever organizes the Vacation Bible School in your community, write an evaluation of the school as an educational activity. Consider the administration, discipline, and the values of the curriculum to the boys and girls.

2. Make a calendar of activities for a Vacation Bible School for the year, including the selection and training of teachers,

selection, and preparation of materials, the time and place for the school, and the follow-up work.

3. How can cooperation be developed between the homes and the church on the Vacation Bible School program?

4. What are the social needs which are met by the Vacation Bible School?

5. How can the problems of housing, transportation, and curriculum for week-day Church schools be met?

6. Investigate the legal status of Bible teaching in the public schools in your state.

7. Make a survey of the communities in your state which have week-day schools.

CHAPTER 17

UTILIZING THE MEN OF THE CHURCH: THE BROTHERHOOD

Most of the early church work in America was unconsciously influenced by the patriarchal pattern of the home, as were our first laws. That is, the man had charge of all important matters, and the woman came second in consideration. The modern democratic conception of the home, in which everyone is regarded as a personality with his or her own individual rights and privileges, had not yet arrived. Consequently, no one raised a question about man's place in the church. It was tacitly understood that he would manage the institution down to the smallest details and would see that his household discharged their religious duties by attending all services. In other words, as far as administrative and official functions were concerned, the church was a man's institution. If there happened to be an equal number of women in the congregation, no one raised a question about the equalization of power, for numbers did not count in this matter of male supremacy, anyway. The result of all this was that there did not exist a need for a separate church organization ministering specially to men and catering to timid males who might have a feeling of inadequacy in the presence of efficient and articulate women. The men were managing everything already.

DEVELOPMENT

Present Situation

Today the situation is different. Many men do not attend church or actively participate in its program and often frankly say that they leave religion to their wives. Also, in some quarters, writers speak of religion as belonging to one of the creative, tender, and feminine arts — meaning, of course, to compliment it. On the side of the church, too, much of the hard work, no little of finance raising, and the bulk of teaching, lie in the hands of the women. But this is not due to a preponderance of females in our population. It is because the men have not been reached. According to J. P. Edmunds, Secretary of Research and Statistics, Southern Baptist Convention:

> There are now approximately twenty-two million men in our Southern Baptist Convention territory, of which eighteen million are unreached by any church. Our population is increasing at the rate of three million a year. In addition our territory is expanding. . . . To meet this tremendous challenge Southern Baptists are engaged in a campaign to start at least 10,000 new churches and 20,000 new stations by 1964. Can we do it? We can if our men are mobilized, if our men are used, if our men will accept their rightful place in the undertaking.[1]

Sixty to 70 per cent of the men belonging to the rural church were entirely unenlisted. The town and village church show a somewhat similar though slightly improved situation, for only 62 per cent of their men are enlisted. Now, there are over eight million Southern Baptists, more than one and a half-million of whom are men whose names are on the church rolls. It is estimated by the Department of Survey and Statistics, Baptist Sunday School Board, that 70 per cent are wholly unenlisted in the work of the churches. The purpose of the Brotherhood is to enlist these men. The slogan for enlistment is "A Million Men For Christ." This does not mean a million new men; but the enlistment of the

[1] J. P. Edmunds, "Key to Southern Baptist Advance," *Brotherhood Journal*, XXVIII, 2 (1958), 62.

potential man-power already in the church membership. The power thus released would be felt in every phase of the local church work and the world-wide co-operative mission program of the denomination.

Origin and Growth

Contrary to the idea of many, the Brotherhood is not a new organization of Southern Baptists. It started during the meeting of the Southern Baptist Convention, Richmond, Virginia, in May, 1907. The original purpose of the movement was to set up an organization for the men to parallel Woman's Missionary Union. It was called the Layman's Missionary Movement of the Southern Baptist Convention. In 1926, upon recommendation of the executive committee of the Layman's Missionary Movement, the name was changed to Baptist Brotherhood of the South. At the 1950 meeting of the Southern Baptist Convention, the status of the denominational movement was changed from that of a committee to a commission. It is now called the Brotherhood Commission of Southern Baptist Convention. All these changes have contributed to making the Brotherhood an integral part of the denominational program. The members of the commission are elected by the Southern Baptist Convention on a rotating three-year term basis as are the members of all commissions and boards of the convention; and the operating expenses of the Brotherhood, since it is a part of the convention organization, are now provided through a regular percentage of the cooperative program receipts. In 1954 the Southern Baptist Convention transferred to the Brotherhood Commission, from Woman's Missionary Union, the responsibility of promoting Royal Ambassador work in the churches, which is for boys nine to sixteen.[2] According to the *Southern Baptist Handbook 1956*, the enrollment of the Brotherhood was reported as 289,307 men and 114,974 boys in Royal Ambassadors.[3]

[2] *Southern Baptist Convention Annual* (Nashville: Executive Committee, S. B. C., 1954), p. 46.
[3] J. P. Edmunds, *Southern Baptist Handbook, 1956* (Nashville: Executive Committee, S. B. C., 1956), p. 32.

Purpose of the Brotherhood

The chief purpose of the Brotherhood is to bring all the men of the church together to inform them of the work of their church and denomination and to enlist them in active participation in the total church program. One reason men have appeared so indifferent in their attitude toward the church and denominational work is their lack of information. Informed men can be more easily enlisted. The Brotherhood program will inform and enlist them and will strengthen every phase of church work.

To achieve these aims the Brotherhood will seek to discover the talents of each man, to challenge him to enthusiastic participation, and to utilize each man in the organization. The officers are urged to always keep the activities within the program of the church. In order to accomplish this purpose, the objectives of the Brotherhood, as set forth in the *Brotherhood Guide Book*, are:

1. Loyalty to Christ, to the church, and to the pastor as leader of all its work.

2. Cooperation with every agency and organization of the church and denomination.

3. Constant emphasis upon the necessity of personal consecration for worthy Christian stewardship of home, self, substance, and service.

4. A greater emphasis upon individual and group effort in evangelism.

5. Increased circulation (and use) of our denominational papers and publications.

6. A wider and deeper study of the missionary, education, and benevolent work of Southern Baptists in the state, homeland, and the world.

7. An aggressive effort by men to reach, win, and develop boys through Christian companionship and guidance.

8. Tithes and offerings brought regularly to the church, and increased offerings in emergencies.

9. Progressive advance in church budgets both for local needs and denominational causes in order that the gospel may be proclaimed to the uttermost parts of the earth.

10. An increasing proportion of church receipts distributed through the co-operative program for denominational causes.

11. Liberal support and patronage of denominational institutions.

12. A continuing effort through the Brotherhood to promote

Christian fellowship and to enlist, organize, and utilize all the men of all our churches in active Christian service.[4]

ORGANIZING THE BROTHERHOOD

In setting up a plan of work, the Brotherhood has followed the general plan of other successful church organizations, which is natural and wise. Taking its cue here, it has developed local, associational, district, state, and Southwide units. The work of the Brotherhood, being modeled thus, is easy to understand as to its organization, grading, program, etc. All other units exist for the purpose of making the local unit effective in achieving the purpose. Above all, its purpose is, first, to contact and enlist the inactive men of the church; second, to develop them into useful Christian stewards; and third, to utilize the manpower of the church in service activities through the church, and into the community and world-wide missions.

Preliminary Steps

In organizing a Brotherhood in a church the preliminary steps may vary from place to place. The conditions in the local situation will greatly affect the structure of the organization. Usually the idea of organizing the men originates in the mind of the pastor. But when it begins in the minds and hearts of some other men of the church, they should first talk it over with the pastor and secure his enthusiastic support. He is the leader of all the church activities. His attitude toward the movement will largely determine its success or failure. The Brotherhood always works with and through the pastor, never around him. When the pastor initiates the movement, he should call a meeting of three or four of his laymen who might be interested and after careful explanation of the aims and purposes of the Brotherhood, and a prayerful discussion of the local needs, together they can make plans for organizing the men of the church.

Next, the plan should be presented to the church by the

[4] George W. Schroeder, *The Brotherhood Guidebook* (rev. ed.; Nashville: The Broadman Press, 1955), p. 11. Used by permission.

pastor and the other interested men, and the church should be asked to vote favorably upon its establishment. A special committee should be appointed or approved by the church for the purpose of working out the details for the first and second meetings, or until the officers are elected and the Brotherhood begins to function properly.

When the committee has made careful plans, the first meeting should be called. All the men of the church should be invited and urged to attend. Many churches have found it desirable to serve a dinner at the church for men only. Announcements should be made in all adult men's classes of the Sunday school, and in the adult unions of the church. The pastor or the committee chairman should write a letter or a post card to each man in the church. Posters and bulletins should be used. The committee should secure the best speaker possible to present the purpose and aim of the Brotherhood. He might be the state Brotherhood secretary or the associational president. It is essential that he be an active leader in Brotherhood work who believes in it and has been successful in its promotion. This meeting is most important. The impressions which the men receive at the first meeting largely determine the future of the Brotherhood in the church.

First Meeting

This meeting should be in charge of the chairman of the special committee named by the church. The program usually follows the meal while the men remain seated around the table and should include the following:

Song service,

Devotional, led by a sincere Christian layman or the pastor.

Message, concerning the purpose, work and aims of the Brotherhood. This message should be from a warm-hearted man who is enthusiastic in his presentation and a firm believer in the need for a Brotherhood; one who can answer questions and clearly explain the organization and purposes in a convincing manner.

Discussion period, in which the men are called upon to express their opinions on the values, the needs, and the possibilities of such an organization in the church. If the discussion is not spontaneous, the chairman may call upon several of the leaders in the work of the church to express their opinions. It is better to secure short expressions from as many men as possible than to have several long speeches. After thorough discussion they should be asked to express their desire to organize by a voice or a standing vote. Then enrollment cards may be signed by all who wish to become charter members of the Brotherhood. (If deemed wise, a motion might be made to extend the privilege of charter membership to those who attend the second meeting at which the formal organization will take place.)

Business period, during which the following items should be acted upon:

1. Time of next meeting to complete the plan of organization.
2. How often shall the meetings be held.
3. Naming of a nominating committee of three or more to work with the pastor in recommending at the next meeting the officers of the Brotherhood. The man who is selected for president should work with the committee in choosing the other officers who will work with him. Each man should be contacted and should agree to serve if he is elected by the Brotherhood and approved by the church.

Organizational Meeting

At the second meeting the formal organization takes place. It is in charge of the special committee first named by the church, and should be as carefully planned as the first meeting. At the business period the nominating committee presents its recommendations. Opportunity may be given for other nominations.

In addition to the pastor the committee should nominate the following:

President;

Membership vice-president, whose duties are to build and sustain attendance;

Program vice-president, who plans and presents all programs at regular meetings;

Activities vice-president, who promotes all the activities adopted by the Brotherhood, checks and reports on progress being made in promotion of all activities;

Song leader, who discovers and develops the musical talents of the men, and arranges music for all meetings;

Secretary-Treasurer, who keeps records and performs the customary duties of treasurer.

Upon election, the officers should be recognized and formally installed. The pastor of the church should bring an inspirational message as a challenge to the newly elected officers, and the president should make the response. All the members may then pledge their support, and a prayer of dedication may be offered by the new president or the pastor. These officers, together with all committee chairmen, constitute the Executive Committee of the Brotherhood. This committee is the planning and steering committee of the organization. It meets each month at a definite time to plan and pray for the meetings and activities of the Brotherhood. A wise president will contact, or have the secretary call, each member a few days before each meeting of the committee and urge them to be present. It is the president's responsibility to plan for this meeting, which is the generator of power for the organization.

ACTIVITIES

No Brotherhood can be a success unless there is a live program of activities. Men do not grow into strong characters by attending meetings and listening to speeches but by participation in some form of Christian service. Without activity it will soon die. Accordingly, the membership is divided into committees, and each man is placed where he can serve best and where his particular interests are centered. New interests may be discovered by placing men on committees where their talents may be discovered, utilized, and developed.

The number of committees needed is determined by three factors. They are: (1) The needs and program of the church; (2) the activities adopted for promotion; and (3) the number of men available for committee assignments. Ordinarily, no man will serve on more than one committee at a time; but at each change of officers, men may be transferred from one committee to another in which type of work each has developed a new and greater interest.

Regular Committees

The chairmen of the committees are appointed by the

president and work under the supervision of the activities vice-president, to whom they make regular reports. There is a working committee to promote each of the activities adopted by the Brotherhood. The regular committees are:

1. *Royal Ambassador Committee* — which seeks to teach missions to the boys of the church;
2. *Evangelism Committee* — which promotes continuous soul-winning activity and cooperates with the church in plans for the revivals;
3. *Worship Committee* — which promotes attendance to all the regular worship services of the church;
4. *Stewardship Committee* — which keeps before the men of the church the Christian doctrine of stewardship of money, time, and abilities, and leads them to cooperate with the church in promotion of its financial program;
5. *Benevolence Committee* — which seeks to extend the benevolent care of the church to the sick, aged, needy, and bereaved people in the community;
6. *Education Committee* — which keeps continually before the men a program of information concerning the work of the church and denomination. When men have the knowledge of the program of the church and the denomination, they will support it wholeheartedly.

Special Committees

In addition to the regular committees, as new activities and objectives are adopted by the Brotherhood special committees are set up to promote each activity. The chairman is appointed by the president; and men who are interested in the new activity are named as committeemen. The chairman of each becomes a member of the Executive Committee and should meet with them at regular monthly meetings as long as the activity is an objective of the Brotherhood. Suggested special committees and their duties are listed below:

1. *Social Committee,* which plans for special social occasions, banquets, ladies night, man and boy dinners, family picnics, etc. (In some churches this is a regular committee, but it is sometimes wiser to have a special committee for each occasion.)
2. *Juvenile Delinquency Committee,* which seeks to work

with juvenile courts and county judges in the rehabilitation of boys who have run into difficulty with the law. This type of activity may be needed only in city and town churches, but it occasionally is needed to help boys in smaller communities.

3. *Military Service Committee*, whose purpose is to keep in touch with young men of the church who are serving with the armed forces of our nation; not only in sending them forth, but by keeping in close touch with each one through regular correspondence; telling of all the church news and helping find a place for him in the work of the church upon his return home from the service.

4. *Extension Committee*, which assists in organizing Brotherhoods in neighboring churches and conducting services in pastorless churches.

Other committees may be appointed as the need for some special activity arises in the church and community and is adopted by the Brotherhood. When the objective has been attained, the committee makes its report to the activities vicepresident and is dissolved.

Through the committees the work of the Brotherhood may be adapted to the needs of any church, whether large or small. The larger churches may have more committees and larger committees and may sponsor a greater number of activities. In a small church with fewer men in its membership, it is wiser to center on a few major activities. This plan of organization makes it possible to fit the program and objectives to the size and needs of each church. The use of this plan also makes it possible for the Brotherhood to expand its work as more men are reached, or additional objectives are adopted for promotion.

THE ORDER OF ROYAL AMBASSADORS

The Order of Royal Ambassadors is an organization for the boys of the church. The boy nine through twelve begins his experience as a junior ambassador. At thirteen he becomes an intermediate ambassador. The purpose of the order is to teach world-wide missions and to make Christ challenging in every phase of a boy's life. Woman's Missionary Union began sponsoring this activity for boys in 1908.

In 1939 the women suggested that the Brotherhood could help promote the Royal Ambassadors.[5] At the Southern Baptist Convention meeting in St. Louis, June, 1954, it was voted on recommendation of a joint committee from the two organizations to transfer the Royal Ambassador work from Woman's Missionary Union of Southern Baptist Convention to the Brotherhood Commission. The final step in the transfer was completed in 1957.

A new Royal Ambassador ranking system was prepared at the request of the Southern Baptist Joint Committee on Royal Ambassador Promotion.[6] This system, which became effective October 1, 1955, provides a uniform plan for Royal Ambassadors throughout the Southern Baptist Convention. The boy enters the order as a candidate. Upon completion of requirements for each rank, he may advance through the ranks of page, squire, knight, and ambassador. It is necessary for a boy to complete each rank before starting on the next. There are three divisions for each rank. They are: (1) The boy and his chapter; (2) The boy and his denomination; (3) The boy and his Bible. Each division offers challenging requirements plus activities for developing well-rounded Christian personality. Additional information on ranking may be found in the *Royal Ambassador Manual* and the *Guide for Counselors of Royal Ambassador Chapters*, which are available at all Baptist book stores.

In assuming this responsibility the men of the Brotherhoods are urged to make this work with boys one of their major objectives. A Royal Ambassador Committee should be appointed by each Brotherhood, a suitable counselor secured, a meeting place provided, and the necessary supplies and equipment purchased. Every boy should be encouraged to

[5] *WMU Yearbook, 1955–56* (Birmingham, Ala.: Woman's Missionary Union, 1955), p. 74.

[6] *Southern Baptist Convention Annual, 1956* (Nashville: Executive Committee of the S. B. C., 1956), p. 312.

subscribe to the magazine *Ambassador Life*, and copies should be provided by the Brotherhood for those who cannot afford it. This monthly magazine is filled with adventure stories and articles of general interest to boys. It devotes space to hobbies and handcraft and is planned on the level of boys' interests.

Recreational activities and camps are a vital part of the Royal Ambassador program. The Brotherhood can see to it that every boy has an opportunity to attend associational, district, and state-wide camps and conclaves. In 1955 twenty states reported a good year in Royal Ambassador camps. The report for that year shows seventy-nine state camps were held with 8,629 boys attending state camps in twenty states; there were 16,200 boys attending associational or district camps — a total of 24,829 boys in Royal Ambassador camps in 1955.[7] There were 4,349 decisions for Christ, of which 1,393 were professions of faith. It is the aim of the Brotherhood Commission to provide a camp program for Baptist boys equal to any in leadership, facilities, and equipment. The Brotherhoods in the churches can see to it that every boy who so desires may attend one of these camps.

Each year a young men's mission conference is held for boys above sixteen years of age at Camp Ridgecrest. Leaders from Home and Foreign Mission fields conduct the conferences. Fellowship with young missionaries home on furlough is provided. The Brotherhood should lead the church to send its outstanding young men to these conferences. Such an experience will most likely make them more faithful Christian laymen, give them a world-wide vision of Christ's Kingdom, and make them more loyal to their church and denomination. No group of men in any church could devote their time, energies, and money to a more worthy cause than the Royal Ambassador movement, and no activity can provide greater satisfaction than the enlistment of boys in the Lord's work.

[7] *Ibid.*, p. 312.

THE ASSOCIATIONAL BROTHERHOOD

The associational Brotherhood is the next unit of work for men beyond the activities promoted by the local church. It is a part of the county or district association. Its officers and activities are approved by the district association of churches. Its purposes are: to promote fellowship of men throughout the association; to promote the organization of a Brotherhood in each church of the association; to co-operate with the associational mission program of evangelism and stewardship; and to enlist the men in churches which do not have a Brotherhood. It is chiefly promotional and inspirational and need not meet more frequently than once a month or even once a quarter. There are no special activities or objectives other than promotion of the associational and convention activities. The enthusiasm and interest created by this unit will be reflected in the activities and life of the church Brotherhoods.

Beyond the associational and district units of work are the state Brotherhoods which meet annually in each state, and the National Conference of Baptist Men, which meets at the call of the Brotherhood Commission of the Southern Baptist Convention. The first meeting of the National Conference was called to meet in Oklahoma City in September, 1957, which marked the fiftieth anniversary of the men's movement. There were more than six thousand men, coming from the thirty-three states, registered as delegates.

BROTHERHOOD LITERATURE

Three types of literature are published by the Brotherhood Commission which every Brotherhood should use. They are: (1) program materials to aid in presentation of good programs for the regular meetings; (2) organizational literature to help in establishing a Brotherhood and making clear the objectives and duties of the officers and committees; and (3) a system of records and reports so that accurate minutes may be kept and reports made to the church and the other units of Brotherhood work. This literature is published by the Brotherhood Commission of the Southern Baptist Convention, and it is distributed by them free or at nominal cost, upon request of church Brotherhoods. It may be secured from the State Brotherhood secretary in any state or from Baptist Brotherhood Commission.

Program Materials

For program material the *Brotherhood Journal* is highly recommended. It is published quarterly and contains materials for regular programs. Not many churches will have weekly meetings, so the program vice-president must select the material which will be best suited to meet the needs of the church. It contains other material and information written especially for men and should be made available to all the men of the church Brotherhood. The circulation of this journal now exceeds 100,000 each quarter. The aim is a total annual circulation of a half-million by the celebration of the fiftieth anniversary. Supplementing the *Journal*, other program materials are available in the form of pamphlets which deal exclusively with some specific phase of Brotherhood work. These aids are most valuable when the program vice-president carefully selects the subject matter to be used in the local brotherhoods. Variety should be used in presenting the materials. The programs must be made interesting or the men will lose interest and attendance will decrease. Long speeches should not be permitted. Use men who are enthusiastic and believe strongly in the objectives of the church and denomination.

Organizational Literature

This is provided in the form of tracts which are published by the Brotherhood Commission and the state offices. There is a separate tract on the duties of each officer which should be given each one at the time of his election. There are tracts for each objective and activity. These should be placed in the hands of the committee chairman and used in guiding the activities of each committee. Special tracts are prepared for special state-wide and denomination-wide emphases. The *Brotherhood Guidebook*, by George W. Schroeder, was revised in 1955. It should be carefully read by each officer and should be made available for all the men of the Brotherhood. Each member of the Royal Ambassador Committee should study, along with the counselors, the *Guide for Counselors of Royal Ambassadors* and the manuals for the Junior and Intermediate Royal Ambassador chapters.

Records and Reports

Good records are essential to good work. They are used to measure progress toward objectives and to evaluate the various activities of the Brotherhood and to guide in making plans for the future. The record system includes the following: the Brotherhood record book; enrollment cards; individual's report of activities; monthly report to the church, copies of which should be sent to the association and state Brotherhood leaders. A good secretary will see that all those reports are properly made and records carefully kept.

To summarize the work of the men, we quote from the *Brotherhood Guidebook*:

The key words to success of the Brotherhood movement are "activity" and "teamwork." Activity, because the men of the church Brotherhoods — the basic Brotherhood unit — must carry through in the adoption and promotion of a church and denominational-centered program of work; one that will challenge men to action. Teamwork, because the officers of the church organization must work together as a team to present, project, and promote effectively such a program of endeavor.

As the officers of the church must work as a team, so must the various organizations in the Brotherhood movement work together in accomplishing their respective purposes and the overall objectives of the Brotherhood. The work of the church and associational Brotherhoods and district organizations, the district organizations and state unit, and the state units and Brotherhood Commission offices must be so co-ordinated that they will function as one great team to achieve one great purpose — the promotion of the cause of Christ in and through their churches and denomination to the uttermost part of the world. ALL THE MEN OF ALL THE CHURCHES IN ALL THE WORLD FOR CHRIST.[8]

QUESTIONS FOR DISCUSSION

1. What percentage of the men of your church attend the meetings of the Brotherhood? Make suggestions for enlisting the inactive men.

2. What is being done by the Brotherhood of your church to develop the men into more useful stewards?

3. Organize a Brotherhood team for a revival in a nearby community. Plan the week of prayer, the music, and the messages.

4. Attend a school of missions and describe its value to the church and to the denomination.

5. How does your Brotherhood help to implement the total program of the church? Suggest ways in which the brotherhood can cooperate more fully with the total church program.

[8] George W. Schroeder, *The Brotherhood Guidebook* (rev. ed.; Nashville: Broadman Press, 1955), pp. 179-80.

CHAPTER 18

SUPPLEMENTAL EDUCATIONAL AGENCIES

Many churches feel the need for additional educational emphases to supplement the regular educational agencies. Special weeks are set apart for enlisting the membership of the church in intensive specialized study and service. Possibly no church will feel the need for all these special agencies every year, but most churches will need to include some of them at some time in their program. Each church must form its own calendar of special events to meet the specific needs of its constituency.

THE CHURCH SCHOOL OF MISSIONS

Nature

The Church School of Missions is a planned week of intensive missionary study for the whole church membership. It is led by the pastor and his co-workers as a church program. It is not sponsored by any single educational organization of the church; but the Sunday school, Training Union, Woman's Missionary Union, and Brotherhood all join forces under the leadership of the pastor for this special week of mission study. Classes are graded by age on the same class and department basis as the other agencies of the church. Each age group studies missions in separate classes and hears visiting missionaries at the Sunday services and at the general assembly each night.

Grading

Mission study is more practical and enjoyable when conducted by classes. There should be one or more classes for each age group: beginners, age four and five; primary, age six through eight; junior, age nine through twelve; intermediate, age thirteen through sixteen; young people, age seventeen through twenty-four; young adults, twenty-five to about forty or forty-five; and adults, above forty or forty-five. It is best to have separate classes for men and women. Teachers may be secured from the local church membership. Reports show that attendance is always larger when study by classes is provided. Some churches hold the classes for primaries and juniors in the afternoon after school is dismissed.

Schedule

A properly conducted school has two major periods each night at the church from Monday through Friday. The first is a forty-five minute class period. Following this is the general assembly of all classes for a missionary address. About ten or fifteen minutes are needed for the classes to assemble in the auditorium for a brief report, introduction of the speaker, and promotional period each night before the missionary speaks. This schedule is suggested:

    Class period: 7:30 — 8:15
    Moving to assembly: 8:15 — 8:20
    Song, prayer, reports: 8:20 — 8:30
    Address: 8:30 — 9:15

The schedule may vary to meet local conditions, but there should be a full forty-five minutes for class study and a full forty-five minutes for the address by the missionary.

SIMULTANEOUS SCHOOLS OF MISSIONS

Nature

The name "School of Missions" used in the singular denotes the program in one church. When referring to a school in which two or more churches in the same association or city participate, the plural term Schools of Missions, Simultaneous Schools of Missions, or Associational Schools of Missions is used. The name is used primarily for promotion. Other names sometimes used are: World Mission Week; Missionary Emphasis Week; World Mission Conference; Forum on World Missions; Missionary Revival. In some cases a different term is used each year, but in most states only the term Schools of Missions is used. Each church (or group of churches) should use whichever term would attract the most people.

In the simultaneous schools each church plans for its class study. All the churches use the same graded textbooks. Each church should secure its own faculty from its members. The teachers should be the best in the church; thoroughly missionary in spirit and in practice. Only in extremely rare cases should the classes be taught by the visiting missionaries. Local people need the blessing which comes from preparation to teach the book. A new set of graded mission study textbooks is published each year for these schools.

In some associations a one-day institute is held for training the teachers. A specially trained instructor is provided for teachers of each of the groups from beginners through adults. This instructor will not attempt to teach the entire book but will show the teachers how to teach one chapter and to use pictures, songs, games, objects, and maps as teaching aids.

The visiting missionaries speak in a different church on Sundays and each evening. Thus each church may have six or seven speakers within the week. Southern Baptists have no other program for bringing so many missionaries who are home on furlough to speak at the churches. The arrangements for such a program should be made through the director of schools of missions in your state or the state mission secretary.

At a conference of state directors of schools of missions in January, 1956, it was reported that in 1955, 177 simultaneous programs, participated in by 3,257 churches, resulted in a total attendance of almost one and one-quarter million.

The demand for missionaries to help in this work is so great that the schools must be planned many months, if not years, in advance. If an active missionary or missionaries on furlough cannot be secured, each of the mission boards has suitable motion picture films or film strips which may be secured from the various boards.

Values

According to Lewis W. Martin, Secretary of Missionary Education, Southern Baptist Home Mission Board, "the simultaneous program, city-wide for large cities, county-wide and association-wide for others, commends itself for many reasons:

— It encourages the individual church to plan definitely for a missionary education program.

— It helps churches planning for Schools of Missions to avoid conflicts with other associational and convention-wide programs.

— Smaller churches are privileged to have what they could not and would not procure alone.

— It personalizes the Cooperative (Mission) Program.

— It permits the few available missionaries to reach, in one week, a larger number of people than would otherwise be possible.

— It affords a co-operation of churches and denominational agencies.

— It permits a valuable fellowship of foreign, home, and state missionaries in a common task.

— It is economical in that several churches and perhaps two or more associations share in the expense which would be prohibitive for a single church.

— From the concerted study, greater benefits will come for mission projects within the city and association.

— It helps to keep churches and associations centered on the main task of evangelism, stewardship, and cooperative missionary endeavor.

— A correlated churchwide study course on missions is encouraged for each church."[1]

TRAINING IN WORSHIP

Christian worship means, at its highest and best, intelligent worship. Magic and superstition, personality-destroy-

[1] Lewis W. Martin, *Church School of Missions Manual* (rev. ed.; Atlanta: Home Mission Board, Southern Baptist Convention, 1956), pp. 10–11.

ing practices, low motivation, and whatever tends to make religion a show, are beneath the dignity of intelligent Christian worship. On the positive side, worship is recognizing and appreciating the presence of God and responding adequately in terms of what Christ and the Bible have taught us about God.

However, there are differences in Christian outlook. One person is so constituted and habituated that he finds satisfaction in song, prayer, sermon, gifts, and a modicum of architectural helps or ritualistic instrumentation. Another feels that the sermon is human intrusion, and enjoys the richness of color and music which are found in authorized forms and ceremonies. Nevertheless, in spite of the wide range in the manifestation of Christian worship, all are agreed that worship is essential for the Christian — it is the one experience without which he cannot live creatively.

Avenues of Worship

The chief avenue to worship has always been prayer in some form, whether the frenzied rhythmical expression found in primitive forms of religion or the refined ethical type of the sincere Christian. Also there are symbolic rituals or ceremonies, song and instrumental music, scripture reading, meditation, contemplation, offerings, sermons or testimonies, and various kinds of service activities, all of which are expressions of worship in varying degrees.

With Protestants, two trends are dominant: one characterized by ritual and symbol, and architecturally framed with the altar and communion table at the center; the other vocalized in sermon, song, and prayer, with the pulpit and the open Bible holding pre-eminence. In the north and eastern United States and in Great Britain and Europe, a combination of the two types is not uncommon. In this instance, architectural modifications are effected, with the pulpit only slightly raised above the communion table, and both at the eye-center of worship.

Generally speaking, it seems that the democratic free worship of evangelical Christian groups is moving more and more toward a beautifully satisfying service; in which shortened sermon, more elevating music, and a planned order of worship are appreciated. Also, prayer, testimony, conversion and consecration experiences tend to comply with these new and more orderly developments. What is most needed is some recognition on the part of all educational organizations of the church for training in the meaning of worship and a growing appreciation for the use of all materials used in the various expressions of worship.

Agencies for Training in Worship

Some agencies which have a definite responsibility for improving worship are the denominational schools, all the educational organizations of the church, and the Christian home. Improvement must begin with the top-flight leadership, the *denominational schools.* The seminaries and the colleges, where leaders are trained, must take the initiative. All too often in the past, these schools have been absorbed with mere knowledge-getting and fact-cramming. The time demands a different approach, where the curriculum will be reconstructed in such a manner as to allow for and encourage more worship, and where personality enrichment — set in a Christian atmosphere — will be given more attention.

The Sunday school, the Training Union, the Vacation Bible school, and the educational organizations for all age groups of the church should guide pupils in the experience of worship. Too often these activities have been noisy and disorderly — with little or no worthy recognition of the Divine Presence. This has been somewhat offset by having a special worship period in the assembly and a "devotional" or prayer in the class period, but there is need for a more spontaneous worshipful atmosphere which should pervade the whole hour. In these graded group meetings the church has its best opportunity to train in the meaning and purpose of worship and the form and content of the materials to be used in the experience of worship. The discovery of a new truth revealed in Bible study and the deeply felt emotion, accompanied by an individual dedication to the Christian movement, may constitute an act of worship. Such momentary individual responses to divine illumination are of greater spiritual significance than opening exercises and pious sermonettes.

In planning for the worship experience in the various departmental programs as well as the general assembly of the congregation, the following principles have been found of value in the conduct of worship:

1. The culture level of the group or congregation should determine the form or content of worship. Responses, for example, would help in one group and hinder in another. The selection of hymns and the order of service should be made on the basis of the tastes of the people.
2. Familiarity with words, music, and order of service is essential to true worship. Strange or unusual elements hinder the release of will.
3. Participation by the congregation is generally imperative.
4. Preparation in advance is best for those taking part. Notice to a person that he will be called on to pray enables him to think of the needs of the worshippers and to put himself in the mood of worship.
5. Unity in a service safeguards against confusion and failure in worship. It is helpful to select an objective for the service and to reveal that fact to the worshippers. Even a hymn announced as for those in sorrow or those facing great temptation becomes tremendously moving.
6. Massing the worshippers for singing, for prayer, or for reading is important. A scattered or divided group lacks unity and sensitivity.
7. Dependence upon the spirit of God will create greater results than all else combined. "God moves in a mysterious way, His wonders to perform. He plants His feet upon the seas, And rides upon the storm."

Finally, though first in importance, is the *Christian home*, as an institution for training in worship. The church can and must help the newly formed families in such a high and holy enterprise. Many of the larger denominations have set up some plan whereby the churches may help the home to plan and conduct family worship. Much is being said about reviving the family altar and saying grace at meal times. Such expressions of worship are exceedingly important, but it is even more important to promote these activities in the right manner. They must be sincere and genuine; otherwise, they are hollow forms which mock religion, and the real essence of worship is not experienced. But from homes which are genuinely Christian — in which God's presence is realized — come the finest and best people. Further discussion of family worship will be found in Chapter 19.

The Mid-week Prayer Service

Because of waning interest in the mid-week prayer service, due to a number of conditions — some local and some general — and in the face of its great importance, it deserves special emphasis here. One approach is to trace the rise of the mid-week service historically and to show that the early Christians held prayer meetings daily. In this instance far less importance would be attached to a special day and time of worship spaced in the middle of the week. Such an interpretation would be in line with the view of many modern evangelicals that holy days and hours have a tendency to confine religion to special buildings and formal services.

Another approach is to accept the mid-week prayer service frankly as a modern institution and see in it great possibilities for genuine worship. In this instance perhaps a good start would be to make a survey of the local situation and plan for a panel discussion on some such subject as "What is Wrong with the Mid-Week Prayer Service?" Then, the leader might gather materials on the content of prayer services in other churches and obtain valuable suggestions. Armed with this information he could set about establishing a real mid-week prayer service in his own church. Every one knows that too little time is devoted to prayer, fellowship, and worship in modern life. Where a creative service is planned, it is sure to meet with a hopeful response in most situations. The average prayer service lacks previous preparation, is haphazard and meandering, and fails to challenge the general membership of the church. Perhaps this is why so few attend it.

Some distinct advantages of the mid-week prayer service over the Sunday services are informality, more personal fellowship in worship, opportunities for spontaneous expression of the soul in testimony, song, and prayer; occasions for Bible study, and greater evangelical opportunities — especially where the church leans toward formal worship on Sunday. In Great Britain and on the Continent evangelical churches have utilized the mid-week service for great Bible study and periods of prayer. The local minister sees here the one big occasion to pour his rich experience into teaching and into training his membership in worship and Bible study. Is it too much to hope that American preachers may do the same? Too little time is spent in the study, and any added stimulus will be a great improvement. Furthermore, useless or pointless field calls are less likely to be expected of the minister if his congregation knows that he has spent many hours in Bible study in order to be prepared for more teaching services.

TRAINING IN MUSIC

Attitudes are all-important in character building. Stimulating the emotions is just as essential as enlightening the intellect. Hence music has always been and will continue to be a necessary part of the experience in which the development of strong Christian character takes place. If anyone doubts this, he may recall readily how argument and smooth oratory at one time or another failed to impress people, while a hymn or a gospel song was moving and creative in its influence. The hymn was one of the most effective means of indoctrination in the hands of the Protestant reformers. The apostle Paul urged the use of music in the early churches. "Speaking one to another in psalms and hymns and spiritual songs, singing and making melody with your heart to the Lord" (Eph. 5:19).

Values

Some of the ways in which music helps to develop attitudes are:

1. Stimulation of the imagination and heightening of religious sensibility

2. Glorification of the commonplace and elevation of life through association with poetry and musical ideas
3. Creation of aspiration and summoning of the best within the individual
4. Recapitulation of gospel truths and creation of convictions and decisions through hymns and songs which carry messages of faith, repentance, salvation, and hope
5. Accessory values making for integration of life, release of energies, and harmony of living

The Protestant evangelical churches are emphasizing the ministry of music, perhaps more than ever, because they realize that the gospel is sent abroad on its wings. Also, a new appreciation of beauty in worship has added to the volume of this emphasis and has created a demand for the highest type of sacred song and musical accomplishment. Almost every theological seminary has definite training in music for ministers, and specialized courses leading to musical degrees are offered in many religious schools.

The ministry of music is a new vocation, and many large churches have employed specially trained leaders to direct their music. In some instances these workers do nothing else but promote the musical program of the church, while in others their duties are combined with those of specialized religious education. The Baptist Sunday School Board of the Southern Baptists has a department of music, and it seems that evangelical denominations, as well as individual churches, are becoming highly conscious of the subject. This is a giant stride toward a higher quality of music and a better type of worship.

Graded Choirs

So great an emphasis has been placed on the value of sacred music as an educational aid that the more progressive churches not only employ a full-time minister of music, but have set up a graded choir program for all age groups. The grading follows the same general pattern as in all the organizations of the church. Appropriate names are sometimes selected for each department choir. The following have proved popular: Sanctuary choir, for adults, which is used for the Sunday morning worship service; Youth choir, for young people, age seventeen to twenty-four, frequently used at the Sunday evening services; Concord choir, for Intermediates; Carol choir, for Junior boys and girls; Cherub choir, for Primaries, ages six to eight; and Music Activities for Beginners, ages four to five. In addition to the choirs, special vocal and instrumental groups may be formed. On special occasions, such as Christmas time and Easter, the combined choirs may be presented in a special Sunday service.

Types

Vocal, instrumental, and special features are the usual types of church music. The piano, electric organ, pipe organ, and string and wind instruments are now rather generally employed. As to vocal forms, the gospel song, the hymn, and the anthem are most universally used. A balanced church music program requires the use of all three forms. Song services, song sermons, cantatas, and oratorios also have their place in the church music program.

As the church of the future assumes a greater share in shaping the recreational program of the community and in raising the cultural standards for its membership beside constructing its own worship program, it will make greater use of music as the handmaid of the church.

RELIGIOUS DRAMA

Nature

Today drama is coming to have a large place in the religious educational work of the church. From earliest Biblical times religious truths were taught by dramatic presentation. Religious rites and ceremonies were used by the prophets and priests of Israel to illustrate spiritual truth. Dramatizing the gospel through the church ordinances, such as baptism and the Lord's Supper, has been used since New Testament times; though few have thought of them as art because of the reality and seriousness of the occasions. Also, the extremes to which the secularized stage has gone have turned the church leaders' attention away from the use of drama. But mystery and miracle plays are beginning to come back again, as in the Middle Ages; and educational dramatics are now being used in church schools.

Types

There are two types of educational dramatization — informal and formal. The *informal* type is used in working with children. A biblical, missionary, or character building story is told by the leader, and the children are allowed to represent the various characters and to act out the story just as it was told. After the simple dramatization, the story and acting are discussed. Then the children may be allowed to repeat the dramatization. This form of expressional activity helps to fix the facts of the story in the memory of each child. It has had a prominent place in vacation schools and Training Union. The entire group should take part. It is not presented to an audience but is used as a means of teaching. Its greatest values are to those who participate in the dramatization. No properties, stage setting, or costuming is required. The imagination of the children supplies all that is needed. When the informal is used with intermediates or young people, the story may be acted out, discussed, repeated; and a special committee may be named to write the play, build stage settings, make costumes, memorize the parts, advertise the performance, and present a formal play.

Formal dramatics include plays, tableaux, pageants, pantomimes, and puppet shows. Each of these forms has a technique of its own, but it can be learned through personal application and patient practice. Since many older intermediates, seniors, and young people are so vitally interested in this activity, some churches will find it most profitable to organize a religious drama club. The first step is for the church to secure from its own membership or church staff a director who has the technical skill, the proper appreciation for the use of drama as a means of teaching religion, and genuine loyalty to the church's total program. When the right leadership is available the church may proceed with the organization of one or more dramatic clubs for its young people.

VISUAL AIDS

Place

The value of visual aids in religious education has been conclusively tested and can no longer be questioned. Churches are making provision for purchase of equipment and rental of films. In planning new educational buildings it is wise to make certain the architect has included special wiring and adequate facilities for darkening departmental and classrooms. Some churches have constructed a projection room, but it is wiser to plan for use of visual aids in the regular departmental rooms. This avoids conflict in schedule and makes possible the use of visual aids in several departments at the same time.

Visual aids are never to be used chiefly for entertainment. They should be used as aids to better teaching and should never be thought of as substitutes for teaching. When any form of aid is used it must be combined with the usual methods of teaching. Each teacher or superintendent should be trained to use visual aids. One thing is essential: an adequate plan of administration must be set up to insure proper utilization of the equipment owned by the church and available to it from outside sources. The plan of organization should be simple, yet it must meet the needs of all organizations in the church: Sunday school, Training Union, Woman's Missionary Union, and Brotherhood.

Administration

Most churches should name an advisory committee to promote the use of visual aids in the church. Experience has established the need for a director of visual aids who shall serve as chairman of the advisory committee. He must have a genuine interest in the use of all forms of visual aids — from the use of chalk-boards, maps, and pictures, to the more complicated electrical projectors now available to most churches. He must also be a promoter. His duties are (1) to give general direction to the advisory committee; (2) to promote the use of visual aids throughout the church; (3) to consult with teachers and leaders in the choice of materials and the best ways to use them; (4) to train the church leaders to operate the projectors or train older intermediates and young people as operators; (5) to see that all equipment is properly stored where it will be safe and yet available to all who have been scheduled to use it; (6) to lead the church to realize the values of visual aids and lead them to provide more and better equipment when it is needed.

In addition to the director of visual aids there should be at least one operator and two or three people who are thoroughly familiar with the work of all the organizations of the church. There is no need for a large committee. A small committee of people who really have vision and are willing to work with the regular leaders of the church will be more successful than a large committee. It must be remembered that visual education is not another *program*; it should be a service which may easily be correlated with the total educational program of the church. It may be used by the choir, for missionary education, and for training teachers and officers. It has been used in promoting the church budget. The director of visual aids can become one of the most valuable officers of a church. He must be loyal to the whole program of the church and always lead his committee to understand their service relationship to the church.

Work of the Committee

The committee should be willing to *study* its work. Many of the larger denominations have an audio-visual aids department which will be glad to supply materials for the committee to study. The Visual Education Service, Baptist Sunday School Board, publishes free literature, and a catalog of visual aid supplies and films, which will be sent to any church upon request. The committee should meet regularly to study and plan for its work. A good time to meet would be during the regular weekly teachers and officers meeting. At least there should be a regular time each week for meeting.

Another responsibility of the committee is to lead the church in the purchase of the needed equipment. The church should start out with a slide and filmstrip projector and learn how to use it before getting additional equipment. Few churches will need a motion projector at first. The committee should study the needs for various forms of visual education and the church should be led to purchase it as needed, only upon the recommendation of the director and the committee.

Financing the Service

This is another important task of the committee. The church should set up an item in the budget for this phase of its work. The director should be on the budget committee or at least should be permitted to present in person the needs of the audio-visual service of the church to the budget committee. There should be a definite amount for purchase of new equipment and rental of films. Another method is to have special groups or interested individuals purchase the equipment and give it to the church. Of course gifts thus designated should be over and above the regular tithes and subscription to the church budget.

Every church should send the members of its visual-aids committee to one of the visual aids workshops which are being held by the visual aids service of its denomination. Baptists conduct such a workshop at Ridgecrest and Glorieta assemblies each summer, at the seminaries and colleges, and at some of the larger city churches. These workshops are directed by the Visual Aids Service of the Baptist Sunday School Board of Southern Baptist Convention.

The prospects for the future are hopeful. Encouraging results have been achieved by many churches through careful selection of materials and skillful use of equipment. Churches are more willing to include the visual education materials in the annual budget. More and better aids are available to the churches. It is reasonable to expect more effective religious education through the use of this new implement which modern invention has placed within the reach of any church.

The interest of the church in visual education is primarily religious and educational. It also may be used as a recreational feature. Every minister and religious worker should have good books on the subject in his personal library and should be well informed on the possibilities of the various forms of this means of religious education.

QUESTIONS FOR DISCUSSION

1. Make a list of those who have gone out from your home church to the home and foreign mission service. Name the fields in which they serve.

2. Give a report on what your church gave last year to state, home, and foreign missions.

3. Visit some churches who are using dramatic activities. What effect has this activity had upon worship? Upon the lives and habits of those participating?

4. Plan to present a religious play at a Church Drama Festival. Write to your denominational Board of Christian Education or to Church Recreation Department, Baptist Sunday School Board, Nashville, Tennessee, for further information.

5. Outline a graded music program for your church, using volunteer workers.

6. How much money is included in your church budget for special agencies as compared to the regular educational activities? Could they be more closely correlated?

Part III

BIBLIOGRAPHY

Barnard, Floy. *Drama in the Church.* Nashville: The Broadman Press, 1950.

Barnes, William W. *The Southern Baptist Convention, 1845–1953.* Nashville: The Broadman Press, 1954.

Barnette, J. N. *A Church Using Its Sunday School.* Nashville: Convention Press, 1937.

_____. *The Pull of the People.* Nashville: Convention Press, 1956.

Briggs, Argye M. *A Question Asked.* (WMU) Grand Rapids: Eerdmans Publishing Co., 1957.

Brown, Archie E. *A Million Men For Christ*. Nashville: Convention Press, 1956.

Brown, Thelma, editor. *Treasury of Religious Plays*. New York: Association Press, 1947.

Burnett, Sibley, *Better Vacation Bible Schools*. Nashville: Convention Press, 1957.

Cox, Ethlene Boone. *Following in His Train*. Nashville: The Broadman Press, 1955.

Dillard, J. E. *Building a Stewardship Church*. Nashville: The Broadman Press, 1956.

Eastman, Fred. *Christ in the Drama*. New York: The Macmillan Co., 1947.

Ehrensperger, Harold. *Conscience on the Stage*. Nashville: Abingdon Press, 1947.

Fallaw, Wesner. *The Modern Parent and the Teaching Church*. New York: The Macmillan Company, 1946.

Flake, Arthur. *Building A Standard Sunday School*. Nashville: Convention Press, rev. ed., 1952.

Grubb, Kenneth G. and Bingle, E. J. *World Christian Handbook*. New York: Friendship Press, 1952.

Harner, Nevin C. *Youth Work in the Church*. Nashville: Abingdon Press, 1942.

Holcomb, Clifford A. *Methods and Materials for Graded Choirs*. Nashville: Convention Press, 1948.

Homrighausen, Elmer. *Choose Ye This Day: A Study of Decision and Commitment*. Philadelphia: Westminster Press, 1943.

Lambdin, J. E. *The Baptist Training Union Manual*. Nashville: Convention Press, rev. 1952.

_____. *Building A Church Training Program*. (For small churches.) Nashville: Convention Press, 1946.

Latourette, Kenneth Scott. *The Christian World Mission in Our Day*. New York: Harper & Bros., 1954.

Lobingier, John L. *The Better Church School*. Boston: The Pilgrim Press, 1952.

Lotz, Philip Henry, editor. *Orientation in Religious Education*. Nashville: Abingdon Press, 1950.

McKibben, Frank H. *Christian Education Through the Church*. Nashville: Abingdon Press, 1947.

Miller, Randolph Crump. *Education for Christian Living*. Englewood Cliffs: Prentice-Hall, Inc., Inc., 1956.

Munro, Harry C. *Protestant Nurture*. Englewood Cliffs, N. J.: Prentice-Hall, Inc., 1956.

Schroeder, George W. *The Brotherhood Guidebook*. Nashville: Convention Press, rev. 1955.

Vieth, Paul H. *The Church School*. Philadelphia: Christian Education Press, 1957.

_____. *The Church and Christian Education*. St. Louis: Bethany Press, 1947.

Part IV

RELIGIOUS EDUCATION
BEYOND THE CHURCH

CHAPTER 19

THE CHRISTIAN HOME

Among all social institutions the family holds first place as the creator and guardian of human values. Randolph Crump Miller, in comparing the home with other agencies, says: "The way in which the family is unified is the chief factor in the integration of a child's personality. The family initiates motives, manners, prejudices, and ideals. The examples of the parents and other children have various effects on the learner. The general atmosphere of home-life is a determining influence in the development of attitudes. The basic stuff of religious belief and faith is established in early home experiences."[1]

What are the main characteristics of homes — good influences, bad influences, advantages, disadvantages? What do homes mean, and what should they mean to human life and civilization? What are the distinguishing marks between a home that is Christian and one that is not Christian? What activities and practices have bearing on Christian education and development? What definite activities and programs can be provided for the improvement of the home as a religious educational institution? How may the home be made more Christian, more wholesome and effective as a Christian institution?

[1] Randolph Crump Miller, *Education for Christian Living*, p. 93. Copyright, 1956, by Prentice-Hall, Inc., Englewood Cliffs, N. J.

ORIGIN AND FUNCTION

Origin

The home is man's oldest social group and institution. The origin of the home is found in the experiences of Adam and Eve in the Garden of Eden. "Therefore shall a man leave his father and his mother, and shall cleave unto his wife: and they shall be one flesh" (Gen. 2:24). This quotation from Genesis gives the origin and nature of the home. The home and the family are fundamental to the life of human society and civilization. Jesus himself bases his teaching on the permanency of marriage and against divorce on the fundamental biological make-up of the human race — "Male and female made he them." Coupled with this, the idea of abiding love between one man and one woman, with the birth and rearing of children, makes the home basic and fundamental for the safety, security, and progress of the human race.

Function

One of the strongest and most fundamental impulses of human nature, *love between one man and one woman, forms the foundation* for the home physically, psychologically, emotionally, and religiously. The home and family are basic and fundamental in human life. The procreation and perpetuation of the human race depend on the home. The home is a place to be born, to live, to be nurtured, and to nurture, and therefore forms the most natural and vital human group. It is in the home where real living goes on, and a normal human being could hardly live at all without some kind of home.

Looking at it *from the physical standpoint,* the home is recognized as the place of *birth and growth of human beings.* Also it gives us the ideal social group, with loving and sharing among members of the family a central feature. Despite serious weaknesses and faults in many homes, the average human being finds in the home love and confidence, protection and security. The basic economic needs of human beings are found in and through the home: food, clothing, and shelter. People make a living together in the home.

Education goes on in every home and all the time, and that of the most abiding and effective kind. Members of the family are teaching each other constantly. The children inevitably learn from the parents, and the parents pass on to the children practically all that they have known and experienced in human living. Religion, or the lack of religion, is unavoidably passed on to the children. The home was the first school and continues to be the most vital and real school in the lives of all human beings.

Education and Religion Meet

In this chapter the home is considered from the standpoint of religious education. Most certainly, education and religion meet in the home. The customs, habits, and traditions of each generation are passed on to the next in large measure through the influences and teaching in the home. In some ways the important question is not how shall religion be taught the children but what shall they be taught. Consider carefully the place and function of the home in the religious education of people from the standpoint of what the home is doing, and what perhaps it can do and ought to do. Consider also what the church can do to help the home. In and through the home bad education is carried on as well as good. By taking thought, both the quality and the content of our teaching can be improved.

ADVANTAGES

What are some of the advantages in the home for the teaching of religion and the development of character? The preceding paragraphs help to answer this question and show the power and prominence of the home in human life and destiny, but there are yet other advantages which require emphasis.

Ideal Teaching Situation

The family group provides the most ideal teaching situation. People teach and learn under the normal and natural conditions of living and making a living. The child is born into the home and for several years is dependent upon his parents and other members of the family circle for physical and economic survival. He has the experience of loving and being loved by members of this intimate circle, and quite early he learns close cooperation and sharing in the struggle for existence. The roots of religion go deeply into the experience of the child in being dependent on his parents. This experience transferred to the larger universe, with God as the supreme Creator and Preserver, gives the child the foundation for true religion. Also, he learns the basic social virtues of cooperation and sharing. The good family gives the patterns for the ideal society. The attitudes and virtues developed in the good family, when transferred to the larger world, become the qualities which are most needed for building the best human civilization.

As has been indicated in the preceding paragraph, in the home education is experienced under the most natural and normal conditions. If the parents and other older members of the family have Christian character and a good understanding of the fundamental Christian virtues and teachings, they have the best opportunity in the world to pass these on to the younger generation. In the home there is much more than formal instruction. There is a natural situation in which to practice the basic Christian virtues, such as loving, sharing, and helping, virtues which are most vital in Christian living.

Most Important in Character Building

Many authorities contend that behavior problems and delinquency get their start in and near the home; apparently, they do not begin at the play area or school, although symptoms may crop up there. It follows, therefore, that anything done to strengthen a youth's home life and his immediate environment can prove of inestimable worth. It is commonly agreed that the first six years of life are the most impressionable in determining attitudes, moods, emotional stability and the life. The home should be a pleasant place to come to and at which to stay. The need for a nook to call one's own where one can work, study, or just be alone, is recognized as an essential of home life. Further, the feeling of belonging and being wanted in a secure setting cannot be ignored.[2]

[2] H. Dan Corbin, *Recreation Leadership*, p. 120. Copyright, 1953, by Prentice-Hall, Inc., Englewood Cliffs, N. J.

The family still provides protection for the child, his care and nurture, his concepts of right and wrong in his relations to the outside world, and cultural guidance in protecting him from influences and conditions that are to his disadvantage. . . .

As an educational and social, emotional conditioning influence, the family has always been important. Besides the actual physical care and help in attaining proper physical development, the family educates the child in every area of his life and reinforces the formal education he receives from outside agencies, including the school. This function is just as important today as it ever was.[3]

The careful studies by educators and psychologists have shown unmistakably the primary and vast importance of the home in character building and religious education. Nor can the responsibility for character development be delegated to any other institution. This obligation of the Christian home is clearly set forth by Ernest M. Ligon:

Many parents still suffer from the delusion that they can delegate the character education of their children to such institutions as the school and Sunday school. It is astonishing how many honestly believe that if their children go to Sunday school with fair regularity and memorize a golden text from time to time, they — the parents — can be completely confident of their future adult integrity. Not infrequently the Church has encouraged them in this belief. Surely no more cruel deception can be practiced on parents, even if they are partners in the deception. The laws of character education are inviolable. They demand seven-day-a-week effort. Principles must be taught until thoroughly understood and enthusiastically accepted. Then they must be applied in every relevant phase of daily life. This must be continued until the principle involved becomes an integral part of the child's personality. When parents realize this fully, they will steer clear of the short-cut methods of character education, whatever they are.[4]

No other institution can do so much to shape human destiny for good as the home, for the following reasons:

1. The first five or six years of a child's life are the most impressionable. It is during these years that many of the basic emotionalized attitudes are formed for life.
2. These early years find the child almost entirely under the influence of the parents. Here are both a golden opportun-

[3] Robert Geib Foster, *Marriage and Family Relationships* (New York: The Macmillan Co., 1944), pp. 232–33. Used by permission.

[4] Ernest M. Ligon, *A Greater Generation* (New York: The Macmillan Co., 1948), pp. 110–11. Used by permission.

ity and a great obligation to lay a solid foundation for
happy, progressive maturity.

3. Love for father and mother surpasses all other love. The
child's confidence in his parents is unbounded. Their deeds,
words, and emotional responses are imitated in ways that
are startling.

Basic in Religious Education

The statements in regard to character education apply just
as truly to religious education. A child is rooted in the religious life of the family of which he is a dependent member.
His ideas, habits, and desires concerning God and things religious are derived largely from the current spirit and practice of the home. This obligation of the parents is described
by Harry C. Munro:

Since the family is the primary source and agency of religious
nurture, is not this problem of incorporating religion in the total
growing experience of children a responsibility of the family? Does
this not place definitely upon the parents the responsibility for providing children with a well-rounded education which includes such
religious teachings and viewpoints as the parents desire? Isn't the
problem of integrating into a unified and consistent total philosophy
of life for each child, those experiences which are provided by home,
church, school, and community, a problem which is up to the home?
What teacher, other than the parent, is in such a favorable position
to guide and help his child to "see life steadily and see it whole"?

Theoretically this is by far the most obvious solution to our problem. But unfortunately, for several generations past, trends in American family life have been in the opposite direction. Technological
developments, making for an industrialized and urbanized society,
have encouraged the family to give to specialized agencies function
after function in economic, vocational, educational, health, and recreational activities. This might have set the family free from its traditional load of providing economic and physical welfare, to specialize
even more fully in the realm of moral and spiritual nurture. Such
ultimately might be the outcome of technology and specialization.
But, so far, the trend seems to have been for the family increasingly
to abdicate its moral and religious role, and to look to specialized
agencies like church school, and club to provide for these functions
also.[5]

[5] Harry C. Munro, *Protestant Nurture*, pp. 232–33. Copyright, 1956, by
Prentice-Hall, Inc., Englewood Cliffs, N. J.

In every way possible increased effort should be put forth to improve and make permanent the religious character of the home and to help teachers and parents to discover and to use the best methods as school and church work together educating children in religion.

PROBLEMS

The old American family with its homestead and its emphasis on training in religion is almost a thing of the past. In the earlier days the family was compelled to live together as a social unit. All the needs of the group were met by working together. Today the average family has delegated almost all of its functions to other agencies. Wesner Fallaw describes the modern family thus:

Children, youth, and adults customarily go outside the family for education, religion, health care, recreation, and work. The traditional functions of the family have declined or vanished. Neither the family group nor the home base has remained magnetic enough to hold the interest of any given member of the family when he wishes to enjoy or enlighten himself. For many families eating out seems to have greater appeal than eating at home. And when people do stay at home, they bring in the world by way of radio, telephone, newspaper, comic book, magazine, and television. Separately and together the modern family seems incapable of developing its own resourcefulness so that work, play, learning, and religion can be a family-group affair.[6]

Many authorities attribute the rapid increase in juvenile delinquency to the passing of the old American home with its religious influence. Just what are the differences from the stand-point of religious education between the old home and the new?

The Old American Home

Perhaps the differences between the religious influences of the old home and the new have been exaggerated; for the halo of age is about the old home, and it is pictured in memory as ideal in its religious character and emphasis. But un-

6 Wesner Fallaw, in Philip Henry Lotz (ed.), *Orientation in Religious Education* (Nashville: Abingdon Press, 1950), p. 236.

doubtedly there were advantages in the home of the past. For one thing, the home of the past had fewer distractions, and the life and interests of parents and children were centered in the home. All the members of the family circle shared together in the duties and responsibilities of the home, and thus the children learned in a most wholesome way through actual living. They learned to do by doing. Fathers and mothers, if they were Christians, naturally taught their children what religion they knew and actually guided them in the practice of it. They felt the responsibility for the spiritual development of their children, for one thing because there were no other agencies, such as the Sunday school and the public school, to which they could turn. The father was the priest of the family. He had the old-fashioned family altar, reading the Scriptures daily and praying with the family. Also he and his wife felt the responsibility for the discipline of the children, teaching and practicing the fundamental Christian virtues in connection with the task of living and working in the home and on the farm.

The Modern Home

Now the situation in the modern home is usually quite different. Too often the home is not much more than a place to eat and sleep; the center for recreation, education, work, and worship usually being in some institution outside of the home. Too, the distraction of the modern movie, comic book, radio, television, and many other forms of amusement and entertainment take the time of the members of the family and, to say the least, do not contribute directly to the spiritual and moral development of children and young people. Even if the parents are anxious to stress religious training in the home, practically they find it difficult to do so. However, "Where there's a will, there's a way."

Constant Teaching

Parents, as a matter of course, teach their children all the religion that they really have and believe in. They teach every day by what they say and by what they do not say;

by what they do and by what they do not do. In perhaps millions of homes there is not only a lack of any positive teaching of the Bible and religion, but the moral and spiritual conditions are bad. Often there is a lack of love and confidence between father and mother, and even between parents and children. There is even constant fussing and fighting where there ought to be genuine love and mutual sharing. Multitudes of homes are broken up by divorce, and that is a serious problem in America today; but, perhaps the greatest need and opportunity, from the standpoint of religious education, lies in the direction of the thousands of homes which never reach the divorce courts but are in imminent danger because of the very low plane of living experienced in these homes. Indeed, the home has great influence in shaping character, and many times the influence is very bad instead of in keeping with the fundamental Christian virtues.

Ignorance and Poverty

Ignorance and poverty, even in these prosperous times, are great evils afflicting American life and the American home. Ignorant parents, as well as wicked parents, make immense blunders in the training and nurture of their children. Poverty is a constant handicap. Millions of homes have difficulty in providing the minimum essentials of good health and education for their children because they cannot provide the means for medical attention, nourishing food, warm clothes, good books, music, and art. These things are not luxuries but necessities. A public conscience is being developed on the matter of providing better living conditions as well as emphasizing the more formal side of religious instruction.

Positive Teaching of the Bible and Religion

However, in the definite sense of religious education, a greater emphasis should be given to the positive teaching of the Bible and religion in and through the home. The most serious problem in the modern day is that so few homes give definite attention to matters of character and religion. The rest of this chapter will attack more directly the problem of stimulating interest in the practical living and teaching of religion in and through the home.

CHRISTIAN ACTIVITIES

In meeting the situation in the home from the standpoint of religious education, there are two approaches to the problem: the informal and formal Christian activities. Both types of activities and emphases are very important.

Informal Activities

The very atmosphere of the home is a matter of great importance. This may be intangible, but it is very real just the same. It comes through the genuine Christian character and living of all the members of the family. The right Christian atmosphere cannot be created merely by taking thought, but in a thousand different ways the right atmosphere is developed by the private devotions and thinking, by the reverence, the genuine love of God and man, and the practice of the fundamental Christian virtues in the "give and take" of daily living. The Christian mother praying for and with the infant makes a large contribution to the life of the child. In such a home the child breathes and drinks in the Christian things of life long before he can understand them or is ready positively to yield his own life to Christ.

The child begins to learn the nature of religion through loving and being loved in the home. Here are the roots of true religion. Later he learns that "God is love" and that the two great commandments are to love God supremely and one's neighbor as himself. After all, love is the greatest thing in the world, and it is at the heart and center of the Christian religion. It finds its highest human expression in the really Christian home.

Sharing in Christian living is an important phase of religious education in the home. This sharing finds expression in the actual work and duties of the home in practical ways, as well as in formal religious exercises like Bible study and prayer. True education comes through living and sharing. Not only are children taught the contents of the Bible but how to practice the fundamental Christian virtues in daily work and play.

Among these informal activities are *conversation in the family*. Ordinarily children are influenced more by informal conversation than by formal lectures or preaching. Members of the family are constantly teaching and influencing one another by what they say and by what they do not say when it comes to spiritual matters. Parents, as well as the children, should be taught to make the ordinary conversation in the home wholesome and uplifting. References to the pastor, the Sunday school, and church, playmates, and neighbors, and evaluation of human character and conduct should be in keeping with Christian ideas and teachings.

Underlying and running throughout these informal Christian activities must be listed the important matter of *personal example*. It is still true that what we do speaks so loudly that often our children cannot hear what we say. "Not everyone that saith unto me, 'Lord, Lord,' shall enter into the kingdom of heaven; but he that doeth the will of my Father who is in heaven" (Matt. 7:21).

Formal Christian Activities

Formal Christian activities should hold an important place in the home. *Family worship* is essential to the maintenance and propagation of religion. There is no substitute for it. Sunday school and church worship cannot take the place of it. It is not merely the forms of prayer or the words of the song which is sung. Primarily it is the attitude of reverence which displays itself when speaking of God, the Bible, the church, and sacred things. It is the attitude and spirit which members of the family show at all hours of the day in the work and play of life and in crises which may come at times in the life of the home.

But there is real need for formal and definite *religious instruction* and worship. More is required than just silent influence, however important that may be. Religion is "caught" but it is also "taught." The basic truths of the Bible must be learned by the children. Family worship expresses itself in three main forms: grace at table; bedside prayers of the children; general family prayers. Other formal activities would include Bible study and teaching in the home, cooperation with Sunday school and church; and sharing in and directing Christian service in the church and community.

The regular custom of having *grace at table or prayer at meal time* is a natural and helpful one. Here God is recognized as the giver of all good things, including "our daily bread."

> Come, be our guest, O Lord of good,
> And bless to us Thy gift of food.

"In the same manner in which we express appreciation to one another we can express our gratitude to God. . . . This brief pause as the meal begins is a meaningful recognition of Divine care. Throughout the day it will help the family to remember that 'every good gift and every perfect gift is from above' (James 1:17)."[7] Such prayers give a devotional and uplifting tone to the family circle at mealtime.

Usually the blessing may be asked by the father or mother. Often it is wise to allow the children to do it in turn. Sometimes beautiful prayers will be repeated together by the whole family circle. In any case, the grace should be short, simple, and sincere, and not stilted or over-pious. Some simple but beautiful prayers for mealtime are suggested here:

A CHILD'S "THANK YOU"

> Thank You for the world so sweet,
> Thank You for the food we eat,
> Thank You for the birds that sing,
> Thank You, God, for everything.

> God is great and God is good,
> And we thank Him for this food;
> By His hand must all be fed;
> Give us, Lord, our daily bread.

[7] Arthur B. Rutledge, *Homes That Last* (Nashville: The Broadman Press, 1952), p. 65.

Heavenly Father, bless this food,
To Thy glory and our good.

The bedside prayers of the children. Even the tiny infant in a sense absorbs the spiritual atmosphere when the mother kneels and prays by its cradle; and the heavenly Father hears the prayer of the godly mother — "for I say unto you, that in heaven their angels do always behold the face of my Father who is in heaven" (Matt. 18:10).

Later the mother or father will have the child repeat simple prayers and gradually teach the child to form his own original prayers. Following this will come instruction in the meaning of prayer. The child can be saved from taking a rather mechanical view of prayer, expecting to get everything for which he asks. He will learn that prayer is not merely asking for things and that the ideal prayer breathes the sentiment, "Not my will, but Thine, be done."

General family prayers. The old-time family altar may be disappearing, but its modern counterpart can and must be preserved. The father and mother will lead in this, but the children will participate as they get old enough. Just as in prayer at meal time, reading the Scripture, leading in prayer, and other parts of this service can be performed by different members of the family group. Some of this can be done reverently in concert. Various methods will be used. Sometimes the main part will be the reading of the Bible in a connected way through many books, with simple explanations for the children. At other times devotional books will be used as guides. Many good books and manuals have been prepared in recent years by various publishers. *Open Windows*, published by the Southern Baptist Sunday School Board, and *The Upper Room*, by Abingdon Press, are illustrations of excellent publications along this line. A monthly magazine, *Home Life*, published by Baptist Sunday School Board, gives excellent suggestions for family devotions for use of parents. Most of the leading denominations publish a similar periodical. The International Council of Religious Education has some manuals and guides for worship in the family, as well as a commission which is leading in the study of this matter and in the help of families in this important function.

It is difficult to find a satisfactory time for family worship, but the earnest parent will find some time. Ten minutes just before or just after the evening meal will be found to be a very good time for many. Other times will suggest themselves according to the situation and needs of the family.

Study of the Bible

In addition to the more formal religious exercises of the home in the way of family worship, there will be a place in the best Christian homes for teaching and guiding the child in the study of the Bible. Graded Bible stories will be helpful for very young children, and various books and manuals will be used by older members of the family. The parents and older children will help the younger ones in the preparation of Sunday school lessons and other programs and services of the church in which the children participate. The home will cooperate with the church in all of its activities, and in turn the church will cooperate with and support the home in this vital matter of Christian nurture and guidance. This will involve, also, guidance in real Christian service in the school and community during the week. Children must learn not only to worship, to study the Bible, and other matters of like nature, but to engage in the real tasks of Christian living and in building a Christian world.

The Church and the Home

Parents and church-school teachers need to unite in order to nurture young and old in the Bible and in the Christian faith. In this the church and the home are engaged in a common enterprise. There should be close cooperation between teachers and parents in this important task. During the past two decades increasing emphasis has been placed on the education of parents for the teaching of their children, on parent-teacher conferences, and on short-term serious study courses for parents.

Paul H. Vieth presents the results of a two-year survey

of religious education made by sixty Protestant educators and other religious leaders, wherein a call is made for the implementation of what many have been saying about the primacy of the home in Christian learning and living:

> It will be no easy task to revolutionize the thinking and practice of Protestantism so that the cultivation of family religion shall become a major concern of the entire church. The enlistment of millions of parents in an effort to provide sound Christian education for their children and to continue in a process of learning throughout all the years of adulthood is an undertaking which will take all the resources of national agencies, denominational and interdenominational, as well as those in the local church. But it is doubtful whether any other effort will ultimately accomplish as much for the young and old and for the Kingdom of God.[8]

A large percentage of parents are weak in interest and dependability and in preparation for Christian teaching and guidance in the home. But they can learn, and they must learn. Pastors and Christian teachers must rise to meet the need. There is an increasing interest in, and emphasis on, adult education. Here is a need and a chance for important work in this field in the enlistment and training of parents for church-family education.

Practically all leading Protestant denominations have made good progress in this field of church-family education. The Sunday School Board of the Southern Baptist Convention has a Department of Home Curriculum. Joe W. Burton, director of this department and editor of *Home Life*, a magazine going into approximately 800,000 homes each month, wrote in his report to the Board, December, 1955:

> This department has no direct connection with the organizational life of the churches, but rather its work is done in cooperation with the existing organizations. Thus the home emphasis in our total program of Christian education in the churches is achieved through cooperation with the other departments in the Board's life. That this cooperation has been cordial and effective gives evidence that we are working in an area of vital need.

This work is based on two propositions or "self-evident

[8] Paul H. Vieth, *The Church and Christian Education* (St. Louis: The Bethany Press, 1947), p. 186. Used by permission.

axioms," Dr. Burton says: (1) "The chief influence in the life of a child is the home"; (2) "We are duty bound to do our utmost to train fathers and mothers for Christian parenthood." The Methodists have a department of the Christian family which prepares an impressive offering of special materials for private and group use. The Presbyterian Church, U.S.A., also has a major functioning committee on family life education. In 1948 they reorganized their entire church school curriculum, one major purpose being to implement this key idea that parents are the chief teachers of their children. The title of the curriculum is "Christian Faith and Life: A Program for Church and Home."

SOME PRACTICAL SUGGESTIONS

Some practical suggestions which have bearing on formal as well as informal Christian activities in the home are given here. After all, the important thing is to be more practical and to do definite things toward the positive guidance of our children in Christian living. All of these things involve also the Christian training and development of the parents.

Begin Early

There is real point in the remark that the time to begin to train a child is a hundred years before it is born. There must be a real connection between the marvelous strength exhibited by Samson and the fact that his mother refused to drink wine or to eat anything unclean after his conception (Judges 13:3-4). The first-born of a happy young couple had just been delivered. The physician had picked up his hat to leave. "Shall we put out the light, doctor?" inquired the young father. "That depends on how you wish to train the baby," was the reply. "If you allow the light to burn tonight, he will cry for it tomorrow night."

Dr. George A. Gordon, for forty years pastor of the Old South Church, Boston, says in his autobiography that a child learns more during the first year of its life than in any ten years afterwards. There has been much and sad blundering at this point. The main tendencies of character and life are fixed during the first three or four years of babyhood, being absorbed from the atmosphere and picked up from the conversations and the actions of those about the child.

Don't Shift Responsibility

It is clear that the Creator has charged those who bring children into the world with the responsibility of at least directing their "first steps" with as much care as possible. The nursery school, the Sunday school, the graded school, the Boy Scouts, the community clubs are all good, but they should be used only to supplement and reinforce the central point in all the child's life, the home. No parent can afford to turn over to any outside agency the task and the privilege which God has in the nature of the case committed to him.

Be Consistent

One of the greatest shocks that a child can be called on to meet comes when he first finds a parent speaking or acting insincerely or even carelessly as, for example, giving the wrong age of the child on the train to avoid paying a fare, or having the maid report the parent out when he or she is at home.

Let Children Share in the Daily Tasks

Do this as early and as rapidly as possible. Of course, they will break dishes, soil carpets, bruise their fingers, cut their toes, and bring trouble in a thousand other ways. It will be so much simpler and easier for mother and father to do the tasks themselves. But to do this is to rob the child of his birthright.

Give Each Child a Definite Assignment

For this makes him responsible and holds him to his responsibility without exception. The Jews of the Old Testament time were very careful in training their children. One of the Rabbis in the Talmud says, "He that has a trade, to what is he like? He is like a city that is fenced." Another Rabbi says, "He that fails to teach his son a trade has done the same thing as if he taught him to be a thief."

Practice Democracy

The home should be neither a monarchy nor a "duarchy." It should be a democracy in which each member shares according to his ability. And the "share" here should include all duties, privileges, responsibilities, cares, burdens, sorrows, joys, and all the rest. In this way each will come, by degrees, to know what life means in its deepest and most meaningful aspects.

Guide Table Talk

Three times a day the family gathers at the table. This period should never be a hurried one. Here is a great opportunity to talk over all sorts of things. With a little encouragement each one will be glad to bring in a worthwhile contribution. It should be understood by common consent rather than by formal agreement that nothing of an ugly or unpleasant nature will ever be alluded to at the table.

Have Special Time for Fellowship with the Children

One family has what they call "The Golden Hour." This comes in the evening when the day's work is done and all can get together for reading a story, for learning the best poems, for singing hymns, for selecting television shows, for the cultivation of the best that our civilization has proposed insofar as the parents have themselves been able to acquire this. One mother through her life as a mother has had with her children what she calls "The Confidential Hour." With her this hour comes generally just before the bedtime prayer. Here the mother shares with her child all that she knows as the child develops and is able to comprehend. The child in turn tells the mother all that he knows — all of his thoughts, feelings, experiences of the day. It is understood that nothing said here is to be alluded to elsewhere nor is anything said here to be used as a basis of condemnation. Here the mother is the true priest mediating the things of God. This is the true confessional. Here is the place to create attitudes toward things fundamental — God, home, sex, church, community, Bible, Sabbath — all the things that mean most in our life. Here character is created.

Make Use of Special Occasions

As they arise, such events as birthdays, holidays, Christmas, Easter; sickness, sorrow, death; special joys, perplexities; local, state, and national elections, inauguration of a governor or a president; anniversaries, centennials, special trips afford opportunities for forming religious associations. The home should make use of all such to teach the background and the meaning of each as it comes.

Study Nature Together

What can be more fascinating than to study the stars, the planets, the birds, the flowers, the insects, the animals, the soil, the streams, and a thousand other objects of God's handiwork that either lie about our feet or stretch out before our eyes? Why not encourage the children to save their nickels and invest in a simple nature book.

Enjoy Good Music

A Confucian canon says, "Music has its origin in heaven. Virtue is the strong stem of man's nature, and music is the blossoming of virtue. Music embraces what all can share equally. To go to the very root of our feelings is its province." The Christian religion is peculiarly rich in its great hymns and tunes. A good hymn book — better, several copies of it — should be a part of the equipment of every home. The family should sing together. Albums of good high fidelity recordings are available at moderate prices. A very discerning man has said, "Let me write the hymns of a nation and you may let whomsoever you will write its philosophies."

OUR GREATEST OPPORTUNITY

An adequate family program of religious education, with all that is involved in the way of church and community cooperation, not only will mean the Christian nurture of our children but will contribute to the training and enrichment of the lives of the parents as well. The parents have a chance to live over their youth again and make good some of the failures of their lives in the blessing and development of their children. The blessing to parents in many cases will even be richer than that visited upon the children. And here is the point at which perhaps richest contribution can be made toward building a Christian civilization and the Kingdom of God.

The fundamental Christian point of view and emphasis in the home which makes up the ideal school and human society, transferred to the big world outside, will make the ideal world-society, "wherein dwelleth righteousness" and world brotherhood. After all, the supreme Christian task and challenge is to learn how to live together as human brothers in the heavenly Father's world.

QUESTIONS FOR DISCUSSION

1. Discuss the significance of the shifting of many of the family's traditional functions to society and the change of emphasis from familism to individualism. Study ways and means of bringing back again more unity and comradeship for the members of the family.

2. Discuss methods and programs for teaching religion and making it more vital in the home.

3. Outline a plan for closer cooperation between the home and the church in the promotion of religious education.

4. How can your church educate parents to teach religion in the home?

CHAPTER 20

LEISURE-TIME ACTIVITIES

Play will influence life, either for good or bad. It is not only a possible but an inevitable factor in the formation of character. Character is not only tested by play, but it is largely made during play. The use or misuse of leisure time is both a test of civilization and a determinant of it. The importance of play and recreational life in the development of the child is generally recognized. Froebel called play "the highest phase of child development." This was considered true because play is the "self-active representation of the inner." Luther H. Gulick, the American philosopher for the play movement, says: "If you want to know what a child is, study his play; if you want to affect what he will be, direct the form of his play." He suggests that man's long period of immaturity is given in order that the child might have ample time for play and thus get the preparation for the complex life of adulthood.

Joseph Lee, who was one of the pioneer leaders of the National Recreational Association of America, once made a splendid statement of the place of play in child life. He said: "The thing that most needs to be understood about play is that it is not a luxury, but a necessity. It is not simply something that a child likes to have; it is something that he must have if he is ever to grow up. It is more than an essential part of his education; it is an essential law of his growth, of the process by which he becomes a man at all."

Recreation also has a place of ever-increasing importance in adult life. It is being recognized that some form of recreation is not only natural to man but necessary for man. The normal attitudes toward life and the proper relationships with others are impossible without some place for play and social life. This is especially true now when large numbers of people have reached age sixty-five or more and have retired from active employment. The churches must give increasing attention to the welfare of older people and their guidance in recreation and other worthwhile activities. So play and social life have come to be recognized not as unimportant activities in the life of children and young people, but as important experiences of all life; not as a sort of necessary evil, but as a necessary good; not as a thing to be condoned and put up with, but as a thing to be enthusiastically accepted and intelligently planned; not as something that merely contributes to a healthy bodily growth, but as an activity that makes a definite contribution to the development of character and the whole of life.

INCREASING IMPORTANCE

There is more interest in, and opportunity for, recreation. Modern athletics and commercialized amusements are attracting millions of people, in fact nearly the whole population. People are interested in social and recreational life. They give their time and their money for those things which contribute to entertainment and amusement. There is a deep-seated desire and need which is met by such activities. There is nothing fundamentally wrong in this situation except that this important phase of life has been left to commercialized amusements and worldly interests instead of being utilized by the church to provide for a more wholesome social-recreational life.

The Short Work-Week

With the speeding up of production by the machine, there has to be a shortening of the hours of labor to prevent overproduction and unemployment. The limit has not been reached yet in the shortening of work time. Some economists predict the three- and four-day week in the future. What will this extra time be used for — to build or to destroy character? Time is not the only thing conducive to play. For play to be prominent in life, there must be a relatively high standard of living. There must be freedom from the fear of need and poverty.

Greater Need for Recreation

Specialization in modern industry has been carried to such an extreme that there is little opportunity for the expression of idealism. Industrialism "pays a premium on monotony." This monotony is an enemy of idealism and endangers moral character. All of this modern specialization means that work contributes less to satisfactory living than in the past. Formerly the worker had the joy of creation, when he completed the whole product; but now his part is so small that he does not recognize the car or machine as his creation. Also, in mass production there is little opportunity for close personal relationship between employer and employee, and a sense of oneness is not developed. The employee works to make a living and rarely thinks of making a contribution to life. Often the employer thinks of those working in his factory as so many machines who are contributing to the dividends of his plant. There is lacking a sense of moral responsibility.

There has also been a speeding up of all life. People live intensely. This is not conducive to the most satisfactory life. Neither does it furnish the best basis for the building of intelligently directed character. The increase in city population, a result of the industrial development, means a shifting of moral standards. Traditional moral ideals are less respected. There is not so much social pressure in the city as in the country. There are few people who know and care what one does.

Modern Education Magnifies Play

The trend in modern education is away from the transmissive to the creative idea and method. The formal recitation method has been supplanted by the fellowship of teacher and pupil in a common search for truth. This has meant more freedom in the teacher-pupil relationship. As a result, the problem-discussion, dramatization, and project methods of teaching have become more prominent. These represent the play and socialized method in education. In addition there has been a new appreciation of the educational value of the playground and the athletic field. This is inevitable when the child is made the center of the educational process. This additional leisure time with the demand for more recreation and an increasing emphasis on the play method in modern education provides an opportunity for good or ill. Shall this added leisure time and increasing emphasis be used to build good or bad character. Release from work is a curse to an individual or a civilization that has not learned how to use leisure time. This leisure time will in the future enrich or destroy civilization.[1]

RECREATION AND RIGHTEOUSNESS

Recreation may make a worthy contribution to the building of character if it has the right content and is properly supervised.

Health and Morality

Play of the right kind contributes to health of body and mind. This is just as true of the adult as of the child. A healthy body furnishes a better basis for moral living than a sickly body. Rousseau said: "The body must be vigorous to obey the soul. A feeble body weakens the mind." John Locke expressed it thus: "A sound mind in a sound body is a short but full description of a happy state!" A healthy body and a healthy mind make for better attitudes toward life and toward other human beings. This makes health a moral responsibility in itself.

[1] For discussion of the dangers of increased leisure time, see Charles K. Brightbill and Harold D. Meyer, *Recreation* (Englewood Cliffs, N. J.: Prentice-Hall, Inc., 1953), pp. 2-19.

The Playground and Crime

Undirected play in a bad environment is a most powerful factor for evil. Thus the playground may develop criminal impulses and contribute to antisocial conduct. Neumeyer warns:

Society may find its greatest asset in the constructively used leisure of its citizens, but too much free time without adequate preparation for its use also may become a serious problem. The increase of leisure has been heralded as a blessing to mankind. [But] if people . . . indulge in useless and destructive activities, the social order deteriorates and social progress is retarded.[2]

J. Edgar Hoover has vividly described the possible use of playgrounds as a deterrent for juvenile delinquency. He records this case in an interview with Clarence Woodbury:

Not long ago police in a small Eastern community rounded up a gang of teenage boys who had staged a series of "scientific" burglaries and thefts which had victimized virtually every merchant in town and netted the juveniles between $1,000 and $2,000 in loot. When asked to explain his behavior, one 15-year-old member of the gang gave a very revealing answer. He really preferred sports to all other activities, he said, but the community offered no organized sports for boys of his age, so he had gone in for burglary because there was nothing else exciting to do.

Had some organization made it possible for this youngster to engage in all the athletic games he desired, he probably would not have turned to crime. If communities throughout the nation provided more wholesome recreational activities for their young people, delinquency could be curtailed.[3]

He further challenges all social institutions, including churches, to organize programs of leisure time activities as a curtailment of crime, in these words:

There are signs of leveling off in juvenile delinquency in many areas. Those areas, however, in which concerted action has proved effective are counterbalanced by too many areas in which too little is being done. There is a real need for more dynamic programs in

[2] Martin H. Neumeyer and Esther S. Neumeyer, *Leisure and Recreation* (3d ed.; New York: The Ronald Press Co., 1958), pp. 3–4.

[3] J. Edgar Hoover, "You Can Help Stop Juvenile Crime," (*American Magazine*, 159:15 Jan., 1955), pp. 91–92. Used by permission of J. Edgar Hoover and Clarence Woodbury.

which parents, police, schools, churches, and community groups combine to promote plans of positive action designed to meet the needs of each area. Once there is widespread community mobilization to meet this challenge, the present unwholesome picture of youth in crime could change incisively.[4]

Play and Morale

The individual is greatly influenced by his loyalties. Loyalty may not be the chief virtue, but it should be numbered with the leading virtues. Play, more than any other activity, builds group morale. One of the secrets of the success of the Scout Movement is the fact that Boy Scouts have built a high sense of group unity and individual loyalty to the standards of Scouts. College loyalty is largely built around the intercollegiate athletic contests.

The qualities developed in team games are loyalties to the other fellows, to the team, and to the institution, the habit of respecting authority, mental alertness, and co-operative response, self-control, and good sportsmanship. The values of team games have been described by Neumeyer:

> The intimacy of the recreation group can be seen in team play. The members of a team, if it is a real team, function together as one, each playing his part but all working toward a common goal. The friendliness, loyalty, *esprit de corps*, and morale of a team can seldom be found elsewhere. Jealousies and conflicts may occur among the members of a team, but, if so, the group becomes demoralized and team-work ceases.[5]

Games of simple organization and those activities ordinarily used in church life are also valuable in the development of loyalty. Church groups that frequently play together have a sense of oneness and a spirit of friendliness not found in groups without these social activities.

PROGRAMS OF PROMOTION

With the increased demand and need for recreation and with the greater opportunity for participation there have

---

[4] J. Edgar Hoover, "Why Crime is Dropping," *U.S. News and World Report,* 39:45 S 30 (1955), p. 45. Used by permission of J. Edgar Hoover.

[5] Neumeyer, *Leisure and Recreation,* p. 256.

come several attempts to meet the need. These attempts might be divided into: commercialized amusements, and socialized amusements. The latter includes recreation under governmental auspices and church recreation.

Commercialized Amusements

Those providing commercialized amusements were the first to recognize the modern demand for increased recreation and have made millions of dollars by this discovery. These amusements have a tremendous grip on modern recreational life. Many of these are unsafe and some are positively harmful.

Motive wrong. One thing that makes commercialized amusements dangerous is the fact that they are dominated by the "profit motive." The main consideration is not the influence of life but the money in hand. Those who control the commercial amusements cannot be relied upon to give the people what they need most.

Participation lacking. For play to contribute much to the building of character, it must secure active participation. There is not much value physically, mentally, or morally, in watching someone perform, regardless of how skilled the performer may be. But for amusements to furnish the greatest financial returns there must be a large number of spectators.

Destructive Rather Than Constructive

While it cannot be said that all commercialized amusements are destructive morally, the accusation would to some extent be true. Most amusements, dominated by the desire for profit, are in the main unwholesome in their influence on the participants, spectators, and society in general. Gambling is prevalent, evil associates are common, evil thoughts are encouraged, the passions and desires unduly stimulated. The commercial spirit is constantly encroaching upon supposedly socialized fields. The commercial spirit is frequently found in the programs provided by industries and municipalities. There is also danger that the commercial spirit will dominate college athletics.[6] In the commercial spirit in college athletics some have recognized one of the major social conflicts — a conflict between business and education. The domination of college athletics by the professional spirit will mean the ultimate destruction of college athletics and the loss of the fine character-building values that come from intercollegiate athletic competition.

Recreation Under Governmental Auspices

The paternalistic function of government has been emphasized more in recent years. The responsibility of the government is recognized not only to protect but also to promote. Cities, as the smallest, most compact unit of government, have given most attention to this phase of government. Public libraries and parks are provided. These serve a large constituency and, in the main, are very helpful in their influence. A renewed emphasis on physical training as a feature of the public school curriculum has been given. But the major recreational program of municipalities is fostered by city recreation boards.

Under the inspiration and guidance of the National Recreation Association most of the large municipalities in the United States have provided for city supervision of playgrounds. Others have provided for swimming pools, athletic fields, golf courses, tennis courts, and field houses with provision for basketball, volleyball, softball, and indoor baseball. This municipal program of play is the most extensive socialized program found at the present time. There is also a trend toward state and federal provision of recreation facilities.

Major Types of Church Recreation

Three or four major types of recreation are promoted by the churches: (1) physical activities, such as athletic games, swimming, playground activities, hiking, camping, and so forth; (2) the more intellectual or mental types of activities, such as the library and reading rooms, art exhibits and literary clubs; (3) creative activities, such as dramatics, hand-

[6] Brightbill and Meyer, *Recreation*, pp. 201-8.

craft, hobbies, and the various uses of the project method in teaching; (4) social features such as banquets, teas, picnics, and parties. These divisions are more or less arbitrary, but they are at least helpful and practical for descriptive purposes.[7]

While the churches will promote to some extent all of the above types of social and recreational activities, the major emphasis will be placed on the social and certain other educationally valuable agencies and activities such as the library and dramatics. Great hosts of people, especially in rural and village communities, need a richer and more wholesome social and recreational life. When people learn to play together and have good fellowship, they learn to work together and to appreciate each other more highly. There are great moral and spiritual values in a good old-fashioned Sunday school picnic. Churches need to plan for more and better social activities of the various church groups and organizations.

ADOLESCENT RECREATIONAL ORGANIZATIONS

There has grown up a group of organizations independent of institutional control that has provided additional character-building opportunities for adolescent boys and girls. The leading organizations are the Boy Scouts, Girl Scouts, Camp Fire Girls, 4-H Clubs, FFA, Hi-Y. The Boy Scouts and the Camp Fire Girls also foster pre-adolescent programs — the Cubs and the Blue Birds, respectively.

A Guiding Principle

The adolescent recreational organizations have been built on the theory that education comes by doing. There has been a minimum of instruction and a maximum of expression. The instruction has always been kept secondary to activity and often it is so mixed with expression that the boy or girl is unaware of its presence. Character is not only tested by free expressional activities, but it is largely made by these activities. There is a place for formal instruction in the

[7] E. O. Harbin, *The Recreation Leader* (Nashville: Abingdon Press, 1952), chaps. vii, viii, ix.

building of character, but it alone will never build character. Permanent impressions are never made without expression. The youth organizations magnify the informal in character education.

Religion Out-of-Doors

All of the major recreational organizations for adolescent young people magnify the out-of-doors. Hiking and camping are regular features. Such contacts with nature furnish a splendid source of religious impressions. These organizations are not sectarian in their religious beliefs, but they are dominantly religious. The Camp Fire Girls give honors for church activities. The organization is characterized by high idealism. The laws of the Camp Fire are:

Worship God
Seek beauty
Give service
Pursue knowledge
Be trustworthy
Hold on to health
Glorify work
Be happy

Scouting, for both boys and girls, has a wholesome attitude toward religion. The Scout Oath is:

On my honor I will do my best —
1. To do my duty to God and my country, and to obey the Scout Law.
2. To help other people at all times.
3. To keep myself physically strong, mentally awake, and morally straight.

The Scout Law also shows this same high moral and religious idealism, emphasizing that a scout is trustworthy, loyal, helpful, friendly, courteous, kind, obedient, cheerful, thrifty, brave, clean, and reverent. The Scout Constitution illustrates scouting's attitude toward religion. Article 3, Section 1, reads as follows: "The Boy Scouts of America maintain that no boy can grow into the best kind of citizenship without recognizing his obligation to God. In the first part of the Boy Scout's pledge the boy promises, 'On my honor I will do my best to do my duty to God and to my country, and to obey the Scout Law.'" Included in the constitution is this paragraph on religious policy:

The recognition of God as the ruling and leading power of the universe, and the grateful acknowledgement of his favors and blessings, is necessary to the best type of citizenship, and is a wholesome thing in the education of the growing boy. No matter what he may be — Catholic or Protestant or Jew — this fundamental need of good citizenship should be kept before him. The Boy Scouts of America therefore recognize the religious element in training the boy, but it is absolutely non-sectarian. Its policy is that the organization or institution with which the Boy Scout is connected shall give definite attention to his religious life.

Relation to the Church

The Camp Fire Girls are usually organized with the home as a meeting place. Home Craft is the first of the seven crafts it teaches. However, frequently the organization is under the direct auspices of the church; and usually where the home is the meeting place, the leadership and inspiration for the organization comes from the church.

Scouting does not attempt to provide religious training in its own name but turns this responsibility over to the churches. In line with this policy, a National Protestant Committee on Scouting and a Catholic Committee on Scouting have been established. The Lutheran churches also have a special Committee on Scouting. In each case official sanction is given to the Scouting movement, and a separate manual is published describing the values of a church-centered troop and outlining the procedures to be followed. In the Protestant manual, the emphasis is placed on integrating the Scouting program into the church's total program of Christian education. Provision is made for a special church-Scout award known as the "God and Country Award." These standards include regular attendance at Sunday school, regular Bible reading and personal prayer, knowledge of the books of the Bible, a specified number of hours of assigned personal service to the church.[8] The "God and Country Award" is coordinated

[8] Philip Henry Lotz (ed.), *Orientation in Religious Education* (Nashville: Abingdon Press, 1950), pp. 315-16.

with the Royal Ambassador program of The American Baptist Convention so that a Scout or Explorer Scout may apply the knowledge and experience he has gained in the R. A. program toward the achievement of the "God and Country Award," and certain work done in the Scout program may be applied toward R. A. awards.

ACTIVITIES UNDER CHURCH AUSPICES

With more attention given to children and young people and with a larger appreciation for the educational method, churches have come to give more place to play in their programs. In response to the demand of the young people, practically all churches provide at least simple social activities. The programs range all the way from simple activities to elaborate programs of physical, mental and social activities. Gymnasiums are provided; athletic teams are fostered; dramatic clubs are featured; libraries are furnished; and complete recreational buildings are now being built by city churches.

Purpose of Church Play

The ultimate goal in the church's program of religious education is the development of Christ-like character. This does not mean mere faithfulness to the services and activities of the church but also the living of the Christ-life in everyday contacts. While play is to add to the joy of life, the ultimate purpose of church play is a strengthening of Christian character. This is the only real justification of play under church auspices. It must culminate in good to those touched.

Contribution to the Church

The church in this industrial age finds itself greatly handicapped in its character-building program. With the complexity of modern life the church's influence on personal morality has been lessened. The church members' week-day tasks and contacts are so far separated from the Sunday activities that it is very difficult for the church's teachings to carry over into workaday relationships. There is no realm where this lack of carryover is more noticeable than in the amusement field. Church members participate in large numbers in all the questionable amusements. This fact greatly handicaps the moral and spiritual development of the individual and the influence of the church. Much of the conflict that hinders the development of well-rounded, integrated personalities is the clash of ideal and practice.

Recreational activities, well selected as to content, carefully supervised and properly motivated, will increase the church's influence for good over those touched. The play hunger will be satisfied and members will choose church-sponsored leisure-time activities rather than participate in questionable amusements. This will make the Christian different and will give greater spiritual power individually and institutionally. By mixing religion and play, religion will be made a more vital part of life. This will tend to make religion a more dominant influence in life and will suggest a center for life's integration.

In addition to the more direct personal results, play will tend to unify group participation, build a spirit of friendliness and good will in the church and unit organizations, cultivate the democratic spirit, and stimulate group loyalty.

A Part of the Educational Program

If play is to be a vital factor in the building of character and is to make a worthy contribution to church life, it must not be an attached activity. It must be made an integral part of the educational program. It must be thought of primarily as an educational method rather than as recreation. This means that most of the leadership for church play will be the leadership of the Sunday school, Baptist Training Union, The Youth Fellowship, and other established agencies. Officers and teachers will receive training along recreational lines as a feature of their preparation. This unity of leadership will mean a better carry-over. It will also contribute to a better direction of teaching and training. The close relationship of the play leader with the participant also gives an increased opportunity for wholesome influence. Some of the larger churches are now adding a Director of Leisure-Time Activities to the church staff.

Additional Principles

There are other principles that should be followed in the promotion of church play. These will assure more satisfactory results.

Questionable amusements should be avoided. A good environment will not assure a good product. An incorporation of questionable amusements will hurt the church's influence. There are plenty of wholesome, character-building activities.

Leadership is more important than equipment. If the right kind of leadership is not available, the right activity will not be promoted. Native ability and training should be sought, but especially character.

The church's program should be one of participation. A minimum of attention should be given to spectators. There is little character development without active participation.

Persons and not programs should be the main consideration. The individual will be at the center of the program. Activities will not be promoted for their own sakes, but because of what they will do for individuals.

A balanced program should be promoted. Different types of activities should be provided, and all ages should be reached.

The Church's program of play should be adequately financed. If it is a part of the educational program and if it is a valuable character-building activity, then its financial support by the church is as justifiable as the purchase of literature or equipment for Sunday school or young peoples' work. If any feature of the program cannot conscientiously be supported by the church, such a feature should not be fostered.

The program of play should be actively promoted. If play under church auspices has a contribution to make to the building of Christian character, then the play program should be actively promoted, just as is true with the Sunday school and other church organizations. Effort should be put forth to enlist the church members in active participation. This will be true because it is realized that the play program will make a worthy contribution to their lives.

An Appraisal of the Church's Program

Some churches that have put on an extensive program of play have been disappointed in the results attained. This has been largely due to two or three things. Play has been considered primarily as a means of enlistment and enlargement. That should not be its main purpose. Often features have been provided without the proper leadership. Then there has been an attempt to duplicate the activities of the public schools and the community recreation board. The church's program to succeed must be distinctive in emphasis, purpose, and leadership.

The major emphasis in church recreation should continue to be on the simple social activities. These are more easily supervised, enlist more people, are already tied rather definitely to the existing organizations. Whatever physical or other activities that may be provided will be secondary to the educational phases of church life.

Mrs. Agnes Durant Pylant, secretary of the Church Recreation Service of the Baptist Sunday School Board, sets forth the credo of the church recreation worker:

I believe that our churches should promote and provide recreation for the members. I believe that recreation should be an integral part of the entire church program and not a side issue. It should be a part of the already existing departments and not set up as another department sufficient unto itself.

I believe that church recreation should include parties, banquets, and other "eating affairs;" athletic activities; Sunday night fellowships; drama; crafts; camps; hobby groups, and all cultural and creative activities that have no taint of worldliness.

I believe that, through a church recreation program, individuals will be blessed with enriched personalities and strengthened characters. In addition, the fellowship of the entire church will be lifted to a higher, sweeter plane and cemented together with stronger ties.

I believe the slogan, "My Leisure for My Lord" will be a safe criterion for those entrusted with the planning of the recreation program.[9]

QUESTIONS FOR DISCUSSION

1. Formulate your own theory of play and philosophy of recreation from the Christian standpoint.

2. Analyze some present trends in leisure and recreation, and list their implications for religious education.

3. Evaluate the recreation program of a local church as to objectives, program, leadership, facilities, finance, and results in character and conduct.

4. Build an improved recreational program for the church which you examined and give reasons for suggested changes.

5. List the main social-recreational agencies in your community, and evaluate their programs and activities. This might be adopted as a special project for the class.

[9] Agnes Durant Pylant, "I Believe," *Church Recreation* (Nashville: Baptist Sunday School Board, April, May, June, 1954), pp. 1, 6.

CHAPTER 21

RELIGION IN PUBLIC EDUCATION

CHARACTER EDUCATION IN
ELEMENTARY AND SECONDARY SCHOOLS

The American Revolution brought into existence a new nation dedicated to liberty with political and religious freedom uppermost in the minds of its leaders. There followed as a natural consequence the separation of church and state. Almost from the first the question as to the control of education constituted a serious problem. In a social order in which church and state are one, it is a simple matter to teach religion to the youth and to develop character in connection with the general educational program. With the separation of church and state and the establishment of state schools, there has been a growing tendency toward the separation of religion and education.

Elimination of Religious Material

With the separation of religion and public education, it came to be regarded as an inevitable necessity to rewrite all texts and materials used in the state schools. The religious and ethical material of books like the *New England Primer* tended to be supplanted by stories which, though more interesting and greatly improved pedagogically as texts for teaching reading, often contained little character-forming material. This was not only true of readers but of all texts used. The old "Blue-back Speller" was a veritable manual of religious and character-building materials; Peter Parley's *Geography* was also a treatise on religion. Histories never failed to point to the hidden hand of Providence back of all human achievements. These religious and moral materials are not to be found now. The public school has sought to be nonreligious but often has become irreligious. The omission of religious teaching from the public school curriculum is itself an admission that religion is not a part of the educational experience of the individual. Dean Weigle vividly describes it. "The ignoring of religion by the public schools inevitably conveys to children a negative suggestion. It is natural for them to conclude that religion is negligible, or unimportant, or irrelevant to the real business of life."[1]

Effects upon Character

There has been a growing uncertainty in the realm of religious convictions and ethical standards. Ethics is truly in a chaotic condition. As such it lacks its binding force in this twentieth century which longs for the strange and the new. All phases of human conduct tend to be left to the thinking and the feelings of the individual as sole arbiter. Ethical anarchy threatens as a result and crime is the inevitable consequence of a state of ethical anarchy. In fact, the underworld threatens to set up its own "rules of honor," and by establishing its own law, to become respectable. The whole world, including America, is in a state of unrest. In big cities, those who would be secure have often been compelled to purchase this security, not so much by the paying of taxes to guarantee for themselves police protection, as by the payment of bribes to leaders of gangs to prevent the attack of their henchmen. According to "Uniform Crime Report, F.B.I.," April, 1957, "major crime in cities increased 12.7 per cent over the preceding year." This was the largest increase in the twenty-six year records of the F.B.I.

[1] Luther A. Weigle, in Philip Henry Lotz (ed.), *Orientation in Religious Education* (Nashville: Abingdon Press, 1950), p. 91.

Inability of Home and Church

During the period just described, the American home was undergoing a rather marked transformation. The lad formerly had worked side by side with his father in the field or in the small shop or place of business. With the coming of a rapidly developing industrialized type of life, there came to be a tremendous migration from the isolated pioneer farm community and small town to that of the larger town or city. Even farm workers have become migratory. In the tasks of the city, the father was no longer able to spend much time with his son. And as women have entered the business world the same has often become true of the mother. So the home has been handicapped in character building.

The church has probably never reached with its message of salvation and its challenge to high ideals more than a third of the youth of the land. Many of those attending its classes of instruction do so very irregularly. Those that do attend get little of the Bible, and much of what they do get is not applied to moral problems. Thus it may be seen that the church cannot guarantee character and that the character-forming ability of the home tends to decrease from year to year.

RECENT AWAKENING

Realizing the need for character education and the limitations of the home and church, there has been an awakening along this line on the part of the school. Especially has this been true since the enormous increase in crime that came in the wake of two world wars. A long period of comparative silence has been broken. Numerous books on character education have come from the press. Practically all magazines that enter the field of education are presenting articles on various phases of the subject. Everywhere educational leaders have turned their attention to the development of character.

Emphasis on Character

Leaders in the National Education Association have long

insisted on the need for character education in the public schools. Ethical character has been listed as one of the main objectives of education. Some have suggested religious activities for the public schools as the most favorable soil for the nurture of character. One of America's leading educators has said that the supreme problem in education is that of character development. Dean Weigle aptly sets forth this obligation of the public schools:

> The public schools should aim at the development of a citizenship which is founded upon character; and they may, in their efforts to educate for character, give due place to religious motives. They can teach that morality is more than custom, public opinion, or legal enactment; they can point to its grounding in the structure of the universe and in the nature of God. In the teaching of history, literature, and the social sciences they can afford to religious faith its normal and proper place.[2]

Ever since the disappearance of *McGuffey's Eclectic Readers* from the public school early in the twentieth century, teachers have been stumped by the problems of instructing the pupils in character without sermonizing. A new approach to this problem is offered by the appearance of a set of readers called the *Golden Rule Series*,[3] with the subtitle of the *Modern McGuffey's Readers*. The readers are available for grades one to six. Their stories are built around eleven moral themes: cooperation, courage, fairness, friendliness, honesty, kindness, patriotism, perseverance, responsibility, reverence, and unselfishness. The chief difference between the old McGuffey readers and the new is the manner in which the truth is presented. These readers are intended to help build character and help curb juvenile delinquency.[4]

Demand for Scientific Study

In view of all that has been said it would seem that a scientific study of character formation is imperative. Almost

[2] *Ibid.*, p. 94.

[3] Ullin W. Leavell, Mary L. Friebele, and Tracie Cushman, *Golden Rule Series (The Modern McGuffey Readers)*, 6 vols. (New York: American Book Co., 1956-57).

[4] "A Modern McGuffey," *Time* (New York: Sept. 30, 1957), p. 72.

everywhere educators are interested, but there is a feeling of helplessness. The great question asked invariably is "how?" It must be admitted that a fairly good technique for teaching geography or mathematics has been developed, but entirely too little is known about how to form character. Much effort in this direction is wasted because of lack of aim or objective. Little is accomplished in any field without definite aims or goals.

While there is practically a common agreement concerning some of the objectives or component factors of character, it must be admitted that this agreement is by no means universal. Such a simple prohibition as "Thou shalt not lie" passed unchallenged yesterday. Under the influence of the relative theory of truth, many are disturbed as to what truth is and as to whether it may not be ethical in some situations to falsify. The modern conception of morals as *mores* or customs is an equally disturbing factor, especially in an age when it is popular to break with custom. In fact the answer with reference to the right and wrong of many situations would be given in various ways by various individuals. The first essential in character formation and the greatest need of this century is to determine what constitutes good or desirable character. After objectives have been defined, the right method may be developed. The tendency to reverse the order in education is too often the case. To know what is wanted in the way of an educational product must come before that product can be intelligently produced.

A SUGGESTED PROGRAM

It appears that the public school is considering seriously today its obligation to develop character. More and more it is attempting to work out an adequate program for character development. Some progress is being made in devising plans, but there is much yet to be done. Various methods and plans have been suggested and have been put into practice in various ways. No one plan, and perhaps not all of them put together, will solve adequately this supremely important matter, but progress is being made, and educators will press on in every way possible. In such a brief treatment as this, only certain main factors can be stressed; but in conclusion, largely by way of synthesis, some suggestions are offered with the hope that they will prove of practical value. The student should by all means read some of the latest and best books on character education and week-day religious education in order to understand better the needs and problems in this field (see Part IV, Bibliography, p. 460).

Maintain a Religious Atmosphere

As has just been stated, the public school should not ignore religion. As a rule it has not done so. It has tended to maintain a religious interest and a religious atmosphere. Religion can be instilled without sectarianism. The public school chapel is an outstanding example of this. It is a lamentable fact that the religious chapel is being supplanted today in many instances by the nonreligious assembly, which may have a place as a pep meeting for developing school spirit, but should not supplant the religious influence of the chapel program. The nonsectarian religious chapel service should not go. That it should be fairly conducted scarcely needs saying. Those of all religions should be welcomed there. As Max Muller well says, "There is no religion . . . which does not say do good, avoid evil." Some might even be invited to appear on the chapel program who profess no particular religion if they attempt honestly to inspire higher ideals and not to engage in sectarian propaganda.

Utilize the School Subjects

All literature abounds in materials that inspire to nobler conceptions of living. In the "Literature and Life Series" for high schools, one of the main objectives given is that of character formation. More character-forming literature should be chosen. Literature is being taught in the more progressive schools from the viewpoint of appreciation and with character as a definite goal. Latin literature abounds in biographical sketches of great character-building value. The teacher interested in character may prophesy to the valley of mathematical dry bones and make them live. Mathematics may be so taught as to form habits of perseverance and accuracy. If related to life, budgeting and thrift may result. The social studies should not make their greatest contribution on the factual plane but as means of inspiring attitudes and ideals. Their main goal is coming to be and should be the growth of personality or character. Many other subjects present excellent opportunities for character development.

Use Discipline

Originally school discipline was maintained with three main objectives in view: retribution, the good of the school, and the good of the pupil. More and more alert educators are realizing that the supreme purpose of school discipline is the good of the individual. In other words, the purpose of school control is to develop the individual who can control himself. Herein lies one of the advantages of student government. Whatever the form of government, this conception of discipline should become a universal aim of all school administrators and teachers.

Socialize the Individual

Since "No man liveth unto himself," every individual must be developed into a social being who is able to live with his fellows and get along with them. But this is not enough. Moral responsibilities are not simply negative. They have a positive element. If progress is to be made, society must develop those personalities who will feel a responsibility for bettering the social order. In anything that approaches an ideal or Christian society, there must be developed a keen sense of the brotherhood of man and a feeling that every individual is his brother's keeper. This is coming to be the primary objective of the social studies and of citizenship in its broadened sense as taught today.

Personal Counseling

Provision is being made for character guidance in an ever increasing number of schools. Deans of girls who guide developing womanhood through the dangerous maze of adolescence render an invaluable service and prevent many a shipwrecked life. Counselors of boys perform this same type of service. This type of service is being rapidly increased. In smaller institutions, and to some extent in all schools, it should be performed by the teacher. It would seem superfluous to add that this demands a teacher of a higher type than a mere hearer of lessons. It demands a teacher who lives what he teaches. The example of the teacher means much.

Cooperate with Church Schools

A regular course with the Bible as a text is not required in the public school. On the other hand, the utmost cooperation should be given by public school administrators and teachers to the work of the Sunday school, the Vacation Bible School, and week-day religious education programs.[5] Former public school teachers may be secured to teach in these schools. In the truest sense, the entire religious educational program is outstandingly character-forming in purpose, or should be. Any school or educational agency of the Christian religion misses the mark greatly if it fails to establish as a main goal the highest in Christian character. Cramming the head with biblical facts with no definite purpose in mind is not sufficient. All biblical facts, all religious teaching should be purposive. Certainly one of the supreme purposes should be the highest in Christian personality and character.

RELIGIOUS EDUCATION IN STATE COLLEGES

Beginnings

It has been truthfully said that higher education in America is the "child of the church," since an overwhelming number of institutions of higher learning actually were founded by the churches. It is a historical fact that the impelling motive for the foundation of Harvard, William and Mary, Yale, and King's College was the desire to provide religious

[5] On week-day religious education, see Chapter 16 in this text.

education in its highest form. Consequently, the curriculum of these first institutions showed a predominant emphasis upon Hebrew, Greek, ethics, philosophy, and Christian evidences. Thus America's first colleges, as well as her first grammar schools, were mainly schools of religious education.

Secularization

Schools founded and fostered by churches were destined soon to share the stage with an ever-increasing number of schools founded and supported by the state. The establishment of the University of North Carolina in 1789 marked the opening of the significant era of state emphasis upon higher education. This does not mean, however, that there came a diminution in the work of the formerly established church schools, for as late as 1850 there were approximately 6,000 church-supported schools and colleges, including academies, with an enrollment of more than 250,000 students. The churches continued to be the chief support of higher education until well past the period of the Civil War. In 1870 the total enrollment of all of the colleges and universities erected by the state was only about 6,000.

Since that date, however, state-supported schools and colleges have sprung up with almost magical profusion, so that today all of the states have state universities and state colleges, or have educational institutions adopted and subsidized by the state. Today the ratio of increase in enrollment is much more rapid than the increase in population of college age. Fred Lindsey, writing for *Nation's Business*, said:

A larger proportion attend college. In 1900 higher education enrollments equaled two per cent of those aged 18-24. The figure increased to nine per cent in 1940. It is twenty per cent today. The trend shows no signs of diminishing — last year 18-year-old youths increased 2.4 per cent, but first-year college enrollments were up seven per cent.[6]

In 1956, there were in operation in the United States 1,936 colleges and universities of all kinds with a total en-

[6] Fred D. Lindsey, "Crisis Building up in College Classrooms," *Nation's Business*, 44: 56, 1956, p. 56.

rollment during the previous college year of just above 2,700,000 students. Of these 1,936 institutions, 679 were state-supported colleges and universities, having a total enrollment of approximately 1,375,000 students, representing 55 per cent of the total. Approximately one-half of these state-supported institutions were two-year or better known as community colleges. The remaining 1,257 colleges were divided between those privately endowed and those church-related. The distinction in many instances is difficult to make and the Office of Education in Washington classified them as private and church-related colleges. As a group, these 1,257 colleges have a total enrollment of 1,125,000 or 45 per cent of the total.

Present Dangers

The late President Faunce of Brown University once pointed out the subtle danger of a church policy of noninterest in religious education in the state schools in these words: "The Church may say, 'Education is no longer in our hands,' The State may say, 'On all religious matters we are silent.' Thus millions will grow up — yea, are actually growing up in America today — without any genuine religious training." The result of such a situation usually proves to be indifference on the part of the student, which is a stronger influence upon youths in college than skepticism or atheism. There is danger, however, that with a secularized curriculum and with a materialistic emphasis in psychology, biology, and elsewhere that worse than indifference will result with the student. J. Paul Williams describes the condition as follows:

> It is said that no doubt sectarian domination of the schools is a danger, but that it is not as serious a danger as the threat of religious vacuum. Religious disintegration furnishes the opportunity for the totalitarian demagogue. When the barometer really drops, hurricanes follow.[7]

Fraught with the keen consciousness of the fact that the state schools hold at least one-half of the potential leadership

[7] J. Paul Williams, in Lotz, *Religious Education*, p. 474.

of the nation as well as of the churches and that there is resident in the hearts of the great masses of these university students an interest in religion and religious education which cannot be stifled, various forces are now at work within the state schools to provide some form of religious education for the students of these schools.

STATE EFFORTS

On the state school campus of today there is a stronger emphasis upon religious training than there has been since the establishment of state colleges. This has come to be true because the administrations of the universities recognize that the absence of instruction in religion in schools which claim to teach all the sciences is incongruous.

Through the Curriculum

The state schools are today placing much more emphasis on religious education through curricular activities. Formerly, on the basis of separation of church and state, there was much objection by denominational leaders to the teaching of Bible and other courses in religion in the regular curriculum of a state school or university. But one hears little objection to this today. Responding to a growing demand for religious courses, two-thirds of all state universities now give academic credit for such courses. Yale University in 1957 began offering undergraduates a major in religion for the first time. Elimination of religious teaching from the curriculum is not maintaining a neutral position. By this omission it indirectly and forcefully teaches that religion is not important enough to be included in the education of the individual.

Edward W. Blakeman gives a fair picture of the curricular status of religion within the tax-supported centers of learning by reporting on one large university within each of fifteen representative states.[8] In the fifteen state institutions used in the sampling procedure, he found courses in religion

[8] Edward W. Blakeman, "A Realistic View of Religion in State Universities," *Religious Education*, November-December, 1948, p. 356.

are part of the liberal arts curriculum except in Illinois, Iowa, Montana, Texas, and Virginia. In these states the denominational bodies supplement the university programs by creating foundations, schools, or Bible chairs in which teaching faculties offer courses, and students taking such courses receive credit for them in the universities concerned.

Dr. Blakeman outlines briefly four main approaches or methods whereby state and church converge on the question of religion as a subject for study in a state school or university.

1. Where religion as a phase of culture is more or less presupposed. This view or method holds that religion by its very nature is an inclusive orientation and therefore calls for treatment in each of the major courses of study — history, literature, philosophy, sociology, and so on. This method has the advantages of offering a challenge to the faculty of each department and eventually to each professional college to treat religion and spiritual experience in its own way and in connection with the study of any course in human culture and development. This is the prevailing pattern in state centers. D. D. Parker, in a survey[9] conducted in 1946, reported that Ohio State, one of the stronger land-grant colleges which has become a university, offers the "English Bible" in the Department of English, "Crusades and the Reformation" in the History Department, and 11 courses of specific religious interest in the Philosophy Department.

2. Where the affiliated denominational college is a second form of administration. In Columbia, Mo., and Grand Forks, N. D., are church colleges especially designed to complement, not duplicate, the state curriculum. This plan enables students of a particular faith to get their general education at a state school and get religious education in an affiliated college of their own denomination.

3. An interfaith school of religion constitutes a third system. For instance, the state university of Iowa at Iowa City has had an interdenominational school of religion for more

[9] D. D. Parker, "Religion at Land Grant Colleges, *Religious Education*, March-April, 1947, pp. 80-85.

than two decades. Its director and its Jewish, Catholic, and Protestant faculty are selected and supported by a board of trustees representing the university and the churches. This school of religion has been unusually successful. No formal objection to the school has been brought before the courts of the state, and there has been a steady growth in its enrollment and influence. In 1947-48 the curriculum was pursued as a whole or in part by twelve hundred different students, the course registration climbing to two thousand.

4. Ecclesiastical or denominational foundations offer a plan extensively used. In many state centers, as at the universities of Illinois, Montana, Texas, and Kansas, certain religious bodies have stationed teaching ministers or regular faculty members in a local church adjoining the campus. A "Bible chair" or "foundation" is incorporated and supported by a particular denominational body or church interested in the matter or by any number of denominational groups which decide to undertake the project. Here, again, the particular student can get his general education in the state school, and his denomination has to supply his courses in Bible and religion.

Through Religious Services

In times past state schools had regular chapel services and sometimes maintained a chaplain. Occasionally this is still found to be true. But for the most part in recent years there has been an almost complete abolition of compulsory mass chapel services. An estimate based upon the survey of representative colleges indicates that not more than half of the state schools with compulsory chapel services have more than one such service each week. Some state schools maintain full-time chaplains, while others depend exclusively upon student pastors or local ministers for chaplain services.

Thus the need for religious instruction is amply met in neither the curriculum nor in the official services of the state school. The need must be met, if at all, therefore, by forces which, though not completely independent of the state schools, are yet partially or completely supported by funds from without the university. Among the sources of this support are the Y.M.C.A., Y.W.C.A., Bible chairs, denominational student workers, local churches, and a few minor forces. And let it not be thought that the state school administrators are antagonistic to these forces because they are not officially a part of the schools. Virtually all the heads of state schools endorse the student organizations, and well they might, since without such organizations the religious education of state schools would be negligible. In looking into the student religious movements of the state schools, it should be remembered that they are the strongest forces for religious education within these schools. To approach the state school campus from this angle compels religious educators to place more than a casual mark of importance upon the leadership and work of these student forces.

INTERDENOMINATIONAL ACTIVITIES

For many decades the strongest forces at work in behalf of Christianity and religious education on the state school campus were the Young Men's Christian Association and the Young Women's Christian Association. Until the advent of the denominational student organizations, these Christian associations stood virtually alone in championing an organized religious program for the state school campus, and the work which these forces have done in creating and strengthening the religious life of college youth deserves more comment than this brief treatise permits. Though the denominational student organizations are meeting a need which the essentially interdenominational nature of the Y.M.C.A. cannot meet, there will always be a sphere of usefulness for the Christian Association on the state school campus.

The first Y.M.C.A. established on an American university campus was organized at the University of Virginia just past the middle of the nineteenth century. The early organizations functioned chiefly on the prayer meeting and student volunteer plan. From the beginning of its American collegiate career, the Y.M.C.A. has set itself to tackle the problems of the state school in a sympathetic manner, and the triumphs of this challenging task are numerous. From the early, simply organized Y.M.C.A. has grown an organization which today embraces many departments of work and which is cared for with superior equipment in well-constructed buildings and which is stabilized with large financial support.

The work of the Y.M.C.A. and Y.W.C.A. was flourishing on practically every college campus, including state, independent, and denominational colleges, thirty and forty years ago. But in recent years the major religious work on the campus has been taken over by denominational groups and foundations, and an increasingly large amount of curricular courses in Bible and religion are being offered in these institutions.

These Christian associations even today, however, are rendering a valuable service as coordinating agencies for the denominational groups on state college campuses. The emphasis on religious education in all types of colleges today is greater than ever before — much greater perhaps — but it is taking a new course and, there is a different pattern. More and more the religious denominations will not be able to provide general education for all their young people. They will have to depend more and more on state and private colleges and universities for general education; and, in turn, the work of such organizations as the Baptist Student Union and the various denominational youth fellowships will become increasingly important and valuable.

DENOMINATIONAL WORK

A survey of state schools in the South will reveal that approximately 83 per cent of the students are members of churches and for the most part, members of Protestant churches. A leading editorial in *The Christian Century* (April 11, 1956) states that of the nearly two thousand colleges and universities of all types in the United States in 1956, five hundred were Christian colleges. The 500 Christian colleges enrolled about 20 per cent of the college and university students in the United States. That means that 80 per cent of the students get their education in state or independent colleges and universities. For the South in particular, a major portion of these students are members of Protestant churches. It is only logical, therefore, that the Protestant denominations should come to recognize their responsibility in the state school to the extent of promoting a definite program of religious education for the student members of their churches. This recognition was somewhat slow, however; and for decades the various churches left the full field of such endeavor to the interdenominational Y.M.C.A. Of course, churches for each denomination existed at the state school centers, but student programs were largely incidental in the work of such local churches.

The years since 1920 have seen a remarkable change in the situation, and today the chief Protestant churches have well-organized departments of student work, a chief part of whose work is the promotion of a program of religious education for their particular students on the state school campuses. A brief survey of this will help the reader to understand and appreciate the indispensable impetus given to religious education by this means. Since the Southern Baptist Department of Student Work is the earliest and one of the most fully developed of the various student movements, it is described as characteristic in this discussion. The Methodist Church through its Wesley Foundation and the Presbyterian Church through its Department of Christian Campus Life are doing a similar work for the students and faculty of their respective denominations.

A Typical Program

From various studies it is estimated that approximately 20 per cent of Southern Baptist students are enrolled in Southern Baptist colleges and universities. This means that 80 per cent are enrolled in state and privately endowed institutions. The Department of Southern Baptist Student Work recognized its responsibility to the entire group of Baptist students but particularly for those enrolled in schools of independent and state control. The work of this department began in 1922 under the supervision of the late Dr. Frank H. Leavell who, with two assistant secretaries as a rule, conducted full supervision of Baptist student work on virtually all state campuses of the South as well as on the campuses of Baptist institutions. Dr. Leavell did pioneer work, laying solid foundations and leading in the expansion of the work for 27 years until his death in 1949. His successors are carrying on the same general type of work, but on a larger scale. There are seven assistant secretaries who stay on the field a large part of the time and lead in special programs on the campuses and serve as speakers and leaders in state conferences and summer assemblies.

The organization through which this department works is known as the Baptist Student Union — popularly, "The B.S.U." It is actually not an independent organization but rather a corporate name for the sum total of all Baptist student activities on a local campus and in the local churches. On the campus Baptist Student Union Council sits a representative from each of the unit organizations of students, usually its president. A president and other officers are elected from a mass meeting of all Baptist students of the college. This elected group sits in council meeting once each week to plan the activities for the week ahead. Since representatives from all the unit organizations are participating, there is a correlated program with no overlapping. The unity of movement thus afforded is indispensable.

Special weeks and days suggested by the Department of Student Work are observed on each campus. Some of these special weeks and days are join-the-church Sunday, student evangelistic week, vocational emphasis week, missionary week, study course week, and similar emphases on other weeks. The special week devoted to conferences and discussions on deepening the religious life on state and privately endowed college campuses is called "Religious Emphasis Week," and the visiting speakers sometimes include representatives of other denominations as well as Baptists. On Baptist campuses this week is called "Religious Focus Week."

Here the team is usually made up of Baptist leaders, who have been chosen by the Department of Baptist Student Work. Similar programs are being projected by other denominations and as interdenominational activities.

Student Directors

In many instances the work of the local campus is under the direction of a skilled student director who lends a remarkable impetus to the religious life of the campus because of consecrated character and masterful preparation. There are 275 full-time Baptist student directors now in the South. In many instances a faculty advisor gives much of his time to the assistance of the student work. There are 22 Southern states with state student secretaries and some part-time secretaries.

Along with the work of these secretaries should be mentioned the student conventions and conferences for leaders which help so much to give inspiration and morale. Special retreats are held for leaders, such as those at Montreat, Lake Junaluska, and Ridgecrest, North Carolina, and Glorieta, New Mexico, for Presbyterians, Methodists, and Baptists, respectively. State conventions, retreats, and conferences and occasionally those for larger areas are held for leaders and other workers, rendering invaluable aid to the denominational student work.

Material Equipment

In recent years splendid progress has been made in building student centers for denominational work. On many state school campuses are to be found "Workshops," "Cottages," "Student Centers," and similar arrangements for the promotion of student work. Some of these buildings have been built at a cost exceeding $100,000. The support for the work of a local campus comes from the local church, the state convention, and from independent individual contributions.

Steps have also been taken to provide dormitories under

the Christian influences for the benefit of students. Instances of this are at the University of Missouri and the College of Industrial Arts in Texas. This is very important, especially in the light of the poor provisions by state schools and the inability to adequately supervise private boarding places.

Bible Chairs

Along with student work, and in fact preceding it, has come the Bible chair provided by the denominations at the state colleges. This was Jefferson's idea for the University of Virginia in 1822, when he suggested that the denominations "establish each for itself a professorship of their own tenets on the confines of the university — preserving, however, their independence." The Disciples did this as early as 1893 at the University of Michigan; Baptists through the Francis Wayland Foundation and Methodists through the Wesley Foundation have done the same at a number of schools in the North. Various denominations have done so at the University of Texas and elsewhere. It is a movement fraught with tremendous possibilities.

Other Forces

Among other forces which have helped greatly in the organized student work of the denominations are the local ministers and their churches. The original approach to a campus is made through the local minister or ministers, and all subsequent work is done with their cooperation and approval. Many ministers have been virtually student secretaries. The local churches have thrown open both doors and hearts to the warm reception and assistance of the college and university students. The religious education program of the local church often includes departments of work for the students. These together with the intensive enlistment and supervision of the denominational student directors, student unions, and unit organizations have resulted in the enlistment of an ever-growing percentage of students of the state schools in the local churches. Such a program not only will mean an immeasurable contribution to individual lives but will also bolster the denominational fiber with the strongest leadership.

QUESTIONS FOR DISCUSSION

1. Write out a statement as to the meaning of "separation of church and state," and "religious freedom." Discuss the meaning of the First Amendment to the Constitution of the United States.

2. How would you assign responsibilities among American institutions — the home, the church, the public school, the week-day church school, and others — for teaching religion and preserving our religious heritage?

3. Discuss the difference between teaching religion *in* the public schools and *in connection with* the public schools. Define carefully the different plans used in so teaching religion.

3. Outline and evaluate the different plans for teaching religion *in* and *in connection with* tax-supported colleges and universities in the United States. See Edward W. Blakeman, in Lotz, *Orientation in Religious Education,* Chapter 29, "Religious Education in Tax-Supported Colleges and Universities."

CHAPTER 22

THE CHRISTIAN COLLEGE

Among the important agencies of religious education stands the denominational college. What its particular function is, how its work is related to the whole program of the Christian movement, and how it is measuring up to its task are some of the questions which are being asked of the denominational school. The best way to begin to seek answers to these important questions is to study the historical development of these schools.

DEVELOPMENT

Early Christian Schools

The Christian movement, quite early in its history, developed two types of schools. One of these was the *Catechumenal*, the purpose of which was to train or prepare novitiates for church membership. The second type was the *Catechetical*, the function of which was to train for church leadership. Among these early schools were two celebrated missionary training schools, that of Pantaenus, in Egypt; and the other on the island of Iona, on the coast of Scotland. The *cathedral* and *monastic* schools of the Middle Ages belonged to this latter type. (See Chapter 4.)

Beginning of Denominational Schools

The denominational school proper is a child of the Reformation. This movement was quick to seize upon education as a means of perpetuating its religious principles. Luther urged the founding and the maintenance of Christian schools throughout Germany. Calvinism also included a program of general education in its scheme of religious, political, and social reform. Hence, the Pilgrims tell that as soon as they had settled safely in New England, "one of the first things we looked for and longed after was to advance learning." Accordingly, Harvard College was founded in 1636 to perpetuate their faith and provide for a trained ministry. The religious motive which led to its founding was back of the founding of every New England college which came into existence before the year 1800. Education in this early period was the servant of the church. The culture of the time was religion-centered and church-dominated.

Growth of Denominational Colleges

Nine colleges were founded during the colonial period. All but one of these were denominational. In the other the Bible was used as a textbook. Fifteen others were founded before the year 1800. Of the first 119 colleges in America, 104 were church-related institutions. Of the 246 in existence in the year 1860, only 17 were state institutions. More than half of the higher institutions of learning in this country at the present time bear some relation to a denomination. Many of the existing independent institutions owe their origin to some denomination. Thence the strength of the religious motive in establishing and maintaining Christian schools in this country is clearly demonstrated.

Beginning of State Schools

About the middle of the eighteenth century, the theory

began to be advanced by French thinkers that education was essentially a civil affair to promote the interests of society and the welfare of the state rather than the interests and welfare of the church. These views had considerable influence in this country where practical tendencies and the rise of the new national spirit were already leading many to feel that education should answer the needs of all the people rather than of groups or factions within the state. They thought that the kind of education given in the schools must ultimately influence the welfare of the state itself and that it could not, therefore, be regarded as a private matter.

One of the results of this feeling was the attempt to take over some of the denominational colleges and make them state universities. King's College received revised charters from the New York legislature in 1784 and 1787 and the name was changed to Columbia. In 1819, the alumni of Dartmouth College, led by Daniel Webster, fought an attempt by the state legislature to alter the constitution of the college, finally winning the decision in their favor from Chief Justice Marshall in the Supreme Court of the United States. This decision saved the day for independent educational institutions and committed the country to a dual system of education — state and independent, or public and private. It also had the effect of stimulating the building of state universities, the University of Virginia being founded in the very year of the Dartmouth decision.

Founding of Baptist Colleges

The idea that education was essentially a civil affair began to gain ground in the latter part of the eighteenth and the first of the nineteenth centuries. Religion was brought to a low ebb, producing a lull in the founding of church-supported colleges. After 1820 this activity was renewed by the denominations. Among Baptists this was largely due to the influence of Luther Rice who toured the country in the interests of the new Baptist Mission in Burma where Adoniram Judson had begun his great work. Seeing, in his travels

up and down the country, the educational destitution of the
Baptist ministry, Rice became active for education as well
as missions.

At the first General Convention of Baptists ever held in
America, afterwards known as the First Triennial Convention, called to organize cooperative support of the new missionary enterprise, Richard Furman of South Carolina who
had been elected president of the body, after the business
of the meeting had been transacted, made an address in favor
of education. He outlined a plan for a system of Baptist
higher education which included a national university to be
located in Washington which was to be fed by colleges
founded in the various states. The state Baptist schools were
slow in getting started, due partly to the fact that the institution which was founded in Washington absorbed all the
funds that could be raised for higher education. The Triennial Convention severed its connection with the Columbian
College in Washington in 1826. From that time begins the
fruitful era in the founding of Baptist colleges.

At the beginning of the nineteenth century, there was
only one Baptist college. By the end of the century the number of Baptist colleges and academies had increased to 200.
The number of students increased during this period from
92 to 40,000. Endowments had grown from $50,000 to about
$44,000,000. By the middle of the twentieth century the en-
rollment in Baptist colleges alone was about 75,000, and the
endowments exceeded $198,000,000.

Other Denominational Schools

Other denominations also became active in the founding
of schools during the first half of the nineteenth century. It
is said that during the two decades from 1830 to 1850 more
colleges were organized than had been established in the
previous two hundred years, and that the rate of founding
new colleges continued to be high up to the end of the century. By far the larger number of these institutions were
denominational and looked upon their functions as largely
religious.

The Secularizing Tendency

In the meantime many influences were combining to secularize state institutions of higher learning, particularly those in the East, causing them to eliminate religion entirely from their plans and activities. Religion was associated in the thought of the time with sectarianism and, therefore, could not be allowed where all faiths had to be educated together. This tendency in state institutions caused many who were interested in higher education to fear grave dangers from a completely secularized culture and thus increased the zeal for the founding of denominational schools. Practically no settled policy was followed by the denominations in founding these institutions; hence a needless multiplicity of colleges resulted, many of them perishing within a few years for lack of adequate support and many others surviving only to eke out a precarious existence.

This lack of system in the founding and locating of denominational schools has furnished one of the greatest impediments to denominational education. Great sums of money have been expended in starting new educational enterprises, doomed to failure from their inception. It would have been better if it had been spent in adequately strengthening existing institutions. As a result, there are many small, weak, struggling schools and but few strong ones. This confusion and lack of wise policy of early years has given way to greater prudence. Most of the large denominations now have education boards to which are committed the policies and the programs of the denomination in the educational field. There is now, also, an organization which undertakes the correlation of the policies of all the church boards.

Problems

Granted that Christian schools are still necessary, as most Christian leaders believe and the discussion further on seeks to show, they face yet other grave problems as to whether they can continue their existence. Many of them are finding it increasingly difficult to *meet the standards* which are set for them largely by the state universities and the accrediting agencies. But to fail to attain and maintain standard rating means eventual elimination from the field of higher education.

The effects of two world wars focused critical attention upon the colleges. A great many felt that there was something vastly wrong with education that the so-called enlightened nations of the world should be engaged in the most destructive wars of history. Sporadic complaints had been heard before of the influence of the colleges upon the faith and morals of students. It was held that *rationalism* was rampant in the colleges. Immediately many became alarmed. A veritable wave of popular suspicion directed against the colleges swept over the country. Peculiarly, the denominational colleges suffered more from this than state institutions. Little was found to justify criticism in most of the denominational colleges, but great damage was done them in the loss of the confidence and support of large numbers of their constituency.

Some Tendencies Noted

Competition with state institutions, criticism, and the demands of the church itself have produced some results with respect to these schools which are eminently worthwhile. There was a time when some of them sought salvation by imitating the state universities. This *secularizing* tendency among denominational colleges was quite strong not so very long ago. The influence of the Carnegie Foundation for the Advancement of Teaching helped in this direction.

There has been, more recently, a notable tendency in the *contrary* direction. This movement has been helped by such organizations as the Council of Church Boards of Education and other agencies within the denominations themselves. As a result the denominational colleges have been taking stock of themselves more closely. One effect of the secularizing tendency was to raise the jolting taunt — "Why have denominational schools been paralleling state institutions, if there is to be no difference between them?" This question, and others, forced the attention of the colleges in upon themselves. Had they a distinctive mission in the field of higher education? Can there be a Christian type of education which meets the highest academic standards and at the same time answers the deepest needs of the Christian movement? If this is possible, then what are the essential characteristics of this distinctly Christian type of education?

DIFFERENTIATION

What makes a school Christian? Some years ago this question was put by the editor of *Christian Education* to a number of prominent men, including the secretaries of the various church boards of education. Their replies were quite interesting. These men said that what makes a school Christian is not the mere fact that it was founded by Christian people for Christian purposes; nor the mere fact of its attachment or relation to an ecclesiastical organization; nor any label; nor the theological position of the faculty; nor the fact that the Bible is read and prayer offered at the opening of the session each day; nor even the fact that the faculty are professing Christians. Some, or even all, of these characteristics may be true of an institution, but they do not in themselves make it a Christian school. Then what are the traits of a Christian school? Gleaning from their replies, the following points are noted. The Christian schools have:

A Christian objective, aim, purpose
A Christian faculty and Christian teaching
A Christian viewpoint
A Christian spirit, atmosphere, life
A Christian program
A Christian product

It is evident that a college, if it really is to be called Christian, will have most of these characteristics.

A Christian Objective

Some, perhaps, will say at once that the denominational school has always had a Christian objective. Nevertheless, there are those who ask, "Is it any different in its real objectives from many other schools which make no such lofty pretensions?" It must not rely upon the purpose of its founders, nor upon its connections, nor upon its label to be counted Christian. For what goals is it striving? The answer to this question will determine whether it is really Christian or not. If it does not itself have a clear-cut Christian purpose, it has no right to claim to be a Christian school. It must so relate itself to the whole program of the Christian movement that it fulfills a distinctively Christian mission.

Christian Teachers and Christian Teaching

Another differentiation with respect to the Christian college is that it has Christian teachers and Christian teaching. Without a Christian faculty, it cannot be Christian. It cannot have a Christian atmosphere or spirit unless the lives of the teachers radiate it. A recent writer in *Christian Century* said: "The faculty should share a common concern for the religious growth of the students and of each other, while at the same time intellectual diversity should be expected."[1]

The Christian teacher is the crucial factor in the process of Christian education. There are other factors, to be sure, but the teacher is the prime factor. It is more important to have Christian teachers than Christian textbooks or Christian trustees. Students largely absorb the views and acquire the outlooks of their teachers. They unconsciously imitate them, especially if the teacher is a combination of splendid character and attractive personality. This is perfectly natural. It must have been partly in this way that Jesus incarnated himself in his disciples so that they became Christ-men. Even Paul, after long spiritual fellowship with the risen Lord, could say, "It is no longer I that live, but Christ liveth in me." There is no contagion like that of a great personality. Teachers and teaching must be Christian in the Christian school. This does not mean that theology is to be taught in every classroom nor does it mean that there is such a thing as Christian chemistry or physics. President John W. Raley

[1] Arlow W. Anderson, "Christian Educators Confer," *Christian Century*, 72: 806-7, 1955, p. 807.

defines the function of the teacher thus: "From Christian teachers the student learns that God moves in history, that He is the author of science, and the true inspiration of all great literature, art, and music. Only the Christian college voices these concerns and affirmations as an official policy."[2]

Christian Worship

Another differentiating characteristic of the Christian school is to be found in its chapel service. Vital Christian worship will be a part of the program of the Christian college. Investigations made in recent years reveal that, in some quarters at least, college chapel is not what it once was. In some institutions it has lost all religious significance and is nothing more than a student assembly. In other schools, where the religious form is still retained, it does not function as an important factor in college life. Some of the reasons given for this state of affairs are:

1. Students object to compulsory religion.
2. Chapel is not an expression of campus religion.
3. Chapel is too much like church.
4. Chapel talks are too often poorly prepared and, therefore, are of little interest or value.
5. The whole chapel is so much boredom.

It would probably not be difficult to find students in most colleges who object to chapel. The remedy lies not in giving up the worship period or in modifying or eliminating its distinctly religious character, but in making it more vital. If there are any points at which the Christian college differs from secular institutions, one of these ought to be its chapel.

The Christian school will use its chapel as a means of bearing *witness* to its claim and aspiration to be a Christian institution. In the services, it will be proclaiming its own faith and its own conception of what is highest and best. Furthermore, it will be seeking to impress its conceptions of the highest values upon its students in order that they may

[2] John W. Raley, *Beyond These Gates* (Shawnee: Oklahoma Baptist University Press, 1957), p. 4.

have a constant enrichment of their religious experience. The Christian college will use its chapel as a means of *worship*. The late Dr. Robert E. Speer said of the Christian school, "The institution will meet regularly for worship and prayer." As to the content of the service, there is considerable difference in various schools. In some, there is Bible reading, one or two songs, and prayer. The service lasts only fifteen or twenty minutes. No announcements are made, and no itinerant speakers are allowed. In other schools, in addition to the above, the president or some designated member of the faculty makes a short talk on some religious topic. Some colleges arrange a yearly schedule of addresses by outstanding speakers. These addresses may not necessarily be on distinctly religious subjects but on vital problems with Christian interpretations and applications. The idea is to present religion to the students as it comes to grips with the practical problems of life in order that they may thus learn to appreciate Christian values and see the Christian way more clearly.

The Christian college will also use its chapel as a means of promoting student *morale*. One of the reasons why chapel is retained in colleges where it has lost its religious significance is for promoting unity and morale. A religious program is better for this than a nonreligious one.

Christian Activity

In addition to the Christian objectives and atmosphere provided by the Christian college, there are a number of student religious activities that are very definitely Christian. One of these is the *Baptist Student Union*, a student organization, which seeks to correlate and foster all phases of Christian life on the campus and to enlist each student in normal church activities in the local church in the college community.

As integral parts of this general organization, the *unit organizations* are promoted for the different groups of religious workers. One is the ministerial group, made up of the prospective or actual ministers with stated meetings for mutual counsel and inspiration. Another is the volunteer band, composed of those who are volunteers for home or foreign missions. Often there is a special workers' group for those planning for religious education, sacred music, and other church work. Most Baptist colleges maintain a College Young Woman's Auxiliary and some a Baptist Brotherhood. Sometimes there is an organization for lay workers.

Along with these general and departmental organizations, there are several very definite *service activities*. One of these is the annual revival meeting which is a distinctive characteristic of the Christian college. In it most of the unconverted are won, indifferent ones rededicate their lives, and others surrender for Christian work. Along with this is the enlistment through the year of the students in the different phases of church work, such as Sunday school classes, young people's activities, mission study groups, and the like. Frequently a daily or weekly prayer meeting is carried on by the students. And extension work is done at jails, homes for the aged, and other needy places.

A Christian Product

The final test of the Christian college is the product it turns out. This is measured by the lives of its alumni; the genuineness of their Christianity; and their participation in the affairs of the Kingdom of God and the welfare of mankind. Each graduate should be ready and willing to find his place in the church of his choice and the community in which he lives. The churches which support the college have a right to expect the college to return to the churches better informed and better trained laymen and women as well as ministers and other vocational church workers.

SPECIFIC FUNCTIONS

The Christian college is essentially an instrument of the Christian movement. The chief business is to prepare young men and women to function effectively in this movement both in churches and in community life.

Training Christian Leaders

There is desperate need today in every field of human

activity for leaders whose outlook, ideals, and purposes are positively Christian. Leadership in every area of social, economic, and political life falls largely into the hands of college trained men and women. This tendency will doubtless increase as the general level of culture continues to rise. Therefore, if Christianity is to have a voice that will be heard, an influence that will be felt in community, state, national, and international affairs, it must get it by supplying to all these important areas of human activity leaders of outstanding ability whose lives are actively motivated by Christian ideals.

Herein lies the work of the Christian college — to equip and send out young men and women who will become great Christian home-makers, Christian teachers, Christian club-workers, Christian doctors and lawyers, Christian public officials, and Christian leaders in the political, commercial, industrial, and occupational spheres. In this way the Christian dynamic will interpenetrate and become effective throughout the entire social order. The college which helps to this end is sharing definitely with the church in the movement for the coming of Christ's Kingdom "on earth as it is in heaven."

Training in Church-related Vocations

There are increasing opportunities today for those who wish to take up some form of religious work, other than the ministry, as a *vocation*. There is need for specialists in religious education who are equipped to teach in college or to direct the educational work of the denomination or in the local church. Field workers, church secretaries, and musicians are needed. Leaders are needed for camp work and other semi-religious movements. Vocational opportunities of a religious character are increasing and offer splendid fields of service to college men and women.

There is need for a far larger number of well-equipped *avocational workers* in the local churches. There are many minor places for religious leadership in the churches. They are minor, though not in the sense of being unimportant. If they are filled with persons who lack needed training, the bad effects will show in the work of the entire church. The Sunday school boards or Boards of Christian Education of the various denominations have done a notable work in improving the quality of Sunday school personnel. Local churches also undertake to train some of their leaders. The denominational colleges are equipped to render the churches valuable service at this point by supplying them with trained leaders for all phases of their work.

Training Leaders in Christian Thought

In addition to filling the places mentioned, there is the necessity of having a group of Christian thinkers in every area of knowledge who will be recognized as specialists in their respective fields and be able to guide the thinking in their disciplines. In other words, there is the necessity of having leaders of thought who can leaven the educational lump, who can write textbooks in every field of knowledge from the Christian point of view. Unless that is true, the time will come when a secularized educational system will lead many away from the Christian view of life and civilization. There is no way of estimating the influence of Christian thinkers not only in the fields of Bible but also in psychology, sociology, the physical sciences, and elsewhere. This is perhaps the Christian college's most indispensable function.

Training Ministerial and Missionary Workers

Christian colleges were established originally for the primary purpose of training men for the ministry. In the colonial period, and for a long time thereafter, there was a shortage of ministers and especially of trained ministers. This was due to the fact that, with the rapid growth of population and its spread southward and westward, churches came into existence so rapidly that the demand for ministers far exceeded the supply, and many men came into the ministry with little or no education.

The Charleston Baptist Association, the General Baptist Association of Virginia, and some others before there were colleges in their sections, developed plans for assisting worthy young men of limited means to prepare themselves for the ministry. They were to study in the homes of older pastors, under their guidance, using their books, while supported by funds raised by these associations. But such plans were unsatisfactory; so attention was turned toward the founding of colleges to train the ministers that were needed so badly. In this way they had the example of New England. Harvard had been founded primarily to train ministers, as the founders said, "dreading to leave an illiterate ministry to the churches when our present ministers shall lie in the dust." Yale and most of the other early colleges were founded for the same purpose.

It is the distinctive function of the denominational college to help prepare young men for the kind of pastoral leadership which is required of them today. It shares this responsibility with the theological seminary and the graduate school. The college furnishes the broad cultural foundations, while the other-named institutions furnish the needed specialization. The colleges also offer pre-theological courses in Bible, religion, or Christianity, and religious education. The ministerial student will need some of these courses; but if the college is truly Christian, the cumulative effect of the entire liberal arts course will be such as to give him valuable religious training and experience as well as a good foundation for his seminary training. Working through the field of history, literature, philosophy, sociology, psychology, and the natural sciences with teachers of deep religious convictions, he will be getting Christian points of view and Christian interpretations and evaluations in all the broad areas of human experience. In this way, he will come to know more of what Christianity really means than if he had a few courses in religion without this broader Christian education. He needs both, as a matter of fact, for the most important phase of the whole educational process comes when the student seeks to synthesize or integrate all of his particular learnings so as to get a true idea of the whole.

OUTLOOK AND NEEDS

What of the future of the denominational college? Is the denominational school passing? Will it be ground to pieces, as one writer puts it, between the "upper and nether mill-stones" of public high school and junior colleges on the one hand, and the state universities on the other? The denominational academy passed, practically, from the field of secondary education because of the development of the public high school. Will not the church college go the same way?

Outlook

There are prophets who are and have been for some time predicting the demise of the church college. About fifty years ago, one of the most outstanding educators in this country predicted that in twenty-five years, 75 per cent of the small colleges either would have ceased to exist or would be transformed into other types of institutions. Since most of the small colleges were denominational institutions, it was a dire prophecy for them. At that time 75 per cent of the institutions reporting to the United States Bureau of Education from the South had less than one hundred and fifty students. Of course, that prophecy missed the mark! There are a third more colleges today than there were in 1900, ten times as many college students, and perhaps ten dollars in college endowment now to one in 1900, and vastly more property and other material resources. True, some colleges have ceased to exist, but so have some churches, and some towns, and some railroads, and some banks and business houses. Many denominational colleges have, in the past century, passed out of existence because they were unwisely founded. Some are merging with others and thus losing their separate existence. But all of this does not signify the passing of denominational colleges.

Values in Denominational Colleges

The values of the church-related colleges to the individual, to society, and to Christianity are so great that these institutions should be strengthened and maintained at any cost. Some of the reasons for their support are here summarized:

1. Forty-five per cent of the college students of America are enrolled in denominational or privately controlled institutions. The states would have great difficulty in providing higher education for all if the church-related colleges fail.

2. The church must maintain these schools if it is to survive, since its future leadership must come from such schools. It is estimated that more than eight out of ten preachers and other vocational religious workers are trained by them at the college level.

3. The church school can teach the Bible and the Christian religion as no other tax-supported college or university is legally permitted to do.

4. The church-related college can accomplish more than any other type of college in the development of Christian personality.

5. The church-related college can give a Christian interpretation of truth in all disciplines in such a way to help keep civilization Christian.

6. The church-related college safeguards the character and faith of youth who come from Christian homes by placing a primary emphasis upon a spiritual philosophy of life in contrast to the materialistic philosophy which is often the emphasis in other schools.

7. The church-related college is primarily a college of liberal arts, and it is to these institutions that the preservation of the priceless heritage of Christian culture has been entrusted. They are the protectors and preservers of that culture in a special way.

It is on the basis of these reasons, and others, that the Christian college must not be allowed to go out of the pattern of the present social order. John Gross most aptly states it: "Because the future of civilization so greatly depends on a spiritual outlook in higher education the church seeks the assurance that its institutions will dedicate themselves to the work of making Christ regnant in all the activities of man and society."[3]

Present Needs

One thing is certain. If these colleges are to survive, they must be cared for now. What are their needs? Upon what factors does their survival depend?

1. Adequate *support*, financial and otherwise. Colleges cannot run without money; and few, if any, of these colleges have enough money to meet their bare necessities. Many of them are in a critical condition financially. They must have more adequate support if they are to survive.
2. A Christian educational *conscience* on the part of the church people.
3. Wise educational *policies* on the part of denominations and their education boards.
4. *Cooperation* among all the friends of Christian education.
5. *Loyalty* to Christ on the part of the denominational colleges themselves.

This last point should be emphasized. Certainly the future of the denominational colleges depends upon it. If they become secularized, they are doomed. State institutions will supplant them. They must be true to their Christian mission if they would survive. "Upon this rock I will build my church, and the gates of Hades shall not prevail against it," Jesus said (Matt. 16:18). That rock was confession of faith and loyalty to Christ. The nation is built upon the belief that the best kind of government is a government "of the people, by the people, and for the people." Destroy that faith, and our government will perish as a democracy. So the church-related college, as also the church, rests upon a faith. In that lies its security. Destroy that faith, and it will perish. The large independent institutions will probably live.

It was stated by an authority some years ago that no col-

[3] John Gross, "Protestant Higher Education," *The Christian Century*, 73: 453-55, 1956, p. 455.

lege with a million dollars' endowment had ever died. But conditions are quite different today. With the increasing financial demands which are falling upon the colleges, even those with much more than a million dollars' endowment will probably find it hard to continue to function in the future in the face of advancing educational standards unless it has great resources in the shape of popular support. The greatest of all loyalties is Christian loyalty. It will outlast every other loyalty. Therefore, in loyalty to Christ lies the hope of the future of the church-related college. Since this is true, every Christian college should put at the heart of all of its activities the splendid motto of MacMaster University, " In Him all things consist."

QUESTIONS FOR DISCUSSION

1. What were the aims or purposes in the founding and development of denominational colleges in the United States?

2. What requirements are necessary for a college to qualify as a Christian college?

3. Define the specific functions of a Christian college.

4. Define the present trends and prospects for the future of the denominational college.

CHAPTER 23

RELIGIOUS LITERATURE

Influence

The power of the printed page over the minds and actions of people was never greater than today. Books, papers, and magazines by the millions are being published every year; and these various publications are shaping the thoughts and actions of individuals and nations. A large percentage of these books and papers are not of the highest type; in fact, many of them do more harm than good. Everything possible should be done to stop the circulation of the cheap and harmful types of books and papers. The baneful effect of such literature on children and youth is seen on every hand.

At the same time the reading and study of the very best literature to be found in the land should be promoted. This applies especially to the importance of getting the best religious literature in the hands of the people. "So great is the power of the printed word," declares Luther Wesley Smith, "that often it is our despair. Yet it ought also to be our constant challenge. God has placed in the hands of the writer and editor an instrument of amazing potency."[1]

[1] Luther Wesley Smith, in Benjamin P. Browne (ed.), *Christian Journalism for Today* (Philadelphia: The Judson Press, 1952), p. 28.

Function

The printed page has become one of the primary means for the communication of religious knowledge, and for the promotion of religion in almost every direction. Religious publications have become one of the most important phases of religious education. This has not been true always. In the early Christian centuries, the church's chief medium of communication, both within its own circle and between itself and the world, was the spoken word. There was writing, of course — a great deal of it. But the oral word was the principal means of instruction, exhortation, and the propagation of the faith. Only a few people read; the multitudes heard public discourse. Even the Scriptures were learned in the main through hearing them read and discussed orally. Hence the importance of preaching and the public services of the church. Winifred Ernest Garrison says,

> The practice of spoken discourse for the promotion of religion has neither ceased nor diminished. But with the introduction of printing, with the increase of literacy and of the habit of reading as well as the ability to read, and with the rise of journalism to the place of primacy as the means of disseminating intelligence upon all kinds of subjects, the press has brought powerful reinforcement to the pulpit as an agency for the communication of religious knowledge.[2]

RELIGIOUS PUBLICATIONS

Religious publications are a mighty factor in the cause of religious or Christian education in particular. The press supplies most of the curriculum materials and a large percentage of all that is involved in study and teaching. No statistics are available to indicate just where in the billions the output of printed pages will stop. From gigantic presses of great publishing houses which operate day and night to the small machines of local shops there flow the constant "black and white" streams of Christian truth.

Kinds

There are three kinds of publications, namely, denomina-

[2] W. C. Bower (ed.), *The Church at Work in the Modern World* (Chicago: The University of Chicago Press, 1935), pp. 236-37.

tional, interdenominational, and nondenominational. These are largely supplemented by general commercial publishers whose fractional religious output is very considerable. Not all so-called religious publications are educational in the best sense, nor is it true that general educational publications are irreligious. The term "religious press" is used in a technical sense. In this chapter it includes publications in any form which set forward the religious education enterprise.

Products

Rather loosely the products of the religious press may be classified as follows: church school or Sunday school periodicals, books, publications for young people's societies and related groups, denominational weekly journals, general religious journals and magazines, professional ministerial magazines, professional religious education journals, missionary and service magazines, publications of Christian colleges, seminaries, and training schools, religious bulletins, pamphlets, tracts. In addition, much space in daily and weekly newspapers is given over to religious matters. In the above classification there is some overlapping. This would be true of any grouping of the products of the religious press.

Measured by the total number of pages, the Sunday school periodicals issued by the several denominational and other publishing houses far outdistance the entire output of all other kinds of religious publications. The total page-output in one single year for any one of half a dozen large denominations would run into the billions. The entire production of Sunday school periodicals is enormous. The vastness of the contribution may be partially realized when it is known that one single periodical may have a million readers a week. There would be no particular advantage in comparing religious and educational values in the several types of publications. Each apparently fills a need. Each makes its own valuable impact upon the religious thinking of its constituency. Each seeks to be true to the spirit and teachings of Christ.

Nine hundred and ninety-nine out of a thousand Christians have very little to do with the actual making of these press-products, certainly with their educational content. However, even if ten out of every thousand church members, able and aggressive, set themselves resolutely to make use of the printed pages of religious education publications, the teaching ministry of the church would make triumphant the Kingdom of Christ in a single generation.

RELIGIOUS JOURNALISM

Brief History

Journalism has had a remarkable development in America since the Revolutionary War. Perhaps the first newspaper in the American colonies was the *Boston News-Letter*, founded in 1704. But it is estimated that there were about two hundred newspapers in the United States by 1800 and one thousand by 1830. Religious liberty and freedom of the press have been two cardinal principles in this country; and consequently, there is a multiplicity of denominations, and these denominations almost from the beginning have made use of journalism for the promotion of their various doctrines and programs. It is said that perhaps the first religious journal in America was started after 1800. These papers were promoted as a part of early missionary work for the dissemination of religious knowledge and for the promotion of various sects and movements. The influence of these various papers has been immeasurable during the last century and a half.

Present Situation

It is said that it is more difficult to maintain denominational papers today than in former years; but still there are many of these religious papers, and they have immense influence in spreading Christian truth and promoting various denominational programs. There has been a tendency toward consolidation of many papers in the direction of the non-denominational paper like *The Christian Century*. However, there are still many denominational papers, especially in the

South. Southern Baptists, for instance, maintain a denominational weekly paper in twenty-five states with a total circulation of 1,290,000. Most of these papers are prospering and are making vigorous contribution toward the promotion of the various causes of the denomination.

Needed Improvements

Some years ago a special committee was appointed by the Southern Baptist Convention to make a study of the various state papers and make recommendations for improvements. Among the suggestions made were that the papers give more space to laymen and their work, that the papers have a more attractive make-up, and that the material in them be of such a nature as to appeal to the whole family circle. Articles should be briefer, of more vital human interest, and with more light and inspiration for the average member of the family circle. The editors should follow newspaper and magazine technique in making up the papers, and the papers should be put in the local church budgets and sent to the homes of the people. "To double the subscriptions to all our papers would mean to double all our work."

It is interesting to note that since that report was made many improvements have been made in religious papers and magazines of all kinds. In fact, the religious press, although it does not have the financial resources to do as much as it would like, has kept up to some extent with the improvements made in secular papers and magazines. More pictures are being used, more human-interest stories and features are being published, and the general make-up of the paper, as a rule, is much more attractive than in former years.

RELIGIOUS NEWS AND THE PRESS

Most large daily papers have "religious news editors." The amount of religious news which they publish, in the aggregate, is very large; and considering their immense circulation, the value of the publicity which they give to religious ideas and enterprises is inestimable. The church should appreciate the services rendered and learn how to cooperate

with the newspapers for mutual advantages of all concerned.
"Our successful use of the press," advises Paul C. Carter, "will
depend somewhat upon our understanding of news-writing
techniques. News writing requires procedures and a style
quite different from essay, sermon, or magazine writing."[3]
He also gives excellent suggestions for the writer of church
news to follow. The larger denominations maintain a press
service to help furnish legitimate news to the papers. Readers should be taught to discriminate between sensational
rubbish and important religious news and movements. Interesting and important religious news should be given to
the newspapers in attractive form, prepared in accordance
with the regular style of the paper, so that it will require
little editing or rewriting; and the church should avoid mere
propaganda under the guise of news. Usually newspapermen
will gladly cooperate with sincere people who are honestly
trying to do the right thing.

PROMOTIONAL MATERIALS

Church Papers

It is well at this point to make special mention of the
matter of church papers, for in recent years there has been
a trend toward using local church papers and bulletins for
promoting educational activities. Apparently this development is on the increase and will so continue, with encouraging improvements in these papers and bulletins. There are
at least two kinds being used. One is the church bulletin,
consisting usually of four pages, giving the order of services
on Sunday, news and announcements about organizations of
the church and activities of the week, and giving a bit of
local church news. It is usually distributed each Sunday at
the worship service. The other type is more of a parish paper,
perhaps giving the order of services on Sunday but giving
much more news of the church and congregation and carrying a few short items about the work of the denomination.
It is usually mailed to each family of the church.

[3] Browne, *Christian Journalism for Today*, pp. 162-63.

There are *three ways of fostering them.* One is for the church to publish them or have it done. Sometimes the mimeograph or multigraph is used for this purpose. Many churches buy from the denominational or commercial bulletin service forms already partly printed and finish them. Another plan is to buy space in a nondenominational church paper such as the *All Church Press.* The space varies from one-fourth to a full page, newspaper size, according to contract. The third is for the state denominational paper to furnish an extra cover page devoted to the local church and usually have the subscriptions provided through the church budget. These local papers have tremendous educational value. More significant however, are the state, national, or sectional papers which can go much further not only in creating religious ideals but also in interpreting current events from a moral standpoint.

Religious Tracts

Various religious tracts are published by denominational boards, by Christian schools and organizations, and by independent religious groups. These tracts deal with denominational programs and work; with doctrines and beliefs; with the message and methods of evangelism; and so forth. Religious tracts have been widely used for the purposes of religious propaganda of almost all kinds. Pastors, directors of religious education, and Christian workers generally should keep informed as to how and where good tracts can be secured and should study how to make the best use of them. They should not be distributed wholesale. This would tend to cheapen the matter and would result in great waste. Giving out tracts to individuals, with an oral or written suggestion as to use, will be found most effective, and this after careful and prayerful study of the real needs of the individual. Some individual in the church might be elected to supervise the use of tracts in the work of the church. Working with him would be those workers responsible for the distribution of the curriculum material in the various organizations and departments.

ADVERTISING THE CHURCH

Between the religious groups that do not have so much as a "name board" on their church buildings and those who sensationally keep themselves before the public eye, are the church people who make known their church, its minister, the regular and special activities of the church and the whole round of religious education by legitimate, common-sense methods of publicity.

The Problem

Do church leaders really believe that Christian truth should permeate all life, reaching down and out into every area of human experience? If so, should it not be made a part of the educational task of the church to make this truth known to the world in all possible desirable ways? Should the church organize through a director of publicity to make known the business of the church as the Divine enterprise? If so, what kind of person should this director be? What should be his duties and how can he best function in honoring the church and setting forward the Kingdom of Christ?

The Director

The ideal director of public relations for a church may not be found, but certainly some of the qualifications mentioned below are essential if he is to make good. He should be one who knows and loves the truth, who recognizes his duty and privilege to propagate that truth, and one who is continually on the alert for new truth which should be made known. He should be loyal to his church. He should be punctual, scrupulous in keeping promises, discriminating, cautious, tactful, correct in speech, devoted in spirit, courteous in manner, a good mixer, poised, genial, original, sane, unselfish in his motives, sincere, impartial, dependable, reverent, one whose character is unimpeachable, who puts his work to one final test — will this piece of publicity honor Christ?

Duties

The following will probably suggest some of the duties

of the director of public relations in an average church or community.

It is well for him to have a desk in the church, making it convenient for him to gather material which should be given publicity. He should put himself in a position to give such publicity as will further the plans of the pastor, recognizing the pastor as the head of the church in all such matters. He should keep in touch with the director of religious education and all other officers and leaders in the church and give to them his full cooperation.

He should be familiar with publications of the Sunday school and all of his own denominational boards, basing all publicity on ascertained facts, he should know his own denominational journals and continually boost the same; he should also know the interdenominational periodicals and be able to publicize them intelligently.

During religious education week, usually observed toward the end of September, in cooperation with other leaders in the community, he may give special publicity, in the local papers and by other means. In largely Protestant communities it will be well for him to seek opportunity to make brief, pointed announcements concerning the work in clubs and other such gatherings. He is the logical person through whom community matters in religious education should be introduced to his church and he will be on the alert to contact all persons and institutions in his community where religious education news may be found. He should contact local parent-teacher associations with religious education materials having special value in character education in the school and home.

He will seek to assist the pastor and director of reading in posting lists of new books and other available material of value. He will be on the lookout for ways and means of making his publicity fruitful, suggesting mechanical devices such as duplicating and mailing machines, etc., for office use in the church. He will perhaps lead in having on the outside of the church building attractive, substantial service boards, and supplying them with items for day and night presentation. He will enlist the aid of the young people in the preparation of posters, and try to stimulate their interest in such work through contests and so forth.

He should prepare concise, timely items for the church weekly calendar or bulletin; he should prepare for the local newspapers occasional human-interest stories, and reports of local, state, or national conventions — especially when "home town" people participate. He may also maintain regular advertising space in the local newspapers.

CHURCH LIBRARY

Statistics compiled annually by the *Publishers' Weekly*, showing the number of books in each general field published during the preceding year, reveal a surprising number of titles classified under religion. As would be expected, fiction is always the most numerous class, but religion generally comes either second or third. The number of books actually read would perhaps not show as large a rating as the above figures might suggest; nevertheless, religious books are published and read in great numbers. Besides, many books not listed as religious actually carry a helpful religious emphasis or message.

Nearly all the leading publishers have religious book departments, and denominational publishing houses send out an immense volume of religious books. Every church should have a library and a good librarian to supervise and promote the distribution of books. Also there is an important place for guiding the people in the finding and selecting of good books for purchase for the home and in borrowing from public libraries. There is no greater service which can be rendered to our people, especially to our young people, than to help get into their hands good books on all kinds of subjects.

The old-fashioned Sunday school library of "goody-goody" books for dear little boys and girls has almost gone — as it should. Many churches now have libraries containing the most up-to-date books of the best literary quality, as well as books dealing with all phases of religious living and service, both of a practical and inspirational nature. The books should be of the highest literary standard, of compelling human interest, and deal with the various interests and needs involved in moral and spiritual living. This calls for a wide variety in the selection of the books.

LIBRARY NEEDS TODAY

Leadership Training

Books for the training of Sunday school officers and teachers, church officers, leaders in young people's societies, in men's and women's church organizations — this is the kind of library which any church should have, even if it must start with only a few books. Ordinarily these books will not be found in a public library. A community board of religious education secured the use of an alcove in the local public library and put in it a most excellent collection of about a hundred of the best books for Sunday school leaders. Lists were prepared carefully and divided among the churches. The books were made available to all officers and teachers of all the churches in the little city of about fifteen thousand population. In such a library would be books on psychology, principles and methods in teaching religion, evangelism, music, worship, missions, recreation and social service, content courses in Bible study and doctrines, and all aspects of the modern program of religious education. Every good church library should have such a collection.

Parent Training

Any church might well establish a small but very valuable library of books for the training of younger parents. Fortunately, very helpful books in this field are now available. One church has about a dozen of the best of these neatly boxed and circulates this library for a month at a time in the homes of young married folks in the church. These may cover many phases of child life and training but particularly those which relate to morals and religion. There is a tremendous need here if the home is to be the ally of the church.

Personal Culture

In addition to the books useful in leadership and parent training, there are many that are valuable in enriching the lives of the members of the church personally. Among these are the ones that deal with personal soul-winning, the devotional life, missionary lands and achievements, church history and doctrines, and present-day social and moral problems. Religious fiction also has a certain place.

General Reading

There are rural communities and even sections of cities not readily accessible to a public library, where good wholesome literature of a general nature may be valuable. Some churches have found it helpful to have on hand some of the best books used as parallel reading in the public schools. These are not only character-building themselves, but also the securing of them may lead the pupils to take an interest in other books in the church library more distinctively religious in nature.

THE LIBRARY DIRECTOR

No group in any church has the right to use church money to purchase books and then put them under lock and key where nobody gets the potential benefits from them. It is one thing to get a church library; quite another to keep it working. All of which points to the church director of reading. In selecting such an officer for the church or church school, the religious education needs of children and young people must be kept in mind although there are many adults who would appreciate kindly, sensible guidance. Especially is this true of parents who are concerned about the best reading for their children.

Qualifications

The director may be a man but frequently is a woman. Manifestly there are qualifications for this office, distinctive and highly desirable in view of the far-reaching significance of it. In no one person can be found all of the things mentioned below. Wise choosers, however, will look for as many of these traits as possible.

1. The director should be one of genuine Christian character, whose personality radiates the spirit of Christ, for, after all, the life back of the book suggestions means much. His judgment should be such as to command confidence when he suggests a book for reading. Most of all, he should be one who is blessed with common sense and the ability to approach all ages tactfully and with an understanding of their likes and dislikes. A patronizing type of character is not the kind to guide people inspirationally in their reading.

2. He should also be a person of broad culture, not only knowing the best of American and English classics but also being able to choose and recommend the best in contemporary books and magazines. Often a former public school teacher will possess this trait. He should know the value of the printed page in the matter of character-building, believing with Browning in "the companionship of good books" and the danger of bad ones. He should know people, both as to the psychology of the age-group, the interests of the individuals of the group, and their nature and needs as related to their reading, being able to suggest the books and other reading material best suited to any particular age and need and tell them where to find it, whether in the church library, the public library, or the book store. It is quite necessary for him to be acquainted with the program of reading in the public schools and know how to accommodate the reading activities of the church library to the development of similar programs in the schools, especially the extra-curricular activities. He should also be familiar with the Boy Scouts, Girl Scouts, Camp Fire Girls, and other youth organizations. He should have both the time and the disposition to keep in touch with the newer books and magazines and introduce the pupils to these.

3. The director in this work should make it his business to keep informed as to the best of the current books and magazines. This will take time, to be sure, but its rewards are more than equal to the effort expended, for his influence

may be next to that of the minister himself. He must make it his business to study to serve all ages and make this his main or sole church duty. He must be willing to begin most often as a pioneer in his field and must persistently work against odds. He must not allow himself to specialize on any one phase at the expense of a well-rounded, comprehensive program of reading. He must be one of vision, seeing the end from the beginning and counting no effort too dear to attain the end desired. He must have more than a self-starter. Rather he must have the spirit of the pioneer who keeps at it week by week. He must ride no hobby horse and be no partisan propagandist. Rather he must see the main task of the church school and of reading and strive faithfully to fulfill his mission.

Counselors

Whenever the church or church school is a large one, the director of reading will have assistants. There may be three such counselors: one who specializes in children's reading, one who gives special attention to selecting books and periodicals for young people, and a third who keeps in mind the reading interests and needs of adults. These counselors should be able to give guidance to readers in each age group.

All library workers will find the following suggestive and helpful. The books should be classified in a card index or loose-leaf notebook. Lists of the best available books should be on bulletin boards in convenient places for the different ages, urging that such books be used. Displays may be arranged. They should be continually on the lookout for new books, scanning current book reviews, stationers' shelves, and periodical publications sent out on request by publishers. Regular reading of such publications as the *Bulletin of the American Library Association*, the *Publishers' Weekly*, and the annual catalogue of the denominational publishing house will be most helpful in the search for new books and old. Suggestions for improvement for the church reading program should be made. Lists of books given in WMU *World in Books* should be followed. The Library Service of the denominational publishing house may be consulted for practical suggestions.[4]

The church librarian should seek the viewpoint of the public school teachers, the public librarian, and the leaders of parent-teacher organizations concerning the needs of the children and the books best suited to the different ages. Occasional visits to the woman's missionary group, brotherhood organizations, and young people's societies, will enable the librarian to know and fill the needs of their various activities. Parents need help in the selection of gift books. The needs of hospitals and other public institutions in this field afford opportunity for extension service. He may assist in helping public librarians to put on their shelves books of religious value. A helpful library of training books for officers and teachers in the church school is an essential service. Effort should be made to enlist the church members in the reading of the state and national religious publications or certain articles therein.

The church library is truly a service agency. The formation of small circulating libraries for the aged, invalids, or other shut-ins, should be planned. A library especially suited to the needs of the ever increasing numbers of active adults who are entering retirement is a challenge to the alert church library staff. Occasional short, pointed announcements concerning the church reading program should be presented in the regular church services and in the meetings of various age groups.

A wise librarian may keep in touch with the local newsstands and know the books and magazines that are being purchased and read by the children and others and, where

[4] Church Library Service, Baptist Sunday School Board, Nashville, can render invaluable service to any church librarian or director of religious literature. Publishes a monthly *Church Library Bulletin* which may be obtained without cost by any church librarian upon request.

necessary, clear these newsstands of undesirable literature and seek the cooperation of leaders in similar work in other churches.

GETTING PEOPLE TO READ

One of the biggest practical problems that faces all leaders in the field of religious education is not the making of more religious books and journals but bringing these into vital, everyday, character-making relationship with Christian and non-Christian individuals and groups in every community. It is important to secure able, acceptable writers. It is necessary to put the thoughts of these writers on attractive printed pages, bound in attractive book or magazine form. But all of this falls short unless the people are contacted; unless those press-products are put in the hands and heads of available readers.

Advertising and Promotion

Practically all religious publishers employ some or all of the following ways of contacting the public with their books and other forms of literature: sales and promotion stores or repositories, sometimes scattered throughout the nation and even with foreign distribution centers; salesmen; advertising through the publishers' own channels or through the purchased space in magazines and periodicals; the preparation and distribution of attractive folders sent out through regular or special mailing outlets; the usual catalog listing and statements; free copies of books or journals to be used for the book-review columns of certain magazines; gratis copies put into the hands of leaders in the religious world who may in turn speak or write a favorable word; and special displays or exhibits at conventions through posters, book flaps, or actual copies. Here are offered only a few hints, for advertising has become a real art, recognized and professionally rated with ample remuneration for industry and cleverness.

Religious Magazine Representative

In every church no matter how large or how small, there

should be an alert man or woman appointed by the church as its official promoter of denominational journals, missionary magazines, and other literature. The same person might also introduce general religious journals. His chief responsibility, however, should be the securing of subscriptions to the regularly endorsed and much needed denominational weeklies and monthlies. Samples will be kept on hand to be seen in the church vestibule or other convenient places. In many churches a table is provided and the representative is there at stated times not only with journals and subscription blanks but also with books, especially of the devotional type. At a leadership training school or institute, a school of missions, or during a special evangelistic campaign, such a helper proves very valuable in setting forward that particular Christian enterprise by making readily accessible the best in books, pamphlets, and journals. Publishers and supply houses generally are delighted to cooperate, furnishing samples or periodicals, price lists, subscription blanks, and other needed information. One such person is all any church needs. Let that person, carefully chosen, be the only religious press representative of the church. Quietly by word or bulletin board notice, such a servant will be welcomed and fully rewarded.

Leading People To Use Curriculum Material

An immense volume of religious literature is distributed to our people monthly and quarterly for use in the various organizations and programs of the church. Much of this material is largely wasted because it is used in a very limited way, or not at all. It is the duty and the privilege of every teacher, worker, and leader to do his best to get his people to make proper use of this material. Every educational agency in the church is vitally interested in this matter.

Constant Emphasis

Pastors, directors of religious education, officers, teachers, and leaders in all phases of church work will find occasion constantly to emphasize good religious literature and the best possible use of it. The library staff will give special attention to the reading of good books. This is a reading age. People will be reading something, but what shall it be? John Ruskin used to say very earnestly to the young people in his day, in trying to get them to read good literature rather than trash, "Don't you know that if you read this you cannot read that?" Our time is limited. We should not waste it in reading worthless or harmful literature but use it well in reading and studying the best that has been thought and written by the great writers of the world.

QUESTIONS FOR DISCUSSION

1. What are some of the strong and also some of the weak points in the average weekly religious paper?

2. Give an outline of some of the major improvements made during the past ten or fifteen years in state Baptist papers of the Southern Baptist Convention. What further improvements could be made?

3. Discuss some of the main ways in which the average church could get more and better publicity in both daily and religious papers.

4. What are some of the best suggestions for building a good church library? Write your denominational publishing house or book store for lists and catalogues.

5. Suggest ways by which to get the average church member not only to read but also to study some of the better books on Christian doctrine, Christian history, and Christian principles and work.

CHAPTER 24

UNIFICATION AND PROMOTION

In a church which maintains all the organizations required for the promotion of a complete program of religious education, there is overlapping of organization and duplication of effort, with much lost motion. So much energy is used in maintaining the efficiency of the various organizations and meeting the requirements of the various standards that frequently the development of individual character is neglected. It sometimes appears that the people are in the church for the purpose of making standard organizations rather than for the purpose of making better individual Christians.

PRESENT SYSTEM OF ORGANIZATION

Multiplicity and Overlapping

There is much duplication in the church. In the majority of churches, at least three organizations are competing with each other for the time, interest, activity, and sometimes the money of the same group of church members. They are the Sunday school, the Training Union, and the Woman's Missionary Union. Many churches also promote a recreational organization for the boys and girls, such as the Boy Scouts and Camp Fire Girls. The vacation Bible School has made a big place for itself in the church's program. In an increasing number of communities, various schemes are to be found for enlisting the boys and girls of the public school in some form of week-day religious education.

In addition to these agencies which have a place in the regular program of the church, there are other educational agencies with paid promotional secretaries whose aim is to give moral training to the youth of America *independent of the church*. The Young Men's Christian Association and the Young Women's Christian Association, with their Christian citizenship training program, and the Hi-Y clubs and the Girl Reserves also make their bid for the time and energy of our young people. In rural communities the Four-H clubs are enlisting many young people. Fraternal bodies also promote organizations which train the sons and daughters of lodge members. These, together with various propaganda organizations such as Junior Woman's Christian Temperance Union, the Allied Youth Movement, Anti-cigarette League and societies for the promotion of world peace make inroads on the time and interest of the church's young people with the stated purpose of character development and moral training.

Functional Origin

Each of these organizations originated and has been promoted, not as an integral part of the church's program, but by movements from without the church. Each has created its own program for its own purpose and has insisted on the cooperation of the churches if they have not demanded a place within church programs. The particular educational function of each is necessary in the development of well-balanced Christian character. Since the churches were not giving sufficient emphasis to each function in their programs, it became necessary for some outside agency to promote a program which would accomplish the purpose.

When *Sunday schools* were first advocated more than a century and a half ago for the purpose of teaching children the Bible, they were often vigorously opposed by the churches, and sometimes even denied the use of buildings. One hundred years later, leaders of young people, realizing that the Sunday schools were not emphasizing the principle of learning by activity, organized *young people's societies* to provide for this function. The general *missionary organizations*, believing that the hope of the future lay in the missionary education of children and youth of the present generation, also constructed a program of missionary education. And so it goes on. Whenever a new function of religious education has been determined, a new organization has been erected.

Each of these organizations has done and is doing great good, and it is not for a moment advocated that there be removed from the educational program of the church any of the functions for which each was originally organized. The church is deeply indebted to the leaders who so faithfully have promoted them.

SOME DEFECTS IN THE SYSTEM

There are some defects in the present church program of religious education. If the aim of the church is to develop mere machines — people who rely upon organization and mechanical efficiency as the expression of Christian life and character — then our present system cannot be surpassed. For whether it intends to do so or not, it places the emphasis on organization. It must do this in order to promote all the organizations which it fosters. There must be provided a set of administrative officers for each and these must be trained for their duties according to the "manual" of each organization, so the church can report to the various state headquarters that all its organizations have "reached the standard."

Overlapping of Function

Is not the true aim of religious education the development of Christian character in the individual? In order to reach this objective, it is necessary that the program consist of the elements of instruction, worship, expression, and social activity. At present, each organization — the Sunday school, the Training Union, Woman's Missionary Union, the Baptist Brotherhood — includes all of these elements in its program in varying degrees.

The *Vacation Bible School* and the *week-day church school* would add other courses of study and other organizations. In these, the emphasis is upon instruction, but the elements of worship and expressional activity are also included. In each of these, the elements of instruction, expression, and worship are all so crowded that none is given sufficient emphasis.

Duplication in Curriculum

Although each has a distinct course of study, there is much overlapping in subject matter. Two of them provide special mission lessons which are not related to either of the other two. Each has its own special study courses, and each its own social life. It is practically a physical impossibility to do all the study required for each if the pupils should be so inclined; but when they see so much overlapping in subject matter they either neglect all but one or else divide their study over so much material that they get only a smattering of it.

Overlapping of Administrative Duties

As undesirable as is overlapping of subject matter, the present program would not be so objectionable if it stopped with that. But each has a distinct plan or organization and administration. Each must have its own president and full quota of officers and committees who are responsible for the promotion of all the elements of religious education in each of their respective organizations.

This administrative work usually falls upon a few choice workers, remarkable for their patience and endurance; so that in the Sunday school one person will be responsible for one form of activity, in the young people's society for another; and the same person will be doing still a third kind of work in the missionary organization. Instead of being concentrated upon one thing at a time, which would be more efficient, his best energy and thought are scattered over so many varied activities that he cannot become efficient in any one of them. This overlapping in organization is one of the most serious defects in our present system. It discourages many of the finest young people who really are anxious to serve in the best way they can.

Not Church-centered

But probably the most serious defect is that the agencies are not centralized in the local church. They might be so organized theoretically, but in reality they are not centered in the church. Instead of feeling responsible to the local church for its work, each organization looks to the office of its state secretary for orders. The church is to blame in that it has been willing to let the various state headquarters direct its programs. As a result loyalty is divided. Instead of being loyal to the whole church, the member usually manifests his loyalty to the particular organization in which he is most interested. Sometimes the state secretary of his organization speaks to him with more authority than does his own church! Happily, this is not always the case, but it might be avoided in a unified program centered in the local church.

Such conditions of overlapping as exist in the present plan of organization in our churches call for a serious effort to find a remedy. Most denominations are facing such problems. Some have worked out a plan of correlation, and experiments are being made by the merging of promotional agencies in general denominational life. Such a plan was adopted first by the General Convention of the Christian Church in November, 1922. Also the interdenominational forces have done much toward unifying the programs through the Division of Christian Education of The National Council of the Churches of Christ in America.[1]

[1] Additional help concerning unification, may be obtained from the Division of Christian Education, National Council of the Churches of Christ in America, in New York.

COORDINATION

Needs

Realizing the need for coordination, the Southern Baptist Convention in 1937 appointed a committee of Coordination and Correlation of church agencies and activities. Through the years some much needed studies and recommendations have been made. Progress is being made slowly. The first step was to combine the various study courses into one correlated course for training all workers in the local church. Another result was the designation of the daily Bible readings of the Sunday school for family worship; the daily Bible readings of the Baptist Training Union are planned for individual devotions. The most recent step in coordination was made in October, 1957, when the new correlated nursery curriculum made its appearance. In cooperation with the Training Union Department and the Sunday School Department, the Sunday School Board projected the new helps for church nursery workers and parents of nursery children. They consist of a forty-eight page quarterly for parents which is called *Living With Children* and a sixty-four page quarterly for the church workers with children below four years of age, called *Church Nursery Guide*. The *Guide* is for use on Sunday morning, Sunday night, and any other time the church nursery is open. This new correlated material takes the place of all nursery curriculum materials. It is hoped that this effort at correlation will be continued until eventually a completely unified course is prepared for each age group of the church.

Among the recommendations made to the Convention were the following: (1) "We recommend to pastors and churches, the formation of a church council, representing the several agencies of the church, to meet as often as may be found necessary, in order to formulate an integrated and comprehensive church program to devise a calendar of activities; to coordinate the work of all the church agencies; and to discover and develop the needed workers and leaders. (2) That the Boards and Auxiliaries of the Convention work together, with the local churches, to the ends of better co-ordination and correlation."

A recent folder on coordination, prepared by the Inter-Agency Council of the Southern Baptist Convention states:

The problem of how to correlate the emphases, activities, and organizations of the church into a unified church program has long been a challenge to patrons and church leaders alike. The accomplishments of churches with councils clearly show that Church Councils provide the most practical solution for the local church.

The average Church Council is composed of key persons representing the church organizations. It is a team as flexible in its procedure and scope of activities as the needs of the individual church dictate. The council may be composed of the pastor, educational director, chairman of the deacons, Sunday school superintendent, Training Union director, WMU president, minister of music or choir director, and Brotherhood president. This council may also include other church officers and chairmen of church committees. Meeting at regularly appointed times, the council co-ordinates the work and keeps the calendar of activities before the church. Thus a team spirit is created whereby all organizations work together to enlarge the church's opportunities and responsibilities as a New Testament church, both in the local community and unto the uttermost parts of the earth.

Plans

There are three plans of organizations. They are a separate organization for each functional activity, correlation, and integration. The first of these plans, *separate organization for each functional activity,* is the plan which is now used by most churches and is the cause of the present over-organization.

The plan of *correlation,* or coordination, which is being studied and promoted to some extent by Southern Baptists has been described previously. A council is formed of representatives of the various organizations for the purpose of working out a program of education for the church which correlates all the activities. This theory sounds plausible. Although it has not so far remedied the situation very much in actual practice, it is a possible solution.

The third plan, *integration,* is considered by many to be the best solution. It is being tried to some extent by the

American Baptists, Disciples of Christ, Methodist Episcopal, Presbyterian, and Congregational churches on a denominational basis. Its distinguishing feature is the merging of the plans and programs of all the educational agencies at work in the denomination into one program with one organization for each age group. This necessitates the merging of the educational departments of all the boards of the denomination into a board of religious education, which prepares one integrated program of education for the churches to be administered by one organization, the church school, or the department of religious education of the church. This program is not a combination of all the programs as they now exist but is a new program into which all the elements and activities of the present conflicting organizations are built as integral parts.

Guiding Principles

There are certain fundamental principles which should underlie and guide in the promotion of such a program for the church: (1) the program should be pupil-centered; (2) it should be church-centered; (3) it should be based on sound educational theory and practice; and (4) it should be integrated. It should include all of the elements necessary to the complete religious education of the individual. Worship, both public worship and private devotions; instruction — biblical, social, and missionary; expressional activity in the form of young people's societies, youth councils, training unions, missionary service, and evangelistic activities; together with social and recreational activities should all be built into the program, not as separate elements, but as integral parts of one unified educational program administered by one organization for each age group.

Integrated Organization

This plan of organization calls for one set of officers and committees to function in the administration of the total religious educational program of the church for each age group.

Instead of selecting a separate set of officers and committees for each type of activity, one set of officers should plan and lead in all the necessary activities of the department. One from each department above the elementary division should be elected by the group as president. He should preside or be responsible for leadership of every meeting of the group as a department, whether for worship, study, expressional activity, or social life. His cabinet should consist of as many additional officers as are necessary, one for the promotion of each activity of the department. Local conditions should determine the size of the cabinet.

The average department would need officers responsible for at least the following activities: enlargement, social and recreational life, worship and devotion, missions and stewardship, evangelism and church relationship. Instead of standing committees, it would be better to have one member of the cabinet be responsible for each particular kind of activity required by the program of the department. These officers might be designated as vice-presidents or leaders. There should be an adult advisory superintendent for the department and adult teachers for the classes, which should meet on Sunday morning and also, if possible, on a week-day for study. In the case of large departments, there should also be adult advisers or supervisors for each special kind of activity. Whenever the church can afford it, a departmental director should be added to the staff to devote full time to the supervision of one age group.

Meetings of the Department

The department as such should have at least three meetings a week, a week-day session and two Sunday sessions. At the week-day meeting, plans should be made for the Sunday sessions, a preview of the lesson should be given by the teacher, and assignments made for the Sunday sessions. The pupils should be assisted in looking up assignments and instructed in matters of biblical investigation. The week-day session should be held at the church on some afternoon or night. All business matters pertaining to the department should be disposed of and all plans for departmental activities should be made at this week-day session.

The Sunday morning session should be given to worship and Bible study. The entire department should engage in the worship service together. The Bible study should be by small groups. Each group should be led by an adult teacher. The Sunday evening session should be devoted to expressional activity. It should usually be a program given by the pupils similar to the Baptist Training Union program, but the topics for discussion should be related to the subject studied at the morning session and the speeches should be an expression by the pupils of ideas received at the instructional meetings of the department and an application of the truths learned by the pupil to his problems and needs. The expressional activity for the older members during the week might take the form of evangelistic services in jails, mission stations, churchless communities, or the organization of mission Sunday schools in needy places.

Integrated Curriculum

The greatest difficulty in undertaking to carry out an integrated program of religious education is the lack of a unified curriculum. Curriculum has been defined by Harry Munro thus: "The Christian curriculum consists of those experiences of the growing person which arise from conditions so selected and organized as to lead him, at each successive stage of his development, into the most Christlike relationships with God and with his fellowmen of which he is capable."[2] As indicated in previous paragraphs, there are three or more independent organizations, each with a separate program consisting of worship, instruction, expression, and social activities in varying degrees. Each has different topics for study, a different plan of daily devotions and Bible reading, and each has a definitely outlined study course or reading course as well as a distinct plan of missionary in-

[2] Harry C. Munro, *Protestant Nurture*, p. 1. Copyright 1956, by Prentice-Hall Inc., Englewood Cliffs, N. J.

struction. Each also considers some form of expressional activity necessary.

What is needed most of all is to build from the nursery up through the adult department an integrated curriculum graded to meet the needs of each department; but in the absence of such material, the workers in each department will be compelled to make their own curriculum if the church feels there is need of such a program.

CORRELATION OF HOME, CHURCH, AND SCHOOL

The home was the first institution of religious instruction, and the church school was established to supplement the training of the home rather than to supplant it. Their cooperation is necessary for the religious education of the child. The influence of the home is more potent than that of the church school in habit formation and character building. Daily activities in the home offer the greatest opportunity for the expression of religious truths, and should be used as a laboratory for such, as well as for helping prepare Sunday lessons.

In order to *secure cooperation between the home and church, each must understand the work of the other* and know what the other is doing for the child. There are three ways to accomplish this. One is for parents to visit the church school so as to know better how to cooperate with the teacher. Another is for the teacher to visit the home so as to better understand the pupil's background and teach in the light of it. And the other is for both to come together in parent-teacher meetings for mutual counsel and aid. Perhaps, also, the home or extension departments could do more at this task.

There is need, also, that the church school teacher as well as the parent shall understand what goes on in the public school and teach in the light of it. To that end, both should keep in close touch with the public school teachers and understand the problems the pupil is facing daily. Also the church school curriculum should be planned more with this situation in mind. If such things are done, the youth of the church will be saved in the future, better than in the past, from religious doubts and moral delinquency.

Churches should also keep in closer touch with their youth as they go away to college, guiding them into the right institutions, keeping in touch with them while they are away, recognizing them when at home during the holidays, using them during the vacation season and helping to keep a guiding hand on their spiritual nurture. This also will save from doubts and delinquencies, bind closer to the church, and develop Christian character.

THE TASK OF PROMOTION

Thus far have been presented the place of religious education in the Bible, Christian history and modern life, some of the principles underlying it, and the agencies involved in carrying it on. It remains to give a general idea of the promotional phase. The more extensive task of administration may be found in the manuals or guides of the respective organizations.

Its Importance

It is very evident that the program of religious education must have some sort of plan for its promotion. No matter how beautiful the ideal, how noble the purpose, or how splendid the program, it will fail unless there is an adequate plan for promotion. For no plan, ideal, or program has ever fostered itself. There must be some person, organization, or activity back of it to give it push and power. Tracks and coaches alone will not run a train.

This is true in every phase of life. In the political world, a candidate for office does not get very far if he waits for the people to seek him out and get interested in him. Rather he must sell himself and his cause to the people. In the business world an invention or new commodity does not go far without extensive publicity and backing. The large industrial concerns spend tremendous sums in setting forth the merits of their products and creating an appetite for them. The most effective psychology is utilized to this end.

What is true in these and other realms is especially true in the field of religion. Those who have the best doctrines or programs are not always the ones who have succeeded best. Rather it is the agency that has been most efficient in promotion. One cannot judge the truthfulness of a cause by its seeming success. Sometimes the worst heresies are the best promoted. In reality it is just this which keeps the issue of intemperance forever to the fore, and also that of war. If the forces of righteousness were as aggressive in promotional activities as those of unrighteousness, things would be different.

Handicaps

In the realm of religious education, there are two definite handicaps that have to be overcome which are not so evident in other realms of endeavor. One is the fact that *church school activity is not compulsory.* People are not required to attend as in the public schools. In other words, there is no ready-made constituency. They must be located, visited, and enlisted. Not only is there no law or custom requiring attendance, but often there is not even concern or example in the home. In many situations, it is left entirely to the child as to what he shall do. So promotion is necessary.

Along with this is the fact of the *natural inertia of life.* People do about what they have to do either from inner constraint or outward pressure. And it is naturally just a little easier to lie in bed on Sunday morning than to get out; and if one is away from home at school, he is free from the constraint of home influence and custom. Furthermore, there is the natural tendency of the human being toward evil — the disposition of the soil to grow weeds — which requires that influence and cultivation be exercised. In other words, the natural conditions of life call for promotional activities in religious work.

CHANNELS OF PROMOTION

There are three possible channels or means of promoting education in religion and morals which may be mentioned. They are being used in one place or another and to some degree are being used or have been used in the recent past.

Secular

One of these is the state educational system. The time was when the Bible and other religious material were a part of the public school curriculum, and the teachers definitely fostered religion. But the separation of church and state and the multiplicity of denominations have gradually changed all of this. This is to be desired, for otherwise the state would become the promoter of religion through controlling the teaching of it.

There has been in recent days, however, some tendency to go back to an educational emphasis on religion through public education, due to the inadequate activity of the churches. In Oklahoma, Mississippi, and other places, the reading of the Bible in the public schools is required by law. In the University of South Carolina, some teachers' colleges in Texas, and elsewhere, the Bible is an integral part of the curriculum. The University of Iowa has established a character-research station and gives graduate degrees to those who major in this field. And the American Association of Universities has urged that Bible study be included. But there are too many dangers in formalism and liberalism for most Christian people to back such plans very far. It is held that religious education must be promoted by religious organizations and not by those of a secular nature, if it is to have the freshness and vitality needed.

Interdenominational

Much also has been done through nondenominational and interdenominational agencies. *Special movements,* such as the Sunday school, started outside the church, through the activities of laymen. The Christian Endeavor, which led to the various young people's societies, through Francis E. Clark's leadership, also got its start as an interdenomina tional agency. The Vacation Bible School movement had a similar beginning, as did the week-day church school in Gary, Indiana, and elsewhere. Organized Bible class work had its greatest impetus through Marshall A. Hudson and the Baraca and Philathea organizations. These facts must not be forgotten. In fact, most forward movements have started outside of denominational channels and often with disinterest or opposition from denominational leaders. Even now many of the ideals and new developments come that way. So out of fairness, credit should be where credit is due. The experiments and developments made by independent leaders should be recognized and utilized.

Promotional organizations as well as individual movements have likewise had such beginnings in this country. The American Bible Society has for more than a century furnished Bibles for Sunday school work and rendered a tremendous service. The American Sunday-School Union for nearly as long has sent out Sunday school missionaries throughout the length and breadth of the nation, establishing schools, starting church libraries, and doing other work. The International Sunday School Association and its successor, the International Council of Religious Education, now the Division of Christian Education, National Association of Churches of Christ in the United States of America, have through their conventions, regularly employed staff, and publications done much to shape Sunday school life. The World Sunday School Convention has likewise done a great deal to promote new schools in the mission fields of the world, develop ideals, and bring about a better world fellowship. These organizations, along with the community movements, the Christian Endeavor Society, International Daily Vacation Bible School Association, and others have done much to bring religious educational development to the point where it is. And most of them are still powerful factors in its promotion. While a denomination may or may not join organically in these movements, there is no good reason why their promotional methods should not be studied carefully and be incorporated, with their permission, into the program of the denomination.

Denominational

The fact still remains that the most effective promotional work is carried on through denominational channels. In fact practically all of the organizations which have started outside of denominational channels have finally been taken over by the denominations and found their most effective promotion after such had been true. This is no argument for a selfish, unchristian attitude between denominational groups. Happily, the day has come when the feeling between denominations is much better than in earlier days, and on matters of common interest they are working together as never before.

But as long as *churches are denominational*, the things that relate vitally to their lives will be denominational. This accounts for much of the failure of Dr. Athearn's community organizations for religious education. It practically ignored the churches and sought to build on a foundation which did not exist. There is a conviction which attaches to denominational life that gives it a warmth and a fervor not found elsewhere. In fact he who has definite convictions is always more aggressive in his activities than he who does not. And along with this, the element of competition enters in, which is not without its value in religious as well as in business life.

Also the organization and integration in denominational life is of special value in carrying on promotional work. The denominations are in a position to train and provide the leaders for promotion and to reach the people to be taught. They have their local churches with good church buildings and pastoral and educational leadership, schools and colleges, their publishing houses with a well-developed literature and stores for its distribution. Their field forces are organized for county, state, and larger units.

Then, too, promotion calls for a considerable amount of *financial resources*. It cannot be done on charity. Money must be provided and this is not easy. The safest, sanest, and surest way to secure the necessary funds for this work is through the denomination, as experience has shown. The people who give most are members of churches, who have a conscience on the matter, and whose budgets and lines of support are already set up. Also the profits that are made on the books and literature used go back to denominational headquarters and are available for new promotional work.

REALMS OF ACTIVITY IN THE DENOMINATION

This work of promotion within the denomination falls in the main upon three agencies; namely, the Christian schools, the field workers, and the local church leadership. In previous chapters, these various realms of activity have been dealt with, and so it is not necessary to say much about them in this last chapter.

The School

There are at least three directions in which the Christian school has functioned in promoting religious education; in providing a vocational leadership; in training lay workers for the local churches, and in evaluating and improving the quality of the work. There is no greater nor more important function of the Christian college than to lead and inspire in this vastly important work. Vision, a public conscience, and a trained leadership are needed. How can the function of the denominational school be realized without including religious education for emphasis and development?

The Field

Perhaps the oldest phase of promotional activity is that which is carried on by the field workers. Much of the credit for today's achievements must be given to these faithful men and women who have left their homes behind and literally gone into the "highways and hedges" throughout the length and breadth of the land, instructing and inspiring the people and organizing the work. They have truly been pioneers and missionaries. Every phase of the educational work of the church has been promoted by these field workers — the work of the Sunday school, the young people's society, the missionary societies, and so forth. Conferences and conventions have been held, training schools, enlargement campaigns, and every type of individual and group work has been emphasized. How poor and inadequate the programs of religious education would be without the inspiration and leadership of this great body of field workers!

The Church

After all, the final phase of promotion rests with the local church. What the school man and field man do will largely come to nought unless backed by and carried on by the local church forces. The school man studies in a wider and deeper way and the field man covers a wider territory, but the local church workers have the responsibility for a longer period — three hundred and sixty-five days out of the year; consequently these workers have the opportunity of seeing and doing some things the other two groups cannot have and have perhaps the most difficult phase of promotion. They are the ones who really know whether or not a thing will work, and especially the vocational leaders in the local church are usually in the vanguard in making improvements. Both the school and the field men will give major emphasis in their work to the training of an adequate leadership in the local church for the promotion of religious education. All of these types of workers will pull together to reach all the people and to provide vital Christian education for all of them.

AN ADEQUATE DYNAMIC

As the whole field has been surveyed with all of the agencies and activities involved, the task of religious education assumes tremendous proportions. It is a worthy program but a hard one. It calls for infinite patience and effort. The question naturally arises, Why go to all of this trouble in time, money, and labor? Who is equal to the task?

It is evident that a strong dynamic is necessary. Several things are involved in it. For one thing, one must *realize keenly the need*. Nothing will be a greater incentive than a realization that civilization and the salvation of mankind are at stake. The let-down in personal morals, the crime wave, the dissolution of the home, the struggle between capital and labor, the menace of race antipathies and war will destroy the nation unless something is done. It must be recognized that a real crisis in civilization confronts the churches. As President Wilson once said, "Our civilization cannot survive materially unless it be redeemed spiritually." This realization is basic to the whole enterprise.

Religious educators must come to *believe fully that Christian education is the way out*. The use of force has failed. Legislation has been found inadequate. Secular education has proven insufficient. These do not furnish the dynamic necessary. Only religion can supply an adequate dynamic, and the best results cannot be secured through inspirational addresses, drives, and crowd pressure, or in later life. It must begin with the child, continue in the youth, and carry on a continuous process of teaching and training to maturity and even old age. As Roger Babson has indicated, "we do not need more battleships and material goods but more religious education." A realization of this fact is absolutely fundamental.

And there must be a *consciousness of being in league with God*. Nothing so stimulates an individual or people as the feeling of a Divine mission. It stood out prominently in the ministry of Christ. It was outstanding in the activity of Luther and Wesley. Every great leader and reformer has had this feeling. The drab routine of continuous effort in good weather and bad, during success and failure, day in and day out, calls for such a sense of Divine compulsion. And indeed it has been given, for the great command of the Master Teacher is "Go ye therefore, and make disciples of all the nations, baptizing them into the name of the Father and of the Son and of the Holy Spirit: teaching them to observe all things whatsoever I commanded you: and lo, I am with you always, even unto the end of the world" (Matt. 28:19-20). In this consciousness we shall not fail.

QUESTIONS FOR DISCUSSION

1. Make a careful outline of the organizations and programs promoted by your local church and indicate where there are overlappings in the work.

2. What is a church council and how can it help in co-ordination and unity in the work of the local church?

3. Make a study of the best plans being used for the co-ordination and unification of the work in the local church as promoted by three leading denominations: for example, study organization and promotion in Methodist, Presbyterian, and Baptist churches.

4. Give three or four reasons why the promotion of religious education is important and indicate ways by which the work can be done.

Part IV

BIBLIOGRAPHY

Brightbill, Charles K., and Meyer, Harold D. *Recreation*. Englewood Cliffs, N. J.: Prentice-Hall, Inc., 1956.

Brown, Richmond O. *Practical Church Publicity*. Nashville: The Broadman Press, 1953.

Browne, Benjamin P. *Christian Journalism For Today*. Philadelphia: Judson Press, 1952.

Corbin, H. Don. *Recreation Leadership*. New York: Prentice-Hall, Inc., 1953.

Cuninggim, Merriman. *The College Seeks Religion*. New Haven: Yale University Press, 1947.

Duvall, Evelyn, and Duvall, Sylvanus. *Leading Parents' Groups*. Nashville: Abingdon Press, 1946.

Foster, Robert Beib. *Marriage and Family Relationships*. New York: The Macmillan Co., rev. ed. 1957.

Harbin, E. O. *The Fun Encyclopedia*. Nashville: Abingdon Press, 1940.
————. *The Recreation Leader*. Nashville: Abingdon Press, 1952.

Harner, Nevin C. *Religion's Place in General Education*. Richmond: John Knox Press, 1949.

Harral, Stewart. *Public Relations for Churches*. Nashville: Abingdon Press, 1945.

Hauser, Conrad A. *Teaching Religion in The Public School*. New York: Round Table Press, 1942.

Johnson, F. Ernest, ed. *American Education and Religion*. New York: Harper & Bros., 1952.

LOTZ, PHILIP HENRY, ed. *Orientation in Religious Education*. Nashville: Abingdon Press, 1950.

MILLER, RANDOLPH CRUMP. *Education for Christian Living*. Englewood Cliffs, N. J.: Prentice-Hall, Inc., 1956.

NIELANDER, W. A., and MILLER, R. W. *Public Relations*. New York: The Ronald Press Co., 1951.

REDDICK, DEWITT C., ed. *Church and Campus*. Richmond: John Knox Press, 1956.

SNAVELY, GUY E. *The Church and The Four-Year College*. New York: Harper & Bros., 1955.

STAUBER, STANLEY I. *Public Relations Manual for Churches*. Garden City: Doubleday & Co., 1951.

THAYER, V. T. *Religion in Public Education*. New York: Viking Press, 1947.

TRUEBLOOD, ELTON, and PAULINE. *The Recovery of the Family*. New York: Harper & Bros., 1953.

WOLSELEY, ROLAND E. *Interpreting the Church Through Press and Radio*. Philadelphia: Muhlenberg Press, 1951.

INDEX